Transoceanic Studies
Ileana Rodriguez, Series Editor

Learning to Unlearn

*Decolonial Reflections
from Eurasia and the Americas*

Madina V. Tlostanova
AND Walter D. Mignolo

THE OHIO STATE UNIVERSITY PRESS • COLUMBUS

Copyright © 2012 by The Ohio State University.
All rights reserved.

Library of Congress Cataloging-in-Publication Data

Tlostanova, M. V. (Madina Vladimirovna)
  Learning to unlearn : decolonial reflections from Eurasia and the Americas / Madina V. Tlostanova and Walter D. Mignolo.
      p. cm. — (Transoceanic studies)
  Includes bibliographical references and index.
  ISBN 978-0-8142-1188-5 (cloth : alk. paper) — ISBN 0-8142-1188-7 (cloth : alk. paper) — ISBN 978-0-8142-9287-7 (cd-rom)
  1. Knowledge, Sociology of. 2. Epistemics. 3. Education—Philosophy. 4. Imperialism. 5. Postcolonialism. I. Mignolo, Walter. II. Title. III. Series: Transoceanic studies.
  BD175.T56 2012
  306.4'2—dc23
                          2011050019

Other identifiers: ISBN 978-0-8142-5875-0 (paper)

Cover design by Janna Thompson-Chordas
Text design by Juliet Williams
Type set in Adobe Minion Pro

CONTENTS

Acknowledgments — vii

INTRODUCTION Learning to Unlearn: Thinking Decolonially — 1

PART I

CHAPTER 1 The Logic of Coloniality and the Limits of Postcoloniality: Colonial Studies, Postcoloniality, and Decoloniality — 31

CHAPTER 2 Theorizing *from* the Borders; Shifting *to* the Geo- and Body Politics of Knowledge — 60

PART II

CHAPTER 3 Transcultural Tricksters in between Empires: "Suspended" Indigenous Agency in the Non-European Russian/Soviet (Ex-)Colonies and the Decolonial Option — 83

CHAPTER 4 Non-European Soviet Ex-Colonies and the Coloniality of Gender, or How to Unlearn Western Feminism in Eurasian Borderlands — 122

PART III

CHAPTER 5 Who Speaks for the "Human" in Human Rights? Dispensable and Bare Lives — 153

CHAPTER 6 Thinking Decolonially: Citizenship, Knowledge, and the Limits of Humanity — 175

CHAPTER 7 Globalization and the Geopolitics of Knowledge: The Role of the Humanities in the Corporate University — 196

AFTERWORD — 217

Appendix	225
Notes	237
Bibliography	253
Index	268

ACKNOWLEDGMENTS

We warmly thank Luis Fernando Sarango—rector of Amawtay Wasi—The Intercultural University of the Indigenous Nationalities and People of Ecuador—for granting us permission to reproduce the diagrams and for providing the updated versions.

We would also like to thank the Academy of Latinity and its General Secretary, Candido Mendes, for his generous invitation to both of us to participate in several conferences in Alexandria (2004), Ankara-Istanbul (2005), Baku (2006), Quito (2006), and Amman (2007). Those were wonderful opportunities for exploring our ideas in the context of international dialogue of civilizations forums in the Middle East, South America, and Eurasia.

We would like to express our gratitude to the Institute of Postcolonial and Transcultural Studies (INPUTS) of the University of Bremen and its current director, Sabine Broeck, for many illuminating conversations and discussions on decolonizing the humanities, as well as for several conferences and lectures she has organized or participated in with us in the recent years. All of them were very helpful for the gestation of our book.

We would like to thank the National Institute for the study of Dutch slavery and its legacy (NiNsee) and Kwame Nimako for a similar invitation to both of us to participate in the workshop "Trajectories of Emancipation" in Amsterdam (2009).

We are grateful as well to the *European Journal of Social Theory*; *Human Architecture: Journal of the Sociology of Self-Knowledge*; *Postcolonial Studies*; *Hispanic Issues Online*; *Nepantla*; and *American Literary History* (The University of Minnesota Press) for granting us permission to use our previously published articles on similar topics. All of the articles were substantially edited to fit the general argument of the book.

INTRODUCTION

Learning to Unlearn

Thinking Decolonially

I.

"Learning to unlearn" grew out of ten years of conversations and collaborations on issues of common interest. As an Uzbek-Cherkess living in Moscow and of an ethnically Muslim family, Madina was concerned with colonial questions in Central Asia and the Caucasus. As a son of Italian immigrants to Argentina and living in the U.S., Walter was concerned with the colonial question in the Americas. It was clear to us that the Russian/Soviet colonies and colonies in South and Central America and the Caribbean have parallel histories vis-à-vis colonial relations and with regards to imperial control and domination. At the same time, in South America, the history of imperial control is tied to the history of capitalism, in the West, while Central Asia and the Caucasus have a different pedigree, due to the subaltern and non-Western or not-quite-Western nature of the empires that controlled them in the past (the Ottoman Sultanate, Russia, the Soviet Union). From the sixteenth century to today, South America and the Caribbean and the Russian colonies (first, the Volga region, Siberia, the Baltic region, the Crimea; and from the late eighteenth to the nineteenth century on, the Caucasus and Central Asia), followed parallel histories vis-à-vis the Western imperial designs (Spain, Holland, France, England, the U.S.) and vis-à-vis the Russian Czardom, the Russian Empire (from Peter the Great onward), the Soviet Union and the Russian Federation today. The U.S. started its advances toward South America at the beginning of the nineteenth century and has continued to advance until today, while the Russian Federation, its current remaining colonies and newly independent post-Soviet states, also have to confront the interests of the U.S. in Eurasia.

As the conversation and collaboration progressed, it began to turn around two key concepts: imperial and colonial differences and their modulations in the modern/colonial world order from 1500 to 2000. The first modulation was the external imperial difference between the Russian Czardom, and later Russian Empire, in relation to Western empires. Consequently, we asked ourselves, what would be the difference between imperial/colonial configurations in the West framed by Western Christianity, secular Liberalism and Marxism and imperial/colonial configurations in Russia and Eastern Christianity, and later on, in the Soviet Union. More concretely, the question turned to the colonial configurations of Central Asia and the Caucasus under the Russian Empire and the Soviet Union, on the one hand, and South America and the Caribbean first under the direct Spanish and Portuguese colonization and, after the formation of the "independent" republics, the indirect colonization by Britain and France in collaboration with the local Creole elites, on the other. Once we reached this point, we moved to the internal imperial difference among Western capitalist empires. For example, the so-called Black Legend that England launched against Spain in the second half of the seventeenth century and the making of the South of Europe through which Latin and Catholic countries leading during the Renaissance were demoted to a secondary role in the second modernity (i.e., the Enlightenment). We arrived at a conclusion that had been expressed historically before: the fact that Russia and Spain became two countries at the margins of enlightened modernity. The core of our argument evolves around this set of concepts. We are not "comparing" Central Asia and the Caucasus, on the one hand, with South America and the Caribbean, on the other, but rather analyzing the underlying colonial matrix of power maintaining the illusion that these "areas" are far apart from each other (and they are, as far as local histories are concerned), while in fact they are linked to Western hegemony by the logic of coloniality.

We are not comparing them, because Central Asia and the Caucasus, on the one hand, and South America and the Caribbean, on the other, are two complex "regions" located *in* the colonial matrix of power. They belong to the same universe. It is only from a modern and imperial epistemological assumption that they are seen as "two distinct areas to be compared." They have local histories for sure. But their local histories are interconnected with the local Western imperial history. This point is crucial in our argument. As both are regions within the colonial matrix, they are entangled with the West. The Central Asia and southern Caucasus entanglement is part of the history of Russia/Soviet Union up to the recent formation of the independent states after the collapse of the Soviet Union. South American and the Caribbean went through a similar process: Spain and Portugal were the imperial countries from which South America and the Caribbean first gained their independence; and later on, the processes continued in the British, Dutch, and French Caribbean. So, what we are looking at here is a complex network of imperial and colonial differences: external imperial differences between the Western empires and the Russian Empire/Soviet Union and internal imperial differences between the South of Europe and the Western post-Enlightenment empires (France, England, Germany), whose intellectuals were responsible for making the European Catholic South an inferior sector of Europe. Furthermore, we take into account the external colonial difference that Europe created in relation to the Indians and Africans. This relation was reproduced by the Russian Empire and the Soviet Union. We are not dealing in this book with the internal colonial difference, which worked in the classification of the European internal "others": Jews and Romany, mainly.

It is necessary to make it clear from the start that, although the point of origination of the particular conceptual structure (modernity/coloniality/(de)coloniality) was located in South America, its scope is not limited to South America and the Caribbean. To think that way would be similar to believing that, if the concept of "biopolitics" originated in Europe, it is valid only for Europe. It is important to make this clarification, because there is an unconscious tendency to think that theories that originate in the Third World (or among Black or gay intellectuals) are valid only for the Third World (or Black and gay people), while theories that originate in the First World (and created by White and heterosexual people) have a global if not universal validity. This modern and imperial way of thinking is coming to its end. But we know that the belief that the Whites have knowledge and the Indians have Wisdom; the Blacks have experience and the Whites have philosophy; the Third World has culture and the First World has science unfortunately is still well and alive. And what we say is that it is time to start learning to unlearn this assumption among others in order to relearn.

The somewhat coeval imperial beginnings of Russia and Spain in the sixteenth century[1] were followed up by Spain's demise in the eighteenth century and the beginning of Russia's doomed catching up race with the great empires of modernity. Russia and Spain "at the margin of the West" (the first because it never got to the center no matter how much it yearned to, and the second because it lost its place there) was a metaphor shared by Spanish, Latin American, and Russian historians and philosophers alike (Ana María Schop Soler (1971), Leopoldo Zea (1958), or Vassily Klyuchevsky (2009)). Paradoxically, when Peter changed his title of the Czar to that of the Emperor (early eighteenth century), the "external imperial difference" between Western and non-Western civilizations was consolidated. Simultaneously, in the eighteenth century, Spain lost its former imperial clout, became the South of Europe, and originated the "internal imperial difference." Both Russia and Spain lost the train of the second modernity, that of the Enlightenment, the Industrial Revolution, and the birth of the secular nation-states.

Consequently, the Russian colonies, on the one hand, and South America and the Caribbean, on the other, were recast according to the new world order dictated by the leadership of England, France, and Germany—the "heart or Europe" in Hegel's metaphor, in politics, economy, philosophy, and sciences. As Russia was getting more and more tightly entangled in the net of intellectual and cultural dependency on Europe, bordering on self-colonization, its methods of conquering the new territories were becoming more and more similar to European ones, and the previous relative tolerance of other religions and ethnicities gave place to open genocide and racism. Ivan the Terrible, three hundred years earlier, was able to have as his second wife a daughter of Cherkess prince Temryuk or a Tatar deputy on the throne, but in the nineteenth century discourses, the inhabitants of the Caucasus or Central Asia were already unequivocally coded as inferior beings. The final conquering of these territories in the middle and the second half of the nineteenth century took place in the context of discourses on racism, Orientalism, and Eurocentrism, which were borrowed from Europe and subsequently distorted by the Russians—due to their own dubious status. The main rival of the Russian Empire then was the Ottoman Sultanate, which shared with Russia its second-rate status, while the Russian inferiority complex with respect to the unattainable Western empires of modernity was compensated in the conquering of the Caucasus and Central Asia, which were racialized in accordance with the notions of the post-Enlightenment Europe in this new colonial period of imperial management.

Meanwhile, in South America and the Caribbean, many countries gained independence from Spain and Portugal in the nineteenth century, just to enter in the first period of imperialism without colonies. England controlled the economy while France had strong political investments (e.g., the name of "Latin" America was a geopolitical move of French imperial expansion; it dominated the intellectual life as well as shaped the state universities). Like

Africa and Asia in the second half of the twentieth century, South American countries gained independence from the former empires, in order to remain dependent on new imperialism.

Thus, while Russia remained and Spain became a marginal empire in the eighteenth century and they were located in the external and internal imperial differences, respectively, the colonies of Central Asia and the Caucasus that were acquired by Russia in the post-Enlightenment phase of modernity were regarded differently from the colonies gained in the sixteenth–eighteenth centuries. The previously existing relations and ways of interpreting the indigenous populations of Central Asia and the Caucasus were completely erased from the Russian memories and replaced with the borrowed Western discourses. This was particularly clear in case of the Circassian genocide and Circassians' subsequent exile to the Ottoman Sultanate in the mid-nineteenth century (Circassian Genocide 2008, Shenfield 2008). As for South America, these ex-colonies were relocated by updating the external colonial difference put in place in the sixteenth century. The colonial difference came into being in the process of debating the humanity of the inhabitants of Anahuac and Tawantinsuyu, renamed "Indias Occidentales" by Spaniards and "America" by a group of intellectuals in northern France and southern Germany, at the suggestion of Martin Waldseemüller. "Indian" as the name of the people and "Indias Occidentales," as that of the place, are two anchors of the colonial difference. Not only was a name that was not theirs imposed onto the people, they were also cast as inferior to Christians and Spaniards. Enslaved Africans transported to the New World were the second group of renamed people: all enslaved Africans became "Black" disregarding their original kingdom of origin in Africa, respective languages, and sacred beliefs.

People of the Caucasus and later Central Asia were also reclassified by the Russian Empire within the frame of the racist logic imported from the West and superimposed onto the existing religious frame. From the "Busurman" of the first modernity (a term originating arguably in the word "Musulman"—Muslim), coming to gradually embrace all non–Orthodox Christian people, the Russian construction of otherness came to the concept of "inorodets" (usually translated as "alien" but literally meaning the one who was born an other), in the early nineteenth century, when the religious difference was replaced with a racial, ethnic, and civilizational one to be essentialized. Thus, in the second modernity, the Muslim confession of Central Asia and partly the Caucasus was turned into the color of skin. So that, on top of the legal term "inorodets" (which included the Pagan nomads, the Muslims, and the Jews alike), there was also the term "Tatar" in use to define all Muslims, similarly to the West, where the Muslims were called Arabs or Turks regardless of their ethnicity. The topographic and ethnic renamings intensified and acquired a more planned strategic element in Soviet nation building in the remapped borders, invented ethnicities and languages, and erased histories. As a result of the Soviet modernization, the religious difference was completely translated into race and the Caucasus and Central Asian people acquired the common name of "Blacks" that they still carry. The Orthodox Christian commonality of Russians with Osetians (until the war with Georgia over South Osetia), Georgians, or Armenians has been systematically downplayed and replaced with racism and Orientalism from the nineteenth century until now.

All of this was taking place at the time when the European philologists and intellectuals were rebuilding and enacting the colonial difference in their definition of the Orientals and the creation of Orientalism. In this move, Muslims became Arabs and Turks and the original imperial difference between the Spanish Empire and the Ottoman Sultanate lost the religious underpinning, while secular ethnicity entered in the Western redrawing of the external colonial difference. It is precisely at this point that the Caucasus and Central Asia entered the imperial imaginary of Russia in the role of Russia's own secondhand Orient. The internal colonial difference was also remapped during the same period: Jews, as a religious group, became secularized as ethnic Jews, a transformation that had its dramatic consequences in the holocaust.

We do not present a new version of historical grand narrative but rather revisit the local histories of different geopolitical spaces, and always within the colonial matrix of power. We do this not with the simple goal of adding certain crucial facts and notions to the existing historical interpretations, although in many cases this is in itself an important and still unaddressed task. Our goal instead is to look at these seemingly familiar historical events from the position of border thinking and border consciousness, sensitive to the colonial and imperial difference, and to do so necessarily in the context of the rhetoric of modernity based on the logic of global coloniality in its various manifestations (Western capitalism and liberalism, socialism, the discourses of subaltern empires, etc.). Border thinking is theorized in more detail later. Since there is no outside position from which the colonial matrix can be observed and described (we are all within it), border thinking emerges in the process of delinking from the colonial matrix and escaping from its control. Suffice it to say here that, by border thinking, we mean a specific epistemic response from the exteriority of Western modernity, a response from the outside created from the perspective of the inside (that is, the exteriority in building its own identity as humanitas). This means that while we are all in the colonial matrix, not everyone belongs to its memories, feelings, and ways of sensing. Many of us have been "trapped" in the colonial matrix but do not "belong" to it. Therefore it becomes essential to delink, and border epistemology-cum-decolonial thinking is one way of doing it. Border thinking is the epistemology enacted in the variegated responses, around the globe, to the violence of the imperial territorial epistemology and the rhetoric of modernity with its familiar defects, from forced universal salvation to taking difference to sameness, from subject-object split to naturalization of Western epistemic privilege. Thus, we perform an act of demarcation or delimiting with the previous principles of interpretation of history and modernity, without which it is not possible to enact the decolonization of being, thinking, and knowledge—another crucial notion and goal that runs throughout the book and connects our otherwise divergent local histories, working for the open utopia of the global decolonial move. We, therefore, enact border thinking in building our argument, which means that we do not place ourselves as detached observers (the myth of modern epistemology) but as involved and embodied in the process we describe. We have this particular step in mind when we speak of the necessity of "learning to unlearn"—to forget what we have been taught, to break free from the thinking programs imposed on us by education, culture, and social environment, always marked by the Western imperial reason.

Therefore, when we say that we became interested in the colonial question, we do not mean that we became immersed in the meticulous diachronic study and detached detailed comparison of the conquest of the New World and the imperial march of Russia taking over Eurasia. Rather we felt that, under all their differences and incommensurability, these local histories that we have just sketchily presented, share some kind of common logic in the way coloniality (the logic under all forms of colonialism since 1500) affected the consciousness, subjectivity, economy, gender and sexual relations, thinking, social and political processes of peripheral Eurasia and South/Central America and the Caribbean. This commonality, as we discovered later and try to demonstrate in what follows, was not connected with the histories of concrete empires and their colonies regarded as isolated and well-formed entities to be compared within the Western comparative studies approach, but rather was a result of what can be called "global coloniality" and defined as a model of power relations that came into existence as a consequence of the Western imperial expansion but did not end with the official end of colonialism and colonial administrations. It survives in culture, labor, intersubjective relations, knowledge production, books, cultural patterns, and other aspects of modern existence (Maldonado-Torres 2007: 243). The word "coloniality" has a specific theoretical and historical meaning for us as members of modernity/coloniality international collective (Escobar 2007, Yehia 2006). Historically, coloniality names the darker side of modernity. Conceptually, coloniality is the hidden side of modernity. By writing modernity/coloniality, we mean that coloniality is constitutive of modernity and there is no modernity without coloniality.

By using the concept of "global coloniality," we want to avoid such terms as "alternative" or "peripheral modernities," at the same time underlying the hidden agenda of modernity, alternative or peripheral. We also intent to go beyond the British colonial history on which postcolonial studies were largely built and attempt to reinscribe the forgotten colonial history of the Spanish empire and take into account the enormous significance of the surfacing of the Atlantic economy (the western coasts of Africa, the western coasts of Europe and the eastern coasts of the Americas), displacing the weight that the Mediterranean had for the Western confines of the world until 1500. Furthermore, we take into account the Russian colonial history, and the split of the Enlightenment project into two modernities (the liberal and the socialist) after 1917. Subsequently, with the fall of the Soviet Union, today's neoliberalism is running wild, creating the conditions for the emergence of what we describe here as polycentric capitalism.

Whether the historical foundation of modernity is located in the sixteenth century, the "discovery" of America, and the European Renaissance or in the European Enlightenment and the French Revolution, modernity has been explicitly and implicitly linked with Western Christendom, secularization, Western types of imperialism (i.e., Spain, Portugal, Holland, France, England, the U.S.), and capitalist economy. In that Eurocentric version of modernity, fashioned from the very imperial history of Europe, coloniality had to remain silenced. But the triumphal march of modernity cannot be celebrated from the imperial perspective without bringing to the foreground that religious salvation implied the extirpation of idolatry; civilization meant the eradication of non-European modes of life, economy, and political organization; and a development within capitalist economy and market democracy in Western political theory. In that version of history, two major issues are left in the background that helps in enhancing the idea of modernity and hiding the logic of coloniality.

The first was the triumphal conceptualization of modernity and its hidden complicity with the spatial and temporal "differences" and with coloniality. Modernity, to be conceived as such, needed (and still needs) a break with the past within internal European history. Therefore, it colonized time and invented the idea of the Middle Ages thus putting in place the historical foundation of modern time. Almost simultaneously, the very concept of "discovery of America" contributed to the historical foundation of modern space. It was a discovery of a continent that did not yet exist, as there was no such a thing as America when Columbus landed in the Caribbean islands. Furthermore, the Christian conceptualization of the "discovery" of a continent that has been inhabited for about thirty thousands years, according to current estimates, was marked by the efforts of Christian intellectuals in the sixteenth century to make the "new" continent and people fit biblical history and the Christian Tripartite geopolitical order. It was from and in Europe that the classification of the world emerged and not from Asia, Africa, or America. The Middle Ages were integrated into the history of Europe, while the histories of Asia, Africa, and America were denied as history. By the eighteenth century, when the "barbarians" in space where transformed (e.g., Lafitau 1724) into the "primitives" in time, the colonization of the world by the European Empire brought together and distinguished the time/space of modernity from the time/space of non-modern Europe and non-modern America, Asia, and Africa.[2] "Modern" imperialism and, therefore, colonialism (as distinct from Roman, Islamic, and Ottoman) rests on two basic and interrelated pillars: the internal colonization of time in the internal history of Europe (i.e., the Middle Ages) and the external colonization of space in the external history of Europe (of the Americas first, by Spain and Portugal; of Africa and Asia since the nineteenth century by England and France; and of strategic places of the globe, mainly since the second half of the twentieth century by the U.S.).

Thus, we make the distinction here between imperialism/colonialism as singular, historical processes, on the one hand, and the rhetoric of modernity/the logic of coloniality, on the other. From the biblical macro-narrative, we inherited the idea that there is a linear history from the creation of the first man and the first woman by God until the final judgment. From Georg W. F. Hegel, we inherited the secular version of the sacred narrative: the idea that History is a linear process that began in the East many centuries ago, then moved West and, at the time Hegel was writing, History was dwelling in Germany, although its future was already destined to move further West to the United States of America (Hegel [1822] 1991). From Frances Fukuyama (1992), we inherited the idea that History has arrived at its end. Although these macro-narratives are Christian and Western, the expansion of the West all over the globe has made these narratives the points of reference (not necessarily of conviction) for the entire world—similar to the way Hollywood and Wall Street are also global reference points. The concepts of colonial and imperial differences alter significantly the calm waters of a linear history that has arrived at its end with the collapse of the Soviet Union, as Fukuyama has it. The rhetoric of modernity (i.e., the Renaissance idea of "les ancients et les modernes") was founded and expanded, in the internal history of Europe and the U.S., in the language of progress and newness. To be modern, people or countries had to be at the tip and the top of history, at the tip and the top of "human" evolution. With regards to the Muslims in the North of Africa, the Indians in America, the Africans in Africa and in the Americas, and the Ottomans, to be "modern" meant to be civilized and distinct from the barbarians (and after the Enlightenment, distinct from the primitives). Thus, the foundation of the rhetoric of modernity consisted of affirming the point of arrival of the societies in which the men who were telling the story and conceiving modernity were residing; it provided and still provides the justification for the continuing colonization of time and space: "bringing" modernity to the world (in terms of conversion to Christianity, to civilization, to market democracy), became a "mission" that, in the name of progress and development, has justified colonization, from the conquest of Mexico to the conquest of Iraq.

II.

Why did we decide to write this book? Several reasons motivated our decision. First and foremost, we did it as a contribution to shifting the geography of reasoning, in Lewis Gordon's formulation (Gordon 2006) and to disengage from the assumption that certain "areas" (Central Asia and the Caucasus; South/Central America, the Caribbean), or certain "minorities" in a developed country (e.g., Latinos and Latinas in the U.S.) are "objects" to be studied. We ask first not what has to be studied but *who* is doing the study and for what? In other words, why has the world been divided into areas of investigation? Who benefits from such investigations? Argentinean philosopher Rodolfo Kusch devoted all his "thinking life" (as a thinker and a philosopher within and outside of the academy) to arguing that we can make no form of affirmation without being involved and transformed in our act of affirming (Kusch 1978).

The argument of our book consists in a sustained effort to shift the geography of reasoning from the enunciated (or object/area to be described and explained) to the enunciator (the subject doing the description and explanation). This is of fundamental importance because there is an ideological assumption in mainstream epistemology according to which subjects who are not Euro-Americans are mere tokens of their own culture. This presupposition implies that knowledge is located in a given "area" (Western Europe and the U.S.) and controlled by certain people (the secular White quantitative minority). The second reason for writing this book is to disobey such taken-for-granted assumptions. We posit ourselves as epistemic subjects who take on the world from our own lived experiences and education. And rather than being tokens of our culture, we take "as our object of study" the Western imperial formations and the Western Christian and secular elites who created institutions of knowledge that became, imperially, the measure of all possible knowledges.

We just wrote "knowledge's" in plural but it came out automatically (Microsoft Word did it) as a possessive case. Word's thesaurus does not accept it. It does not admit the plural of "knowledge," because knowledge is supposed to be singular: It is the singularity of agents and institutions who control and dictate what is acceptable and what is unacceptable. We disobey; we delink from all totalitarian epistemology and claim epistemic equity. Therefore, this book should not be read as a "comparative study" of Central Asia and the Caucasus, on the one hand, and South/Central America and the Caribbean, on the other, because both are located within the colonial matrix of power. How can one compare entities that belong to the same system? Comparing would mean to assume that the two regions are delimited by their local histories and ignore that they are interconnected by global designs: the very constitution of the modern/colonial world and the formation and transformation of the colonial matrix of power.

As we stated, we do not offer a comparative study of Central Asia, the Caucasus, South/Central America, and the Caribbean or Latinos as in the U.S.: We take our experience (not the disciplines) as an epistemic guide. Disciplinary apparati (concepts, narratives, debates, etc.) are tools to build our arguments, addressing problems and issues not framed in the disciplines. This does not mean that we want to represent (describe or speak for) the regions or the people. We just claim that we (Madina and Walter) belong to those regions and not to South Asia, France, or the U.S. Thus, our thinking is in-formed geo- and body politically. No essences are invoked. What is invoked is how we inhabit the colonial matrix and respond to it. Therefore we claim epistemic rights grounded in local histories and in the bodies instead of being grounded in disciplinary principles established in local histories and by body agents with whom we do not identify. A common dictum says that Native Americans have wisdom and Whites have science, that Blacks have experience and Whites have knowledge. We do not recognize such common assumptions. We disobey and delink from them. And we are not claiming for recognition of the right to exist. Our claim is stronger: We claim that future epistemologies are being and will be constructed with their "back" toward the West, not competing with the West but delinking from it. For, if decolonial epistemology engages in competition with Western epistemology, the war is lost before the first battle: "Competing" means playing by the same rules of the epistemic game. We instead conceive the decolonial as an option. By so doing, all "competing" alternatives become merely options. Those options could be at the level of system of ideas (Christianity, Islamism, Judaism, Liberalism, Marxism) or disciplinary formations (Social Sciences and the Humanities, Professional Schools, Natural Sciences). When one looks at a system of ideas or disciplinary formations as options, one realizes that there is no single truth to be defended or imposed. There are only options to be engaged with. The road to pluriversality begins when we accept that there are options to be engaged and no universal truth to defend. The rules of the epistemic game are precisely what we are contesting and disengaging from. At the same time, we look for networking and building solidarity with projects moving in the same direction around the world. "Solidarity" should not be confused with "charity." You can be "in solidarity" with people struggling for food in the world, meaning that you are sympathetic and justify their fight. But they would not care much about your "solidarity," which is indeed a "paternalistic charity." "Solidarity" in decolonial terms is reciprocal: If you are in solidarity, you have to be a partner and be considered as a partner by the institutions and agencies with which you are in solidarity. In sum, we are not claiming recognition, inclusion, or the right to exist—we know that we belong to global trajectories that do not pretend to compete with modern Western epistemology—rather we intend to move in a different direction, to delink, to shift the geography of reasoning.

The third reason for writing this book is in revolt against the organization of the world in boxes, in areas to be studied or their natural resources to be exploited. In such an obviously imperial order of knowledge, what has the Caucasus and Central Asia to do with South America and the Caribbean and with Latino/as in the U.S.? A lot, we sustain, because they all are connected through the logic of coloniality (or the colonial matrix of power) that has guided the world order and Euro-American leadership. What we are saying is that the mentioned areas and people are not linked as objects but through the logic of imperial enunciation.

"Learning to unlearn in order to relearn" is a crucial principle in the curriculum of Amawtay Wasi [The Intercultural University of the People and Nations of Ecuador],[3] aimed at the development of reflective and intuitive practices of wise people rather than Western style professionals, by organizing various "learning environments where the building of knowledge is interrelated with research, dialogue and projects and services" (García 2004: 329). We need to make several clarifying points to explain why our book is titled after the Amawtay Wasi project of higher education and not after some model that Harvard, Cambridge, Le College the France, or Heidelberg (to mention just a few possibilities), may offer.[4]

Amawtay Wasi is a project lead by indigenous intellectuals and activists in collaboration with non-Indians (Ecuadorians of European descent of mixed blood and mind). The project emerges after a long series of claims, from land claims in the 1970s, to bicultural education, from the right of political interventions argued through the concept of "interculturality" (which we explain later), to the right to create institutions of higher education under indigenous leadership. This leadership does not mean that it is an Indigenous university exclusively for indigenous people, as was the case with the national Ecuadorian university created by creoles of European descent and mestizos, which indeed, at the beginning, was meant only for high-class mestizos and European descent students. In 1987, the Constitution of Ecuador was reformed and one of the changes allowed Indians to register at national universities. It should be added that the creation of Amawtay Wasi is part of the political processes led by Indigenous Nations that forced numerous claims into the new Constitution of Ecuador, including reconceptualizing "nature" as life to which we, as humans, also belong, and having done with the four hundred years of Baconian principles according to which "nature" is outside of us to be exploited and dominated. However, Indigenous actors (epistemic and political) soon realized, on the one hand, the disadvantages they had in competing with students who were born and raised in the same spirit that the national university was reproducing. On the other hand, they realized that, whatever effort they make to fulfill the university requirements, they will be learning "how to be according to national expectations regarding the indigenous population" but not learning to "be themselves." For this reason, Amawtay Wasi is open to all Ecuadorians, and not only to indigenous people. The concept of "interculturalidad" was created to highlight the emergence of political and epistemic rights that both the colonial and nation-state administration had denied to indigenous nations.

In addition to that, the institution was conceived as a pluriversity although the Minister of Education did not accept such a denomination. The concept of inter-culturalidad was connected with the indigenous project, working toward the constitution of a pluri-national state; a claim that is also made in Bolivia and has been reinforced by the government of Evo Morales. Clearly then, an institution such as Amawtay Wasi has significant implications in higher education, public policy, and international relations.[5]

The philosophy and conceptual curricular structure is clearly delinking from the history of Western university as an institution, from its origins in the Middle Ages to the corporate university that dominates today in the U.S. and is gaining ground in Europe and other parts of the world (Tlostanova 2004b, Mignolo 2003). "Delinking" does not mean that the university will be driven by "Indian cosmology" or that its curriculum will be structured and based on some ideal perennial "Indian" knowledge modeled before the conquest and colonization, when there was no "Indian" as a concept and the territory of today's Ecuador, Peru, and Bolivia were a part of Tawantinsuyu [the world in four parts] and the major languages there were Aymara (mainly in what is today Bolivia), Quechua (mainly in what is today Peru), and Quichua (mainly in what is today Ecuador). "Delinking" means basically shifting the geography of reason[6] and planning and organizing knowledge from the "Indigenous" American point of view instead of having only one option, that is, the university organized from the point of view of "Creoles and Mestizos," who adopted the model created by the "Indigenous" Europeans of the Renaissance and the Enlightenment. Amawtay Wasi does not reject the existing knowledge (in science, technology, medicine, social sciences, etc.), but it subsumes it within the vision, needs, and life style of Indigenous nations. Amawtay Wasi is founded and grounded not in an authentic or essentialist concept of knowledge, but in border thinking or border gnosis. "Interculturality" is precisely an expression of that epistemic and hermeneutic foundation based on cross-cultural dialogue, a transdisciplinary approach, and an imparative philosophy (from the Latin imparare—to learn in a pluralistic environment) (Panikkar 2000).

In the center of the cognitive and educational matrix of Amawtay Wasi stands a deeper fundamental principle (Kawsay) shared by the Indigenous people—the inextricable link between the "being," the "existence," and the "doing" (the human agency), or the principle of relational-experiential rationality and building knowledge not outside the essence and existence of being, not by presenting a problem outside of its context, but by practicing community learning as an ongoing and never-ending open process, based on complexity and relationism, complementarity and reciprocity, the shift from the subject-object relations to the subject-subject model instead of the dominant fragmentation, to the learning-unlearning-relearning path, and from accumulating knowledge to its critical and creative understanding and integration in wisdom.

The curriculum, very complex indeed, is basically structured—spatially—in the four spheres or spaces of learning and—chronologically—in five years of schooling. Spatially, it is framed in four corners or houses of learning and modeled on the Southern Cross, which in its turn was the spatial model for the territory of Tawantinsuyu (the "map" of the Incanate). At the center stands the house of Wisdom, wisdom being the ultimate goal of the university. In each corner, Western knowledge is detached from Western cosmology and "incorporated" and subsumed in Indigenous cosmology. Obviously, we cannot expect to find here genomic or nanotechnology institutes, not just at Amawtay Wasi but not even in South/Central America and in the Caribbean in general.[7] What we should expect from a project such as Amawtay Wasi is to shift the geography of reasoning and the very goals of knowledge and understanding. Learning is related to doing and experience. From the viewpoint of Indigenous leaders, Western knowledge, both in the colonial and the national period, was an instrument of (epistemic) colonization. As a result, the aim of such a shift is not destruction but rather creation of another model of knowledge and understanding of the world and human beings.

If the spatial structure is organized in four corners or houses of knowledge and a center, the chronological process of learning has five levels. The center of space coincides with the present in time. The first level is devoted to "learning to think doing things as a community." The second level aims at "learning to learn," the third strives for "learning to unlearn and relearn," and the fourth- for "learning to undertake." The last, fifth level, which is also at the center (similarly to Cuzco, the capital of the Incanate, which was at the center of the world but also the present of four previous eras, or "Suns" as the Incas counted each era), is devoted to "Learning throughout life." The university aims at decolonizing knowledge and being and promoting communities of "buen vivir," or "the fullness of life." "Sumak" is better translated into Spanish as "plenitude" or "fullness" in English. "Sumak Kawsay" would be better understood as precisely living the fullness of life rather than "buen vivir" or "living well," where "buen" and "well" are too attached to the materiality of life, to living as possessing things, to surrounding oneself with objects transformed into commodities, and feeling "happy" when life allows us to buy. Living well rather than living better than the other or better than my neighbor means a life in fullness that cannot be achieved within a capitalist economy. This concept necessarily presupposes the assumption that humans, nature, and the entire cosmos are alive to the extent that they are fully related and ontologically existing in this relational dynamic. According to Amawtay

Wasi vision, "education is viewed as learning to achieve relationalism, symbolized experience, symbolic language as a way to advance towards wisdom and to approach an understanding of living well" (García 2004: 288–89).

Such a model of education and cognition is possible to imagine in other locales of the world that have retained the indigenous knowledges (be it India, China, or Central Asia). However, the question is not only to reorganize universities according to the principles similar to Ecuador University and based on local histories and cosmologies but also to go beyond the university and shift the geography of reasoning and the approach to the interpretation of reality, history, philosophy, or politics of intellectuals worldwide. The basic questions are these: What kind of knowledges are produced and transformed? Who produces and transforms them, why, and for whom? What knowledge contributes to management for the benefit of the few, and what knowledges contribute to the liberation of the many from the management of the few? We are not always capable of changing the dominant power machines that run the systems of education or disciplines, in the same way we do not always have simple access to and the invigorating link with the communities and their knowledge and learning practices as with Amawtay Wasi. However, this does not mean that we cannot create the volatile communities of critical decolonial thought, the global coalitions of thinkers who chose as their main principle the Abya Yala's "learning to unlearn in order to relearn."

We take "learning to unlearn in order to relearn" as a guiding principle of this book and assume the goals and consequences of the radical proposal of Amawtay Wasi. We are not Indigenous Americans, but that does not mean that we cannot learn from them in order to unlearn what we have learned through our education or cultural environment and to relearn from the point of view of knowledge and understanding generated by the people and communities that have been disavowed in their participation in education, in the state and public policy, and in international relations and whose view of economic administration has been cast as "traditional" and troublesome for "development" proper. We are not appropriating Indigenous categories to the benefit of non-Indigenous intellectuals and scholars employed by public or private universities. This caveat would have not been necessary, if instead of Indigenous thinkers, we relied on the Frankfurt School or French postmodernism. Would a trans-diasporic multiethnic scholar living in Moscow and an Argentinean living in the U.S. be accused of appropriating Adorno or Baudrillard? If that were the path we had followed, it would have seemed "natural" that a Caucasus-Central Asian scholar in Moscow and an Argentine in the U.S., who became a Hispanic or Latino, learned from critical imperial scholarship. But, to learn from Indigenous thinkers could be rendered as "appropriation." Such biased interpretations are a result of remaining within the limits and blindness of modern epistemology.

III.

What do we mean by "thinking decolonially"? And, how does it relate to the title, *Learning to Unlearn*? Is it an expression parallel to many already existing ones: thinking philosophically, thinking economically, or thinking politically, where invariably, an action is invoked ("thinking") and a field in which the act of thinking is performed (economy, philosophy, politics)? There is a clear difference in the fields invoked here and in the way they can be used: economics, philosophy, politics can refer to academic disciplines; but they can also refer to a wider range of activities, not necessarily academic. The CEO of a corporation thinks economically and politically, too. The next presidential candidate thinks politically and economically as well, albeit not within the disciplines but within a larger field of social actions and discourses, the political field, and so forth.

"Decolonial thinking" is formulating the epistemic, political, and ethical basis for global decolonial options *in* the existing world order, which we all witness or take part in today. Where do "we" (scholars, intellectuals, journalists, activists) operate? Not in the sphere of the state or the market but in the public sphere, in the domain and terrain of the civil and political society, which we explain here. What is the "decolonial field" in relation to which "thinking decolonially" can have a meaning then? "Decolonial" presupposes first that there is another field, the field of coloniality (that is, the colonial matrix of power), from which it is assumed one should delink or disengage: This is the first meaning of decolonial, not anticolonial, but moving away from the colonial. The term "colonial" has a specific meaning in decolonial thinking. It refers not to the Roman Empire's understanding of a colony as a polity built or ruled by imperial order but to the modern meaning of "colonial" as a "conquered and managed territory" linked to the process of European "colonization," grounded in destroying the existing social order and imposing one responding to the needs and habitus of the conquerors. By "colonies," we refer in this book to the type of imperial-colonial interconnections between the imperial core countries of Europe (Spain, Portugal, France, England, Holland, and to a lesser extent Italy and Germany) from approximately 1500 onward. This is a particular type of imperial-colonial relations, classified mainly by the emergence of "capitalism" (as defined by

Max Weber (1904/05) and "imperialism" (as defined by J. A. Hobson ([1902] 2002), later appropriated and altered by Marxist popularizes such as V. Lenin ([1917] 1963), R. Luxembourg (1913), and others). Hence, by the early twentieth century, the legacy of the term "imperium" was translated into modern English as "imperialism" and connected to the already flourishing new type of economy, "capitalism." We ask, at the same time, what kind of imperial-colonial relations characterized the Russian Czardom/Empire and the Soviet Union? How did the colonial matrix "translate" from the Atlantic to Eurasia?

Decoloniality means projecting decolonial thinking over the colonial matrix of power. The latter is an analytic concept, but its very creation already implies decolonial thinking. Liberal and Marxist thinkers, political theorists, and economic experts all accept that the current global economy is capitalist. The only difference is that some of them are happy and want to maintain it (even during and after the crisis and legal corruption of Wall Street in 2007–2008) and others are unhappy and want to dismantle it. A decolonial thinker is with neither of them, and the reason is that "capitalist economy" is not the core analytic concept of decolonial thinking, whereas the "colonial matrix of power" is.

Polycentric capitalism made the modern idea of "revolution" obsolete for two reasons. One is that, in polycentric capitalism, in spite of the competition for control of authority (current conflicts between capital and state and between non-Western states embracing a capitalist economy, like China and Russia), there is no more room for an idea of revolution that consists in taking control of the state (like the bourgeoisie did in Europe over the monarchy; the Bolsheviks over the Russian Czars; like the Creole of European descent (except in Haiti) did in the Americas since the end of the eighteenth century; or the natives did in Asia and Africa, during the era of decolonization, after World War II). The second reason is that all the revolutions we have mentioned were revolutions within the same cosmology, within the same rules of the game. And the word "revolution" itself is meaningful only in the ideology of progress and development within the realm of sameness. At the moment when the colonial matrix of power reached a global scope, from the U.S. and European Union to China, India, and Brazil, one can argue that the very idea of revolution (a keyword in the vocabulary of modernity) lost its historical possibilities. Decolonial thinking offers an essentially different approach— the decolonial option. What is the grammar of decoloniality that could help advance transformative projects beyond the "revolutionary" language and expectations of modernity? Instead of digging into Western archives to find a Saint Paul or a Spinoza who would get us out of the impasse, we would like to dig into derogated archives, abased authors, concepts, and dissenting initiatives, which grew out of dissenting energies and minds that thought the world otherwise, that is, on the basis of a non-Western or not-quite-Western genealogy of knowledge. However, since the West is all over and in all of us, non-Western does not mean outside. It means residing in exteriority, that is, the outside created by the inside, by the imperial reason of Western control of knowledge (i.e., coloniality of knowledge and of being). The historical and logical foundation of exteriority is a Western epistemic construction of racism and the patriarchal control of knowledge and understanding.

Decolonial thinking and decolonial options are projects led and created by the people whom Frantz Fanon called "les damnés de la terre" (1967): all those humiliated, devalued, disregarded, disavowed, and confronting the trauma of the "colonial wound,"[8] a trauma that no modern psychoanalyst can cure, as Fanon himself experienced in Algeria (1967, Chapter V). "Damnés," in the colonial matrix, is a scalar category pervading all spheres of the social and not only the dispossessed. We believe that Fanon (a professional educated in France) placed himself among the damnés. The damnés should not be understood in economic terms (poverty) but mainly in racial terms (inferior human beings). Living experience generates knowledge to deal with the very foundation of a system of knowledge and subjectivity that constructed the damnés. Decolonizing knowledge and being means to generate knowledge to solve the problems in which the damnés have been placed as damnés. "Ending poverty" means maintaining the colonial matrix of power that produced and reproduced the dispossessed damnés. The decolonial intellectual and the decolonial political society link epistemology, politics, and ethics in the process of decolonizing knowledge and being. Radical "social movements" like La Via Campesina and Food Sovereignty are good examples of transnational projects decolonizing knowledge and being (La Via Campesina 2008, Abergel 2005, Desmarias 2007). Still another case is the Indigenous projects across the Americas, which have lately congregated in the annual Americas Social Forum. The project of Evo Morales's government has generated a significant and clear discourse about what it means to decolonize the state and the economy.

These are, in a nutshell, some of the questions that decolonial thinkers ask. By asking these kinds of questions, we start thinking decolonially and engage ourselves in a transdisciplinary analytic in which the problems precede the method. Our approach departs from the canonical scholarly assumptions in the humanities and social sciences and has implications for other areas of knowledge, in natural sciences as well as in professional schools.[9] By switching the emphasis from method to problems, a scholar, intellectual, or researcher is thrown into the world rather than remaining within the discipline. Instead of the study or analysis of the existing postcolonial and neocolonialist phenomena and processes, be it diaspora, exile, nationalism, biopolitics, etc., and maintaining the divide between the known object and the knowing subject, for the decolonial approach to study a phenomenon (idea, social event, art work) is only the first step toward a project, toward *solving a problem, toward answering a question.* The decolonial approach departs from the canonical distinction, in the humanities and social sciences, between explanation and understanding; between nomothetic and idiographic sciences. Studying and investigating are only preliminary steps in formulating decolonial arguments in public policy or education. The problems the decolonial thinkers explore are problems emerging from the modern-colonial matrix of power, that is, from the modern rhetoric of salvation hiding the colonial logic (coloniality) of oppression, control, and domination. Knowledge and understanding for decolonial thinkers overrule and overcome expert knowledge. While expertise is necessary, it is, at the same time, dangerous, for it forecloses dialogue, as the expert is the Deus absconditius, the observer who cannot be observed because, precisely, he or she is An Expert! While disciplinary knowledge in the social sciences and the humanities focuses on objects (culture, society, economy, politics), decolonial thinking shifts the politics of knowledge toward problems and questions that are hidden by the rhetoric of modernity.

To what problems do we refer and explore further later? They are problems emerging from the modern-colonial matrix of power, that is, from the modern rhetoric of salvation hiding the colonial logic (coloniality) of oppression, control, and domination. Thus, the analytic of coloniality is the necessary condition for prospective decolonial arguments—the decolonial option presupposes the analytic of the colonial matrix, in the same way as psychoanalysis presupposes the analytic of the unconscious or the international proletariat revolution presupposes the analytic of the logic of capital. Therefore, while disciplinary knowledge in the social sciences and the humanities focuses on objects (culture, society, economy, politics), decolonial thinking shifts the politics of knowledge toward problems and questions that are hidden by the rhetoric of modernity. For example, the general concern to fight poverty demands from the social sciences to study the conditions under which poverty could be eliminated, while decolonial thinking focuses on the hidden reasons that created and naturalized poverty. Decolonial public policy and education start from this premise.

Decolonial thinking can and should work effectively at any level and sphere of education (schools, colleges, higher education), as is manifested in case of Amawtay Wasi; and it can be very effective in another area of education: the media (particularly independent media, because mainstream media reproduces and perpetuates—in different scale and to a different degree—the coloniality of knowledge and of being) (Decolonizing the Digital 2009). Decolonial thinkers will not be listened to in Davos or among the G8; they will not be invited to a dialogue in the UN (and a wide range of similar subordinate institutions). But decolonial thinking works within the global political society, confronting the consequences of the colonial differences because "imperial international law and corporations are there" and "immigration is here."

"Political society" is a concept introduced by Indian historian Partha Chatterjee (Chatterjee 2004). He refers to a wide range of collective activities that no longer belong to the sphere of the civil society that expresses itself mainly through voting every two, four, or six years. The liberal model of society then begins to crack and distinct spheres emerge between the civil society and the state and between the civil society and the market. Furthermore, the political society no longer keeps the relative homogeneity of the Europe-American civil society, but it is emerging in the non-West and transforming the West through massive migrations from the non-West. Briefly, political society is not a modern concept but a decolonial one. If, within the liberal model of social organization, we can imagine a triangle with "the state," "the economy," and the "civil society" as its angles, in the colonial matrix of power, we have to imagine a tetragon, consisting of the modern/colonial state, the imperial/colonial market, the civil colonial society formed by European migrants, and the political society emerging out of the imperial/colonial history in which these four domains are the sites of struggle for control, domination, and liberation. One of the basic components of the civil society, in the liberal model (modern and Euro-American), which feeds the state and the market, is "education." Education, from a decolonial perspective, is located in the domain of "knowledge and subjectivity" and can be divided between "instruction" (skill, knowledge for practical purposes, as is clear today in the "universities" created in the corporate world) and "nurturing" (knowledge and understanding for personal and collective well-being).

In the liberal model, education and instruction communicate with "the state" and "the market" and are geared toward the instruction of experts, on the one hand, and the education of citizens (in which experts are included), on the other. Consumption is part of the educational process at the moment in which education itself becomes a commodity and sustains the corporate university (see Chapter 7). So we can imagine double arrows connecting the citizens in the civil society with the state and the market. However, the arrows connecting "the state" and "the market" confirm the domain of "the untouchable," to which members of the civil society have little access. The media plays precisely, the role of a "mediator"; in fact, more than a mediator, it is an agent of economic and authority control by the market and the state. In the colonial matrix of power, the liberal model is contested by the emergence of national and global political societies (often referred to as "social movements"). The coming into being of indymedia, filling the gaps and uncovering the silences of official TV channels and newspapers, becomes part of the political society. The role of the decolonial intellectual, in the academia and in the media, is then defined by his or her task in the process of decolonizing knowledge and being. Although the entire sphere of the political society could not be described as decolonial (e.g., the sphere of the political society that makes claims to improve living conditions without questioning the colonial matrix of power is not), we can define a growing sector of the political society as decolonial—the decolonial political society. "Learning to unlearn" describes the future of decolonial education and the problems it has to face. "Education" is not one and universal. It is always entangled with projects of regulation, assimilation, transformation, conservation. Learning to unlearn the imperial education is the starting point of decolonial education (Candau 2009).

Instruction and education, which went hand in hand in both the liberal model and the socialist version of modernity, have as their goal the training of the skillful professionals and the nurturing of either liberal or socialist subjects. In the corporate university, the role of education is the formation of "experts." "Scientific communism" in the Soviet Union was no less compulsive than the presumable liberties in Western liberal societies. After the fall of the Soviet Union, neo-liberalism strengthened its philosophy of education by making the central role of education that of an "expert." In so doing, neo-liberalism merged in the figure of the "expert," both in instruction and in nurturing. Decolonial thinking, instead, follows the philosophical principle set by the planners of Amawtay Wasi described previously, where decolonization of knowledge and being, from an Amerindian perspective, does not mean inclusion in the existing social system, governed by the colonial matrix of power, but instead unlearning what imperial/colonial designs have naturalized as the only way to know and the only way to be. Decolonial thinking and decolonial option are akin and conversant with these transforming processes taking place in the sphere of the "civil society." And, partly, they are an attempt to contribute to both—the conceptual formations for instruction and the transforming of subjectivities in nurturing. But the decolonial option projects itself as an intervention in the sphere of "political society" as well.

As the examples of Fanon and Amawtay Wasi suggest, there is a corridor between the profession, the academy, and the decolonial political society. Decolonial thinking is then transdisciplinary (not interdisciplinary), in the sense of going beyond the existing disciplines, of rejecting the "disciplinary decadence" and aiming at undisciplining knowledge. Thinking decolonially in the academy means to assume the same or similar problems articulated in and by decolonial political society. This is a change of terrain, a shift in the geography of reason: Instead of an object of study determined by disciplinary and academic demands, we face problems identified by les damnés acting in the decolonial political society. Living experiences (which I. Kant identified as preconditions of abstract knowledge) cannot be universalized. The type of living experience that Kant underwent is not the same as those experienced by Fanon. That is why geo- and body politics of knowledge is of the essence in decolonial thinking. And this knowledge is generated in the process of transformation enacted in decolonial political society. Hence, decolonial thinking in the academy has a double role:

a. Its contribution to decolonize knowledge and being.
b. Its joining the processes initiated in and by the actors of the political society.

Decolonial projects in the mid-twentieth century were at first built into the existing system of two modernities. What we encounter in postcolonial countries, after the second wave of decolonization, is mostly neocolonialism. The collapse of the Soviet system, even if incomplete (as Russia retains several of its colonies and clings to the symbolic tokens of its former imperial grandeur), was the next act in this global show of the imposing of the new form of coloniality onto the world. In today's conditions of the tectonic change from one power system, linked to the U.S. as its center, to a new polycentric one, it is crucial that the colonized or better, the damnés, the nodes of border thinking in the world, could establish a dialogue and create networks globally. What is crucial here is not to try to find a better place in the existing global coloniality but to destroy this coloniality and create an other world. It is an unavoidable process because coloniality carries in it the seeds of the decolonial agency.

Decolonial options orient the acts of delinking (at the same time being constituted by them) from the rhetoric of modernity and the logic of coloniality. Today's global coloniality has slipped out of Western imperial hands. As a consequence, it becomes a terrain of disputes between Western and non-Western countries (and unions, such as the EU and UNASUR), disputes already at work between the G8 and the G5 (China, India, Brazil, Mexico, and South Africa). The emerging decolonial political society, therefore, faces a situation that goes beyond each nation-state. In this regard, La Via Campesina and Indigenous projects across the Americas, associated with New Zealand and Australian aboriginals, as well as the World Social Forum, are creating conditions for delinking from the colonial matrix of power, at the moment when the colonial matrix of power is "uniting in conflict" the G8, G5, and BRIC countries (Brazil, Russia, India, China). If, then, these countries and unions are operating within the rhetoric of modernity and the logic of coloniality, the decolonial political society is working toward the mutation of the colonial matrix of power into different forms of communal (not communist) social organization, in which the role of the economy will not be that of accumulation and the economy will not be the site of competitiveness and exploitation but the site in which human beings work to live rather than live to work for others who accumulate.

The control of the economic sphere in the colonial matrix of power (referred to as "capitalism" in liberal and Marxist terminology), is now disputed by several countries (U.S., China, Japan, the formation of oil-based Middle East countries, etc.). As the control of the economy (and therefore the control of labor and natural resources) is disputed by several countries, the spheres of the control of authority (political and military) become contested and off-centered as well. Instead of liberalism versus socialism, the rivalry over the control of authority in a polycentric capitalism has multiple orientations and leads to the re-inscription in the political arena of the conceptions of society and life that have been pushed aside, disavowed, or marginalized by imperial expansion of Western Christianity and liberalism (South America, India, North and Sub-Saharan Africa) and by Orthodox Christianity and socialism (Central Asia, the Caucasus). The dispute for the control of knowledge is also at work: The geopolitics and body politics of knowledge are the emerging sites contesting the Western imperial hegemony of theo- and ego-politics of knowledge (we come back to these categories).

Networking across the globe, across languages and religions, and across institutions is one of the major tasks of decolonial thinkers and doers working toward global futures no longer controlled by the colonial matrix of power, once in the hands of Western empires but today being disputed by different centers grounded in a capitalist economy. Even though the government of Evo Morales, in Bolivia, introduced decolonial thinking in the sphere of the state and the economy, a series of events around the highway across the Amazon prompted a protest by the Indigenous communities living in the area. Such a heatedly debated march against Evo Morales as the "TIPNIS case" demonstrated the limits of decolonization in the sphere of the

State (Friedman-Rudovsky 2011). For the time being decoloniaity remains exclusively a project of the political society. Recently, it authorized the creation of three universities led by indigenous leaders and geared toward an education that brings the needs and interests of indigenous people to the curriculum. These kinds of experience, added to Amawtay Wasi, are the prime examples of thinking decolonially, that is, delinking from the liberal model of education and the growing corporative values invading higher education.

We take the lead from these experiences and link "learning to unlearn" to "thinking decolonially." Thinking decolonially means to feel and live beyond competition and hatred, which nourish each other. However, moving beyond both means delinking from the hegemonic vision of society grounded in corporate values with the support of state regulations. Competition and hatred prevents caring for each other. The Christian ideal of love (love yourself as you love your neighbor) and national state ideal of love (monolingual and monocultural) work in tandem with competition and its consequence, hatred (Mignolo 2000, Chapter 6). Learning to unlearn is basically pedagogical. And although learning to unlearn could be thought out and practiced in a non-decolonial project, there is already a genealogy of thought in which both are closely connected. It is in this genealogy of thought that we place our argument in the following chapters.[10]

IV.

The first part of the book opens with two jointly authored chapters. In the first chapter, "The Logic of Coloniality and the Limits of Postcoloniality: Colonial Studies, Postcoloniality, and Decoloniality," we aim at demarcating decolonial thinking from postcolonial studies and theory. Acknowledging the contributions made by postcolonial studies and theories in bringing the "colonial" into critical debates, we depart from it in two points. We start from the modern/colonial formation, in the sixteenth century, of the colonial matrix of power (Quijano 1992, 2000). The experience of British India and Orientalism, in which postcolonial studies and theories are grounded, is only part of the picture, imbedded in the already existing colonial matrix. Occidentalism, which is the necessary condition for the emergence of Orientalism, is left out in postcolonial studies. And the Russian/Soviet Union history and their respective colonies are also not accounted for.

In the second chapter, "Theorizing *from* the Borders; Shifting *to* the Geo- and Body Politics of Knowledge," we attempt to conceptualize border thinking as a manifestation of today's epistemic shift from the theo- and egopolitics of knowledge to the geo- and body politics of knowledge. The basic idea is that the gradual expansion of Western (Euro-American) concepts of knowledge and life has created borders with the so-called non-Western world at all levels of the colonial matrix. "Theorizing from the borders" is, in our view, a way of dwelling, being, and thinking in the borders. While it is not possible to do away with Western conceptual apparatus and its implementation, it is far from obvious that it should be adopted and adapted by the rest of the world. Hence comes the "double consciousness," as the famous African-American sociologist W. E. B. Du Bois described his experience of being Black and American, a condition under which lives the majority of the world population.

Parts II and III are devoted to exploring these issues in further detail. In other words, our respective histories, languages, memories, sensibilities, academic training, and the like do not correspond to the imperial/colonial legacies of the British Empire and French colonialism in Asia and Africa. Russia and the Soviet Union, and the imperial Iberian histories in South America and the Caribbean (topped at a later date by British and French imperialism without colonies), depart from both European Marxism and postmodernity and the corresponding postcoloniality. In a nutshell, if postmodernity is the internal and imperial overcoming of modernity, postcoloniality is the corresponding version of overcoming modernity/coloniality translated into postmodernity/postcoloniality.

Part II opens with Madina's chapter entitled "Transcultural Tricksters in between Empires: 'Suspended' Indigenous Agency in the Non-European Russian/Soviet (Ex-)Colonies and the Decolonial Option." It starts with a brief critical assessment of the existing area studies research on Central Asia and the Caucasus, taking into account the coloniality of knowledge, with its persistent Orientalism and progressivism and the geo- and body politics of knowledge as the most important yet often neglected defining factors of delinking from Orientalism and progressivism. The chapter argues that a more promising positioning is to be found in research produced by the local scholars themselves, provided they delink from the rhetoric of modernity with its underlying logic of coloniality. One of the basic elements of this sensibility in the making is the vital link with the specific negotiating subjectivity of a trickster that is to be found in such border locales as the Caucasus and Central Asia—the cultural, linguistic, ethnic, and religious crossroads. Being multiply colonized in an epistemic as well as economic and political sense, these regions have developed their strategies of survival, resistance to various regimes, and re-existence through border, transcultural, and transmodern models, which can constitute a way out of the contemporary opposition of the post-Christian West and Islam and find parallels in other instances of border epistemology unfolding in the world.

This chapter briefly traces the complex history of both locales in modernity, trying to understand, under the influence of which factors they turned into, the threatening images of paradigmatic antispaces, fallen out of time, for the West, and how the distorting influence of modernization and modernity endangers the transcultural continuum of Central Asia and the Caucasus. Further on, the chapter focuses on the specific position of Indigenous epistemic and political protest in the Caucasus and Central Asia, contemplating why such movements often remain unheard. It juxtaposes Indigenous movements and epistemologies in the Caucasus and Central Asia with those in South America, striving to understand the internal and global reasons for their failure in Eurasia. This failure is connected with the ways modernity has been manifested in these locales, with the specific influence of the subaltern empires and the imperial difference, with the multiple colonization, and with the brutal experience of the Soviet modernity.

Chapter 3 also touches on the nation-building processes in contemporary Central Asia and the Caucasus and the specific internal neocolonialism as an important agent of indigenous movements' stagnation, repression, or commodification. A crucial complicating factor here is Islam, which has gradually moved into the center of indigenous movements, contrary to the South American indigenous agency. The complex relation of Islam and indigenous decolonial epistemologies is also touched on, as well as the importance of deconstructing developmentalist logic to make the renaissance of indigenous movements possible in the newly independent Eurasian states. Specific attention is paid to the aesthetic and creative ways of resistance and re-existence in various art forms in Central Asia and the Caucasus today as possible preliminary venues for the future political agency.

Chapter 4, "Non-European Soviet Ex-Colonies and the Coloniality of Gender, or How to Unlearn Western Feminism in Eurasian Borderlands" continues to elaborate on the same problematic and epistemic locale but with yet another additional dimension—that of coloniality of gender. It starts and departs from the concept of the modern colonial gender system introduced by María Lugones and interprets racialization/genderization in the non-European former and present colonies of Russia based on the mutant forms of gender discourses. In the Caucasus and Central Asia a successful Soviet zombification of the political and social imaginary has continued until now and has been accompanied by the influence of neoliberal ideologies of globalization. In the focus of the chapter stand the contemporary gender discourses of the Caucasus and particularly Central Asia that have been developing within the well-known frame of coloniality of knowledge and being and within the simplified opposition of modernity vs. tradition, which results in the tripartite scheme or vector of gender development presented in the majority of feminist works written in and about the Caucasus and Central Asia. This scheme moves from local traditionalism through the Soviet half-tradition and half-modernity to today's ideal of Western gender emancipation as an epitome of modernity. Here, we can clearly see how the Eurocentric discourses of Western feminism and its Russian clones dominate in the gender studies of Eurasian borderlands. At the same time, the chapter concentrates on several examples of successful alternative gender discourses coming from China, South America, Africa, and so on. A dialogue with them could be fruitful for the Eurasian gender studies in the future.

Part III is composed of three chapters written by Walter. The first, "Who Speaks for the 'Human' in Human Rights? Dispensable and Bare Lives," takes the questions of subalternity and humanity to the limits. In the last analysis, subalternity, knowledge, and humanity are connected by racial and class hierarchies in the modern world. And, both are hierarchically connected with values placed on knowledge and the question of who can produce legitimate and sustainable knowledge. "Learning to unlearn" is tantamount to thinking decolonially about these commonly held assumptions.

Chapter 6, "Thinking Decolonially: Citizenship, Knowledge, and the Limits of Humanity," brings the question of subalternity to a more basic level: the concept of Human and Humanity in the modern/colonial world. Human and Humanity are linked to knowledge in very complex and ambiguous ways. In fact, there is a direct connection between racism and legitimate knowledge, and between citizenship and education, which, in their turn, impinge on the concept of Human and Rights. This is the topic of Chapter 7, "Globalization and the Geopolitics of Knowledge: The Role of the Humanities in the Corporate University." This chapter connects with the previous two through the concepts of Human and Humanity and comes back to the main thesis of the book, i.e., learning to unlearn, as a basic process of delinking from imperial education and building decolonial knowledges. "Learning to unlearn" means here a double movement: decolonizing the Humanities as inherited from the Renaissance and the Enlightenment and delinking and shifting toward the making of decolonial Humanities the overarching horizon of knowledge under which science, technology, and professional schools should be conceived and enacted. Amawtay Wasi [the House of Wisdom], is the model that provides us with the need of learning to unlearn in order to relearn and to conceive of and enact the decolonial humanities.

PART I

CHAPTER 1

The Logic of Coloniality and the Limits of Postcoloniality

Colonial Studies, Postcoloniality, and Decoloniality

IN JULY 2001, we were teaching a summer seminar, sponsored by Open Society Institute at the European Humanities University, in Minsk, Belarus. During a lunch conversation in which we were talking about "postcoloniality," one of the participants in the seminar asked: "What exactly is coloniality? When you talk about postmodernity," she said, "I know what modernity is (at least I am familiar with the idea and the term), but when you talk about postcoloniality and decoloniality, I haven't the slightest idea what coloniality is or may be."[11] This is a belated response to that question.[12] Explaining to our student what coloniality means, we also lay out the difference between post- and de-coloniality, clarify why we opted for decoloniality over postcoloniality, and outline what are for us the contributions as well as the limits of postcoloniality.

By addressing the limits of postcoloniality, we are not placing ourselves "against" it; on the contrary, we are bringing forward another option—the decolonial option. The term "decolonization" became common currency during the Cold War and was connected to the Third World, particularly to the process of liberation in Asia and Africa. The decolonial option that rejects both capitalist and communist alternatives was introduced in the Bandung Conference, in 1955 (Ampiah 2007). However, decolonial thinking and decoloniality go back to the sixteenth century and cut across the eighteenth to the twentieth centuries. A non-Spanish or, later on, non-British or

31

non-French ruling was one of the first responses given by activists and intellectuals in Tawantinsuyu and the Caribbean to global linear thinking supported by the invention of international law (Francisco de Vitoria and Hugo Grotius) and the *jus publicum Europaeum* described by Carl Schmitt in the early 1950s.[13] Postcoloniality and decoloniality are two different responses to the five hundred years of Western consolidation and imperial expansion. These responses were built on different historical experiences, languages, memories, and genealogies of thought. Our take on decoloniality is built on the historical foundation of the modern/colonial world in the Atlantic (sixteenth to eighteenth centuries) and the history of the Russian Czardom and Empire; its translation into the Soviet Union and the changing roles of the Russian Federation and its ex-colonies in the past two decades.

In building on decolonial thinking and outlining decolonial options, our aim is to delink from the principles and structures supporting the existing system of knowledge in the humanities; we question the rhetoric justifying the role of the social sciences and the humanities as well as their methodology. Drawing on experiences and arguments such as the ones suggested by Maori anthropologist Linda Tuhiwai Smith, we call into question the disciplinary legitimacy of knowledge and the disqualification of knowledge that does not obey the existing disciplinary rules. That is one of the starting points of learning to unlearn in order to relearn—the disciplinary disobedience (Smith 1999). This is a qualitative not a quantitative shift, as is often the case with postcolonial studies.

Hopefully now the reader begins to see the different paths followed by decolonial thinking on the one hand, and postcolonial studies and theory on the other. What happens in the majority of postcolonial studies? They start from the version of history that places the British Empire (or, sometimes, the French Empire) at the center of modern/colonial history. It is too late for us. Modern/colonial history originated in the Atlantic, in the complexity of European imperial formations (Iberian Peninsula) and would-be empires (Holland, French, England), in the dismantling of Tawantinsuyu and Anahuac and the massive capture, transportation, and exploitation of enslaved Africans. This is one of the limits of postcoloniality seen from the historical perspective of decolonial thinking and struggling much before the advent of European postmodernity that makes possible the emergence of postcoloniality.

Sometime around the 1970s, due to the impact of decolonization struggles in Asia and Africa, the emergence of dictatorial regimes in South America, and the Civil Rights movement in the U.S., a radical transformation of intellectual and scholarly fields took place. In the "Third World," the concern was with the *geopolitics of knowledge* and, consequently, with decolonizing of the imperial knowledge. In the U.S., the concern was with the *body politics of knowledge*.[14] It was the moment when a new organization of knowledge and understanding came into being: women's studies, ethnic studies, Chicano/Latino/a studies, African-American Studies, Queer Studies, Asian-American Studies, and so forth. Postcolonial studies emerged mainly in the U.S. in this particular context. The novelty was that they put the geopolitics of knowledge on the table of an already subversive scenario centered on the body politics of knowledge. Postcolonial theories and postcolonial studies, instead, entered the U.S. carrying in their bags the last word by and about postmodern thinkers; the bags were *le dernier gadgé-d'outre-mer*. Postcolonial contributions are obvious: they brought into U.S. humanities scholarship the relevance of the world beyond Europe and the U.S. The influence of postcoloniality was felt also in the social sciences, particularly through the influential work of Edward Said (1978). All in all, postcolonial studies and theories are connected to the splendors and miseries of French poststructuralism through which colonial experiences in British India were filtered. Parallel to that development, the Subaltern Studies, initiated by Ranahit Guha in London in the mid to late 1970s took Antonio Gramsci to India, i.e., an ex-British colony. It was Said who brought with him the British Maghreb and the Palestinian question and connected it to postcolonial debates. However, if in *Orientalism* Said fits the discourse and goals of postcoloniality, his book *The Question of Palestine* (1978), published in the same year, reads today as a decolonial critique parallel and complementary to Frantz Fanon's *The Wretched of the Earth* (1967 [1961]), Albert Memmi's *The Colonizer and the Colonized* (1957 [1991]), and the earlier José Carlos Mariátegui's *Seven Interpretative Essays on Peruvian Reality* (1928[1971]).

In a nutshell, postcoloniality presupposes postmodernity, while decolonial thinking and decolonial option are always already delinked from modernity and post-modernity. It brings to the foreground a silenced and different genealogy of thought. The decolonial option originated not in Europe but in the Third World, as a consequence of struggles for political decolonization. And it emerged among "minorities" in the heart of the U.S. as a consequence of the Civil Rights movement and its impact on decolonizing knowledge and being through gender and ethnic studies. Furthermore, if we take into account the history of the Russian Empire, which was the first not-quite-European imperial formation following the European model and, in case of the Soviet Union, the first non-Christian European formation modeled on the European Marxist ideas and ideals, we would have to deal with the imperial difference (and imperial differentiation, since "differences" are never static). Thus, decoloniality works on specific sets of issues built on particular historical legacies, languages, sensibilities, experiences, and senses affected through smells and food, bodies and sexualities, music and everyday life.

It is also through these routes that decolonial thinking enters the ex-Soviet world after 1991. *We* (Madina and Walter, as well as the collective modernity/coloniality/decoloniality) do not derive our ideas from European post-structuralism but from the colonial histories of South America and the Caribbean and of Central Asia and the Caucasus under the Russian Empire and the Soviet Union. In building our arguments, we may or may not use some of their concepts for convenience, but not the epistemic principles on which those concepts are grounded and the historical foundation of post-structural arguments. Our subjectivities, experiences, languages, histories, desires, frustrations, and angers are different from the ones expressed by Foucault, Lacan, or Derrida. Theirs is a different history; their problems are not our problems; and we surmise that our problems are not necessarily theirs.[15] For this reason alone, geo- and body politics of knowledge is of the essence. This is what we meant when we made a distinction between focusing on objects and focusing on problems. Postcolonial theories and decolonial thinking are interrelated at the level of the enunciated (i.e., the content, the concern with colonial histories and their consequences for the present) but they do not intersect at the level of the enunciation (i.e., the terms of the conversation).[16] Furthermore, imperial differences, encroached on colonial differences (e.g., racialization of China and Russia) and the way these encroachments engender and shape enunciations, are highly relevant in understanding the global coloniality (the darker side of global modernity). They are "next to" the encroachment on which postcolonial theorists and critics dwell.

While anti-colonial struggles were shaking up the Third World, the Soviet Union and the U.S. (with the support of western European countries), were engaged in the Cold War. If, in the U.S., the Civil Rights movement opened up the waters for the decolonial body politics (e.g., for Chicanos and Native Americans as well as for African Americans in the 1970s, when the expressions such as "decolonization" and "internal colonialism" were already a common currency), the Soviet Union was successful in repressing the internal decolonial openings, particularly in racialized non-European colonies devoid of any agency, where the empire destroyed, bought up, or exiled most alternative voices in order to wipe off any traces of heterodoxy on cultural, ethnic, or religious basis. The collapse of the Soviet Union resulted in an unwanted independence of most of its colonies, but the process was quickly strangled, while Russia together with the whole post-Socialist space became a large arena for global coloniality (embracing the (neo)liberal version of the colonial matrix) and neocolonialism.

Decolonial thinking was also available (Aimé Césaire, Frantz Fanon; the journal *Presence Africaine*; etc.) but silenced in places where Marxism, structuralism, and poststructuralism occupied all the intellectual debates at the time. Decolonial thinking was going on in Maghreb, in sub-Saharan Africa, and in India but not in France or England. Decolonial thinking entered Europe with the massive immigration from South Asia, the Middle East, Maghreb.[17] In today's U.S., the massive migration is just joining decolonial thinking processes that can be traced back—in their conceptual awareness—to the 1970s, if not before. The field of "education" has changed radically. A diversity of "conceptual tools" became available, no longer controlled by canonical disciplines and transforming the instructional dimension of education, mainly in the humanities and the social sciences but already entering into other fields as well. Most important, however, it had and continues to have a strong influence on "nurturing," shaping, and transforming subjectivities disputed in other realms by religious orders and market gurus.

It seems to us that postcolonial studies bring forward a change in the content but not in the terms of the conversation. The latter presupposes delinking and shifting the geography of reasoning, which is not obvious to us in various manifestations of postcolonial studies. One can reformulate Jacques Lacan's ideas and create on their basis the new concepts in the vein of Homi Bhabha, but one can also start not from Lacan but from Gloria Anzaldúa, from the Zapatistas, from the Caucasus cosmology, or from Nakshbandi Sufism. These are options that already distinguish decolonial from postcolonial trajectories. It depends, in the last analysis, on how the world is inscribed in your skin rather than on how the novelty of post-structuralism affects your mind. Postcolonial studies seem to dwell in a skin different from ours and in need of the epistemic frame of Eurocentric modernity: the distinction between the knowing subject and known object is implied in both the notion of "study" and the notion of "theory." For that reason, postcolonial studies do not alter the internal discourses inherent in and fundamental to modernity, such as progressivism and developmentalism: both are implied in the prefix "post." Gandhi, Fanon, and Anzaldúa did not "study" or "theorize" British imperialism in India, Black experience in the Caribbean, Berber and Arabic existentia in North Africa, or Chicana trajectories in the U.S. Their political stance went together with a decolonial shift in knowledge production. Their thinking is "actional," as Lewis Gordon describes Fanon's work (Gordon 1995). What they all have in common, beyond their differences, is that they inhabit the colonial wound. All three of them "thought" and wrote from the "experience" of the colonial wound. And the knowledge produced from the colonial wound is not a knowledge that aims to change the "disciplines" but rather to "decolonize" knowledge, to undo imperial and colonial differences, ontologically and epistemically. Therefore, one of the vexing questions that emerged in the late 1980s about the relations between identities and epistemologies becomes a mute point: Fanon is not "studying the blacks" but instead, "thinking" ethically and politically from the colonial wound and shifting the ethics and politics of knowledge articulated in the distinction between the knowing subject and the known object. Learning to unlearn confronts us (scholars, intellectuals, students, professors, professionals of all sorts, officers of the state, and corporations officers) with the necessity of delinking from the naturalized vision of society (the idea of Humanity, of happiness and reward, of a vertical structure of power) that was created in the sixteenth century by monarchies and the Christian church, then mutated into the secular project (secularism) that brought the European bourgeoisie into the state and the Industrial Revolution and into reframing of the economy.

What about post-Socialist Russia? Who are the equivalents to Gandhi, Fanon, or Anzaldúa? The complication in Russian history is that the Soviet revolution turned Marxism into a model of imperial domination and Marxism became as oppressive as Christianity and liberalism. Post-Socialist Russia is facing the dilemma of having burned out one of the "hopes" still alive among Western Marxists and not having another way out of joining the new philosophy of Western empires—neoliberalism, which is only dusted today with the moth-eaten imperial nationalism and isolationism. Consequently, whereas decolonial projects and practices emerged in the colonies of Western empires as early as the sixteenth century, in Russian modern/colonial history, the anticolonial sentiment proper was less pronounced than the one linked to the imperial difference with the West. So, within the history of today's Russian Federation, the decolonial attitude starts, paradoxically, with the imperial wound. Intellectuals and writers such as Fyodor Dostoyevsky in the nineteenth century and Victor Yerofeyev today describe this as follows: "In Europe we were hangers-on and slaves, whereas in Asia we shall go as masters" (Dostoyevsky 1977 [1881]); and "From Moscow I can go to Asia, if I want, or to Europe. That is, it is clear where I am going to. It is not clear—where I am coming from . . ." (Yerofeyev 2000). It is not clear yet what will come from the ex-colonies of the Russian and Soviet Empires, as well as from some of the colonies that remain under the Russian Federation (such as Chechnya, Tatarstan, or, Buryatia). What is clear, however, is that a shift in the ethics and politics of knowledge that would cast Russian history beyond the Hegelian dictum and beyond its double dependency with the West—liberal and Marxist—will emerge at some point at some place, because neither Christian Orthodoxy (very much like Christian Catholicism and Protestantism in the West) nor second-class liberalism offers a promising future. Marxism as a model for the organization of society has also run its course in Russia as well as in Western industrial countries (Europe and the U.S.) and their dependent states (Latin America and the Caribbean).

The Colonial Matrix of Power

The analysis and understanding of the logic of coloniality presupposes a reframing of the current view of history and of modernity. The very concept of post-coloniality (and its corollaries, postcolonial studies and theory) would also have to be reframed once the logic of coloniality is brought out of its invisibility and placed side by side with the rhetoric of modernity. The idea of modernity, to begin with, has been conceived from the perspective of European history and framed based on the historical process and subjective experience of Western European countries and people—more specifically, on the complicity between Western Christendom and the emergence of capitalism as we know it today. Europe and modernity have become synonymous and essential components of modern European identity. Coloniality, instead, has been swiped out and made invisible in the Eurocentric narratives as an encumbrance for the glorious march of modernity. Where coloniality is visible every day is in the colonies, semi-colonies, and ex-colonies of Western empires. For that reason, it is not surprising that the concept of "coloniality" has been brought out in Latin America, whereas the concept of "modernity" is a European invention. These are not, however, concepts that stand at the same level in power relations. We can talk about modernity ignoring coloniality, as it has always been obvious. But you cannot talk about coloniality without invoking modernity.

"Development" is a companion concept to modernity. "Underdevelopment," however, is not the equivalent, in economic terms, to coloniality in historical and philosophical terms. Underdevelopment is what development proposes to overcome. In other words, underdevelopment is an invention of the discourse of development to justify economic and political interventions, with a good cause. Instead, modernity does not propose to overcome coloniality but rather tradition, barbarism, fanatic religious belief, and the like. Coloniality is what development needs to overcome under the guise of underdevelopment. Coloniality is indeed the hidden weapon behind the rhetoric of modernity justifying all kinds of actions, including war, to eliminate barbarism and overcome tradition. Thus, coloniality is, like the unconscious, the hidden weapon of both the civilizing and developmental missions of modernity.

The imbalance in power relations brings about—this time—the splendors and miseries of coloniality. The misery is its dependency on modernity. The splendor is that the concept reveals the colonial matrix of power, illuminates colonial and imperial differences, makes understandable the colonial wound, and delivers epistemic energy for a radical shift in the geo- and body politics of knowledge. The history and interpretation of the world can no longer be achieved from the universal perspective of the modern social sciences and humanities. Perspectives from modernity (from the left and from the right, from neoliberals or from neo-Marxists) provide only half of the story—hence the perplexity of the student in Minsk who was familiar only with this half. Telling the other half is our task then.

The logic of coloniality (the colonial matrix of power) is the "missing" half in current definitions of "modernity," which passes for the totality. Take, for example, Anthony Giddens's short description of modernity: " 'modernity' refers to modes of social life or organization which emerged in Europe from about the seventeenth century onwards and which subsequently became more or less worldwide in their influence" (Giddens 1992: 1). Giddens's concept of modernity is very shortsighted, for he sees only one side of it—the European imperial side. From the perspective of coloniality, however, world history since the sixteenth century has had different colors and shades, different geohistorical locations for accumulations (of money as well as of meaning), enjoyments, and sufferings. We can therefore paraphrase Giddens's description of modernity to render visible the logic of coloniality, as follows:

> "Coloniality" refers to the modes of control of social life and economic and political organizations that emerged in the European management of the colonies in the Americas and the Caribbean from around the beginning of the sixteenth century onwards and that subsequently have become more or less worldwide in their influence. This associates coloniality with a time period and with an initial geographical location but for the moment leaves its major characteristics safely stowed away in a black box. Yet, they are being applied today in Iraq and the Middle East and North Korea, in Georgia (Transcaucasia) and Chechnya; in redefining the internal imperial difference between the U.S. and the European Union,

and the external imperial difference between the U.S. and the European Union on one side and Russia, China, and Japan on the other. Coloniality, indeed, has become since the sixteenth century more or less worldwide in its "influence." (Mignolo and Tlostanova's paraphrase of Giddens's (1992) definition of modernity)

Let us now explore further coloniality as a concept, rather than the set of historical processes that the concept uncovers. It is a disturbing concept indeed. Coloniality invokes colonialism, which is the complement of imperialism. Thus, whereas "imperialism/colonialism" refers to specific sociohistorical configurations (i.e., the Spanish and British Empires' colonies in the Americas and Asia), "modernity/coloniality" refers to the conceptual and ideological matrix of the Atlantic world that, since 1500, has expanded all over the globe. Third, coloniality or the colonial matrix of power, describes a specific kind of imperial/colonial relations that emerged in the Atlantic world in the sixteenth century and brought imperialism and capitalism together. The Roman Empire, for example, was not a capitalist empire, neither was the Ottoman Sultanate that coexisted in the sixteenth century with the Spanish Empire. The colonial matrix of power explains the specificity of the modern/colonial world and the imperial/colonial expansion of Christian, Western, and Capitalist empires: Spain, England, and the U.S.

Coloniality is disturbing because it forces you to move back the clock of "modern" history, because "modernity" has been self-fashioned on the French Revolution (politics), the Industrial Revolution (economy), and class struggle (the logic of history and the future of the world). Historically, coloniality is the hidden logic of control and management, underlining (invisibly) the European appropriation of land, the massive exploitation of labor, the slave trade, the extraction of gold and silver, and the plantation economy. It was not at that time a projected global design. Western Christians, after losing Jerusalem, where concerned about how to expand Christianity over the world—the oecumene that then did not include what would become "America." Coloniality as a specific set of processes started with the Spaniards and the Portuguese. The world we live in today is, decolonially speaking, a consequence of the "colonial revolution" rather than the French or Industrial ones. The colonial revolution or revolution of coloniality started in the sixteenth century and does not consist in overruling something previous within the same history but in erasing to build something new: the New World, metaphorically, the modern/colonial world. This kind of revolution took place later on in Asia and in Africa, when European powers arrived with the tools of the empire; and when the U.S. and transnational corporations, today, arrive with their juggernaut to dismantle the environment in search for natural resources and the colonization of the last remaining subject of colonization: life itself.

In the seventeenth century, Dutch, French, and British merchants and entrepreneurs took advantage of the Caribbean lands and enslaved Africans to settle a plantation economy that contributed to increase the wealth and authority of Western European monarchies and created the conditions for the Industrial Revolution. The Dutch created the East India Company. The British soon initiated their own commercial relations with the Mughal Sultanate; after Napoleon, France started its commercial and colonial contacts with Maghreb. From the late eighteenth century on, the colonial matrix of power was expanded, transformed, and enacted by the emerging European imperial nations of the western and Atlantic coasts. This story is well known. Less attention has been paid to the commonality, the three centuries after the "discovery" of America, of the underlying structure that united the Portuguese, the Spanish, the Dutch, the French, and the English and also, with a few important provisions, the Russian.

Eastern Christianity housed among other spaces in Russia had its own historically unsuccessful global pretensions of the specific Orthodox Christian kind (based on aggressive Russian Orthodox universalizing the ideal of a particular spiritually, taking over the whole humanity) and also, its own New World—first Siberia, which was colonized by the Russian equivalents of the conquistadors (the Cossacks) and under the supervision of the proto-capitalist merchant families like the Stroganoff, from the late sixteenth century on—and in the second modernity—the Caucasus and Central Asia (the Russian Orient or the hot Siberia, as it used to be called in the nineteenth century). In spite of lacking classical capitalist model, in the first modernity, Russia had its own variant of coloniality, with Orthodox Christianity in its center (Moscow as the Third Rome) and all the commercial and geopolitical reverberations, except for the ingenious "discovery" of Western modernity—the firm link between racism and the shaping of the capitalist exploitation of labor in the colonies. Thus, already at that point in history, it became obvious that coloniality is wider and deeper than just "capital/modernity,"[18] it cannot be taken exclusively to the economic sphere, and it allows us to conceptualize not just the West and its colonies but also the rest of the world, particularly Eurasia, which was later mentally colonized by the discourses of modernity. This deeper nature of coloniality, rather than capitalism, would keep coming forward again and again—in the Soviet modernity and in the late twentieth century, when capitalism would become polycentric and travel to non-European spaces.

It is disturbing, finally, because it forces you to a new beginning of modern/colonial history, to see the foundation of capitalism in the very "primitive accumulation" that Karl Marx, with his progressive view of history, saw as a precondition of *real* capitalism in the northern European Industrial Revolution. Globalization, as it is understood today, goes hand in hand with coloniality, with the foundation of the colonial matrix of power. Postcolonial studies and theories, as currently understood in the U.S. and certain European countries, start from a different historicity and genealogy of thought, which places the British Empire and, sometimes, French colonial expansion at the center of modern/colonial history. This is one of the limits of postcolonial studies seen from the perspective of global coloniality. Equally misleading and simplified are the attempts of certain scholars to apply postcolonial studies and theory to the analysis of the post-Soviet space, without paying attention to the differences both within their varied local histories and configurations and vis-à-vis the rest of the world.[19]

Defining Colonial and Imperial Differences

Colonial and imperial difference(s) are not fixed, stable walls. They change through time and space. What is maintained is the coloniality of both. If modern/colonial empires are one and the same with the foundation and history of capitalism and the idea of Europe, then the question is this: How does the colonial matrix of power, thus defined, relate and explain the Russian Empire and the Ottoman Sultanate, to take the examples of empires coexisting with the capitalist and Western Christian ones? To answer this question, we need to unfold the concepts of the "colonial and imperial differences" introduced previously. Both are implied in the very structure of the colonial matrix of power. Imperial discourses are built on the bases of the differences with people, languages, religions, economies, and political organizations of the colonies. To exploit, it is necessary to dominate, and to dominate, it is necessary to build discourses and belief systems that produce the imperial image as the locus of the right and unavoidable march of history and the colonies as the locus of the erroneous, the inferior, the weak, the barbarians, the primitives, and so on. To conflate differences with values in human beings' hierarchical order is not just to *identify* "cultural" differences but to *build* "colonial" differences, justified in a "racial" configuration of human beings on the planet, their languages and religions, their economies, and their social organizations. That is, modern imperial discourses have been founded on the basis of "colonial differences" at all levels of the social. On the other hand, to maintain the control vis-à-vis competing empires, it is also necessary to assert the superiority of imperial hegemony and to found the "imperial difference" with coexisting and imperial formations. Thus, the Russian Empire that took off with Ivan the Terrible toward 1555 and the Ottoman Sultanate, whose moment of splendor with Suleiman the Magnificent coincided with Charles V of the Holy Roman Empire and I of Castile, were soon located in the margins of the Western Christian imperial discourses. The Russians were Christian but not Catholic, their alphabet was Cyrillic, and their language was Slavic (linked with Greek literacy and not Latin), whereas the Ottoman Sultanate was Muslim and its language was Turkish and Arabic. The Russian and the Ottoman may have been empires, like the Spanish one, but certainly only second class. That is, the imperial difference recognizes the similar but immediately reduces it to a second-class empire by extending to it the features of the colonial difference.[20] That is to say, both the Russian Empire and Ottoman Sultanate were inferior in terms of religion and language. Consequently, the imperial difference was constructed on the same principle of the colonial difference, except that it was applied to sociohistorical configurations that were not reduced to colonies.[21]

Zero-Point Epistemology

The foundation of knowledge was and remains territorial and imperial. The world map drawn by Gerardus Mercator and Johannes Ortelius worked together with theology to create a zero point of observation and of knowledge—a perspective that denied all other perspectives. Modernity in this respect is not a historical process but an idea that describes certain historical processes. This idea needs a system of knowledge that legitimizes it. Simultaneously, once the idea was created, it legitimized the system of knowledge that created it (Mignolo 1992, 301–30). By the same token, the idea of modernity and the system of knowledge that legitimized it became a mechanism to disavow other systems of knowledge and to make other historical processes non-modern. The system, in which coloniality is embedded, also created a meta-language wherein its own affirmation went hand in hand with the justification to disavow systems of knowledge that the meta-language described as non-modern. Meta-languages have the peculiarity of detaching the known from the knower, the said from the act of saying, and create the effect of an ontology independent of the subject. Modernity then is the construction of a meta-language that originated the European Renaissance (rebirth) coupled with European imperial expansion. Through the centuries, the meta-language was transformed and at the same time maintained during the Enlightenment and adjusted during the period of neoliberal globalization, to become globally hegemonic.

The hegemonic system of knowledge production, transformation, and transmission is grounded today in what Colombian philosopher Santiago Castro-Gómez described as the hubris of the *zero point*. The coexistence of diverse ways of producing and transmitting knowledge is eliminated because now all forms of human knowledge are ordered on an epistemological scale from the traditional to the modern, from barbarism to civilization, from the community to the individual, from the orient to occident..... By way of this strategy, scientific thought positions itself as the only valid form of producing knowledge, and Europe acquires an epistemological hegemony over all other cultures of the world (Castro-Gómez 2007: 433).

The hubris of the zero point is the place of the observer and the locus of enunciation that, in Christian theology, was taken by God and, in Secular Philosophy, by Reason. The zero point is the limit in which there is an observer than cannot be observed, the God of Transcendental Reason; that is, zero point epistemology is theologically Christian and egologically secular. Once a mortal human claims that he or she occupies that space, either in communication with God or in assuming the position of the observer at the top of the hill looking down the valley, a secure locus of enunciation is created that is hard to dispute. This happens because he or she observes not just with his or her eyes, but within certain languages and in certain linguistic tradition in the categories of thought; and consequently, whoever comes from knowledge systems incorporated in non-Western languages and relies on different principles of knowledge has a hard time entering the house where the hubris of the zero point dominates.

Epistemological frontiers were set in place as a result of this move. These were the frontiers that expelled to the outside the epistemic colonial differences (Arabic, Aymara, Hindi, Bengali, etc.). Epistemic frontiers were rearticulated in the eighteenth century with the displacement of theology and the theopolitics of knowledge by secular egology and the egopolitics of knowledge. Epistemic frontiers were traced by the creation of the imperial and colonial difference. Both epistemic differences were based on a racial classification of the population of the planet, where those who made the classification put themselves at the top of humanity. The Renaissance idea of Man was conceptualized based on the paradigmatic examples of Western Christianity, Europe, and white and male subjectivity (Las Casas [1552] 1967, Kant 1798).

Global Coloniality: The (Four) Spheres of the Colonial Matrix of Power Revisited

The colonial matrix of power emerged and was founded as a consequence of the Christian and Castilian colonization of the Americas. Radical changes took place during that period in the history of humankind. The changes in scale and orientation could be described in four interrelated spheres of social organization.

In each sphere, there is a struggle, conflict for control and domination in which the imposition of a particular lifestyle, morale, economy, structure of authority, and so on implies the overcoming, destruction, and marginalization of the existing one. The four interconnected spheres in which the colonial matrix of power was put together in the sixteenth century, and has operated since then, are the following:

1. The struggle for the economic control (i.e., the appropriation of land and natural resources and the exploitation of labor) oriented to produce commodities for the global market. As Anibal Quijano and Immanuel Wallerstein (1992: 134) suggest, the Americas were not incorporated into an already existing capitalist economy, but on the contrary, a capitalist economy as we know it today could not have existed without the discovery of America. The complementary movement of land appropriation and labor exploitation meant, simultaneously, the dismantling and overruling of other existing relations between human beings, society, land, and labor, such as the one already in place in the so-called Inca and Aztec Empires.

2. The struggle for the control of authority (setting up political organizations, different forms of government, financial, and legal systems or the installation of military bases, as it happens today). Thus, in the Americas, the Spanish and Christian institutions were established to dismantle and overrule the existing forms of control of authority between Incas and Aztecs.

3. The control of gender and sexuality—among other ways, through the nuclear family (Christian or bourgeois), and the enforcing of normative sexuality and the naturalization of gender roles in relation to the system of authority and principles regulating economic practices, the third sphere of the colonial matrix of power. It is based on sexual normativity and dual "natural" gender relations. Christian morality, the idea of the family, and patriarchal superiority were imposed at the same time that homosexuality was condemned and placed on the side

of the Devil. The control of gender and sexuality also overruled gender relations and sexual practices existing among Aztecs, Incas, and other communities reached by the spread of Christian itinerant missionaries. A decolonial gender theorist and activist, María Lugones, recently summarized this sphere in the concept of *coloniality of gender* (Lugones 2008), which we explore in more detail in Part II.

4. The control of knowledge and subjectivity through education and colonizing the existing knowledges, which is the key and fundamental sphere of control that makes domination possible. The control of knowledge and subjectivity was part of the package of the colonial matrix of power on which the imperial control of the colonies was organized. Christian colleges were created all over the Spanish dominions. The Renaissance University, already at work in places such as Salamanca and Coimbra, were installed (like McDonalds today) in Santo Domingo, Mexico, Peru, and Argentina during the sixteenth century; and in the seventeenth century, Harvard (1636) was founded as the first university in the British colonies. The control of knowledge goes hand in hand with the control of subjectivity, from the Christian subject, modeled according to theological principles of knowledge to the secular subject, modeled according to the egological, emancipating, and sovereign principles. Obviously, the control of knowledge and subjectivities was accompanied by the dismantling and overruling of Aztec and Inca systems of knowledge and formation of subjectivity, which were framed neither on Christian theological principles nor on secular egological ones. From the late eighteenth century onward, the colonial matrix of power that was put in place during the sixteenth century under Christian and Iberian forms of governments and economy was translated and adapted to the needs of the new emerging imperial powers, mainly France and England. Myriads of examples illustrate the transformations of the colonial matrix of power at the level of economy, authority, sexuality and gender, and subjectivity and knowledge in both local and global histories in the last five hundred years. We refer to a number of such examples in the following chapters of the book. Here, we should also consider the imperial aesthetic in molding colonial subjectivities contested within Western civilization by always rebellious artists and, more recently, specifically by decolonial art and decolonial aesthetics (Tlostanova 2005, Mignolo 2007).

These four spheres describe a) the totality of the social where the struggle for power takes place and b) the interconnectedness among the four spheres.

But, what holds them together? The enunciation—categories, institutions, and actors in a position to manage and legitimize each of the spheres including knowledge itself—is precisely what "barbarians" and "primitives" and "Orientals," underdevelopment, and the like mean: people, institutions, languages, religions, economies "behind" modernity.

The colonial matrix went through successive and cumulative periods, in which the rhetoric changed according to the needs and the leading forces shaping the spheres of economy, authority, public realm (gender and sexuality), and education (knowledge and subjectivity). And so, secularism displaced theology; development displaced the civilizing mission, and so forth. In the first period, knowledge was framed by theology and the *mission of conversion* to Christianity. That period dominated the scene during the sixteenth and seventeenth centuries and was in the hands of the Catholic Christian and southern European monarchies, although the Orthodox Christianity also had its limited success. It was marked by the compromises between the Roman Papacy and the Crown of Spain (from 1480 to 1555, from Ferdinand and Isabelle to Charles I of Spain and Charles V of the Holy Roman Empire). By the end of the seventeenth century, a secular and commercial language emerged in England, based on the profitable plantation economies. The combination of a growing economic discourse and an increasing secularization of life was a step toward the second stage, the *civilizing mission* led by England and France. When imperial leadership changed hands again after World War II, the U.S. *development and modernization mission* displaced the British Empire's mission. It was in strong competition with another modernizing and developmental mission called *Socialism*.[22] When development and modernization failed because it was not possible for a capitalist economy to develop underdeveloped countries, the mission changed again to market democracy as the supreme point of arrival of neoliberal philosophy. Approximately from 1970 to 2000 was the moment of consolidation of neoliberalism that, after the collapse of the Soviet Union, translated the previous mission of *development and modernization* into the Washington consensus of the priority of market economy over social regulation. Through five hundred years of Western capitalist empires (Spain, England, the U.S., and their supporters), the rhetoric of modernity (i.e., the different types of "salvation" that the elites in power articulate in their discourses) has at once justified and hidden the logic of coloniality implanted during the sixteenth and the seventeenth centuries.

Historically, the colonial matrix had a serpentine, not a vector, history. It unfolded not just in the Western empires, from Spain and Portugal, to Holland, France and England, to the U.S., but also—in a transmuted form—

in the Russian and, particularly, Soviet modernity. Starting from the sixteenth century and more intensively, from Peter the Great, Russia has been transforming gradually into a subaltern, second-rate empire that adapted the Western model of modernity, civilization, and later, progress, pushing the global expansionist Orthodox Christian project more and more aside or suppressing it in the collective unconscious. This only intensified Russia's historical failure, as it could not possibly compete with the West in secular areas and was doomed to remain within the catching-up and resentful discourse that it is trying to overcome only today. Besides, adapting the rhetoric of modernity (as Russia did) went hand in hand with the logic of coloniality, but it certainly went unannounced and was not properly conceptualized. Efforts at revamping the aggressive Russian claims to world domination would take place in the nineteenth century as well, but only Soviet modernity would rebuild itself as an integral and seemingly secular system in which the rhetoric of modernity would change but the logic of coloniality would remain intact, altering only in its content. Thus, modernity in the twentieth century was implemented in two forms: the liberal/capitalist modernity and the Socialist/statist one. The Soviet modernity refashioned the rhetoric of modernity in the language of Socialism versus capitalism, but it reproduced the logic of coloniality in the control and management of its colonies, particularly the non-European racialized colonies of the Caucasus and Central Asia. As has been demonstrated by a number of scholars, the Bolsheviks wanted to build Socialism and have the colonial empire, too, and it would be sentimental and misleading to believe in their anticolonial rhetoric, particularly when it referred to the spaces that were historically claimed by Russians as their "own."[23]

Soviet modernity was an ultimately unsuccessful attempt at creating an alternative world, where nonetheless we can find the distorted reflections of all the elements of liberal capitalist modernity. Parallel to its rival, the socialist world had been building its own successive forms of coloniality, which in the end proved only the derivative and mimicking nature of Soviet modernity. Thus, the Soviet division of labor was also based on a racial hierarchy with a seemingly lacking idea of race (it was replaced with the specifically understood "nation"),[24] but with a developed racial politics, the Bolsheviks inherited Eurocentrism, Orientalism, and racism from Western Socialism, albeit in distorted derivative forms. The Soviet modernity had its own developmental and progressive ideals, as well as a theatrical form of multiculturalism based on double standards similar to those of its liberal cousin and a caricature halfway decolonization (fashioned as the rehabilitation of the "enemy nations") after Stalin's death. In the realm of coloniality of knowledge and being, based on the erasing of memory, history, literacies, and alphabetic traditions of the colonized and creating docile intellectual slaves, the Soviet modernity proved to be even more effective than that of the West. It is clear that the Soviet Union was a colossus with feet of clay and could easily collapse because of its own contradictory strategies and the time bomb of its ill-designed federalism, but it is also clear that the lack of immunity in the face of intellectual and cultural colonization by Western modernity, which the USSR inherited from Russia, was systematically used during the Cold War for the gradual disintegration of the Soviet Union from within. The collapse of the Socialist system coincided with the beginning of a new époque and became in itself one of the many manifestations of the new face of the global coloniality. In a way, Soviet modernity fulfilled its part and was dismantled.

The second crucial moment is taking place in front of our own eyes: the reproduction of the colonial matrix is being "diversified," so to speak, in the struggle for the control of authority and economy. Diversification means that the colonial matrix is slipping out of control of Western imperial states that created it and made it work in the last five centuries. A common global economy goes hand in hand with global racism and the struggle for the control of authority. Diversified or polycentric capitalism means that, in contrast with the world order that existed thirty years ago, the emerging economic nodes no longer follow the instructions and recommendations of the World Bank and the IMF; they are already unfolding globally.[25] This also means that the struggle for authority and control is no longer between the European imperial centers (World War I), or the European imperial center and a peripheral one (Japan), or the conflagration between liberal capitalism and Socialist economy that polarized the world during the Cold War and opened up the space for the nonaligned countries (basically the Third World).

No matter if the diversification of capitalism takes sometimes more and sometimes less successful forms in various parts of the world (from China and Russia to Southeast Asia, from India to Brazil and the Middle East), it becomes clear that, in a polycentric world, the type of economy described by liberals and Marxists alike as "capitalist economy" is hegemonic.[26] But that is not all, because economic transactions impinge upon and are modeled by the state competition in international arena, and state competition is not exempt from racial tensions, religious struggles, and rivalry for the control of knowledge. The colonial matrix of power is still at work but now outside its place of origin: the Atlantic economy from the sixteenth century on, and the European political theory, philosophy, and science since the eighteenth century. And no mater how great Western contributions were to the world history in the past half a millennia, the West is losing its global authority and, therefore, the expectation that the rest of the world would follow the path of Western Europe and the U.S. is vanishing. It is clearly seen in the politics of the aforementioned locales that refuse to receive orders and recommendations from the IMF, the White House, or the European Union.

While the era of liberal and secular civilizing missions opened up the doors to its opposite, the Socialist civilizing mission, the Washington consensus, and the invasion of Iraq disguised as a war against terrorism (an example of rhetoric of modernity to justify the control of authority and natural resources), *took the colonial matrix of power out of the Western hands, including its Socialist version.* We do not know how polycentric capital/modernity will manifest itself in different locales in the future. But, what seems to be clear is the decline of the era of peaceful coexistence between theology, mercantilism, and free-trade capitalism in the sixteenth- and seventeenth-century Western nations; of the cohabitation of secular liberalism and industrial capitalism after the eighteenth century, when England became the dominant empire; and the emergence of the nation-states that replaced communities of faith (religions) by communities of birth (ethnicity), of coexistence of Western imperial nation-states under the leadership of the U.S., centered on global designs of modernization and development, translated into neoliberal projects of market democracy in the end of the twentieth century. Polycentric capital/modernity means, in short, that the five hundred years of Western domination is ending and the colonial matrix of power—created in the process of Western global domination—is now the terrain of global dispute.[27]

Yet the colonial matrix is not going away. Coloniality will remain as long as the final horizon of human life is guided by the desire to accumulate capital, as long as the economic gains and benefits continue to define "development" and the pursuit of happiness. The control of authority will continue, disguised by a rhetoric of progress, happiness, development, and the end of poverty and will justify the huge amounts of energy and money spent on the conflicts between the centers ruled by the capitalist economy.

Next to and beyond Hegel: Coexisting Imperial Formations, the Colonies, and the Mutations of Colonial and Imperial Differences

We have thus far argued around the constitutive complex modernity/coloniality and described the colonial/imperial differences, the production and reproduction of the colonial wound in the name of the achievements of modernity. There are no nor can there be any modern achievements without inflicting colonial wounds. It is necessary now to displace Hegel's version of world history anchored in modernity, to shift the geo- and body politics and to anchor new world histories from the perspective of coloniality. We suggested how the implementation of the colonial matrix of power created the conditions for the emergence of spatial epistemic breaks that emerged around the world in the form of decolonial projects and orientations, silenced in the map of world history by the rhetoric of modernity. We move now to the complex imperialism/colonialism as far as the imperial and colonial differences have been defined by the rhetoric of modernity and implemented within Western, capitalist, Christian, and secular empires. The imperial and colonial differences are not, of course, "matter of fact" and ontological realities but imperial constructions on which the entire racial matrix of the modern world has been and continues to be built. Think, for instance, of the characterization of Islam in sixteenth-century Christian Spain and its counterpart, the interpretation of Islam in the twenty-first century U.S. Or think of the Circassian (Cherkess) people, who went from being treated by the Russian Empire as possible military allies and equals in humanity in the first modernity, through being racialized and dehumanized in the second modernity, during the conquest, then through their Soviet treatment as internal others and to their total othering and symbolic blackness today. Hence, the paradoxical metamorphosis of Circassians from the quintessence of the Caucasian race, in the German anthropologist Blumenbach's ([1795] 1865) quasi-scientific interpretation, still around in some of the U.S. questionnaires, to their becoming subhuman in today's Russian neo-imperial discourse.

In the unfolding of the linear history of Western empires that coincides with the history of capitalism (Arrighi 1995), the making and remaking of the imperial and the colonial differences became the empire's companion, as Spanish philologist and grammarian Elio Antonio de Nebrija said when Queen Isabella asked him what would be the use of the grammar of the Spanish language.[28] The foundation of imperial and colonial differences were articulated in the sixteenth century from the privileged perspective of Western Christendom and with the imperial foundation of Castile, with the "discovery of America" in 1492, and with the kingdom of Charles V of the Holy Roman Empire, which occupied almost the entire half of the sixteenth century. It was in Christian Castile and the historical role it attributed to itself in the simultaneous events of expelling Moors and Jews from the Iberian Peninsula, conquering two empires in what became the New World, and initiating a massive appropriation of land and exploitation of labor (followed by Holland, France, and England) that created the conditions for a theological discourse in which the imperial differences with the Ottoman and the Russian Empires were established. Simultaneously, the colonial difference was articulated in the process of colonization of the Indians and the massive trade of African slaves.

A genealogy of the word "imperium" is of the essence here. Imperium has sovereignty and management of the colonies as one of its basic meanings. These legacies were handed down to Spain, particularly through Charles V, Holy Roman Emperor (1519–58), and later on were appropriated by the kings and queens of England and France. In a nutshell, the genealogy goes from the foundation of the idea of empire in Rome to its continuation in Spain, England, and France. That is, in the foundation of Western capitalist empires, there are legacies of the noncapitalist Roman Empire. This narrative is quite well known in the West, but it is particularly interesting that the Russian Empire has been left out as a silent and absent historical agent. The imperial difference begins, from the perspective of modernity, with this silence, which implies the inferiority of those who are, if not altogether out of history, then on its very margin, even if they are also imperial people. At the beginning of the sixteenth century, when Spain was not yet an empire but just a kingdom that happened to "discover" America, Russian imperial vision declared itself an heir of Rome and of Constantinople (the second Rome), self-defining and christening Moscow as "the Third Rome." A British scholar of Russian descent, Dominic Lieven, wrote a book, *Empire: The Russian Empire and its Rivals* (Lieven 2000),[29] which begins with the analysis of the coetaneous existence, toward the first century of the Christian era, of the Roman Empire and the Chinese Dynasties, and of Latin and *Hanyu* (Han language) as the two languages and carriers of a complex system of knowledge. Second, Lieven moves to the three heirs of the Roman Empire: the Islamic Caliphate that arose toward the eighth century A.D.; the Russian Czardom, rising at the end of the fifteenth century; and the Western Christian empires (as Lieven puts it), which carried the torch for the rise and growth of Western empires (capitalist, Catholic, and Protestant).

The connections between these two genealogies (the Roman Emperor and the Chinese Huángdì, and their respective dominions) were forged in the eighteenth century. At this point, the imperial difference is not only crucial to understand the historical changes but also to reread Hegel´s imperial version of world history. The Russian Czardom was translated into Empire and began a process of affirmation of sovereignty and establishment of colonies that transformed "frontiers" into "borderlands" (i.e., the political divisions with adjacent empires, such as the Ottoman Sultanate and Persian domains under the ruling of the Shahanshah in the south, Qing China in the east, and Europe in the southwest). The Caucasus developed into a borderland between Islam and Orthodox Christianity as well as, later on, into a colony of the Russian Empire. Thus, imperial and colonial differences were established in the very act of setting up the physical and geographical borderlands—the colonial difference with the Caucasus was simultaneously the locale of the imperial difference with the Ottoman Sultanate. The Russian Empire that, from the eighteenth century on, imitated and followed the imperial, sometimes capitalist, and often liberal patterns emerging in England, France, and Germany—at least on the surface—had a local history that prevented its governors, intellectuals, scholars, and civil society from feeling that they also inhabited the house of the "Absolute Spirit." Thus, the imperial difference was established and Russia became a lesser empire in the ascending history of "European modernity." Russia and the Soviet Union as empires had their own colonies subordinated through their own adaptation of the colonial difference that in this case can be called a secondary colonial difference. The colonial difference in Russia and the Soviet Union was subordinated to the imperial difference and subjected to the superiority of Western imperial rhetoric.

Modernity/Coloniality and the World of Imperial Differences

The imperial difference brings its own configurations into modernity/coloniality picture. For instance, in those locales where the projection of modernity was not direct but mediated by the presence of a secondary empire that created its own distorted, mimicking, and ineffective variant of modernity, the history, the genealogy of humanities, and the ways of their regeneration would be quite specific. The humanities as we know them are indeed responsible for the shaping of the Western imperial reason, but in certain locales, this formula has to be complicated. For example, in Russia, this knowledge is not quite Western but imperial and its non-Western nature does not save it from a discriminatory stance toward its own internal and external others.

All the Atlantic empires that came into power through the exploitation of labor and extraction of natural resources from America were Catholic or Protestant, whereas the Ottoman Sultanate was Muslim and the Russian Empire was Orthodox Christian. Historically, then, capitalism was complicit with the materialization of the Atlantic economy, with Catholicism and Protestantism. If the very idea of "modernity" thus became part of the vocabulary and the rhetoric that went together with the coming into sight of the Western empires of the Atlantic and their colonies in the Americas, the colonial control of labor that materialized in the Atlantic was based on two systems of exploitation of labor to produce commodities for the world market. Western exploitation of labor was organized around encomienda[30] and slavery, of which the Spanish, Portuguese, French, and British took ample advantage. The implantation of labor systems that founded colonial capitalism displaced and destroyed the labor system in the Aztecs and Incas, which, whatever it was, was not capitalist. In contrast, Russia was not largely involved in the type of exploitation of labor that the encomienda and the transformation of the slave system implanted in the Atlantic (i.e., the triangle trade) during the sixteenth and seventeenth centuries. In contrast with the Spanish colonization of America, Russian colonization did not take the shape of massive exploitation of labor to produce commodities for the global market. Geopolitical, military, and religious goals prevailed, as Russia did not find itself in the situation of having to deal with a "new" continent and its natural resources, and the only massive labor force it could exploit was that of its own serfs. Thus, if Spain and Russia had a similar beginning in their road to empire (e.g., "liberating" themselves from the Moors and the Mongolians), soon the differences became apparent: Russia was not part of the Atlantic monopolistic capitalism, and therefore, it found itself on the margins of European modernity and the emerging logic of coloniality.

Through modern/colonial (that is, decolonial) analysis, the world of imperial difference is dominated by two recurrent motifs: the problematic of subaltern empires (Austria-Hungary, the Ottoman Sultanate, Russia), which act as intellectual and mental colonies of the first-rate capitalist Western empires in modernity, and, consequently, create their own type of secondary colonial difference; and a forceful Socialist modernity, which is a mutant, marginal, yet decidedly Western kind of thinking and acting, an emancipatory global utopia, gone conservative and reactionary.

In works touching upon the typology of empire(s) (Hardt and Negri 2000, Ferguson 2004a, 2004b, Smith 2003, Spivak 1999), Russia/Soviet Union remains nonexistent or at the border, which, however, does not mean that its experience is not relevant for other locales. In fact, because of their uniqueness, the discourses and practices of the Russian and Soviet Empires, the "dark other" of Western Europe, can be used to illustrate and partly reformulate the problematic of modern colonial and imperial differences throughout the world. To understand from a border epistemic perspective how the European colonial model was replicated and transformed in subaltern empires such as Russia is one of the goals of this argument. To do so, it may be interesting to briefly trace the main aspects of modernity/modernization in Russia/Soviet Union interpreted both internally and externally. By "internally" and "externally" we do not mean ontologically existing entities but imperial inventions and creations. These terms mean indeed the self-making of the interior space and, by the same token, the invention of the exteriority that makes possible the construction of the interiority. So by "internally" and "externally" we mean both the frame of Russia's complicated relations with the capitalist empires of the West and the frame of its no-less-complicated and varied imperial discourses with respect to its own quite different colonies. Khazhismel Tkhagapsoev, an intellectual from the northern Caucasus, mapped the making of the imperial difference in the relationship between Russia and the West, starting from the "beginning," that is, the adoption of Christianity, to Vladimir Putin's presidency:

> In general the Russian reality appears as an existence of "transmuted forms" on all crucial and turning points in its history. For example, in the ninth century, Russia adopted Christianity, but it got so transformed within the Russian social-cultural context that it became very much imbued with the spirit and forms of pagan culture and it acquired a "transmuted nature (form)" in relation to Western European Christianity, based on the systemic-rational philosophy of Aristotle and Aquinas. In the eighteenth century, Russia began to assimilate European economic, political, and cultural ideas and forms of modernity—the ideas and forms of capitalism, market economy, and technological culture. However for another two hundred years (up to the beginning of the twentieth century), Russia preserved the dominance of the political class of landowners (*latifundium*), while the capitalist (bourgeois) class was denied access to the political decision making. So capitalism also acquired in Russia a transmuted nature (form) as it was driven not so much by the rules of the market as by the subjective will of the main landowner of the country, the "tsar-autocrat." In 1917 a new turn took place in the history of Russia—the Bolsheviks pushed it into the new historical trajectory, that of Socialism. But, as is well known, Stalin's model of Socialism, which had never undergone any principal changes under other Communist party general secretaries from Khruschev to Gorbachev, had little to do with the Swedish social political system. (Tkhagapsoev 2006: 519–20)

The exemplary case of Russia shows how the canonical concept of "universal history," a Christian invention and a fundamental tool of modernity/coloniality later secularized by Kant and Hegel, could be reframed in terms of borders and differences—imperial and colonial. Universal history in this sense is none other than the history of the world from the epistemic perspective of European modernity (Christian and secular), fashioning itself as such and building on the imperial difference with other rival empires and on the colonial difference with subjugated people.

Within the world of imperial difference(s),[31] modernity discourses acquire secondary and mutant forms. This refers to secondary Eurocentrism practiced by people who have often no claim to it (like the Russians), to secondary Orientalism and racism that flourish particularly in relation to the non-European colonies of subaltern empires, such as the Caucasus and Central Asia, giving them a multiply colonized status and a specific subjectivity often marked with self-racialization and self-Orientalizing (Tlostanova 2008). Without these additional categories, we cannot rethink humanities, social movements, or subjectivities in these spaces. At the same time, the Central Asian and Caucasus people would be unable to decolonize themselves without a robust reconceptualization of their location in the world history of the past five hundred years and the history of their relatively recent colonization by Russians and Soviets. This unstable and blurred world of distorted reflections and Janus-faced subjectivities produces a specific kind of scholar and humanities marked by only virtual, imagined belonging to modernity, based primarily on intellectual colonization, which is the most serious impediment for any decolonization of thinking, of knowledge, and of being in the world of imperial difference.

Racism:
A Criterion for Deciding Who Belongs to Humanity

The struggle for the economic control, the control of authority, of gender and sexuality, and finally of knowledge and subjectivity that the colonial matrix of power rests upon are interrelated and interdependent. Each of them impinges on the other. But, what glues them together? The answer is racism. By "racism," we do not mean a classification of human beings according to the color of their skin but rather a classification according to a certain standard of "humanity." Skin color was the secular device used since the eighteenth century when the religious racism based on blood purity was no longer sufficient to accommodate, in the classification, peoples around the world that were not Muslims or Jews. In the sixteenth century then, while Christians in Europe were building a discourse that disqualified, in religious terms, Moors and Jews, the same Christians were building in the Americas a discourse that disqualified not only Indians and Blacks, but also mestizos and mulattos, that is, the mix between Spanish and Indians and Spanish and Black. Although this classification was necessary for Spanish and Creoles of Spanish descent in the Americas, Spaniards from Spain introduced a new distinction to cast Creoles of Spanish descent in America inferior to those Spanish born and raised in Spain. Thus, *racism* is an instrumental term in which the colonial difference is built and the colonial wound infringed: Racism is a device to deprive human beings of their dignity. The logic of coloniality is implied in the racialization of people, languages, knowledges, religions, political regimes, systems of law, and economies. Racialization of the sociohistorical spheres on a world scale means to degrade whatever does not correspond to the imperial ideals of modernity and to persecute and destroy whoever disagrees with the racial classification of the world. That hidden logic, justifying killing in the name of modernity, is precisely the constitutive logic of coloniality.

Racism, in the final analysis, rests on the control of knowledge/understanding and subjectivity. The modern imperial missions were as much about the control of economy and authority as about producing new subjects, modeled according to Christian, liberal, and Marxist concepts of society and the individual. Knowledge has been, together with language, the companion of empires and, in the case of Western empires founded in capitalist economy (from mercantilism to free trade, from monarchy to nation-states), knowledge has been under control of theology and egology. By "Egology," we refer to the new principles of knowledge ("I think") and subjectivity ("I am"), which were both twisted by René Descartes (1596–1650) in his well-known "I think, therefore I am." One cannot exist without the other, although Knowledge was placed before and above Being. And both contributed to a new direction in European thought and subjectivity that was already in place, for instance, in Miguel de Cervantes Saavedra's *Don Quixote* (1605, explicitly stated in the Preface). The Cartesian thinking subject and constitutive being was not supposed to be a black African or a brown Indian from the Americas, a brown Indian from Asia, or a brown Arab from North Africa and what is today the Middle East. The Cartesian subject was immaterial and disembodied, without color and odor—an empty signifier of a sort (controlled by the principles of the theo- and egopolitics of knowledge) that embraced all, every skin color and religious belief under the control of the experience of white European man and Christian religion. Immanuel Kant was clear, following Descartes's route, that "these" people were not yet ready to reach the highs of the Beautiful and the Sublime and, even less, of Reason (Eze 1997: Part 4).

Nelson Maldonado-Torres conceptualized this ontological dimension of coloniality through the idea of misanthropic skepticism, that is, a doubt in the humanity of the other, who is marked by constant violence and death. Therefore, he questions the Cartesian logic of the "ego cogito" that hides its darker side—the *ego conquiro*—as a crucial element of European consciousness that led to global naturalization of the subhuman status of the colonized and racialized peoples. "If the ego cogito was built upon the foundation of the ego conquiro the "I think, therefore I am" presupposes two unacknowledged dimensions. Beneath the 'I think' we can read 'others do not think,' and behind the 'I am' it is possible to locate the philosophical justification for the idea that 'others are not' or do not have being ... should not exist or are dispensable" (Maldonado-Torres 2007: 252).

Shifting the Ethics and Politics of Knowledge

The control of knowledge in the colonies implied, simultaneously, the denial of knowledges and subjectivities in Nahuatl, Aymara, or Quechua languages. In the sixteenth century, Arabic had been already cast out, and in the nineteenth century, Hindi, Urdu, and Bengali would follow the same path. The denial of knowledge and subjectivity created a *spatial epistemic break* that cannot be captured by Tomas Kuhn's (1962) paradigm changes or Michel Foucault (1968) epistemic breaks. The panorama we face as scholars and intellectuals concerned and critical of the formation, transformations, and current persistence of the colonial matrix of power is not so much the "study of colonialism" or "postcolonial studies" around the world but the need to "decolonize knowledge." And decolonization of knowledge can be hardly attained from within Western categories of thought—neither Spinoza nor Nietzsche will do. We need to move in different directions.

Today, the spatial epistemic break is turning into geo- and body political epistemic shifts: those managed by the body politics of the state (unveiled by Foucault) are turning miseries into celebration and claiming the geo- and corpopolitical epistemic rights of enunciation. Both "breaks" are chronological and remain within the regional history of Europe. The spatial break emerged in the decolonial attitude which can be traced back to the sixteenth and seventeenth centuries (Waman Puma de Ayala in the Viceroyalty of Peru) but became more visible in the nineteenth and twentieth centuries (Gandhi, Mariátegui, Césaire, Cabral, Fanon, Menchu, Anzaldúa). Mariátegui, Cesaire, Fanon, or Anzaldúa become the equivalents of Descartes for the decolonial epistemology that is already well underway, although not visible in the publications of university presses, which are more and more attentive to the market. The concept of coloniality is not only a concept that describes a reality but also a concept that affirms its own locus of enunciation; a concept that anchors the shift in the geo- and body politics of knowledge. This argument not only describes a phenomenon but also argues mainly from the new perspective that the phenomenon described allows us to create.

Decoloniality (as synonymous with decolonization of knowledge and being) cannot be a knowledge at the service of the monarch, the church, the state, or the corporations, but knowledge that comes from the perspective of and empowering of the "the colonial subalterns"—that is, those whose languages, religions, social organization, and economic production have been denied and suppressed by structures based on the theo- and the egopolitics of knowledge. The first took away the geographical and biographical locations of knowledge and the knower in the name of God; the second—in the name of Transcendental Reason. The epistemic imperial and colonial differences were the instruments through which theo- and egopolitics of knowledge were established. The decolonial shift relocates the geo- and body politics of knowledge and reveals that both the theology and egology implemented a philosophy of knowledge that denied its own geographical and biographical location while projecting, as universal, what was indeed anchored and located at the geographical and biographical location of imperial agencies. Decolonial projects and actions cannot be subsumed under paradigmatic or epistemic *breaks* within the universal time of Western modernity but should be considered as a *geo- and body political epistemic shift* fracturing a cosmology with no alternatives other than Christian, liberal, and Marxist.

The spatial epistemic shift generated by the repressive logic of coloniality engendered, as we suggest, decolonial projects and practices, including knowledge and subjectivity, and prompted the question of the ethics and politics of knowledge: Where do intellectuals stand in this enterprise? How do their subjectivities formed by ethnic belonging and discrimination based on race, gender, languages, regional histories, and so forth impinge on how they think, how they are seen, and how they want to imagine and create a future beyond discrimination? Imperial and colonial differences inflicted wounds and created borders—physical and mental lines that can be policed between one country and the other, between one neighbor and another, between an employer and an employee, between the population of ex-imperial countries (such as Russia) and the immigrants in imperial ones (such as the core countries of the European Union and the U.S.), between the police and the civil society. Borders are lines that divide people in the street and allow the police and the embassies of dominant countries to control entire populations in other parts of the world. And borders are also conceptual and mental lines that divide different types of knowledge. What we need is the *epistemic geopolitical and body political potential emerging from the borders (in the ex- and neocolonies as well as in the ex- and neoempires) to displace the epistemic privilege of modern epistemology* (theo- and egological; Eurocentrically oriented). The line of the colonial difference is common through time and space to all those who have been wounded by the coloniality of knowledge and being, one domain of the colonial matrix of power. Silenced through the history of modernity told from the perspective of modernity, those who have been wounded are taking the lead, not in the academicism of postcolonial studies but in the ethical and political arena of the epistemic decoloniality. Decoloniality (the undoing of the colonial matrix of power) implies two simultaneous moves: to unveil the hidden logic of modernity (i.e., coloniality) and to work toward another globalization, as the World Social Forum has it.

CHAPTER 2

Theorizing *from* the Borders; Shifting *to* the Geo- and Body Politics of Knowledge

BORDER THINKING and theorizing emerged from and as a response to the violence (frontiers) of imperial/territorial epistemology and the rhetoric of salvation that continues to be implemented on the assumption of the inferiority or devilish intentions of the other and, therefore, continues to justify oppression and exploitation as well as eradication of difference. Border thinking is the epistemology of the exteriority and, as such, is the necessary condition for decolonial projects. Recent immigration to the imperial sites of Europe and the U.S.—crossing the imperial and colonial differences—contributes to maintaining the conditions for border thinking that emerged from the very inception of modern imperial expansion. In this regard, critical border thinking displaces and subsumes Max Horkheimer's "critical theory," which was and still is grounded in the experience of European internal history ([1937] 1999). "Decolonial border thinking" instead is grounded in the experiences of the colonies and subaltern empires. Consequently, it provides the epistemology that was denied by imperial expansion. "Decolonial border thinking" also denies the epistemic privilege of the humanities and the social sciences—the privilege of an observer that makes the rest of the world an object of observation (from Orientalism to Area Studies). It also moves away from the postcolonial toward the decolonial, shifting to the geo- and body politics of knowledge.

Why do we need border thinking (border epistemology)?[32] Where is it taking us? To the decolonial shift as a fracture of the epistemology of the zero point. Decolonial border thinking brings to the foreground different kinds of theoretical actors and principles of knowledge that displace European modernity (which articulated the very concept of theory in the social sciences and the humanities) and empower those who have been epistemically disempowered by the theo- and egopolitics of knowledge. The decolonial epistemic shift is no longer grounded in the Greek and Latin categories of thought that informed modern epistemology (since the Renaissance) in the six European imperial languages (Italian, Spanish, and Portuguese for the Renaissance; French, English, and German for the Enlightenment) but in the epistemic borders between European imperial categories and languages and categories that modern epistemology ruled out as epistemically nonsustainable (e.g., Mandarin, Japanese, Russian, Hindi, Urdu, Aymara, Nahuatl, Wolof, Arabic). The epistemology of the zero point is "managerial," and it is today common to business, natural sciences, professional schools, and the social sciences. Border thinking is the epistemology of the future, without which another world will be impossible.

Epistemology is woven into language and, above all, into alphabetically written languages. And languages are not something human beings *have* but what human beings *are*. As such, languages are embedded in the body and in the memories (geohistorically located) of each person. A person formed in Aymara, Hindi, or Russian who has to learn the rules and principles of knowledge mainly inscribed in the three imperial languages of the second modernity (French, English, and German) would of necessity have to deal with a "gap"; while a person formed in German or English who learns the rules and principles of knowledge inscribed in German or English is not subject to such gap. But, there is more, since the situation is not just the one that can be accounted for in terms of the universal history of human beings and society. Knowledge and subjectivities have been and continue to be shaped by the colonial and imperial differences that structured the modern/colonial world.

Consider, on the one hand, knowledge in the modern and imperial European languages, and on the other hand, knowledge in Russian, Arabic, or Mandarin. The difference here is imperial: In the sphere of knowledge, scholars, diplomats, and intellectuals in China, Russia, and the Arabic countries have to know English. The reverse is optional, not necessary. However, these languages are not just different. In the modern/colonial unconscious, they belong to different epistemic ranks. "Modern" science, philosophy, and the social sciences are not grounded in the Russian, Chinese, and Arabic languages. That of course does not mean that no thinking is going on or knowledge produced in Russian, Chinese, or Arabic. It means, on the contrary, that in the global distribution of intellectual and scientific labor, knowledge produced in English, French, or German does not need to take into account knowledge in Russian, Chinese, and Arabic. Furthermore, increasingly since the sixteenth century, knowledge in Russian, Chinese, and Arabic cannot avoid intellectual production in English, French, and German. Strictly speaking, societies in which Russian, Chinese, and Arabic are spoken were not colonized in the way the Americas and South Asia were. Thus, any languages beyond the six imperial European ones, and their grounding in Greek and Latin, have been disqualified as languages with worldwide epistemic import. And, of course, this impinges on subject formation: People who are not trusted in their thinking are doubted in their rationality and wounded in their dignity. Border thinking then emerges from the colonial and the imperial wound.

If we consider, instead, Hindi or Aymara, the epistemic difference with modern European languages and epistemology is colonial. In both cases, the coloniality of knowledge and being goes hand in hand with modernity's rhetoric of salvation. Today, the shaping of subjectivity, the coloniality of being/knowledge are often described within the so-called globalization of culture, a phrase that in the rhetoric of modernity reproduces the logic of coloniality of knowledge and being.

Borders Are Not Only Geographical but Also Epistemic

"Borders" are not only geographic but also political, subjective (e.g., cultural), and epistemic; and contrary to frontiers, the very concept of "border" implies the existence of people, languages, religions, and knowledge on both sides linked through relations established by the coloniality of power (e.g., structured by the imperial and colonial differences). "Borders" in this precise sense, are not a natural outcome of a natural or divine historical processes in human history but created in the very constitution of the modern/colonial world. If we limit our observations to the geographic, epistemic, and subjective types of borders in the modern/colonial world, we see that they all have been created from the perspective of European imperial/colonial expansion.

"Border thinking" (or "border epistemology)" emerges primarily from the people's antiimperial epistemic responses to the colonial difference—the difference that hegemonic discourse endowed to "other" people, classifying them as inferior and at the same time asserting its geohistorical and body-social configurations as superior and the models to be followed. "These" people (we, Madina and Walter, included) refuse to be geographically caged, subjectively humiliated and denigrated, and epistemically disregarded. For this reason, the decolonial epistemic shift proposes to change the rules of the game—and not just the content—and the reason for which knowledge is produced: Decolonization, instead of working toward the accumulation of knowledge and imperial management, works toward the empowerment and liberation of different layers (racial, sexual, gender, class, linguistic, epistemic, religious, etc.) from oppression and toward undermining the assumption on which imperial power is naturalized, enacted, and corrupted.

Second, border thinking could emerge also from the imperial difference, i.e., through the same mechanism as the colonial difference but applied to people in similar socioeconomic conditions to the ones who are in a dominant position. Western (Christian and secular) discourses about Indians and Blacks (that is, Africans transported to the Americas) founded the colonial difference and the modern matrix of racism. During the same period, the sixteenth–seventeenth centuries, Western Christian and secular discourse founded the imperial difference with the Ottoman Sultanate and the Russian Empires. Turks and Russians, in other words, were obviously not Indians and Blacks from Western hegemonic geo- and body classification of the world. However, it was clear for everybody in the West that, even if Turks and Russians were not Blacks or Indians, they were not European either. Starting at least from Kant and Hegel onward, the Russians are not considered quite white/European and therefore, not quite human. In Kant's classification of the world in a decreasing order of meeting the requirements of the enlightened Reason, Russians held a very modest place, to put it mildly. In *Anthropology from a Pragmatic View*, he simply says that "since Russia has not yet developed definite characteristics from its natural potential; since Poland has no longer characteristics, and since the nationals of European Turkey never have had a character, nor will ever attain what is necessary for a definite national character, the description of these nations' characters may properly be passed over here" (Kant [1798] 1996: 231). Hegel, reflecting on the universal history, was writing about the Slavs, who in his opinion were ahistorical people: "This entire body of peoples remains excluded from our consideration, because hitherto it has not appeared as an independent element in the series of phases that Reason has assumed in the World" (Hegel [1882] 1991: 350). However, "second class" empires also had to deal with colonies. The Russian/Soviet Empire, Japan between 1895 and 1945, and the Ottoman Sultanate, before its demise, are all Janus-faced empires: One eye points toward Western capitalist and dominant empires; the other toward their own colonies (Tlostanova 2003).

Zero point epistemology manifests itself in the theo- and egopolitics of knowledge. Both Christian theology and secular philosophy and science are grounded in the Rationality of Ego rather than in the Wisdom of God. By so doing, the zero point epistemology posited itself not just as the right way of knowing but as the only way. Whatever did not fit the demands of theological and egological principles was relegated to the world of the barbarians, the not quite yet or those who maybe, some day will. Both, Christian theology and secular philosophy and Western science shaped Western imperial expansion throughout the last five centuries. Border thinking began a process of detachment from the magic effect of theological and egological imperialism. Border thinkers dwell in *the difference* (colonial and/or imperial), and dwelling in the borders, border thinkers look at, watch, ponder, examine, and study imperial thinkers. Imperial thinkers are not necessarily imperialists. Imperial thinkers think within theological and egological premises: They inhabit the house of zero point epistemology.

Thus, border thinkers ask first, what are the relations between geohistorical locations and epistemology, on the one hand; and between identity and epistemology, on the other? Border thinkers do not believe that Aristotle's or Kant's ideas and reasoning were detached from their bodies and their geohistories, where their senses were soaking. Consequently, decolonial intellectuals do not believe in the universality of statements made from any local history. And there is nothing but local history. The ideas of global or universal histories are just an imperial epistemic euphemism. Border thinkers quickly bring to the foreground Ibn-Sina, al-Gazhali, Ibn-Rushd, Guaman Poma, Ottobah Cugoano, Mahatma Gandhi, Nawal el Saadawi, and many others next to Aristotle and Kant. Border thinkers seat next to those in the "second row" (seen from the perspective of zero point epistemology) and watch and contemplate those sitting on a pedestal and looking down the valley, classifying the creatures who are in the valley and not on pedestals. The issues and questions deriving from them are never asked by theological and egological epistemologies.[33] The array of possibilities for border thinking is indeed vast, but they all have one thing in common: How do people in the world deal with Western economic, political, and epistemic expansion if they do not want to assimilate or remain passive and if they/we choose to imagine a future that is their/our own invention and not the invention of the empires, hegemonic or subaltern? Someone born and raised in British India has little in common with someone born and raised in Spanish America; languages and religions are different, histories are incommensurable.

However, they have a common history: the imperial/colonial history of Western capitalist and Christian empires—Spain and England. From the imperial perspective—either of the dominant empires (England, U.S.) or the subaltern empires (Russia, China, the Ottoman Sultanate of the past)—border thinking is almost an impossibility (one would have to give up the epistemic privilege of Western modernity and admit that knowledge and understanding are generated beyond institutional norms and control), and from the colonial perspective, border thinking is straightforwardly a necessity. Dwelling and reflecting in the borders does not take you to comparative studies but to border thinking. Comparative studies presuppose that the knowing subject dwells in the zero epistemic point; places himself on the top of the hill, observing from above the movements in the two valleys, one to his right and the other to his left. The observer is in neither of the valleys but remains detached on the top of his hill.

The next question is whether border thinkers could dwell in the borders and emerge from the borders of subaltern empires or are their chances for emergence better in the colonies, and what kind of colonies at that—the (ex-)colonies of a subaltern empire (e.g., Uzbekistan, Ukraine) or a hegemonic empire (e.g., India during the British rule, Iraq under U.S. imperial moves, Bolivia and Ecuador in the history of the Spanish empire and the present of the U.S. domination in Latin America, or South Africa in its past and present).[34] In the case of Russia, border thinkers have to deal with imperial borders—the borders between Russia and the West are not quite the same kind of borders as those between Mexico and the U.S. But, on the other hand, border thinkers also have to deal with borders between the Russian Federation and the ex-colonies of the Russian Empire and the Soviet Union. Uzbekistan is not exactly India; the Caucasus is not exactly the Andean region of South America. Border thinkers walk away from imperial abstract universals (e.g., critical theory, semiotics of culture or nomadology for everyone in the planet) that will account for all experiences and geohistorical violence and memories. They/we assume that border thinking is one way toward decolonial options and the promotion of pluriversality or, if you wish, the coexistence of universals. Global futures would be a world where universals coexist because, otherwise, there may easily be no future, global or regional. Pluriversality, and not universality, is the major claim made by border and decolonial thinkers, since, once again, there is no pluriversality from the perspective of theo- and egopolitics of knowledge. And without pluriversality and the decolonial coexistence of universals, the blinding impulses to domination and personal gluttony, prevail. Pluriversality is possible only from border thinking, that is, from shifting the geography of reason to geo-

and body politics of knowledge. Because, if pluriversality is coopted from the perspective of theo- and egological thinking (from the left or from the right), it will become an imperial abstract universal. This is precisely the logic of multiculturalism. Multiculturalism is based on a pluriversal content controlled by a universal epistemology. Pluriversality predicated from the perspective of zero point epistemology (liberal, Christian, or Marxist) ceases to be such and becomes a mask, a content of imperial epistemic appropriation. Thus, learning to unlearn is essential and becomes a road to decolonial options.

Whereas imperial epistemology is based on theological and egological principles, as we stated already, the shift to geo- and body-political principles is indeed a decolonial move. Geo- and body politics are the "displaced inversion" of theo- and egopolitics of knowledge. It is an "inversion" because it is assumed that John Locke's "secondary qualities" cannot be bracketed in the process of knowing and understanding. In a world order in which the imperial and colonial differences establish all hierarchies, from economy to knowledge, "secondary qualities" that matter are colonial local histories (geopolitics) subordinated to imperial local histories, on the one hand, and colonial subjectivities (Fanon's "wretched of the earth"), on the other. Colonial subjectivities are the consequences of racialized bodies, the inferiority that imperial classification assigned to everybody that does not comply with the criteria of knowledge established by white, European, Christian, and secular men. "Displaced inversion" changes not only the content but fundamentally the terms of the conversation: the geo- and body- political perspectives delink from the imperial and totalitarian bent of theo- and egological principles. It is hardly enough to question the secularity of the social sciences from the perspective of theology, as John Milbank does. It is of the essence to move away from inversions internal to imperial epistemology and to shift the geography and the biography of reason.

These positions are hard to reconcile, which is clearly seen in any juxtaposition of Western and radical non-Western theorizing of borders. From the perspective of the imperial difference, the conditions and possibilities of border thinking and decolonization are not only different but also more difficult. If, in the history of borders marked by colonial differences, the opposition to the empire is clear and loud, in the history of borders marked by imperial differences, the *assimilation* (e.g., Peter the Great in Russia) and desire to become the West or *competition* (the Soviet Union confronting Western capitalist empires) takes precedence over *decolonization* (which would be a sort of deimperialization), as we see in the case of Russia today. China offers still another example of border thinking through the imperial difference: *adaptation* without *assimilation*.[35] Overall, the conditions for decolonization seem to be more promising in the colonies and ex-colonies or in empires that had been reduced to colonies (e.g., the Islamic Empire, which, by the nineteenth century, was already subdivided and found itself at the mercy of the new imperialism, England and France).

In the Eurasian space, sporadic instances of border thinking were practiced by people who experienced double and multiple marginalization and discrimination by several imperial (at least in their form) or quasi-imperial interventions at once. But, these histories largely remained undocumented. The views of these people (if ever they were put on paper) were erased by the empires and Western modernity, for instance, nineteenth-century Caucasus anticolonial movement activist Saferby Zan or late-nineteenth-century secular intellectual, journalist, and Tatar enlightener Ismail Bey Gasprinsky. In most cases, these border thinkers had to ultimately make a compromise with the dominant power(s) by manipulating in between them or choosing the assimilative position of Ariels, as it happened in the case of the Kazakh writer and intellectual Olzhas Suleimenov.

In his book *Az I Ya* (Suleimenov 1975), he retold the Russian foundational epic *Lay of Igor's Campaign* from a Turkic viewpoint and stressed a utopian possibility of creating a great secular Eurasian Slavic–Turkic confederation or polity based on common history and culture. It is a meditation created similarly to Anzaldúa's text, on the border of the generally accepted genres of the scholarly and fictional discourse. Suleimenov presents a cultural manifesto that incorporates in a discursively unstable way elements of historiography, poetry, etymological problem, and a traditional novel. The Soviet scholarly establishment was infuriated with this book and regarded it as an infringement on the grandeur of the great Russian national tradition, with its fake secondary Eurocentric myth. Suleimenov got out of the prescribed role of a secondary colonial other who, within the Soviet system, had to follow a simple rule: Soviet in its essence, ethnic-national in its form. What is more important, however, is that Suleimenov's positioning in the long run is not so similar to Anzaldúa's mestiza. The difference is that Suleimenov's subjectivity is traditional for the Russian/Soviet Empire's internal assimilated other. It is based on synthesizing and not on border impulse, in relation to the Russian and "Asian" nomadic traditions. In contrast with Anzaldúa, Suleimenov is not living in the border, constantly juggling traditions and identities. He is rather a subaltern brought up on the Russian dominant culture, viewed as the champion of (Soviet) modernity. By looking for similarities between the Russian and the nomadic traditions, he is trying to upscale the Nomadic one instead of denigrating the Russian or draw attention to its colonialist nature. Thus, what is at work in case of Suleimenov is a forbidden (for the late Soviet period) ethnic-cultural revivalist impulse of rewriting the dominant tradition by means of looking for similarities between the imperial and the subaltern cosmologies and origins. Thus, he is not negating or rejecting the colonizer but rather trying to integrate into the sameness in yet another way. This is possible in a limited number of imperial/colonial configurations, mainly those that originated in the subaltern empires and their colonies. We cannot imagine an African writer proving the common roots of his native culture and the British one. But we can imagine a Circassian slave in the Ottoman Sultanate looking for a kinship with the Turks. Suleimenov seems to be a Soviet Ariel who suddenly made a Caliban-like move and was punished for that by the empire. In post-Soviet period, when the ethnic political pendulum, in Emil Pain's words, goes from minority ethnic nationalism to the predominance of fundamentalist Russian chauvinism, Suleimeinov's utopian, but global and positive, model is equally unattractive to both parties.

The world marked by imperial more than colonial difference lives on/in the border, yet instead of border thinking, we mostly find blurred, in-between, self-Orientalized models (the Ottoman Sultanate, Russia/USSR, central and southeastern Europe). It is difficult to conceptualize such locales and epistemic and existential configurations from the viewpoints of either the West or the radical non-West, as well as from the viewpoint of the very people who were colonized by Western thinking, infected with secondary Eurocentrism and unable to analyze their own split subjectivity (their *double consciousness*, as a necessary condition for border thinking), because it is always easier to analyze binary polar structures than soft and blurred difference—the same but not quite, different but too similar. The geo- and body politics of knowledge as well as border thinking implies the awareness of the double consciousness, which is not the case in the world of imperial difference that longs to belong to modernity's sameness so much that it often erases it own difference.

Double consciousness, as conceptualized by W. E. B. Du Bois lies in the very foundation of border thinking: One is not possible without the other. Imperial consciousness is always territorial and monotopic; border thinking is always pluritopic and engendered by the violence of the colonial and imperial differences. Internal imperial critique (be that of Bartolomé de las casas or Karl Marx) is territorial and monotopic and assumes the "truth" of abstract universals (peaceful Christianization by conversion, free market, international revolution of the proletarians, etc.). Double consciousness emerges from the experiences of being someone (Black, inscribed in the memory and histories of the slave trade in the Atlantic economy) who was classified by the imperial-national gaze (European imperial frame of mind, U.S. emerging imperial nationalism at the turn of the twentieth century). Thus, the problem of identity and identity politics is a direct consequence of imperial knowledge making all the inhabitants of the New World Indians and Blacks and all of Asia the Yellow Race. Identity in politics is a step forward: It means to build transformative projects on the identity infringed on "us" by the imperial "them." "Infringed on us" means that identity is not ontological but conceptual and that identities are imposed by imperial discourses rather than emerging from the soul of those who have been classified and identified. If border thinking is the unavoidable condition of imperial/colonial domination, critical border thinking is the imperial/colonial condition transformed into epistemic and political projects of decolonization. Hence, identity emerges in politics. For that reason, decolonial thinking is always already critical, it is border thinking and it is double consciousness. Hegel, Kant, and Marx, to name just three European luminaries, at different times denied internal others—be they Slavic people or Turks—a place in the universal history, in the march of modernity, in the unfolding of global proletarian revolution, and so forth. Their disincorporated epistemology and their belief in a universal parameter blinded them to the subjectivity of otherness and more so to internal others. It was beyond their scope to understand why a Russian feels himself as a cockroach in Europe,[36] while a Turk buying a coat from a French store is in fact buying a European dream.[37]

The reaction of internal others to this rejection has been that of an unconscious border, divided between the First and Third worlds, wanting to see itself as part of a center. The painful border splitness is being masked and at once reinforced, when in Istanbul they change the alphabet to Latin or make slightly crooked but recognizably Parisian boulevards, when in Moscow they speak only French or destroy their own economy in order to please the IMF. Today, the split configuration of internal others is expressed in the continuing hierarchy of othering: The world of imperial difference, on the one hand, plays the role of unwanted and threatening immigrant into the West; on the other hand, the West guards its own borders (including epistemic borders) against the unwanted immigration from the ex-Soviet republics and the ex–Third World. However, when border thinking does not emerge, the alternatives are competition, assimilation, or resistance without a vision toward the future.

For instance, when the European imperial/colonial model was replicated and transformed in subaltern empires or empires-colonies, like Russia or the Ottoman Sultanate, which became mirror reflections of each other, it led to ideological and intellectual dependency on the West and the epistemic colonization by the West, which resulted in the phenomenon of two cultures—the culture of European-oriented imperial/national elite with secondary Eurocentric inferiority complexes and the impenetrable culture of people, that the elite is either ashamed of or attracted to, in the importing of the Western discourses of nationalism, cosmopolitanism, liberalism, socialism, modernization, progress, and the like (Tlostanova 2004a). The two empires shared the subaltern status in relation to the Western empires of modernity, but each had its own configuration of imperial subalternity—Russia was a quasi-Western subaltern empire that, in order to survive, had to put on different masks for different partners and the Ottoman Sultanate was a quasi-Islamic one that also had to have multiple faces and in a sense, in contrast with Russia, even practice tolerance as the principle of survival. But, in both cases, paradoxically, the hierarchy of otherness was built exclusively in accordance with Western European racial, cultural, linguistic, and religious norms, which deliberately put both the Ottoman Sultanate and the Russian Empires into the situation of empires—colonies, creating peculiar inferiority complexes and specific transitory, in-between and underconceptualized cultural, social, epistemic, and political forms.[38]

The imperial and colonial epistemic differences create the conditions for border thinking but do not determine it. In the hierarchical structure of the modern/colonial world, we can identify the four main types of dependency relations:

1. The oppositional attitude consisting in total rejection of Western epistemology and subjectivity based on fundamentalist defense of languages, religions, knowledges, and the like.
2. The assimilating attitude, consisting in wanting to become like the superior other and, therefore, yielding to the imperial language, knowledge, and subjectivity at the high price of alienating oneself into the imperial other. This is the case of the trickster empire Turkey, making its own subaltern status work for its benefit, through transcultural and transreligious mediation of Western ideologies and establishing new alliances based not on abstract principles of democracy and freedom but on religious, linguistic, indigenously economic and cultural expansionism, and soft penetration, which today turns out to be more effective than many European and American strategies (Özbudun and Keyman 2002).
3. Competition within the capitalist rules of the game or adaptation without assimilation (e.g., China or modern defeated Russia, to some

extent, which is still grounding itself in the doomed imperial myths of grandeur and dominance, finding solace in understanding the border as an aggressive expansionistic "third way," and reviving the dusted ideology of Eurasianism).
4. Border thinking and critical border thinking, which consist in the incorporation of Western contributions in different domains of life and knowledge into an epistemic and political project that affirms the difference, colonial or imperial, to which most of the population of the world has been subjected throughout five hundred years of economic, religious, epistemic imperial expansion and its consequences in the formation of split subjectivities.

Dependency relations with the exteriority of Europe are established through the imperial and colonial differences. But these dependency relations with the colonies, revert back to its internal others like the Jews, the immigrants, and the states, ex-Soviet colonies, now joining the European Union. Aimé Césaire clearly saw, in the 1950s, that the colonial matrix of power set up and implemented through the four hundred fifty years of colonization, were implemented by the Nazi regime in Germany and by the Communist regime in the Soviet Union ([1955] 2000).These are all different historical conditions from where border positions could be developed as active decolonizing projects, both epistemic and political from the lived experiences (i.e., subjectivity) of diverse communities. The geo- and body politics of knowledge would be of the essence to disengage from the epistemology of the zero point in which the geo- and the body-political have been repressed. The epistemology of the zero point that privileges political economy and political theory continues to repress the geohistorical and body-graphic politics of knowledge in which critical border thinking is founded. The interconnections between geohistorical locations (in the modern/colonial order of things) and epistemology, on the one hand, and body-racial and gender epistemic configurations, on the other, sustain "the inverted displacement" we describe here as geopolitics and body politics of knowledge. If, say, René Descartes or Immanuel Kant suppressed (in their theo- and egopolitical epistemic foundations) the geo- and body-political component of their thinking, Frantz Fanon and Gloria Anzaldúa brought both (geo- and body politics) wide and loud into the open.

Border thinking needs its own genealogy and its own history; a history and genealogy that emerges in the very act of performing border thinking. Without it, border thinking would remain either an appendix of modern Western imperial epistemology and the variants of canonical history of

Western civilization told from the imperial perspective (from the Renaissance, to Hegel, to Marx) or an object of study for the social sciences (like the savage mind for earlier anthropologists). And decolonization runs the risk of being appropriated and immediately trivialized not only by the World Bank but also by the so-called progressive European intellectuals who prefer to see it as emerging from their own European history and out of their own epistemic universality. These champions of Eurocentered epistemic universality tend to "re-write" in their own terms the concepts, projects, and categories of thought that have emerged precisely to delink from both right and left Eurocentrism (Driscoll 2010). If border thinking is ever to emerge in the world of imperial difference today, it would have to happen in the colonial and ex-colonial locales of the subaltern empires, among the people who were multiply marginalized and denied their voice by Western modernity—directly and through subaltern imperial mediation. These are the Caucasus and Central Asia (in connection with Russia); the Kurds, Greeks, and Armenians (in connection with the Ottoman Sultanate); the Yugoslavian bundle of contradictions in the Balkans; and the like. But these voices will hardly be heard soon. These mute colonies of the subaltern empires are split in between the Western culture (now also directly accessible to them) and its bad subaltern empire copies, the ex mediators of civilization. Plus their own native ethnic traditions continue to play their part in the process of further disintegrating their already split selves, being shattered into even smaller pieces. That is why the manifestations of the "multitude" (in Georgia, the Ukraine, or Kirgizstan) have been so far geared more by a desire to assimilate to the West than to engage in imagining a possible future beyond the options offered by Communism and its aftermath and liberalism and is aftermath.

Thinking from the Borders

Borders could be "studied" from the perspective of territorial epistemology (e.g., Western social sciences; Horkheimer's traditional theory) but the "problem" of the twenty-first century would be not so much to study the life and deeds of the borders but to *think from the borders themselves* and therefore to be the border, in Anzaldúa's words. The main problem of the twenty-first century is not just *crossing* borders but *dwelling in the borders*. We, Madina and Walter, are border dwellers, and hence the argument unfolded here is not an analysis of observers practicing a zero-point epistemology but that of border dwellers engaging in border and decolonial thinking. That is, dwelling in the borders means rewriting geographic frontiers, imperial/colonial subjectivities, and territorial epistemologies. Paraphrasing W. E. B. Du Bois, we can say that the problem of the twenty-first century would be—next to that of the color line announced by Du Bois—the problem of the "epistemic line"(Bogues 2003: 69-94). However, the epistemic line does not replace or displace the color line. The color and epistemic lines belong to different realms of reality, since epistemology is not supposed to have color, gender, or sexuality. In terms of social class, the problems are easier to deal with because it was assumed that epistemology belonged to a division of labor in which the "intellectual workers" do not belong to the same class as the "proletarians." However, intellectual workers, even if they are not proletarians, do have color, gender, and sexuality. Thus, the "borders" between the color (and gender and sexuality) line and the epistemic line are precisely where the "problem" appears and the solutions are being played out. For, there is a shift at work at the moment when the epistemic line is interrogated from the perspective of the color (gender and sexuality) line. It is at this very moment that border thinking or border epistemology emerges: It emerges in the crack and it emerges as an epistemic shift. It is a shift from the theo- and ego- to the geo- and body politics of knowledge.

The question commonly asked is this: How do you engage (in) border thinking and how do you enact the decolonial shift? What is the method? Interestingly enough, the question is most often asked by predominantly white and North Atlantic scholars and intellectuals. It is impossible to imagine Du Bois asking that question, because he prompted it with his own thinking, dwelling in what he called "double consciousness." The question is interesting because it plays like a boomerang and returns to the person who asked it. Why is he or she asking that question? Where is he or she dwelling, in a *single consciousness*? Why was it an Afro American like Du Bois and not a German like Habermas who came up with a concept such as double consciousness? Furthermore, double consciousness would not admit the thesis that promotes the "inclusion of the other" (Habermas 1998). Double consciousness and the inclusion of the other confront each other across the colonial difference. The question is not being asked because modern epistemology (theologically and egologically based) separated the geo- and corporal location of the thinker. The hubris of the zero point—by eliminating perspectives—prevents the possibility of asking, how can I at once inhabit the zero point and what the zero point negates? Asking that question, "feeling" that modern epistemology is totalitarian (that it negates all other alternatives to the zero point) is the first step to border thinking. And, it is also a dwelling that is no longer the House of the Spirit—i.e., the dwelling of modern European philosophy and science.

To answer the previous question, let us look again at the Janus-faced empire of Russia/Soviet Union and think about how border thinking could emerge out of the imperial difference of Russia today dwelling in the memories of subaltern empires, on the one hand, and how could it emerge in the colonies or ex-colonies, on the other? How could border thinking and decolonization of knowledge and being (i.e., the decolonial shift) be thought out and enacted from the histories and perspectives of those locales? The blurred spaces of imperial difference once again link knowledge production and race (accepting as natural the idea that modern epistemology is and should be white). However, no matter how hard "the other" tries to imitate or adapt European or—today—American epistemological hegemony, for the West, the world of imperial difference continues to play the part of culture-producing and not knowledge-generating regions of the earth, never really changing their ahistorical status assigned by Hegel. This scenario is particularly clear in case of Russia and its imperial/colonial interdependence with its colonies in Asia and Eastern Europe. Russia did not have its own theology in the Western sense of the word; philosophy and science were shaped there following the Western model and borrowed from Europe in their already secularized variants, while later on there emerged a double alterity from the old Russia and from Europe that failed to fulfill its universalist promises. Epistemology, philosophy, and science were born in Russia at the point when European modernity had already managed to naturalize its dominance and erase all the inauspicious for itself, the histories and epistemic traditions (such as the Islamic one), while considerably altering and correcting others (like the Antiquity) to its benefit. Russia discovered epistemology as such at that very moment and has not ever since seriously questioned its basic Eurocentric principles, consequently classifying the rest of the world, including its own non-European colonies, according to the Western European racist colonial matrix of power.

The most promising case for border thinking in Eurasia is to be found in non-European (ex-) colonies of Russia that have managed to preserve their epistemic link with the indigenous cosmology and centers of thought, philosophy, and science. That is why the logical step of the Soviet Empire was to erase completely and effectively all the traces of this link: to deprive these people of their past, epistemology, and culture; to rewrite history in such a way that their antiquity would be negated; to ban the previous (Greek or Arabic) alphabetic systems and make them start anew with the Cyrillic. Border thinking, in other words, could not be acknowledged by the territorial epistemology of the state without loosing its imperial control of knowledge and subjectivity. It is also symptomatic that virtually all instances of border thinking in Eurasia come in fictional or semi-fictional forms, especially in the post-Soviet period. That is, border thinking presupposes the transgression of genre and disciplinary boundaries. Here, border thinking creates border or transcultural aesthetics with specific narrative viewpoints, discourse, and optics (Orhan Pamuk in Turkey; Milorad Pavič in Serbia; Zorikto Dorzhiev, Afanasy Mamedov, or Vyacheslav Useinov in Russia and the ex-Soviet republics).

Let us explore a different local history. In North Africa, the Moroccan philosopher Mohammed Al-Jabri asked an interesting question: Muslim philosophers of the past as well as Christian philosophers of the Middle Age founded their philosophy on Aristotle's *Physics* (1999). In that line of thought, Descartes built his own philosophy on Galilean physics that, in its turn, was built on Aristotle's. What then happened during the time span between Ibn-Rushd (1128–98), who brought Muslim thought to its most rationalistic point, and René Descartes? Living in Spain, in Seville, and making remarkable contributions to philosophy, logic, medicine, music, and jurisprudence, he wrote his major philosophic work "Tuhafut al-Tuhafut" [The Incoherence of the Philosophers] in response to al-Ghazali (1058–1111), who was born and died in Tus, Iran, and had a profound influence on what would become known as European thought, at least until the beginning of modern philosophy and experimental science. So, then, why, since Descartes, has the epistemic line erased Muslim contributions to human thought?

In trying to understand how the Western Christians won the epistemic battle against the Muslim philosophy, let us remember, as an anchor before René Descartes, the name and works of Desiderio Erasmus, a Dutch humanist (1466 [Rotterdam]–1536 [England]) with a remarkable influence in Spain, during the kingdom of Charles V of the Holy Roman Empire (Bataillon [1950] 1965). Metaphorically, Erasmus was one of the main agents in pushing Ibn Rushd out of the memory of a reconstituting Christian Spain, shortly after the final defeat of the Moors in 1492. There is a straight line between Erasmus's theology and Descartes's secular philosophy; while there is a profound gap between Erasmus and Descartes, on the one hand, and Al-Ghazali and Ibn-Rushd, on the other. A historical and epistemic gap was converted into a mirage and translated into a natural and logical historical continuity. The mirage is that it appears as if "universal history and intellectual history" follow an ascending temporal line, and therefore, it is natural that René Descartes continued and took advantage of an accumulation of meaning that had been taking place in a genealogy that went from the Central-Asian philosopher and physician Ibn Sina (born in a village named Afshana near the ancient Central Asian cultural center of Bukhara (modern

Uzbekistan), to the Iranian al-Ghazali to the Spanish-Morrocan Ibn-Rushd. But that, as we all know, is not the way the history was told. Ibn-Rushd was eradicated from the Universal march of Human thought and Descartes, after Bacon, inscribed a genealogy of thought that was grounded in Galileo and in Aristotle; while Kant followed suit by replacing Galileo with Newton. To redress this history and contribute to a pluriversal world in which many worlds coexist is one of the tasks of the border thinking and the decolonial shift.

The conditions for border thinking illustrated in the three previous configurations and the potential to make the decolonial shift are certainly there. Yet, the dominance and hegemony of Western Christianity (in its diversity) and secular liberalism (in its diversity), managed to engender both assimilation and apartheid, which is illustrated by Muslim and other non-Western forms of fundamentalism today. During the existence of the Soviet Union and its aftermath, Communism, as an alternative to Christianity (including its Orthodox variant) within the modern/colonial world, enacted the same logic of coloniality of Western empires toward the Soviet colonies. But, on the other hand, in the domain of the imperial difference, the Soviet Union remained a second-class empire that implemented the same logic of Western coloniality but altered its content.

Border thinking and the decolonial shift allows to imagine the ways out of the confrontation between Western promotion of its global designs and the Russian/Soviet Empire and colonies, on the one hand, and Islamic/Ottoman legacies in the Middle East, on the other. It has yet to find a way in which "either-or" is at a deadlock, which seems to be maintained by the success of capitalism in wearing different masks (liberal, Islamic, etc.). In Russia, however, there are no efforts at creating any alternative mediating bordering models and the two dominant ones, in this respect, remain the word-for-word repetition of the Western discourses, rapidly going out of fashion today, and the return to the mixture of Russian and Soviet imperial ideology of a besieged camp. As a result we see today the full swing division of the ex-Russian "property" between the more powerful rivals, as we can witness in several minor revolutions going on in the ex-colonies of Soviet Union: Georgia, the Ukraine, Moldova, Kirgizia, Uzbekistan, and so on. What happens here is the redistribution of borders that are changing one master for another. In contrast with Japan, China, or the Islamic world, where the ancient and elaborate native epistemic, cultural, and religious systems did not allow the Western modernization to destroy this basis completely, in such unstable, in-between, and blurred spaces marked with incomplete or partial difference as Russia, central Europe, or the Ottoman Sultanate, the forceful insertion of Western epistemology easily pushed their own problematic roots, which were not very deeply ingrained in the first place, completely out.

Border Thinking at the Crossroad of Local Histories and Global Designs

One of the common views about modernity and globalization (i.e., a later stage of modernity) is to conceive the first in contradistinction with alternative modernities and the second in contradistinction with the local. Local histories/alternative modernities are dependent and surrogate components of the triumphal march of Global history/modernity. The assumed reality in both cases is that globalization "moves" to the periphery, and it is in the peripheries where alternative modernities take place as well. Our three theses are an exercise in border thinking (or thinking from the borders) and they contest both the held view of the global/local and of modernity/alternative modernities.

Regarding the first, the distinction between global and local is based on a territorial, not a border, epistemology that assumes the global emanating from Western Europe and the U.S. to the rest of the world, where the local dwells. In that regard, globalization is seen as a set of processes that engender responses and reactions from those who defend the "authentic cultures" or political sovereignty threatened by global forces. Our theses assume, on the contrary, that local histories are everywhere, in the U.S. and the European Union as well as in Tanzania, Bolivia, China, or Mercosur. But, the question is that not every local history is in a position to devise and enact global designs; the majority of local histories on the planet have had to deal, in the past five hundred years, with an increasing spread of *imperial* global designs of all kinds: religious, political, economic, linguistic and epistemic, and cultural.

The coloniality of knowledge and the coloniality of being, i.e., the spread of global designs from local histories where they emerged to local histories to which they are alien, create the conditions for border thinking (instead of authenticity), for the decolonial epistemic shift aiming at the decolonization of knowledge and being. And, it is in the precise sense of the imperial/colonial conflicts between global designs that spread forms of knowledges and subjectivities from the local histories where they emerge to local histories to which they are alien, that the decolonial epistemic shift is geo- and body-politically oriented in confrontation with the theo-and egopolitics that has sustained the global imperial designs.

From this emerges our second conclusion, our response to the emergence of the idea of "alternative modernities" that are grounded in the territorial epistemology of modernity. In other words, the very idea of alternative modernities makes sense only from an epistemological Eurocentered perspective that looks at the world as if the epistemic gaze was independent of any geohistorical and body-graphic location. That is precisely the epistemology of the zero-point that, historically, has the name of theology and egology. The government of Evo Morales is not claiming a colonial modernity but rather the decolonization of the state and the economy, altogether with decolonization of education (knowledge and being). From the perspective of border thinking and the decolonial shift, the idea of alternative modernities is, as we just said, already embedded in the Eurocentered idea of modernity. There is no modernity, in other words, beyond the macro-narratives, invented since the Renaissance by means of which Europe was invented as geohistorically occupying the center of space and the present in time. From a border epistemology, the idea of alternative modernities is unsound and what is needed instead are "alternatives to modernity," i.e., alternatives to the naturalized idea that the past five hundred years of European history are the point of arrival (or the end of history) of the human race, and as Anthony Giddens has it, it will be modernity all the way down. If that is the case, then, it will be coloniality all the way down, because from a border epistemology perspective, coloniality is constitutive (and not derivative) of modernity.

"Demodernize" in this context would mean to reenact in Europe or in the U.S., decolonial projects that are emerging not as "colonial modernities" but as alternatives *to* modernity/coloniality, alternatives to the perpetuation of the colonial matrix of power. It is clear that decolonization and deimperialization do not mean the same for the U.S. and European Union citizens and for the immigrants to these countries or the citizens of Bolivia, Algeria, and India. In its turn, deimperialization does not indicate the same for the citizens of Germany and France and for those of Russia and China. There is no universal blueprint for either decolonialization or deimperialization. To decolonize means at the same time to demodernize. And demodernizing means delinking from modern Western epistemology, from the perspective of which the questions of "representation" and "totality" are being constantly asked. Demodernize does not mean going back in time as it is usually understood by the proponents of modernity's vector models, who immediately react by refusing "to go back to the Dark Ages." We mean something completely different here, and to understand what is demodernizing, one has to forget the generally accepted juxtaposition of modernity and tradition as its dark other. To do this would already mean a decolonial step.

Border thinking is indeed a way to move toward the decolonial shift; and the decolonial shift, in the last analysis, consists in "delinking" ("desprenderse" is the word employed by Anibal Quijano in 1992) of theo- and egological epistemic tyranny of the modern world and its epistemic and cultural (e.g., formation of subjectivities) consequences: the coloniality of knowledge and being. But to delink is not to abandon, to ignore. No one could abandon or ignore the deposit and sedimentation of imperial languages and categories of thought. Border thinking proposes how to deal with that imperial sedimentation while at the same time getting out of the spell and the enchantment of imperial modernity. The decolonial epistemic shift, grounded in border thinking, aims at processes of decolonizing knowledge and being. Decolonizing being and knowledge is a way toward the idea that "another world is possible" (and not of alternative modernities). That world, as the Zapatistas had it, will be "a world in which many worlds will coexist" and not a world in which there persists "globalization" or the imposition of global designs and "authenticity," nor will fundamentalists responses to imperial global designs reproduce an unending war against the enemies of imperial abstract universals. A world in which many worlds coexist cannot be imagined and predicated on the basis of the "good abstract universal valid for all" but, instead, on pluriversality as a universal project. Critical border thinking and the decolonial shift are one road toward that possible future. Ours was an effort at theorizing *in* the borders and contributing to changing the geo- and body politics of knowledge.

Today, the colonial matrix of power is dominated more than ever in the past five hundred years by the sphere of the economy. Once Christianity wanted to control the souls, now the spirit of economy controls the bodies and souls. The rhetorical promise is not "Paradise after death," but "Happiness after Development." There is nowhere to go from here if we remain within the logic of coloniality.[39] And more and more people realize that it is high time that we reject the rhetoric of modernity and, subsequently, the logic of coloniality and attempt to shift the biography and geography of reason from its established Western place to the locales marked by the colonial difference. Here, the most instrumental concepts would be that of political society bursting the harmony of the liberal model apart and the new subject of the decolonial agency: the *damnés*. Modernity/coloniality inadvertently generates critical dimension from within and on its colonial side, it nourishes the seeds of the decolonial consciousness and the future development of *demodern* agency, while the very concept of the colonial matrix of power is the first basic critical step in decolonial thinking.

PART II

CHAPTER 3

Transcultural Tricksters in between Empires

"Suspended" Indigenous Agency in the Non-European Russian/Soviet (Ex-)Colonies and the Decolonial Option

I.

Non-European Russian/Soviet (ex-)colonies such as the Caucasus and Central Asia are one of the typical subjects of area studies research—the proverbial subalterns who were taught to speak in the language of the Soviet modernity but presumably retained a number of unchangeable characteristics pointed toward a negatively marked "tradition." Their interpretation within the global and local configuration of knowledge in the Soviet time and today is an interesting subject in itself. The history of the Soviet anthropology, race studies, and ethnography has been recently put at the center of the heated discussions in Russia, in the ex-colonies themselves, and in the West (Bertran 2003, Solovey 1998, Tishkov 1992, *Ab Imperio, Slavic Review* 2009). The development of these social sciences was marked with coloniality of knowledge within the twentieth-century Western taxonomy of disciplines and was closely linked with the construction of the social, cultural, and ethnic matrix of the Soviet Empire, with its sanctification of primordialist theory of ethnos (from the 1960s onward), peculiar federalism, theatrical multiculturalism, and hidden colonialism. Today's critical reassessment of these concepts is important for nation-building and identity construction of the ex-colonies, for the continuing post- and neoimperial politics of Russia, and for the Western efforts to know the other, which still mostly fall into two categories—alienation and appropriation.

After the collapse of the Soviet Union and the following ideological decline, area studies both in the West and in the ex–Soviet Union hastily reoriented in their interpretation of the Russian/Soviet (ex-)colonies. They stopped to erase the ethnic-racial and religious differences and hierarchies for the sake of ideological conformity in the interpretation of the former national republics. In the West, the old Sovietology could not exist any more, because its ideological core, which glued together the heterogeneous material it studied, simply vanished. Russia proper rapidly lost its significance as an object in the Western area studies configuration (Kotkin 1995, 2003, Dawisha and Parrot 1994, 1996, Aranaga 2009, Slezkine 1994, 2000, Suny 1997), while the interest in the newly independent states grew and resulted in the emergence of Eurasian studies.[40] This was a geopolitical more than a purely scholarly endeavor, while the new Eurasianists in the West, largely remained innocent Orientalists of a sort with few exceptions (Suchland 2011).

In many cases, scholars who did this new Eurasian research were the same old Sovietologists or their pupils. I do not mean to criticize them but just would like to draw attention to the fact that their ideological clichés (many of which they shared with their Soviet equivalents) turned out to be deeper rooted than it seemed and linked not even with a particular kind of ideology, be it Socialism or liberalism but rather with the rhetoric of modernity as such. What lay in its basis? The familiar cult of progress and development, the false but powerful opposition of modernity and tradition and the ideal of newness, the comical scientific pretensions and the hubris of the zero point. The political scientists both in Russia and in the West are the most vulnerable to criticism (Olcott 1993, Malashenko 1993), as they reproduce either Orientalism as an alibi for the lack of real interest in comprehending the non-Western other in its own terms, reducing the other to the site of difference to explain away the need to attend to its opacity and complexity; or modernist ideology, which sees history in linear terms as moving from the primitive to the developed, confering similarity on the other as the past of the self (Shu-mei Shih 2005: 5).

In such works the Eurasian borderlands continue to be regarded within the Orientalist or progressivist frame that according to Shu-Mei Shih, cloaks the lack of the desire to know the other (Shu-Mei Shih 2005: 5). Therefore, Central Asia and the Caucasus are still largely seen as a source of exotic culture or dangerous terrorism and instability, as a new risk factor in the world after the collapse of the Soviet Union, as a sinister "dust of empire" (Meyer 2004) of which the West has to be aware. Russian political scientists also suffer from this disease, but they are marked with the victory in defeat rhetoric and often continue to practice assertive imperial revivalist discourses.

If we consider historians, literary and cultural critics, sociologists, and anthropologists, the situation is different. A number of scholars looking for a new paradigm to interpret the post-Soviet ex-colonies, turned to the ready-made model of postcolonial studies, which, as was pointed out in Part I, is hardly adequate to define the post-Soviet experience and local histories.[41] But most of the scholars attempted to abstain from theorizing and remain within the limits of description and meticulous source study and field study. Starting in the early 1990s, Central Asia and the Caucasus have become a popular place for Western field work specialists, who produced a considerable amount of mostly descriptive works within a wide range of quality (Sahadeo 2007, Adams 2005, Kandiyoti 2002, Kamp 2006, Northrop 2004, Beissinger 2008), typically published in journals defined as "Survey" or "Review," which betrays their disciplinary and ideological framework. Russia, as usual, lagged behind and has started to slowly revive its interest in the study of Central Asia and the Caucasus only relatively recently (Kosmarsky 2004, Kosmarskaya 2006, Abashin 2007, Tishkov 2003, Tyomkina 2005).

Some of these new types of area studies scholars are marked with the coloniality of knowledge syndrome in a milder form and retain their ability at transcultural pluritopic hermeneutics when they "study" an alien "tradition." This refers mainly to historians and anthropologists, particularly of the younger generation, in the West and Russia who are less contaminated by the Cold War mentality and more attuned to questioning and rethinking of historical meta-narratives. Their works are often examples of honest research that is still limited by their excessive reliance on often-biased archives (Russian, Soviet, newly (re)created national, seldom diasporic). Second, such works are still restricted by their Western methodology and primarily by the zero point epistemology lying in its basis, as well as the cult of objectivism and empiricism. Moreover, the very categories of analysis being used in such research distort the local histories they "study." For example, they assume that the ideal for any kind of society is a well-developed Western-style civil society with clearly articulated forms of political and social struggle and resistance. All other forms of agency, historical or contemporary, are automatically discredited as marginal, pertaining to the sphere of the nonrational and therefore subhuman. Consequently, any scholar who attempts to present these irregular forms of agency or indigenous epistemology not as traditionalist archaic survivals to be marveled at, but as a serious form of agency projecting into the future, is automatically accused of Orientalism, romanticism, sentimentalism, and other such vices.

Finally, the limitations of even the new generation of area studies specialists of the Caucasus and Central Asia in the West and in Russia are connected with their authors' body politics of knowledge, which alienates from them the world they strive to describe and define. Their mode of analysis is far even from "participatory anthropology," which still may remain within the object/subject divide, to say nothing of the epistemic and political projects with indigenous agendas working *with* anthropologists, such as THOA (Taller Historia Oral Andina) or the Zapatistas (Cusicanqui 1990). Therefore, these works still describe Central Asians and Caucasus peoples as insects. However, there are a few exceptions, most of which belong to diasporic and border intellectuals living in the West (among them Adeeb Khalid 1999, 2007, Jeff Sahadeo 2007, Sada Aksartova 2005 and several others). For them, the problem remains their need to obey and mimic the Western scholarship rules to survive as academics in the West, which leaves them a rather narrow space for maneuvering. Some of these limitations can be eventually overcome by the scholars from Central Asia and the Caucasus provided they stop being regarded as native informants and are not restricted by Western scholarly rules in their own research. At this point, there is less than a handful of such scholars (among them Svetlana Shakirova 2006, 2007, 2008, Marfua Tokhtakhodzhayeva 1996, 1999, 2001, Sofia Kasymova 2005b, Madina Tekuyeva 2006a, Elza Bair Guchinova 2005, and several others).

Their position is often marked by the sensibility of internal others, multiply colonized by many imperial traditions and by the global coloniality as a constant reproduction of the imperial and colonial difference (see Part I). Such positioning can be found in bordering spaces, located in between Europe and Asia, Western modernity and Islam, the subaltern empires of modernity, such as the Ottoman Sultanate and the Russian Empire. The Caucasus and Central Asia fall out of the general logic, imposed on the world by several centuries of the Western European supremacy, but also out of the prevailing Arabic Muslim tradition. Moreover, being doubly or multiply colonized in epistemic as well as the economic, cultural, and political sense, these regions developed throughout the centuries their specific techniques and strategies for survival, resistance, and in some cases, positive models of thinking and subjectivity formation, which even if virtually unknown in the West and in the Muslim world at large, can constitute a way out of the contemporary dilemma—the West versus Islam.

II.

Central Asia and more so the Caucasus are paradigmatically border spaces. "Border" in this case is a geographic, geopolitical, and ontological phenomenon, as these locales are positioned on the cracks of not just mountain ranges or deserts, caravan crossroads and between the seas, but also on the borders of empires and civilizations. Political scientist Karl Meyer, in *The Dust of Empire*, points out that "culturally and physically, Caucasia is the prototypal borderland. Its mountains, stretching six hundred miles from sea to sea, not only form the divide between Europe and Asia but also separate the two earliest Christian kingdoms (Armenia and Georgia) from Islam's two major branches, the dissenting Shias, mostly inhabiting what is now Azerbaijan, and the majority Sunnis who predominate in the North Caucasus" (2004: 145).

Both the Caucasus and Central Asia have been always cultural, linguistic, religious, and ethnic crossroads. Various religions and ethnic and linguistic groups came one after another into these locales; some of them stayed and hybridized their cultures with those of the people who already lived there, creating a unique and complex history. For example, in the territory of modern Azerbaijan, antique Zoroastrianism gave way to Christianity, which later was replaced by Islam, when Azerbaijan became a part of the Arabic Caliphate. Central Asia, with its heart in the Ferghana Valley (a place between two rivers Amu-Darya–Oxus and Syr-Darya–Jaxartes), also has been a site of multiple religious, ethnic and linguistic mixing, starting from the same Zoroastrianism, which many scholars believe to be born there, in Khorezm, and to Buddhism and Hellenism, the nomadic polytheistic cultures of the steppe and the metropolitan craftsmen and artisans traditions, the scientific and cultural achievements, borrowed from India, China, Persia, Greece, the Middle East, and Turkey—all of them coming together in the flourishing Central Asian culture, which came under the Arabic control in the seventh through ninth centuries, finally to become Muslim under the Samanid dynasty, and in the thirteenth century, once again, being conquered by Genghis-Khan's army. Both territories, from the start, had been the sites of intense transculturation and took an active part in the precapitalist world economy. They elaborated their own tolerant ways of dealing with this cultural multiplicity as well as strategies of survival under various regimes, which, though transformed, are alive even today in the subjectivity of the people living in these locales, even after the distorting influence of modernity brought with it concepts initially foreign to these territories such as ethnic and linguistic nationalism and the strong sense of ethnic belonging, religious and linguistic purism and intolerance, racialization and ethnization, artificial divisions of major ethnicities and minorities, into "Arians" and "Mongolians," and the like.

Therefore, the geopolitical understanding of the border in this case should be complemented by epistemic and existential rendering of this problematic, similar to the one to be found in the works of a Chicana philosopher Gloria Anzaldúa. Her border sensibility is very much in tune with transcultural multiply colonized subjectivities of Eurasian borderlands. Anzaldúa (1999) states that "a borderland is a vague and undetermined place created by the emotional residue of an unnatural boundary. It is in a constant state of transition. The prohibited and forbidden are its inhabitants" (p. 25) . . . . "The new *mestiza* copes by developing a tolerance for ambiguity. . . . She has a plural personality, she operates in a pluralistic mode—nothing is thrust out, the good, the bad and the ugly, nothing rejected, nothing abandoned. Not only does she sustain contradictions, she turns the ambivalence into something else" (p. 101). Such a border sensibility develops in both Caucasia and Central Asia as these regions happen to be simultaneously inside and outside of the Muslim world, constantly finding themselves in the zone of clashing interests and transcultural processes between various empires and dominant cultures. This positioning gives them the epistemic potential of the border. The Caucasus and Central Asia for centuries have given birth to various models of transcultural mediating thinking and subjectivity that, even if suppressed by various empires, turned out to be impossible to completely destroy. On the contrary, a trickster sensibility of a particular kind, incorporating various cultural, ethnic, religious, epistemic traditions and demonstrating particular intersubjective models of treating the other, managed to survive and was in some cases even strengthened by the imperial control.

By "tricksterism" here, I mean the contemporary understanding of the term, which is linked with yet departs from the classical mythological, religious, and folklore meaning, when it referred to gods, half-gods, anthropomorphic animals, and less frequently, to humans with supernatural characteristics (Hynes and Doty 1993, Ballinger 1991–92). What is important is the insurgent nature of any trickster, his or her tendency to disobey the normative rules and conventions. From the classical understanding of "tricksterism" come such qualities developed and sustained in modern tricksters as ambiguity, deceit of authority, playing tricks on power, metamorphosis, a mediating function between different worlds, manipulation and bricolage as modes of existence. In this sense, trickster becomes not only one of the most ubiquitous figures of world literature in modernity and postmodernity (up to its Internet form as a Troll today) but also acquires specific features in colonial and postcolonial traditions, where tricksterism acts as a form of resistance and re-existence.

This sensibility has a lot to do with the subjectivity of a transcultural migrant of the globalization époque, an individual who lives in the world and not in a particular national culture, who is rootless by definition, who is a wanderer with no links to any particular locality. More specifically, I mean a dialogic concept of a trickster negotiating between Dona Haraway's (1991) and Chela Sandoval's (2000) interpretations and also the real trickster traditions that grew out of the geo- and body politics of particular locales, such as peripheral Eurasia, where we encounter the less known in the West trickster characters such as Hodja Nasreddin, found all over Central Asia, the southern Caucasus, and the Middle East (Kharitonov 1986), and Sosruko, a northwest Caucasus Prometheus (Jaimoukha 2010). Donna Haraway's trickster is a revolutionary form of human being who becomes an amalgam of technology and biology, the machine and the human, but also the dominant and the oppositional, the First and Third Worlds, the men and the women (1991). She takes up the Native American trickster metaphor (that of coyote) to formulate her position of radical critical "mestizaje" or a cyborg machine, which has to do with the indigenous people's resistance, looking for similarity in difference.

In Sandoval's dialogue with Haraway, a differential mode of social movements and consciousness depends on the ability to read a concrete situation of power and consciously chose the ideological position most adequate for opposition to this power configuration. The individual practicing such a mode is required, according to María Lugones (2003), to make a nomadic journey between the worlds of meaning. In her article "Playfulness, 'World'-Traveling, and Loving Perception," she rethinks the concept of the Western *agon* and playing based on agonistics, regarding love as the essence and basis for any successful intercultural and intersubjective communication. Lugones's *homo ludens* is not interested in who wins and who loses and is forever ready to change the rules of the game. Therefore, such a trickster sees others nonaggressively, retaining an absolute flexibility and easily switching from one world to another, as well as a playful attitude to all worlds, including his or her own. Instead of the strict prescription of frozen social roles, Lugones stands for the flexibility and fluidity of one's own images, for the constant process of self-creation and self-destruction as well as the creation and destruction of various worlds. "We are not self-important, we are not fixed in particular constructions of ourselves, which is part of saying that we are open to self-construction . . . . While playful, we have not abandoned ourselves to, nor are we stuck in, any particular 'world.' We are there creatively,

We are not passive" (Lugones 2003: 96). Finally, Lugones sees "world-traveling and identification through world-traveling as part of loving" others, and "a form of disloyalty to arrogant perceivers, including the arrogant perceivers in ourselves and to their constructions of powerful barriers between" people (2003: 98).

Differential consciousness as a trickster's mind inclines to other principles of mobility and to metamorphosis and tranformationism. For Sandoval, a trickster "practices subjectivity as masquerade, a nomadic 'morphing' not performed only for survival's sake. It is a set of *principled conversions* that requires (guided) movements, a directed but also a diasporic migration in both consciousness and politics, performed to ensure that ethical commitment to egalitarian social relations be enacted in the everyday, political sphere of culture" (2003: 62) Turning to the changeable trickster metaphor, which acquires concrete meanings in each cultural-epistemic locale, we can avoid the new abstract universal and attempt a mutual translation between the modern and transmodern idioms.

Sandoval and Lugones's interpretations of trickster consciousness and playful traveling, along with Anzaldúa's new mestiza's consciousness of tricksters dwelling on the borders of the imperial/colonial differences, are among the brightest realizations of border sensibility in the non-West. From such experience emerges a new transaesthetics connecting people throughout the world who have suffered the colonial wound (Anzaldúa 1999). This sensibility finds parallels in the Caucasus and Central Asian subverted forms of agency residing mainly in the aesthetic realm, in the sphere of visual and verbal arts, as I demonstrate next.

III.

For the West, both the Caucasus and Central Asia remain paradigmatic antispaces or nonspaces—ultimately exoticized or demonized.[42] This is quite logical, because the universal Hegelian history never unfolded in Tashkent or Baku. Even a Ferghanian Babur left his motherland in quest of fame; and only after he conquered Kabul, was he able to found the Great Mogul Empire. But in today's global geopolitics, these remote (from Europe and America) spaces suddenly come to play a more important part in the new world order. Hence, there is a new round of struggle for dominance between various forces in these regions, where economic and social factors (from the high density of population to the low economic level, from the limited land and water resources to mass unemployment) are accompanied by ethnic statism and, in some cases, religious extremism. It would be nearsighted to blame only the Soviet Empire for this. The USSR was the latest and most persistent colonizing agent in these locales, but the forceful Soviet modernity/coloniality itself was only an act in the larger Western modernity/coloniality play. Therefore, if we want to understand the present situation in the Caucasus and Central Asia, we would have to frame it within the march of Western modernity in all its forms, which resulted, among other things, in the decline and fall of these previously prosperous and culturally rich places. Thus, the beginning of the end of Central Asian prosperity and its falling out of the future world history was linked with the foundation of the global capitalist world economy and the looming European dominance. It was then, that Vasco da Gama's ships blazed the sea route from Europe to India and further, to China; and the Great Silk route lost its significance, while Central Asia lost its strategic economic importance on which it had rested for two millennia and became a periphery. Even today, when the Eurasian borderlands finally became politically independent, at least partially (in case of the Caucasus), they still cannot leave the vicious circle of multiple colonization.

Up to the establishment of the global Western European dominance, the power asymmetry based on the Hegelian understanding of world history was not yet generally accepted and the "exotic" Tamerlane's empire was not interpreted by Europeans as primitive, underdeveloped, in need of civilizing, or fallen out of history. The figure of Tamerlane is an interesting semiotic sign of transcultural exchanges between Europe, Russia, and Asia, which illustrates how Western modernity gradually turned anyone non-European and non-Christian into a subhuman through demonizing and Orientalizing and how various local versions of modernity, such as the Soviet, the Jadid, and the contemporary postindependent Uzbek one, continue to exploit the Timurids myth, supporting their ideological and geopolitical interests. This is how, from a willy-nilly equal, he soon became a standard manifestation of barbarous cruelty and despotism, marveled at in both the Western and later Czarist Russian interpretations, then went through a period of Soviet positive recycling, and today is once again recycled in Uzbekistan, often turning into a simply masquerade figure dismissed by both Russian and sometimes Western historians, who are trying to diminish Timur's role in history to blame the Uzbek administration for exploiting the myth as a source of the new national identity (Allworth 1998, Marozzi 2006, March 2002, Abashin 2007, Ilkhamov 2005). What is important here is not even the degree of Timur's achievements or failures as such. Tamerlane semiotics is indeed ubiquitous in modern Uzbekistan and takes disproportionate dimensions, but the act of ridiculing this imagery from the side of modernity is not innocent either, as it clearly demonstrates yet another guise of Orientalism. As in case of any historical figure of the same scale, from Henry VIII to Peter the Great, we can equally easily depict Timur as a tyrant or as a benevolent monarch. What is more important is what is behind this black legend mentality, implied today in the Western, Russian, and Uzbek historian debate over Timur and his legacy. It is Eurocentrism, racism, a wish to put a wall between European (or Russian) history and the "barbarous" Orient, in short, coloniality of being and of knowledge struggling to prevent the subaltern from finding any viable historical source of agency by ridiculing it and dismissing as a superstition.

In both the Caucasus and Central Asia up to the second modernity, a variety of independent and semi-independent polities existed that alternatively came under control of various stronger agents, often successfully balancing between them for centuries. When the main colonial spaces were already divided among the large Western capitalist empires, a process of appropriation of the less attractive but still geostrategically important territories, such as Central Asia and the Caucasus, started. In the latter case, the rivalry took place between the secondary empires of modernity, marked by imperial external differences, and mainly, the Ottoman Sultanate and Russia. Both the Caucasus and Central Asia were colonized not directly by the Western capitalist empires but by the second-class empire, which was itself epistemically and culturally colonized by the West and, thus, acted as a mediator of Western modernity, albeit in distorted forms. As a result, the Caucasus and Central Asia as colonies of a second-class empire took a specific doubly subaltern space in the complex global power structure. For example, the Shia Persia, the Ottoman Sultanate, and Russia all competed for Azerbaijan in the second modernity. Russia got it after its victory over Persia in the early nineteenth century. As a result, one of the many Eurasian artificial borders was drawn on the River Arax (echoing Gloria Anzaldúa's border semiotic interpretation of Rio Grande, which continues to bring people death, suffering, and humiliation). Even today it divides the Azeri people of northern Persia and those of Azerbaijan. A similar history is to be found in Central Asia, which after the collapse of the Timurids dynasty and several centuries of decay was conquered by the Russian Empire in the 1860s. Russia imposed on this space its own colonial model of modernization, copied from the West up to minute details, including the famous concept of the "tools of empire" and "*kulturtreger* mission." It is worth noting that Russia almost immediately began making a cotton colony out of Central Asia, intending to shake the cotton monopoly of the U.S. South. This project of Central Asia modernization was continued by the Soviets with larger and more violent excesses, ultimately resulting in ecological and humanitarian catastrophes of the second half of the twentieth century.

It is only natural then that both the Caucasus and Central Asia were torn between modernization via the Russian Empire, via the Ottoman Sultanate model (in the case of the Caucasus) and more traditionalist Muslim Persia, and the countries of the Southeast Asia (in case of Central Asia). Their modernization model came from Russia and later from the Soviet Union, up to the 1990s, when the politically pragmatic secular Muslim state model (such as Turkey) and the renewed attempts at direct Western control, came back. Even if the West never succeeded in directly colonizing these locales, there were several attempts in modernity at establishing indirect rule over both the Caucasus and Central Asia—all of them within the logic of redistribution of colonial spaces when the collapsing empires gave a chance to their more successful rivals to gain control over their territories. This happened roughly in the period 1917–20, when the collapsing Russian Empire slackened its grip and both the Caucasus and Turkistan gained independence, if only for several years. Immediately, the Western European countries attempted to take over, but the strengthened Bolshevik Empire quickly restored its dominance. We witness a more recent example of the same imperial tactic today, when once again the West is trying to establish control over these regions—economically, politically, and culturally. However, neither the Caucasus nor Central Asia is ready to make a final choice, resorting instead to the age-old tactic of balancing, mediation, transcultural sensibility, and trickster resistance that gives them at least some potential for the future.

IV.

Here it is a good place to say a few words about the genealogy of this resisting sensibility going hand in hand with epistemic models of alternative thinking and subjectivities in peripheral Eurasia. It demonstrates some intersections with the dissenting South American indigenous models, even if, in case of Eurasia, they have not yet had a chance to be sufficiently represented on the level of the state, the public discourse, or the social structures, being confined to the sphere of the nonrational, esoteric, artistic. The reasons for such differences are linked with different ways modernity manifests itself in these locales, leading to the emergence of multiple and varied groups of "others" and, at the same time, inevitably generating the effect of resistance, which, as the Latin American experience demonstrates, can eventually become a powerful political force.

Furthermore, our use of indigeneity refers to people who were already in place when the march of modernity (directly by the West or indirectly by second-class empires, like Russia) began to interfere in their places and life. "Indigenous" then should not be limited to people whom the Europeans named "Indians" in the Americas or to Australian and New Zealand aboriginals but should be extended to all people, irrespective of their way of life, religion, or culture, who became a hindrance for the march of modernity and progress.

Therefore, the history of indigenous movements in the Caucasus and Central Asia cannot be taken out of historical context. These movements did not stay the same in some frozen form but changed together with the changing world. They were in the center of geopolitical events of the world history in the nineteenth century, acting as pawns in the struggle of several types of empire for geopolitical dominance. Both regions played a central role in the so-called Eastern question, which was a fight between European powers and Russia for control of the lands of the Ottoman Sultanate and also in the great game between the Great Britain and the Russian Empire over India. While Russia was unsuccessfully trying to win a better place for itself vis-à-vis Europe, its non-European colonies were often used to exercise the Russian imperial self-assertion that could not be expressed in the West. The indigenous people of these locales, even if they were and are used by all fighting sides—from Great Britain to the Russian Empire and from Germany to France, from the dying Ottoman Sultanate to the Bolsheviks reconquering these territories, and finally, by the Americans and the Muslim world and China today—remained completely stripped of human rights and any opportunity of taking part in nation building, generation of knowledge, and local social structures. They were and remain now the hostages of modernity/coloniality great game.

There are many examples of resistance of Central Asian and Caucasus people, such as the Adyghean Princes Union of the 1830s, an anticolonial organization of the leaders of all the Caucasus tribes, which made an appeal to the Russian authorities, asking them to stop the military actions on the lands of Adyghe (Circassians) (Zihia web-portal) and offering a project of a confederation of the Caucasus lands. Later, when their appeal was ignored and the colonization continued in its most cruel forms, they organized a volunteer corps to fight against Russia, as a result of which many of these Caucasus ethnicities were completely wiped from the face of the earth. But, the Caucasus decolonial movement did not end then, continuing well into the twentieth century—in the anti-Soviet movements of the 1920–30s, strangled by Stalin and his local disciples, jealously eliminating all alternatives to

Soviet modernity, such as Nazir Katkhanov's Shariah Column and his vision of the Bolshevik yet Muslim northern Caucasus (Tekuyeva 2003), and today, in the new Caucasus war of the late twentieth to early twenty-first centuries (Sahni 1997, Lieven 2000, *The Circassians 2008*).

The same refers to many instances of Turkistan resistance, from the 1892 uprising in Tashkent and the 1898 Andijan revolt to a more massive Dzhizak uprising of 1916–17, through controversial Basmachi movements and various religious revivals to the late Soviet political organizations and groups protesting against the ecological catastrophe of the Aral Sea. Among them a special place is occupied by the Turkistan National Liberation Movement presided by an indigenous intellectual Zeki Velidi Togan (Togan 1967). Similarly to the Caucasus, this movement also started with legal and nonviolent political actions, but by the end of the second decade of the twentieth century, Togan created a Secret Society for the liberation of Turkistan and the anticolonial struggle acquired military forms (guerilla movements) on the one hand, and the underground struggle and infiltration of the Soviet structures in preparation for the major anticolonial war, on the other. In Stalin's era, this ended with the death or defeat of all of its members except those who immigrated and attempted to continue their struggle from European capitals. Neither the Caucasus indigenous movements nor those of Turkistan ever stopped their resistance—for many decades, they continued to generate oppositional ideologies and leaders who were methodically eliminated by various imperial powers. (Khalid 1999, Traho 1956, Natho 2009).

These histories remained undocumented at large, the views of these people were erased, the oral histories (such as the Turkistan Dastan *Koroglu*, a story of the sixteenth century fighter for independence and freedom, used as a role model and inspiration for the early leaders of national liberation movement and the Caucasus oral history and epic tale of the woman-warrior and healer Khanifa Kazi, to say nothing of the newer documents and oral histories linked with the anticolonial movement of the late nineteenth to early twentieth centuries, such as the *mardikor* songs of the 1916 revolt) were buried, never published or mentioned in the Soviet Union.[43]

Both the Caucasus and Central Asian liberation movements included political and social elements, as they fought to construct Turkistan and Caucasus polities and attempted to open a dialogue with the state, using petitions, declarations, marches, and demonstrations, which always ended in bloody massacres and suppressions by both Czarist and later Soviet powers. The Bolsheviks, when reconquering Turkistan and the Caucasus, did not shun any means—first establishing contact with anticolonial and Muslim reformist movements then destroying them, often with the aid of local feudal and parochial Islamic forces, as well as international pan-Turkic ones, who in their turn were also eliminated later in the millstones of Soviet history. In the Soviet tradition of double standards, which was much more skillful than the Czarist one in the sense of its official liberation rhetoric and the actual repressive and racist acts in relation to the reconquered colonies, the Soviet historians often called the leaders of anticolonial movements "fighters for national liberation against Czarism." But, as soon as they turned to Soviet history, the same people were labeled as bandits, brigands, traitors, "basmachi," "abreks," whose destruction was thus justified. Along with the massive destruction of anticolonial movement leaders and members, the Bolsheviks also generated a massive elimination of indigenous knowledges and cosmologies, which are almost impossible to restore, especially since the new governments of the independent states are not interested in promoting the liberating spirit of these epistemologies. That is why they allow for only particular brands of Islam and sorts of ethnic culture to exist, while repressing all other forms of religious or ethnic-cultural expression today. The new/old corrected historical narrative promoted by the local leaders is often grounded in their efforts to create a strong and unified national identity and pride, which is opposed to the previous scattered tribes, conflicting tensions, small khanates—an easy prey to even such an ill-starred colonizer as the Russian Empire. Behind this postcolonial nationalism, we can easily detect familiar myths of stagism, development, newness, and other elements of the rhetoric of modernity. This creates an aftertaste of déjà vu recognizable in many official educational and cultural institutions (Abashin 2009).

V.

The tactics of the Russian and later Soviet variants of modernization in both regions were strikingly similar. They can be summarized in the motto "divide and rule."[44] The empire was afraid of a pan-Turkic or pan-Circassian unification on any grounds; and this was the reason for Islam being one of the most persecuted religions in the Soviet Union, for the borders drawn by the ruler, for the well-conceived linguistic and alphabetic reforms that deprived them of the continuity, cut off the legacy, and today prevent any possibility of having a dialogue with others of similar cultural, religious, or linguistic heritage. New ethnicities were invented, mosques closed, and the so-called Oriental women forcefully liberated—all that done to ensure the imperial dominance—but at the same time causing, particularly in the Soviet period, passive yet successful resistance to and distrust of any official authority.

Examples of this devastating imperial tactic are abundant. Russians used the Shia and Sunni opposition in Azerbaijan to make sure that they cut off the Sunni Azeris from the possible alliance with Shamil Sunnis and their descendants in the northern Caucasus. The Soviets mapped Turkistan in such a way as to prevent any attempts at Turkic and Islamic reunification, when they once again put artificial borders between artificially created republics and ethnicities, which were soon to be assimilated and dissolved in the Russian majority. Before the Russian modernization of the second half of the nineteenth century, there was no clearly defined idea of ethnicity in Central Asia (although the Jadids efforts to build it from within were already at work at the time). People were much more socially mobile and flexible. They could leave one region for another and easily change their status and identity, entering into different hierarchies, due to specific local mechanisms of mutual adaptation. It allowed for this complex cultural multiplicity to peacefully coexist. Therefore, Central Asians categorized themselves in a cultural, regional, social, economic, and religious but not strictly ethnic or linguistic sense, and only the Russian and particularly the Soviet colonization forcefully and nearsightedly introduced its own idea of ethnicity into this region, together with modernization model, based on the Soviet brand of ethnic-national identity (Northrop 2004, Abashin 2007).

The Soviets divided Turkistan ethnic-religious-linguistic unity into artificial entities. The tactic of Stalin's deportations of the whole peoples into Central Asia (such as Meskhetian Turks, Crimean Tatars, Chechens, and Balkars) and setting artificial borders contributed to the future ethnic and economic tensions in these regions (Karabakh conflict between the Azeris and Armenians, as a result of which over thirty thousand people were reported, according to several sources, to perish and around one million became refugees, the Osh conflict and other ethnic clashes in the Ferghana Valley). This is a direct result of Russian and Soviet imperial tactic of ethnicity building. Although the modern nations in Central Asia and the Caucasus were artificially formed, the result is there nonetheless. The scholarly constructs turned into political instruments that, in their turn, were implanted into the texture of economic, social, and cultural life and began to be seen by the people as ancient and given once and for all. Therefore, for the majority of modern inhabitants of Central Asia or the Caucasus today, nations are not "imagined communities" any more. In Rasanayagam's words, the ethnic divisions that were imposed on this region in Soviet times were not questioned by the leaders of the post-Soviet Central Asian states. Instead they stressed the validity of ethnic-territorial idea of the nation, but replaced Marxist ideology as its glue with ethnic nationalism (Rasanayagam 2004). As a result, nothing changed in the life of the common people, who remained as powerless and vulnerable as before. An important part here is played by Islam, which has been gradually transforming itself into ethnicity both in the metropolis and in the colonies themselves as the idea of race and nation have been replacing the previous theological constructions of the first modernity. This is how from *busurmanin* the Muslim became a *Tatar* (an equivalent of the Western Arab used to define all Muslims) and an "inorodets" (literally, the one who was born an "other") in the nineteenth-century Russian imaginary, and today—simply the *Black*—completely replacing the religious difference with the racial one. A radical ethnization, racialization, and politization of Islam took place in a number of postcolonial spaces with a traditionally weak idea of ethnicity, where ethnic nationalism often takes Islamist forms and Islam is claimed for the new nations and interpreted as primarily a manifestation of the local culture. However, in the case of both Central Asia and particularly the Caucasus, the gap between Islam as such and the indigenous culture, epistemology, cosmology, and ethics is wider than it is often admitted. For a number of politicized studies, it is more convenient to see both regions as a fixed Islamic Orient, while in reality, as a few Western, Russian, Central Asian, and Caucasus scholars demonstrated recently (Abashin 2007, Yordan, Kuzeev, and Chervonnaya 2001, Sahadeo and Zanca 2007, Quandour 2006), religious Muslim identity is only one of the elements in the complex syncretic sociocultural and civilizational belonging of the inhabitants of these ex-colonies. In peripheral Eurasia, Islam originally acted in a similar unattractive role to that of Catholicism in the New World. However, in both locales, the indigenous peoples elaborated specific strategies of domesticating the imposed religions (be it Catholicism or Islam), by means of maintaining their form yet changing the meaning and building these religions into the wider realm of indigenous cosmologies, thus shifting the geography and biography of reason. The Amerindian religious duality, the peculiar symbiosis of Muslim and indigenous beliefs in the Caucasus and Central Asia, and even the Russian "double faith" are all examples of this essentially decolonial sentiment, which was later recast in secular terms and today can be recast once again, in rethinking of humanities from the perspective of these locales.

With the end of the Communist utopia, several models of nation building emerged on the ruins of the Soviet empire, from the meticulous reproduction of Western liberal nation-states in the Baltics to autocratic Turkmenia, to take just the two extremes. The nationalist ideologies, hastily created and put in the basis of ex-colonial countries, mostly use the Western ideological frame of the sovereign nation-state, even if filled with local content, sometimes lapsing into ridiculous examples of totalitarian and militant ethnic nationalism. It is not by chance that all confederation projects in Eastern Europe and Central Asia or the Caucasus, which could potentially lead to a more productive way around and beyond the rhetoric of the nation-state, quickly failed, giving way at times to a maniacal race for ethnic-territorial sovereignty, the quest for roots (and often their invention), the striving to reinvent their own history and make it more prominent within the universal historical metanarrative, and consequently, the careful erasing from the collective consciousness and from the official historiography any alternative models of polity, any different cosmologies, or epistemic systems that did not fit into the new/old idea of the nation-state promoted by the new/old leaders of these ex-colonies. This is particularly sad in case of the Caucasus and Central Asia, both of which have a history of indigenous epistemologies and social models that had diverged from both Muslim or Christian and secular European modernity and later from Russian and Soviet modernization.

If they chose a confederative way of unification on the basis of indigenous social and epistemic models, the political life of eastern Eurasia would have been quite different, the same as in the case of the initial confederative projects of the eastern and central European states (the ex-satellites of Soviet Union), which were never brought to life. However, instead of the revival of indigenous epistemologies, the liberation movements in Central Asia and the Caucasus went mainly in the Islamist direction, in contrast with contemporary indigenous movements in South America. Amerindians struggle mainly for decolonization from the Eurocentered racist epistemologies in their creole rendering, while the multiply colonized peoples of the Caucasus and Central Asia have to decolonize from the overall coloniality of Western modernity in its Eurocentered Western, Russian, Soviet forms and, also, to decolonize from militant Islamism, which uses the economic hardships to gain control over the ex-Soviet territories.

Nation-building processes in the newly independent states have been controlled from the outside and by the "comprador" local elites, as always happened in the imperial times and continues to happen today. Both the Caucasus and Turkistan liberation movements of the mid-nineteenth century to early twentieth centuries were originally local, not precisely religious, and dealt mainly with retaking control of their lands and their future from the Russian/Soviet Empire, seldom venturing in the global pan-Turkic or pan-Islamic direction, instigated later by European emissaries and their non-European helpers (such as the Ottoman general Enver Pasha) to spite and weaken Russia. Today, the logic does not change much, which is clearly seen in the history of the northern Caucasus movements, quickly usurped by the forces of international Islamist organizations, and sometimes indirectly supported by the West. Here, we find mostly transmuted forms of ethnic statism. As the northern Caucasus social philosopher K. Tkhagapsoev points out, the post-Soviet space generated ethnic states based on the ethnic-clan system of power. "The space of freedom of ethnicites" proclaimed with the collapse of the Soviet system and comprising postcolonialism, neoliberalism, and traditionalism, finally resulted in ethnic statism, regionalization, and the ethnization of power. "As a result, in ethnic republics the political instrument for the implementation of reforms—which were manifested as liberal and democratic . . . turned out in fact to be the authoritarian regimes of ethnic statism—which has nothing to do with democratic principles" (Tkhagapsoev 2006).

A citizen of such states today often has to become a new nomad against his or her will (see Chapter 6 on the question of citizenship). The inhabitants of Central Asia or the Caucasus, who are so much hated by xenophobic Russians and constitute a larger part of the labor migration today, go mainly to Russia and not to the West (which is possible only for the chosen few) looking for jobs and better life, because in the modern global configuration of power, entering the world economic system as labor force is still impossible for them. These people can get to Europe or the U.S. through human trafficking or as organ donors, because only for these kinds of activities have the borders become more permeable today if one is an ex-Soviet colonial other. With the present systemic economic crisis, fewer and fewer options are left for these involuntary migrants, even in the world of imperial difference.[45] This problematic has found an interesting rendering in Central Asian art. Uzbek artist Vyacheslav Useinov, in his installation *A Guest Workers Flight*, presents a plane made of adobe bricks, like those still used by the peasants of Central Asia to build their houses (Useinov). The unlikely combination is shocking, as is the forced modernity in this locale. What is awaiting them on the other side of globalization migration? The worker's overalls closely resembling the prisoners' clothes, made of checked plastic trunks—a staple of the post-Socialist shuttle traders and refugee life. They symbolize the illegal migration status of millions of Uzbeks today, who flee their homeland to find low-paying jobs in Russia, Arabic countries, and Turkey. It is an ironic and sad way of telling an alternative history of Uzbekistan: from the adobe house through the high tech modernity to the same age-old status of a low-paid worker with no rights, whose life has no value. The motif of dispensable lives remerges in the works of other Central Asian artists such as Kazakh Said Atabekov, with his almost decolonial project "Observatory of the Bereaved," where the bereaved act as a new subjectivity similar to Fanon's *damnes*, or Yerbossyn Meldibekov's imagined state Pastan, in which the dispensability of human lives is manifested in the image of live people sold in sacks as if they were food in the market (Miziano 2006).

VI.

A telling example of suspended indigenous activism is the northern Caucasus, still remaining in the dubious capacity of a conglomerate of ethnic-federal republics and districts within the Russian Federation. Here, the Russian Empire first performed an artificial selection in the form of genocide and a massive deportation to the Ottoman Sultanate and later (in the Soviet period) "created" artificial small ethnicities and encouraged their hostility toward each other together with their accelerated assimilation. As a result there is really no spiritual reunification or even any dialogue of several million Adyghean Diaspora in the world, who are more inclined to an imagined pan-Circassian identity, and the remaining seven hundred thousand dispersed Adyghe community in Russia, who are divided by the invented ethnic identities and Soviet instigated jealousies. With the collapse of the Soviet Union, a number of Adyghean political associations emerged, aimed at territorial and political unification, sometimes irredentism, and repatriation of several million of diasporic Circassians. It certainly did not accommodate Russia, which was not planning to let the Caucasus go (although the situation and the sensibility started to change when I was preparing the second version of this chapter, so that Caucasus peaceful separation does not look so fantastic any more). For a long time, Russia considered the Caucasus to be an important strategic point and continued its typical politics of keeping the land but getting rid of its inhabitants or keeping them at a low and docile number and preferably in quarrels with each other. The diasporic Circassians, in contrast with those who stayed in Russia, are more articulate in their criticism of Russian colonialism in the Caucasus and in formulating decolonial discourses for the future. They claim the old tradition of unsubdued Circassians and a pan-Circassian identity, and they also retain traces of indigenous cosmologies, at the same time attempting to use the civil society and international organizations to attract attention to the Circassian question.

After the collapse of the Soviet Union, it was initially not religious but rather ethnic-cultural discourses and indigenous cosmologies and ethics that were used to restate the Adyghe identity (*adyghe khabze,* an indigenous ethical code being one such example). However, the local elites who used this sentiment in their fight for power were a typical comprador intelligentsia of Soviet modernity origin and future collaborators in the creations of Caucasus "banana republics." Unfortunately, this virus infected the international Adyghean organizations as well, so that today, in the words of Haci Bayram Polat, the "International Circassian Association acquired an institutional face of collaborationism" (Polat 2008). As a result, the authority of local Adyghean organizations among the people quickly faded and the contesting sentiment was to be looked for in Islamism, starting in the 1990s and particularly now. The legal ways of resistance, including the media, were entirely wiped out by Russia in several years; and today, resistance has no other way than violence and the remnants of still surviving underground activities, internet sites, and the somewhat tired appeals to international organizations, usually initiated from abroad. The two contemporary forms of resistance among the Caucasus peoples are therefore the Islamic one, often on the verge of extremist, and the ethnic-nationalist one, either tamed or no less extremist and based on hostility towards the neighboring Circassian ethnicities. This is a direct result of Russian, Soviet, and post-Soviet colonization of being and thinking.

In contrast with the Zapatistas and other indigenous movements in South America, digging out the erased history is not sufficiently paired with the continuing living tradition in case of the multiply colonized Eurasian spaces. There is a crudely interrupted indigenous legacy that often makes any dialogue difficult and seemingly leaves only the option of going back to a tradition that would be artificially recreated in this case. The colonial minds were systematically fed with the colonialist interpretations of history, Soviet nationalities discourses, lack of continuous literacy tradition that would help to remember, and a constant fear of the cruel master. Therefore, it is extremely difficult to decolonize. A more global power shift and a more visionary leadership are needed to make the two resistance flows—that inside the Caucasus and the diasporic one—reunite and, more important, do it without being manipulated by either Russia or the West. A long awaited process of delinking from both and building horizontal coalitions with other *damnés* of the world needs to be initiated as well.

This problematic has already become a subject of ironic and encoded resistance and creative re-existence in art forms[46] in Central Asia and the Caucasus. For example, contemporary Uzbek artist Utkam Saidov in 2005 exhibited an installation called *To Discover a Hero,* which problematized the erased and forgotten histories inconvenient for the official Muslim interpretation of the Central Asian identity, for the Russian and Soviet modernity, and for today's local autocratic power remake. We see seven human heads covered with a white cloth. It is an allusion to a real historical character—Khashim ibn Khakim, a white-masked leader of a Central Asian revolt against the Arabic contest and forceful Islamization, who was later erased from the history of Uzbekistan. He, as well as dozens of other unknown and erased heroes, symbolized by the rest of the heads, are inconvenient for power and thus remain masked (Kudryashov 2007).

VII.

What makes nearly all of the nation-building models in Soviet ex-colonies similar is the neoliberal and democracy rhetoric, based on the ideology of developmentalism, progress, and the rational building of society grounded in dependency logic, well known in South America. However, the Eurasian dependency discourse is somewhat different and deserves to be addressed. In contrast with the Russian Empire, which rather marginally but still belonged to the world system, the Soviet Empire presented itself as a case of extreme autarchy and implemented the unheard of experiment of a Socialist economic system as opposed to the capitalist one, a system that would be self-sufficient and insulated from the world market. This ideal was certainly never followed word for word, even in the darkest years of Stalinism, but it was the image of the Socialist world that was imprinted into the Western imaginary.

Everybody knows about the fatal shortcomings of an ineffective planned economy, but not many people pay attention to the fact that the Socialist economic system, even if it looked so different from the capitalist one, was based on the same assumptions of progress, teleology, industrialization, and a cult of technological development. Another neglected fact is how, within this system, the coloniality of power was expressed in the phenomenon of chronic dependency and lagging behind, which was typical for the racialized colonies. The collapse of the Soviet Union resulted in the initial stagnation of certain countries (e.g., the Central Asian states) and advantages to others (the Baltics), although in the scale of the global world economy, this advantage is minimal, because even the more successful countries/survivors of the Soviet Union are still of no use to the European Union except in the capacity of cheap labor force and new markets. The hierarchy of colonial economies within the Soviet Union was not openly framed according to racist discourses, but again, through the mediated and blurred Eurocentric rhetoric, so that the more European Soviet colonies (the Baltic states, the Ukraine) were also less mono-economic, while the Caucasus or especially Central Asia were deliberately caught in a vicious circle of dependency that is reproduced today on the global scale in their being completely thrown out of the world system.[47] Their condition copies on the next turn the imperial/

colonial hierarchy shaped in modernity. If the Russian and Soviet Empires were caught in the catching-up ideology of "overtaking and surpassing," the colonies of this second-rate empire, marked by imperial difference, turned out to be third-rate in comparison with the colonies of the capitalist empires of modernity. Their "master" was itself a slave of a more powerful master. As discussed previously, Russia's own status remained dubious and anyone associated with it in the past or today automatically is assigned an inferior status. This is connected to the external imperial difference of Russia. To this general configuration of the wrong master, we must also add the Muslim affiliation of both Central Asia and partly the Caucasus, which however superfluous and marginal, still adds to their stigmatized status. As a result, the inhabitants of both regions reacquire their subhuman status again and again.

Not many theorists or politicians in the ex-Soviet world want to take into account the South American unsuccessful experience of development and modernization programs. The reason lies not only in simple ignorance but also in a peculiar snobbishness of the ex–Second World in relation to the ex–Third World. Thoughtlessly following the logic of modernity with its typical agonistic approach preventing from any meaningful dialogue, the ex–Second World nourishes its imperialist and peculiar nationalist discourses, as well as a strange pride for the previously higher position on the ladder of modernity. It is scared to death to lose or endanger this position in any way, for instance, by associating with those who are still lower in the present hierarchy of humanity. This is clearly the Russian case, a difficult combination of disgust toward the global South and a fear of being associated with it, except in the paternalistic capacity; at the same time, it makes constant efforts to hide behind a rosy imperialist mythology the cruel excesses of Russian and Soviet colonialism.

Practically all newly independent states, including Russia, bought into developmentalism in its neoliberal form, which soon turned into various nationalist models, when all these states realized that they cannot find a place in the new global capitalist market, that nobody really wants them there. While preaching the gospel of the market economy as a global panacea, the West reluctantly allows the survivors of the Soviet Union to enter the world market in any capacity, except for its cheap labor force or raw resources. The non-European (ex-)colonies have been interesting to the West in the last two decades primarily as a springboard for military bases, necessary for the preparations of the righteous wars for oil. This results in devastating consequences for practically all ex-Soviet colonies and satellites, from Central Asia to Central Europe, who have little choice in maneuvering between the West,

Russia, and the economic coalitions and regional agreements of various local kinds, once again, resembling South America. In this context, it is clear why dependency theory re-emerged quite soon in post-Soviet Russia and its ex-colonies. One can often hear today the well-known ideas of protectionism, economic nationalism, boycott of the WTO, banning of natural resources export, and so on—sometimes in the radical form of dependency discourse.

However, economy in this case once again clashes with culture and ideology, when the ex-Soviet colonies follow the well-known Soviet (and modern) slogan "socialist in its essence, national in its form." Today, it changes into "market or developmentalist in its essence, ethnic-national in its form," which does not alter the logic of the formula itself. In the non-European ex-colonies, the ethnic-national element is more pronounced in the nation-building discourses, accompanied by some ideas of dependency theory and by the extreme authoritarianism of the ruling elites. A good example of this is Uzbek President Islam Karimov's rhetoric, which attempts to justify the inefficient economy and authoritarian power of the Soviet type with an appeal to the mythic ancient ethnic solidarity and the construct of "uzbekness" that are largely Soviet products, invented and imposed onto these people by the imperial ideologues (Karimov 1993). The really existing institute of *makhalla* is effectively used by the Uzbek state in its attempts to justify the repressive policies and lack of respect for the individual, while its leader becomes a recognizable and not very appetizing "father of the nation."

VIII.

If decolonial impulses have existed in non-European Eurasian colonies, in some cases, for many decades and even centuries, then why are they virtually absent from the political discourses and nation building today? Here, a comparison with South American indigenous movements could help. In a number of South American countries, such as Ecuador and Bolivia, in the last two decades at least, as a reaction to the multiple failure of both developmentalist projects and dependency theory, an alternative model of *interculturality* emerged, which was connected with questioning the sociopolitical reality of neocolonialism as it manifests itself in the present models of the state, democracy, and the nation (Walsh 2009). Interculturality is linked to decolonization as the goal of indigenous movements, and particularly, CONAIE, in whose political project emerges the idea of a plurinational state, based on "the full and permanent participation of the peoples and nationalities in decision making" and in "the exercise of political power in the

Plurinational State" (CONAIE 1997: 11). What is interesting here is that this initiative is born not on the level of the nation-state but, higher or lower, on a more global and more local level, although it attempts to change the state and the national imaginary the way it needs. According to Catherine Walsh, interculturality acts as an overarching principle signifying the construction of a different society, epistemology, state, political practice, and generally, a paradigm that is other than modernity/coloniality (2009). On the ruins of the Soviet Union are many examples of neocolonialism, discrimination, racism, lack of willingness to hear the voices of indigenous people. However, in spite of the growing grassroots resistance sentiment, the indigenous social or political organizations still do not play any significant part in the decision-making and cannot even attempt to change the state.[48] The allowed official forms of their existence usually come to culture and sometimes to religion. The majority of such organizations and movements play a ritualistic ornamental role, while their leaders are often manipulated and tamed by those in power or destroyed if they refuse to cooperate.

One of the important differences between the northern Caucasus and Central Asia and the Zapatistas or CONAIE today lies in the religious sphere, which brings us back to the question of imperial and colonial difference. A decidedly Muslim basis of a number of indigenous liberating movements, often demonized by the official power as Islamist and terrorist, is a relatively new phenomenon, linked among other factors to the lack or erasing of any coherent other than Islam epistemology and cosmology to ground itself in and to today's special role of Islam as an opposite to Western modernity and the global *damnés*. In spite of the efforts to present this Muslim face of indigenous resistance as an ancient one, it is less than half a century old. Even in the Caucasus War in the nineteenth century, the Jihad banner was not the main element of anticolonial movements, and most of them in all non-European colonies shared a wider than Islam anticolonial sentiment that was subsequently lost. The West is familiar with the story of Chechen and Dagestan resistance and with the name of imam Shamil, who presided over the religiously marked uprising in the northern Caucasus. However, in case of the Circassians, the Islamic element was not initially as important as in case of those people who adopted Islam earlier. Their resistance was persistent and continued for another five years at least, after Shamil was captured and taken to Kaluga (Jersild 2002).

The same is true in relation to the early Soviet period Turkistan indigenous movements. Turkistan National Unity was not in the least interested in the struggle between Socialism and capitalism or in the creation of an Islamic state. They declared in 1921 that they "did not want to sacrifice the future of the old Turkistan to plans in preparation for the deliverance of the Islamic world and to the yet unknown outcome of forthcoming struggle between capitalism and socialism" (Paksoy 1995b). A Bashkir leader of the anticolonial movement, Zeki Velidi Togan, wrote in a 1920 letter to Vladimir Lenin: "You accept the ideas of genuine national Russian chauvinism as the basis of your policy. . . . We have clearly explained that the land question in the East has in principle produced no class distinction. . . . For in the East it is the European Russians, whether capitalists or workers, who are the top class, while the people of the soil . . . , rich or poor, are their slaves . . . . You will go on finding class enemies of the workers, and rooting them out until every educated man among the native population . . . has been removed" (Caroe 1967: 112–13).

Even if often the repressive states in Central Asian countries or the Caucasus exaggerate the Islamist threat, one cannot ignore the growing militaristic nature of anticolonial movements and their consent to Islamism (e.g., Akromiya in Andijan). One of the reasons for this lies in the nature of the Russian/Soviet colonization. It created and intensified the culture of violence in these locales. It pushed the great masses of people out of their previous social hierarchies, legal, and civil systems; it destroyed the traditional economy and imposed a colonial one, leaving no choice for the large groups of people than to join either the colonizers or the guerilla movements. Finally, it removed the indigenous ethics, replacing it by a cynical double standard Soviet servility. But the Caucasus and Central Asian Robin Hoods, as they were often presented by the Russian propaganda, by the early twentieth century, turned into the well-organized and often quite-educated strata of the local elites, who envisioned the future of their homeland as rather secular and egalitarian (not necessarily in Western terms but sometimes in the sense of indigenous social relations). However, this stream of anticolonial movements was strangled by the 1940s, and whenever it raised its head afterward, it was systematically destroyed both by the Soviet and today by the new local governments, which want to promote exclusively their own versions of the state and Islam and are not interested in establishing any dialogue with indigenous movements or the common people, for that matter. The pattern of state violence and instigated fear remains dominant all over the Eurasian space.

The 2005 tragic events in Andizhan (Uzbekistan), when not only the armed insurgents but also a number of uninvolved civilians were killed,[49] and the same year Nalchik (the northern Caucasus) uprising[50] (both with reemergence and relapses in the subsequent years) were presented by official propaganda of Russia, Uzbekistan, and the local governments of the northern Caucasus autonomous republics, as fundamentalist, Islamist, foreign (Western or coming from the Muslim countries), and criminalized, while a number of Western media and human rights activists, on the contrary, overestimated the figures of the death toll and rendered the same events as a liberating struggle of the unarmed population raising their voices against the absolutist power and for their rights and freedoms (Kimmage 2005, Andijan Massacre 2005). Both extremes are biased. Although independent sources show that the action in both cases was indeed initiated by armed and trained insurgents, some of whom came from outside the region, the religious, economic, or even ideological content in both cases were in fact minimal. The socioeconomic demands of the impoverished population of both Uzbekistan and Kabardino-Balkaria and their annoyance with the ubiquitous corruption on every level and the lack of prospects for the future were effectively used by yet publicly unidentified forces to start a coup d'état and, if successful, another flower or fruit revolution. But, no matter what were the concrete rationale and antigovernment forces in both cases, these events reflected how easily innocent bystanders could be victimized and destroyed as dispensable lives by both the government and the insurgents.[51] In neither case, we must admit, did the initiative come from the people themselves, in neither case did they actually raise their voices of their own accord. As Akiner points out, in the vacuum of a political will to solve the problems of the common people in Central Asia, "a coalition of social, political economic and religious grievances will surely emerge. This volatile compound could readily be manipulated and used as an ideological weapon by those who seek to challenge the present regime. . . . If this were to happen, it is the Islamist groups who would be best placed to take advantage of this situation. This is not because of their current strength or appeal, *but because they have goals, commitment, leadership and organization*" (Akiner 2005).

Today, the historical phenomena of both Basmachi and Abreks (Sahni 1997, Bobrovnikov 2000, Paksoy 1995c, Botiakov 2004) arguably anticolonial movements, originally far from religion, are often revived in Islamist forms and in the creation of networks with international Islamism, while the anticolonial resistance and possible coalitions with anticolonial movements of not fervently religious nature are downplayed. This situation is different from the South American indigenous movements, where Catholicism comes from the colonizer and is not used today as an inspiration for anticolonial movements,[52] as happens with Islam, whose expansionistic nature is symbolically forgotten in this case and even forgiven, in the larger dimension, where it lost to Christianity and Western modernity and started to be used as a banner of the global anticolonial movement. However, in the complex imperial-colonial configuration of Eurasian ex-colonies, in order to revive the indigenous movements as a source of viable epistemic models and decolonial struggles, it is crucial to remember, along with the local history of Islam and local Muslim identity, other alternative and forgotten paths of indigenous thinking, to preserve and nourish the pluriversality of epistemic and ethical models that always existed in both the Caucasus and Central Asia. It is also crucial to avoid the pattern of "going back" to true Islam or any other homogenous archaic culture, thus changing the terms of the conversation, questioning the established opposition to modernity and tradition. It is important to occupy instead the position of double translation and double critique of both Islam and Western modernity. Such a position is actively developed among the diasporic Muslim intellectuals living in Europe and the U.S., such as A. Khatibi (1990), A. Meddeb (2003), T. Ramadan (2003), and many others. It is yet to be coherently formulated and expressed politically in Central Asia and the Caucasus.

Newly independent Central Asian and the southern Caucasus ex-colonies are a case of what can be called an indigenous neocolonialism (i.e., internal colonialism). Here, it is not the equivalent of the white creole elites (the Russians) that are in power today, as it seems these regions are in the hands of indigenous people, while the Russian ex-colonizers find themselves often discarded from the society and economy.[53] But, the local regimes that are presided by the representatives of indigenous people turn out indistinguishable from the Russian or Soviet power. They reproduce the logic of coloniality, though in contrast with South America, it is a coloniality with respect to their own people and not to racialized others, which is a result of an external imperial difference with its secondary Eurocentrism as the constitutive element that spreads over the colonized as well as the colonizers. The tradition of educating the local elites as champions of Russian, Soviet, or Western modernity, who would not be interested in the least in the future of the people, coded by the elites as subhuman, is still maintained. It remains the major tactic in the psychological and ethical mechanisms of forging new political identities, a tactic that has not changed much after a caricature of socialism turned into a caricature of capitalism. It was borrowed by the ethnic elites from the colonizer and allowed them to continue the economic, legal, and cultural genocide of their compatriots, hiding behind neoliberal values and marked with suicidal intellectual dependency on the West, even if masked as the revival of ethnic nationalism. Today, when neoliberalism is discredited, this predominant tendency is starting to change. However, the outcome is not clear yet.

We are risking a fall into the well-known mistake of developmentalism if we assume that there are certain stages in the development of other-than-modern patterns of thinking and epistemic decolonization on a global scale; that some time needs to pass before these problems are understood, as happened in South America, which went through a long period of colonization and later independence; that in Central Asia or the Caucasus in due time and at some appropriate stage, the analogues of indigenous movements in other parts of the world will emerge. It is very hard to avoid the temptation of such developmentalist logic. In fact, the difference here lies not in stages but, once again, in the imperial/colonial configuration, burdened by complicated religious and ideological factors.

In the ex-Soviet colonies, the idea of civil society remains nominal, while political society is often being strangled or tamed at birth. The local grassroots organizations cannot make the state and the local power hear them, while more global coalitions invariably fail (except for the Muslim ones) due to the "zombification" of the social and political imaginary, which is tailored to see the ethnic-national project in a Herderian sense of the unity of the people, their territory, ethnicity, and language. This does not allow for the emergence of any intercultural idea of uncoupling the state and one nation. It does not mean that, in the post-Soviet space, there are no examples of border thinking. But the social/political system is constructed in such a way that they remain sporadic and doomed to stay unheard, unless some major social cataclysm takes place. Until the recent global crisis and its aftermath, the latter option did not look feasible, due to the extreme fatigue, apathy, depolitization of the population, which is sick and tired of any reforms and social projects. People are skeptical about power, but they also do not believe in the possibility of any effective resistance based on legal political ways. Hence, the culture of violence, which unfortunately has long historical roots in Eurasia persists, as does the peculiar resistance without dialogue, based on going around and beyond the power, leading a parallel life and often successfully avoiding being reduced to the will of the state (McGlinchey 2007).

IX.

The lack of models similar to interculturalism and the plurinational state in the non-European (ex-)colonies is linked among other things to the "success" of Soviet modernization, with its carefully elaborated strategies of mind-colonization of indigenous peoples, with the Jesuitical nature of Soviet ideology, which surpassed in this respect the clumsy and underreflected double-facedness of the Czarist Empire. The cynicism and many-faced nature of the Soviet ethnic-national ideologies is hard to match, the same way as the repressive mechanisms of the accelerated Soviet modernization, as a result of which even traces of indigenous cosmologies and ethics were erased from the collective memory and replaced with either Soviet Eurocentric progressivist discourse or, today, by ersatz ethnic nationalism. For the external world and mainly for the West, the well-developed rhetoric of proletarian internationalism was manifested, for example, in the affirmative action Soviet quota system in the national republics. The metamorphosis of the local elites into the Soviet nomenclature led to the elimination of all links with indigenous epistemologies and to the purposeful elimination of these ideologies themselves. The children and grandchildren of these elites are largely in power today, even if they turned from faithful Communists into the enlightened Caucasians or neoliberal Central Asians. The nature of this zombificaiton was rather complex—in the West, people assumed that all inhabitants of the Soviet Union were zombified by Marxism. But, in reality, the Communist ideology was just an external shell, while the essence remained Eurocentric, chauvinistic, racist, and based on progressivist modernization, while the resistance shaped itself as anticolonial, antimodern, and often anti-Russian.

Another difference between South America and the Soviet ex-colonies, which is a result of specific Soviet colonialism, is that the latter are alienated from each other and often hostile to each other. They lack the sense of unity, which the empire gave before, but they also lack the sense of the larger community of the *damnés*. This prevents possible coalitions with each other and with other others, while cultural and epistemic community of non-Soviet (also nonethnic and not exclusively Muslim) type, which existed in the Caucasus and Central Asia as specific border civilizational forms before, their linguistic continuum—similar to the Caribbean case—were erased from the social, political, and cultural imaginary in the Soviet years and continue to be forgotten or forcefully replaced with straightforward ethnic and linguistic nationalism today.

The ex-colonial states of the post-Soviet periphery started their independent nation building not of their own accord, not as a result of revolution or a national liberation movement. They were just informed about their new status by Boris Yeltsin and the other two Slavic leaders, who decided to get rid of the Soviet Union without consulting the subaltern Central Asian or southern Caucasus leaders. This collapse, in itself, was an important step in the change of the global geopolitical order and the victory of neoliberal globalization, with its rhetoric of the end of history and the apotheosis of market economy.

These specific conditions also worsened the situation for the non-European ex-colonies. From dependent colonies within the Soviet Union, they turned into spaces, mostly ignored by the rest of the world, spaces inhabited by unrecorded people whose future is not taken into account by the new architects of the world. These countries have not been used for the demonstration of the market economy advantages, as happened in case of several South American countries. The Global North uses them merely as tokens of geostrategic dominance, which does not even require capital investment. As a result of flower and fruit revolutions, the previous Soviet bosses and later presidents loyal to Russia were quickly pushed out and replaced with neoliberal politicians. In post-Soviet Eurasia for more than a decade, an Evo Morales was not possible. Instead, there were the ex-Soviet bosses, the mercenary champions of Western neoliberalism, the representatives of mafia structures, or more often, a combination of all three. Today, it seems it is their turn to be replaced by a new kind of elites who, one can only hope, finally will be more responsive to the needs of the people.

The invisibility of anticolonial sentiment in the indigenous movements of the Caucasus and Central Asia has an ideological explanation as well. As mentioned previously, during the Cold War, the West did not see the anticolonial element, concentrating entirely on its anti-Soviet project. That is why, when the émigré leaders of indigenous movements called for assistance from the U.S. and Western Europe, they faced a lack of understanding on the Western part and an attempt to erase the racial, religious, ethnic, and ultimately, colonial difference. For example, the Turkistan liberation leaders were told to work in Western European centers under the auspices of Russian dissidents, which they refused to do because for them these dissidents were yet another manifestation of imperialism with a different ideology (not Czarist, not Bolshevik but liberal). Today these movements continue to be used in the opposition to post-Soviet Russia, quickly reorienting from anti-Soviet to anti-imperial rhetoric. But the arguments often remain the same, based on persistent stereotypes and old phobias, as well as the black legend logic turned against Russia. The true needs and interests of those who are involved in anticolonial movements or live in those locales are invariably ignored (Paksoy 1995b). Yet, for many Third World intellectuals and leftist thinkers from the West, the Socialist element overclouds everything else in the complex history of the Russian/Soviet Empire. They truly believe in the Bolshevik rhetoric of decolonizing and liberating the people of the "national peripheries." In reality, the Bolsheviks wanted to keep the empire and have Communism, too, hence the massacres in ethnic republics, the persecution of anticolonial movements, labeled by the Soviets as "bourgeois nationalism" (for which no Russian was ever sentenced), hence the economic policy based on the hidden logic of coloniality that perpetuated the chronic dependency of Soviet non-European colonies. The disappointment of many Third World intellectuals in the second Socialist world, which did not cope with its mission, has remained a serious and undertheorized complex. Yet, Third World intellectuals are seldom ready to accept the equation between colonialism and socialism (or Second and Third Worlds).The collapse of the Socialist paradigm was catastrophic not only for the Socialist world itself, it also left many parts of the Third World without a vision. A different vision was soon found (and this is a subject of a separate reflection), but what is crucial is that the ex-Soviet world and particularly Russia have become a new invisible and disabled entity. In this situation of void, it is an urgent task to finally get rid of the mythic Socialist notions and grasp the complex configuration of the Soviet Empire within the logic of the global coloniality and its local manifestations.

In the idea of the plurinational state, the anticolonial struggle merges with the anticapitalist one. But, for the majority of ex-colonial subjects in peripheral Eurasia, the anticapitalist pathos does not hold. In their minds, the only alternative to capitalism is Socialism, which was discredited forever for those who had to survive in it. The presence of other alternatives, not necessarily Socialist or Marxist, remains unimaginable for the people of peripheral Eurasia. One of the important tasks for the indigenous people is to decolonize from the mutant local neocolonial thinking. An epistemic revolution is possible in these (ex-)colonies, but to initiate it, it is necessary to combine the local and the global levels, to stop thinking in the limits of our own countries or even continents, to dismantle the chronically peripheral position of the Central Asian or Caucasus people in the world, to make them part of the informational and political space of alternative thinking and being on a global scale. This is what the leaders of the newly independent states are afraid of, enforcing a statist and clannish form of patriotism instead and plundering their countries, while using anticolonial impulses to their benefit. To build coalitions and open a dialogue with other *damnés* of the world, the Eurasian ex-colonies would have to shape the new elites, who would be grounded in other epistemologies than mimicking neoliberalism or narrow and aggressive nationalism and would attempt a multiple translation between indigenous, Western, and Muslim elements, as happened in case of the Zapatistas in Mexico.

In the world of imperial difference and particularly in the ex- and present Russian colonies, the situation is more complex, and the decolonial impulse is expressed more coherently not in social and political agency but in the areas expelled by modernity from the sphere of rationality and decision making—the arts, the occult, and nonrational knowledge, meaningless in the eyes of analytical reason. Any social and political initiative would be strangled immediately by the strong state, both in Russia and in neocolonial newly independent states. For this reason, often, the diasporic intellectuals from these locales present more interesting and independent examples of decolonial thinking and truly transepistemic, transvalue, transmodern, and not just transcultural humanities and arts.

Such individuals make a virtual or aesthetic link between the erased history and the subaltern modernity. A good example is an Abkhazian by origin artist, philosopher, and spiritual Sufi leader, Murat Yagan, who was born in Turkey as a result of the nineteenth-century genocide of the northern Caucasus peoples by the Russian Empire and their massive exile to the Ottoman Sultanate. Along with being a talented artist, who studied in the West and also knows perfectly the Circassian and the Islamic traditions, Yagan is also an oral transmitter of the Ahmsta Kebzeh, an ancient spiritual tradition or knowledge of the art of living an abundant life, which originated in the Caucasus Mountains but was preserved mainly by the Circassian diaspora abroad. The goal of Kebzeh is to awaken and develop the latent human faculties under divine grace and guidance. It is an oral teaching that has been passed on through story, song, and the way of being. Yagan who received this knowledge from Caucasus elders in exile later immigrated to Canada, and for more than twenty-five years, he has been sharing it with a small group of students in Western Canada. He wrote a spiritual autobiography, *I Come from behind Kaf Mountain* (1984), which has been translated into many languages. Recently invited to Abkhazia, Yagan was hoping to bring back the ancient wisdom. The question remains, however: Would he stay an exotic guru of an unknown ancient philosophy in Canada and no less exotic diasporic intellectual for contemporary Abkhazians or would Kebzeh become a ground for a long-awaited decolonial subjectivity in the Caucasus?

X.

What I just sketched, however, is an open decolonial utopia that can unfold into a specific collective subjectivity only under favorable conditions hard to imagine today. Yet, in what follows, I attempt to demonstrate a few manifestations and traces of decolonial border thinking and border identities in the Caucasus and Central Asia, where for centuries "adaptive and creative resistance" and re-existence (Alban Achinte 2006) have been expressed in the phenomenon of transcultural tricksterism, allowing the "re-appropriation of the spirituality rooted in the soil" (Marcos 2006). After two post-Soviet decades and in spite of the aforementioned problems, the Caucasus and Central Asia still retain their particular transcultural sensibility and subjectivity. This was clearly expressed in such multicultural urban ex-colonial centers as Baku and Tashkent. Their Babylonian hybrid nature was not entirely a constructed proletarian internationalist product or the Czarist Empire colonial creation. The roots of this linguistic, religious, ethnic, and cultural tolerance and dynamic mixture were deeper than that and went far back into history, so that it is possible to talk about specific multiethnic nations of Tashkenters or Bakineans rapidly disappearing today and leaving a trace of nostalgia for the times of fruitful transculturation and mutual cultural penetration and dialogue, captured in various artistic forms, such as a Mark Weil's (1996) documentary *The End of an Era: Tashkent* or Oleg Safaraliev's (2006) film *Good bye, Southern City* and Azeri-Jewish writer Afanasy Mamedov's (2000, 2010) creative Proustian revivals of nonexistent Baku of his childhood.

The big cities of the ex-Soviet Orient are still ready to embrace and accept the Russian/Soviet ex-colonizers as well as dozens of other ethnicities that have traditionally lived here or found themselves in colonial Soviet capitals as a result of major historical cataclysms of the twentieth century. For instance, Tashkent which became an unofficial capital of the Soviet Union during World War II and also a Soviet Hollywood, accepted several large migration waves, from the adventurous Russian settlers of the late nineteenth century to the Russian, Ukrainian, and Jewish families from the West of the Soviet Union, evacuated here during World War II, from Uigurs to Japanese and German POWs, from Chechens to Leningrad emaciated orphans, and later, after the major 1966 earthquake, thousands of construction workers from all over the Soviet Union who came to rebuild Tashkent. Many of them preferred to stay here afterward. The topos of such colonial multicultural cities carries traces of various traditions and imperial models—one can study it as a cultural palimpsest of different, often conflicting or merging meanings—one can find here a governor's palace or a park from the Russian colonial times and traces of secular colonial architecture (which are almost always copies of a copy, meaning that the Russian imperial imagery was itself borrowed from the West and hence its colonial copies were double simulacra). This layer easily coincides with the later Soviet layers and the so-called old town, with its typically narrow streets, adobe houses, and fortresses (like the Bakinean Icheri-Shekher). A visual example is provided by Mark Weil in his tracing of the eleven monuments that replaced one another in the same spot in Tashkent in the course of the twentieth century, including the monument of General-Governor Kauffman, Stalin, Marx, and finally, Amir Timur today (Weil 1996). But what is crucial in all these multicultural colonial capitals is certainly not architecture or monuments but the people. As Afanasy Mamedov wrote in his nostalgic novel about Baku, it is the people that create this transcultural mood: "the old men with their Muslim beards under the palms and the tolling of the bells at the Armenian church that sounds so close from the Jewish quarter Juude-Meilesi—a real present for Shagal" (Mamedov 2000: 110). Ten years later, in his novelette "A Cop Had a Dog," Mamedov imperceptibly changes the mood or, even, the modality of his post-imperial, post-Soviet narrative as one of the last representatives of this fiction and this cultural and linguistic imaginary. He creates a painfully sharp and disturbing image of the lost dog, left by an Armenian family fleeing Baku in fear of massacre. The dog is adopted by the new owner of their empty apartment, an Azeri policeman who is not a nationalist and Islamist monster in Mamedov's rendering but a full-fledged human, imperfect yet prone to love and compassion, guilt and repentance (2010).

It was modernity that ultimately made an antispace out of Central Asia and the Caucasus, a nonspace that can exist in the Western mind only in the form of a conventional topos of some exotic parable, where stereotyped Orientals reside.[54] But who were these people, the West never really wondered. In the case of Central Asia, they were interpreted as Deleuze and Guattari's "nomads" at best, the abstract agents of some conventional speculative history, who just illustrated the concept of deterritorialization. However, in the East, this trickster, wondering, mediating, rootless sensibility is no news—it is just that, under globalization, it acquires an unexpected reification on a global scale. The abstract nomad turns out to be a real new Ahasuerus or, rather, an al-Hadir of the newest époque of the great migration of peoples and transcultural border subjectivities, or in a more pedestrian variant, an ever-wondering Hodja Nasreddin, who brings us back to the problematic of tricksterism.

Saint al-Hadir, or the Green Man—important for several Sufi orders, with their specific culture of respect for the other, standing in the center of the ethics of interpersonal relations—is an initially transcultural personage, a quintessence of the people who for centuries have lived between empires, religions, languages, in a complex imperial/colonial configuration, and have managed to maintain their own system of reference marked with specific philosophy of treating the other. This transcultural personage is to be found in many traditions, from India to Palestine, from the Ferghana Valley to China, and arguably, even in Ireland and the Arthurian tales. Saint al-Hadir or al-Hidr, having a parallel in Christian Ilea, in modern terms, is the immortal protector of all migrants and travelers and is himself constantly traveling around the world, fulfilling his mystical mission. This character is of pre-Islamic origin, and among its sources are the Acadian Gilgamesh epic, the novel of Alexander, the Judaic parable about Joshua ben Levi, and so forth, hence the Central Asian popular belief that hospitality cannot be selective, for al-Hadir can come to your house in any disguise, anyone can meet him, but what one would gain depends on how pure one's intentions are. In this belief, we find a specific philosophy of treating other people and other cultures (Catherine 2004, 2007, Franke 2000) that in Muslim rendering is associated with the concept of *adab* ethics.

A contemporary progressive Muslim intellectual, Omid Safi, claims that "adab . . . that most essential, basic and glorious of Muslim interpersonal codes, is the compassionate, human, selfless, generous, and kind etiquette that has been a hallmark of refined manners in Muslim cultures. Almost anyone who has ever traveled to areas that have been profoundly influenced by Muslim ethics has no doubt seen great examples of this wonderful way of being welcomed and put at ease." But the scholar sadly continues that "it is precisely this compassionate humanness that is missing from so much of contemporary Islam" (Safi 2004: 13). Even if it is missing from many versions of contemporary Islam, it is not missing from such border spaces as the Caucasus and Central Asia and from the sensibility of the people who live in these locales. It cannot be taken to just Islam, however unorthodox. It is this inherent transcultural border element—forever open to the dialogue with the diversity of the world—that can be a way out of the persistent black-and-white binary oppositions.

I pointed out previously that, due to the Western epistemic monopoly, until now the only way of entering the spheres of philosophy, historiography, sociology, or other social sciences for indigenous people in many parts of the world has been exclusively through literature and the arts, the culture of the quotidian, the nonrational and esoteric knowledges, so that, in Caribbean writer and philosopher Wilson Harris's words, the philosophy of history was "buried in the art of imagination" (Harris 1981: 24–25). A peculiar example of contemporary Central Asian realization of border subjectivity is to be found in case of the modern Uzbek "saint" Habiba (Allione 1997), who after a revelation that came to her in a dream, made a connection with Bahauddin Nakshbandi, a fourteenth-century founder of a Sufi order with over forty million followers in the world.[55] The question is not if Habiba has real healing "powers," it is more important to trace how she creatively mixes in her cosmology various cultural and religious sources leading to a tolerant and flexible ludic frame with a well-defined ethics, based on subject-subject relations instead of the usual subject-object scheme. It is not surprising that orthodox patriarchal Islam is extremely hostile to such practices and such "saints."

Several elements of Habiba's cosmology allow us to put it into an imaginary dialogue with voices of Amerindian curanderas analyzed in Sylvia Marcos's book *Taken from the Lips: Gender and Eros in Mesoamerican Religions* (Marcos 2006). The mystical and transcendental dimensions are regarded in both cases as parts of everyday life, demanding from the people a cultivation of their skills and abilities to decipher such invisible signs. In the outlooks of Central Asian and Caucasus healers that I interviewed for my recent book on gender (Tlostanova 2010a), like in *espiritualismo*, a dynamic religious and cultural mélange erases the possibility of any fundamentalist stable interpretation of religious or cultural identity. Various sources coexist and correlate in an explosive and fruitful, essentially decentered, interaction easily combining monotheistic, polytheistic, and pantheistic grounds as only different languages expressing the same thing and serving as a means in the mission of saving people by sharing the healing spiritual energy with them.

Habiba, Lira Karagulova, Fatima Zhakomikhova, and other modern healers in Central Asia and the Caucasus invariably stress the importance of keeping the world's equilibrium by remaining silent when it is needed, talking when it is necessary, and acting when action is called for—always listening to the rhythms of the multiple universe. Each of them, in her own language and semiotic system, refers to the all-encompassing interrelation and interconnection of everything in this world—the people, the nature, the cosmos—where each of us *represents* the other. "Take a hand—we can concentrate on the differences between each of the fingers, marveling how different they are, but then we risk not noticing the movement of the hand as a whole," says Habiba, following Nakshbandi (Allione 1997). In the revival and cultivation of this logic of respect for other cultures, religions, histories, a logic of open dialogue and fairness, still maintained in spite of any historical cataclysms, wars, and colonization, lies a possibility of intercultural understanding in the future.

Such understanding requires the shaping or reopening of a specific transcultural border subjectivity and epistemology grounded in critical thinking, which is born in between various equally questioned and destabilized models. It lacks religious or ethnic-national fundamentalism and is based on pluritopic hermeneutics. Instances of such sensibility are to be found in Central and South America, in some parts of southeast Asia and Africa, and in peripheral Eurasia, with its hotchpotch of various traditions, most of which were doubly or multiply colonized spaces. This new subjectivity and epistemology can be expressed in many ways—from the theology of liberation to progressive Muslims projects, from other thinking to border thinking—but is always based on questioning modernity from an in-between position of transculturation.[56]

Transculturation requires the inclusion of many equal cultural and epistemic reference points, the crossing and negotiation of cultures, a specific state of cultural in-betweenness. In the case of Central Asia and the Caucasus, such subjectivity has been always a norm in an ethnic-cultural, social, and linguistic sense (take, for example, the specialization of languages: Arabic was used for the official sphere and law, Farsi referred to culture and poetry, the local vernacular languages like New Uzbek were connected with the sphere of everyday communication). Here, the imperial assimilation tactic was needed, not as a way of coping with metisation (as in South America) but as a realization of the imperial principle "divide and rule." However, behind the surface, the age-old processes of mutual interaction refusing to accept the imperial cultural hierarchy of assimilation have flourished, giving birth to new meanings and complex codes. To understand them one needs to focus on the texture of transcultural weave and not on the nature of the components, as Eduard Glissant described in relation to Caribbean opacity ([1990] 1997: 190).

Defying the continuing Western and Russian Orientalism, the Caucasus and Central Asia today offer fascinating if not numerous examples of transcultural art, fiction, cinema, and theater as the means through which to channel their border sensibility, critically rethinking the caricature or exoticist image of the East, created by the West, questioning both Western modernity and ethnic nationalist or religious fundamentalist discourses. Such is the case of the famous Tashkent theater *Ilkhom*[57] (Ilkhom 2009). What would happen when the breath of real history and real culture and people flow into the Western Orientalist metaphors and elegant parables, where Asia (e.g., Samarkand) acts as a paradigmatic antispace in which it is suitable to have a rendezvous with Death, to quote Jean Baudrillard's famous essay (1979)? *Ilkhom*, in the words of its director Mark Weil, who called himself a patriot of Tashkent and a human of the planet Earth and was tragically killed in September 2007, mixes on its stage the languages and faces of Tashkenters, their tempers and their ways of life (Antelava 2008). This theater is as transcultural and able to accommodate the unlikely opposites as the city where it stands. It remained so even at the point when Tashkent era ended and it started to change its multicultural nature. This sentiment is particularly clear in the signature 1993 production that still successfully runs today, a Samarkand fantasy based on Karlo Gozzi's comedy *Happy Beggars* (*I Pitocchi*

Fortunati 1764). The show was built on the mutual penetration and hybridizing of totally unexpected sources and traditions—comedia dell'arte and Uzbek street theater, "maskharaboz." In fact, *Ilkhom* negates Gozzi's Orientalism, which presented Samarkand as a fantastic dystopia, a place nowhere, fallen out of time and progress, as well as Baudrillard's beautiful and sad parable of the rendezvous with Death in Samarkand. This production, in contrast with Baudrillard's essay from *De la Seduction,* can be called "Life in Samarkand."

In 2005, Weil came back to this problematic in his controversial and risky *Flights of Mashrab,* dedicated to the 250th anniversary of Wolfgang Amadeus Mozart. Mashrab emerges in this show, not in his "combed" traditional appearance of one of the most talented Uzbek poets of the late seventeenth to early eighteenth century, a contemporary of Mozart, but as a wild, naked-ass dervish of a Sufi order, a heretic castrate born in Andijan and a cheeky and arrogant wanderer who refuses to fear the power in any guise—Muslim or secular—who rejects any organized religion and cultivates intimate and direct connections between the human being and God. His life is a series of small and big acts of defiance similar to those that *Ilkhom* company and its director went through in the preceding two decades. Mashrab is a provocative radical and trickster who jokes with power and urinates on the khan's throne and who does not keep silent if he disagrees, even when it threatens his life, just like Weil himself. The performance is not just transcultural (e.g., Mozart music is played using traditional Uzbek instruments); it is also palpably connected with contemporaneity, as it obviously parallels the situation in modern Uzbekistan (Ilkhom 2009).[58]

The lingering interpretation of Central Asia or the Caucasus as exotic or threatening antispaces is just a continuing Eurocentric practice of pushing the other out of the sphere of the valuable, out of the myths of progress, linear world history, science, and the like. While what is needed is to realize that these are not just fairy-tale spaces, continuously exploited as sources of exotic imagery, but quite real locales with their own local histories and, most important, people. Life never stopped here, even if modernity went around it, leaving it behind and beyond. And to learn what kind of life it was and is, we need to listen to the people who live, feel, and think in Samarkand, Baku, Tashkent, Nalchik, Grozny, or Dushanbe. The problem remains that decolonial and other alterative thinking models are still not properly consolidated in spite of such exemplary events as the World Social Forum. What is needed is the development of coalitions of such border thinkers and transcultural multiply colonized locales on a global scale that, in spite of such technical means as the internet, still remains a problem to be solved. What is lacking is not only financial support but also a sufficient global knowledge and global drive allowing us to embrace into the sphere of decoloniality such "others" as Circassians or Uzbeks, to name just two. A lack of communication and a void among those who have been marked by colonial difference and the colonial wound and have suffered from the same logic of global coloniality is immediately filled by ideologies that normally do not suffer from lack of resources to promote themselves on a global scale, such as ethnic and religious fundamentalism and extremism of all shades and, of course, neoliberal modernization in all its expected forms, from military bases and economic pressure to opening English-speaking universities in the vast spaces of Eurasian steppe.[59] The Caucasus and Central Asian mentality still carries traces of other thinking and the ideal of other transcultural world of harmonious and just social structures and relations. Today, as before, this sensibility is only starting to develop a political manifestation. Yet, mainly, it is restricted to the allegorical language of the arts and the illusive culture of the quotidian, to the nonrational and esoteric realms. Some examples I have touched upon here. This gives a small hope that the voices of Eurasian others will at some point be heard in the global chorus of modernity/coloniality otherness, defying and overcoming this category as such, and that they/we will finally take part in deciding of the future of the unknown world and their/our own future in this world.

CHAPTER 4

Non-European Soviet Ex-Colonies and the Coloniality of Gender, or How to Unlearn Western Feminism in Eurasian Borderlands

I.

In the title of this chapter, I intentionally juxtapose María Lugones's concept of coloniality of gender, formulated mostly in relation to the colonial world and mainly to South America though obviously having a global reach, and the local history and epistemic and ontological conditions of the Caucasus and Central Asia, the two Russian/Soviet "Orients" with a specific local history within the global coloniality. Can Lugones's concept be a traveling theory in this case? How translatable is it in the conditions of imperial difference and its secondary colonial difference complicated by Soviet modernity/coloniality? What problems and issues are important for rethinking gender in this locale, potentially pointing to the possibility of transcultural and transmodern gender coalitions on a global scale, and what assumptions, scholarly myths, and intellectual dependencies have to be unlearned in the process? This chapter traces the sphere of decolonial gender epistemology and adds an emerging yet still problematic voice to the polilogue of decolonial feminism—the voice of the Caucasus and Central Asian gendered others.

María Lugones's concept of the colonial/modern gender system formulated as a critique of A. Quijano's blindness to the multiplicity and complexity of gender issues in the colonial world (connected with the generally accepted biological and heterosexual patriarchal interpretations of gender) (Lugones 2007) was an attempt to get rid of the continuing biologization of gender, which often leads to erasing the epistemic side, knowledge instead of nature. Regarding gender as a colonial concept, she stressed the cognitive and pseudo-scientific mechanisms through which gender (along with race) has become one more criterion facilitating the massive dehumanizing of non-Europeans. Drawing attention to the hidden link between the transference of exploitation from the (European) man to nature and the essentially colonizing invention of gender, Lugones focuses on the intersection of mainly racial, sexual, and gender aspects of coloniality and eventually comes to the idea of coloniality of gender as an overarching category of the modern/colonial world marked with what Nelson Maldonado-Torres named "misanthropic skepticism." It makes colonial subjectivities become invisible as a result of racialized and gendered corporality. And, what becomes invisible in this case is precisely their humanity (Maldonado-Torres 2007).

The concept of coloniality of gender brings us back to Lugones's idea of traveling in other peoples' worlds with a loving perception, mentioned in the previous chapter. Traveling as a mode of existence of a diasporic Third World intellectual sees culture itself as a journey, as a process of social construction instead of any essentialist interpretation of tradition and its myths. This mode is essentially open, unfinished, constructive, and positive in its emphasis of reexistence instead of negative resistance. For Lugones, opposition to coloniality of gender is a complex process that "starts from subjectification and comes to active subjectivity." She accentuates the coalitional opposition to the coloniality of gender from the position of the colonial difference. This is the gist of decolonial feminism, its historical and bodily (in the body, as she puts it) ground, which Lugones sees not as a conceptual foundation but rather as "the peopled ground on which one stands, that runs through one, the ground that one is as an active subject" (Lugones 2008). Similarly to other contemporary theorists (Alexander 2005), she thinks feminism from and at the grassroots and from and at the colonial difference, with a strong emphasis on a historicized incarnate intersubjectivity.

The local histories and the geo- and body politics of knowledge that lie in the basis of Lugones's vision refer mainly to the colonial difference and clearly defined racial hierarchies. However, when we step into the world of external imperial difference and its secondary colonial difference, particularly if we deal with a deviant Socialist kind of modernity, the picture becomes blurred and complicated. In what follows, let us see how the coloniality of gender has been manifested in the Caucasus and Central Asia and what the potential can be for decolonial gender agency in these locales.

II.

Decolonial feminism efforts to delink from progressivism, stagism, and the general enchantment with the myth of modernity translating geography into chronology and into a binary human taxonomy are better realized in those spaces where race was initially put in the basis of the modern/colonial matrix of power—in the Americas and Africa. In these locales, race and gender have been traditionally coupled in a quickly naturalized way in the infamous stereotypes of the Black man that represents the act of rape (of the White woman) and the Black woman who is seen as the most legitimate victim of rape (Maldonado-Torres 2007: 255). Within the modern/colonial gender system, representatives of the non-Western world were excluded from the realm of the human and feminine to facilitate their discrimination, exploitation, and objectification, as several scholars demonstrate in case of indigenous communities and enslaved Africans in the Americas (Lugones 2007, McClintock 1995). But Russia/USSR and its colonies seldom are regarded through the lens of the racial discourses, and gender in these locales in the interpretation of the majority of scholars (Navailh 1996, Wood 2000, Ashwin 2000, Posadskaya 1994, Katz 2001) tends to remain a rather abstract category, controlled through the social and political but not racial engineering of the state and interpreted mainly through the lens of Western feminism without the intersectionality with race (or ethnicity and religion, for that matter). In reality, there was a specific realization of racial-bodily-gender politics in the Soviet modernity that was not openly discussed or even stated,[60] yet rather consistently implemented. Many Bolshevik racial, gender, and body discourses were successors to the Czarist ones because both were the distorted copies of the Western originals (Sahni 1997). In fact, almost all of the forms of treating the gendered other that emerged before continued to exist in the Soviet Union in various forms—from Romantic Orientalism to quasi-scientific and culturalist racism, and from the "commodity racism," in Ann McClintock's formulation (1995), to Soviet theatrical multiculturalism, and to today's zoological forms of othering. Practically all these discourses had women at their center.

The paradox of colonial femininity and masculinity based on blaming the colonial others in mutually exclusive vices at once, thus building a negative self-identification, has been thoroughly discussed by many scholars in relation to the Western empires and their colonies (Alexander and Mohanti 1997, Espiritu 1997, Sandoval 2000). In this case, racialization works through gender, and colonization itself comes to be symbolized as an act of rape or violence. However, this is typical of the *confident* empires with a positive masculine identity, while Russia was far from it. The colonial gender paradox is based on the self-negating definition of the darker side of femininity and masculinity, which prevents working out any successful positive identity. The colonial man is at once feminized (castrated) and presented as an essential rapist and an aggressive animal threatening the chaste White lady. The non-White woman, in turn, is regarded as sexually available and willing to be raped, essentially lacking chastity or honor as such. In the Russian colonization of the Caucasus and Turkistan, this perverse yet naturalized ethics was recast in particular ways, connected not with race but with essentialized ethnicity and Islam, which was early translated into symbolic race (Muslim equaled non-White and often subhuman; Tlostanova 2010b). The paradox of colonial masculinity and femininity was different from the West, because the gap between the Orientalist European fantasy and the reality of the Caucasus and Turkistan conquest was too obvious and based on the secondary Orientalist ideologies always poisoning any victory for Russia.

The women in Central Asia were well protected by Muslim and local ethnic-cultural custom and could not possibly act in the role of the non-White women in the European colonial imaginary. Yet the Caucasus women, for a while played the part of the exotic sexual slaves and even a profitable commodity for the Russian army. They were compared to exotic elegant creatures (gazelle) or dangerous but beautiful beasts (panther), which did not save them from having dispensable lives. Here, the pedophiliac tendencies of Russian officers were often justified by the presumable early puberty and free morals of the local girls (Nortsov 1904). However, there were no Blacks or Indians in Russia, so the European racial classifications were distorted and mechanically applied by the Russians to the newly colonized spaces. A good example is an 1837 diary entry of Lieutenant N. Simanovsky, who was surprised to find that the captured Cherkess princess was "quite attractive and—what is most strange—quite White" (Simanovsky 1999). Since, in his reference system, she belonged to the "savages" and was Muslim, she was supposed to be non-White. Traces of this mutant racism are abundant in the majority of Russian nineteenth-century romantic fiction, from A. Pushkin and M. Lermontov to sexual Orientalist tales of A. Bestuzhev-Marlinsky.

The local men in the Caucasus and Turkistan alike refused to be interpreted within the Orientalist docile stereotype, and any comparison with them was not to the advantage of the much more tepid Russian masculinity. The erotic element of Russian imperialism was expressed in the male form and extrapolated into the Russian male anxiety and fear of the Caucasus machismo in war and sex (Sahni 1997: 33–69; Tekuyeva 2006a). In Russian colonization, only one side of the colonial gender paradox was at work: the association of the local men with violence. Post-Soviet society retains this stereotype of the Caucasus man, which today is used as the basis of the standard racist accusations—from his desire to possess a Russian woman and humiliate Russian men, to his presumably dangerous tendencies of reckless courage and readiness to sacrifice lives, his own or other people's, including women. The Caucasus man was used by the Russian officers as an attractive sexual role model—they massively changed into Cherkess traditional dress to borrow some of the aura of Caucasus masculinity. In this theatrical metamorphosis into a noble savage, there was a clear Rousseauistic touch in the interpretation of those fallen out of modernity and progress. In spite of all their borrowed enlightenment discourses, the imperial ideologues imbued the Caucasus people with inherent, stable, and given once and for all characteristics, later reproduced in the Bolshevik constructions of the Orient. Here, the two sides of the medal—the light (modern) and the dark (colonial)—merged in the interpretation of the colonies. On the one hand, they were racialized and presented as unreformable; on the other hand, it was assumed that, under the influence of the Russian/Soviet civilizing efforts, the mountaineers would gradually turn into another sort of people (Jersild 2002: 9–125).

As for the female colonial stereotypes in Turkistan, the local culture reacted to the Russian colonization by intensifying the defense of their culturally valuable women by making the veiling codes much stricter than before (Northrop 2004: 44–45). Here, the logic of blaming the victim for her own rape could not work, neither did the gendered variant of the "black legend" in general (which in this case means the accusation of the Islamic culture in sexual deviance and lack of morals), by contrast with the proliferation of such discourses in the interpretation of Muslim northern Africa by Catholic countries (Jiménez-Lucena 2008).[61] The Russian/Soviet Empire did not go as far as to accuse the Muslim women in Turkistan in sexual dissoluteness. Any erotic relations of Russian men with the colonized women remained adventures outside the realm of the metropolis morale. These women were not turned into an important part of the economy of sexual and labor exploitation (until the Soviet colonial cotton industry emerged in Central Asia, with its decidedly racist and misogynist division of labor). So the gendered black legend took a more restricted form, of associating the Muslim Oriental women with backwardness, illiteracy, and lack of hygiene. As neither in the Caucasus nor in Turkistan was there a system of direct colonial slavery, it was impossible to create a unified and coherent system of labor and sexual exploitation of the colonized women. Moreover, the role of the sexually, economically, and psychologically exploited female compared to an animal and taken out of the realm of the human and feminine, here, was performed not by an African slave but by an ethnically same and socially other Russian serf woman. With the borrowing of Orientalist discourses in the nineteenth century, when the Russian Empire was colonizing the Caucasus and later Turkistan, this problematic acquired the typically European racist forms of interpreting local women as animals. Yet, by contrast with African slaves, even the Caucasus women, who for a while played the role of the exotic dehumanized others, stood at the erotic Orientalist extreme of the racist hierarchy in which sexual exploitation was not directly linked to the labor one.

Thus, the modern/colonial gender paradox functioned with a twist in the case of the Russian/Soviet non-European colonies: Men were seldom feminized or symbolically castrated and their aggressive macho overtones were consistently stressed, while the Russian colonizer was often paradoxically prone to mimicking the Caucasus savage, compensating his own need for masculinity. The Oriental beauty stereotype functioned almost identically with its Western master narrative version in the Caucasus (women as sexual goods), while in Turkistan the colonizer's disappointment from the lack of access to harem erotic exoticism led to a discourse of "the fox and the grapes," grounded in inferiority complex in relation to Europe and its original Orient. The labor economic exploitation element of gender/race discrimination was absent until late.

Finally a specific role was assigned to the Russian woman in the Caucasus and Central Asia. The Western myth of the White (European) woman as innocent, docile, and sexually passive was clearly transformed in this case, as up to today, it is the local woman that manifests purity, sexual passivity, and piety in the Caucasus and Central Asian mentality, while a more modernized Russian one often stands for the stereotype of aggressive sexual promiscuity. But, even so, the gist of this configuration lies in the same ideology of modernization based on racial differences. Symbolically, the Russian (i.e., more European) woman is forgiven her dissoluteness precisely on the grounds of her being Russian (i.e., superior).

III.

As stated previously, modernity in the twentieth century was implemented in two forms: the liberal/capitalist modernity and the Socialist/statist one. Each had a sunny side and a darker side, each had its own kind of coloniality of being and gender. The understudied darker colonial side of Soviet modernity generated a second-rate type of Soviet citizen, in spite of the proclaimed internationalist slogans and overt goal of racial mixing of the population to create a future Soviet mestizo/a with an erased ethnic element brought up on Russian culture and on Soviet ideology. In the gender variant of this ideology, a "metropolitan" (Russian) woman was opposed to the stereotyped colonial female, who was in need of civilizing and reinvention as the New Woman of the East or a New Mountain Woman. These identities turned out highly problematic and self-negating at times. We cannot ignore the responses of the colonial women themselves and their efforts at negotiating their subjectivities often around the paths offered by Bolsheviks and escaping their initially prescribed roles of the "surrogate proletariat" or the "liberated Oriental" (Massel 1974). In the dominant Soviet gender logic, the women representatives of the colonized people were accepted into the public sphere only within the frame allowed by the colonizing culture and in points of a particular understanding of the Soviet colonial woman, which was regarded as being fixedly determined by her culture and could be later redeemed by the Soviet enlightenment. This was a specific form of Soviet anthropological primordialism mixed with a daring social engineering strike, both based on humiliation, primitive stereotypes, and dehumanizing. If an indigenous woman did not follow the rules of the game and did not allow the Russian/Soviet civilizers to regard her as a mentally retarded "savage" in need of modernizing, if she did not correspond to the physical and behavioral stereotypes of predictable exotization, she was and still is immediately marginalized and seen to be in need of taming by means of forced assimilation or rejection. This issue of effective stoppages put in front of the colonial women who refused to correspond to the Soviet models of either complete assimilation or the exotic (subhuman) colonial is seldom discussed in the works of gender theorists and historians of gender in the West or in the Caucasus and Central Asia.

The reason lies in the continuing enchantment with the myth of modernity and its presentation as the only and best option for all women. Any alternative women's roles, such as the institute of *otins* (woman clerics and healers) in Central Asia or folk medicine women in the Caucasus who carried an *other* knowledge, are quickly pushed into invisibility. The same thing happened with those who carried a different idea of modernity that was for various reasons inconvenient for the Soviet Empire. This was true in the case of the Jadids and their rendering of gender problematic and in the corresponding Caucasus modernizing discourses, which also attempted to fuse local cosmologies and ethics with modernity. What is important here are not even the concrete details of these struggles, which are often meticulously rendered in the historical descriptive works of both local and Western scholars (Kamp 2006, Tokhtakhodzjayeva 1996, 1999, 2001), but rather the stubborn clinging to colonialist racist stereotypes in the Soviet Union at any stage of its development. This gap between the law and propaganda and the everyday discrimination taking myriads of hidden and open forms is especially hard to analyze, as it can be captured only through the voices of the real colonial women who went and continue to go through the ordeal of surviving as others in Russian, Soviet, national, or global modernity today.

IV.

In gender discourses, no matter where they are created—in the West, in the non-West, in Central Asia or in the Caucasus—one can trace the underlying logic of modernity based on coloniality of knowledge, of being and gender. Its sources lie in the very fact of the invention of modernity and its opposite, tradition, that changed the course of universal history. The social sciences and the humanities, including Western feminism, were shaped in accordance with the spatial-temporal matrix of modernity (Mignolo 2002a). The main feminist arguments of gender egalitarianism and the struggle with patriarchy were formulated precisely in connection with the invention of secular modernity as a questionable ideal of emancipation and negatively marking all other models as traditionalist and patriarchal by default, particularly if they were connected with non-Christian cultures. As a number of scholars demonstrated in the last two decades (Oyěwùmi 1997, Marcos 2005, Lugones 2007), the patriarchal nature of traditionalist society is a Western myth. In many cases, the patriarchal binary structures were introduced by and with colonization and modernization, together with the invented concept of tradition. But, in work after work, we still find the worn-out mutually exclusive oppositions of emancipation and backwardness, neo-Orientalism and religious extremism, paranjee and mini-skirt. Svetlana Shakirova and other Central Asian gender activists attempt a nuancing of this simplified model of gender relations and stress the lack of negative or positive emotional characteristics in the interpretation of traditional and emancipated women (Shakirova 2005). But, if we continue to use the binary opposition of modern vs. traditional, we cannot avoid the Eurocentric bias. In spite of the author's good intentions, the binary model is inevitably grounded in vector teleology—from the tradition through the Soviet half tradition and half modernity to today's Western emancipation. Any alternative and in-between forms are seldom analyzed or regarded independently, which is symptomatic in itself. Behind this selectivity is again a particular established scholarly tradition, which artificially creates certain points of reference and codes everything else as a deviation.

Western feminisms sometimes tend to ignore the difference between freedom and liberation, and its non-Western clones repeat this mistake. The history of Soviet gender discourses shows the nearsightedness of this position. Soviet state feminism indeed liberated women, sometimes against their will, but this liberation led not to freedom but rather to more dependency on other factors and preserving the fundamental discrimination in all spheres intact. The woman had to perform both the feminine and the masculine roles in economic, social, professional, and other senses. In colonial spaces, in addition to that, she also had to keep at least minimally her role of the traditional Oriental female and her difference with the Russian emancipated one. In contrast with China, where the principle of equality was fulfilled almost literally (Li Xiaojiang 1999, Wu 2005, Shu-mei Shih 2005), in the Soviet Union, women faced a more complex task: They had to never yield to men in public and professional spheres, remain a motherly and nurturing figure in private family realm, and on top of that, look and behave as a traditionally feminine woman, corresponding to the stereotypes of patriarchal society.

Egalitarianism, often considered to be an essential element of all feminisms, is not viable in communitarian or mixed societies, where the ideal of equality is either nonexistent or coded negatively. An example of this is described by S. Marcos in her analysis of the Zapatistas women (2005), by a number of Chinese feminists (Wu 2005, Li Xiaojiang 1993), but it can also be found in the women voices from the Caucasus and Central Asia, who, taking an intermediary position between individualism and communitarianism, reluctantly accept the separatist Western ideas of the exclusion of men.

Traditional feminist wars against sexism in language make sense in the majority of Western European and, wider, Indo-European languages, yet they would not hold for grammatically genderless or gender-neutral languages and those that started to develop gender-specific words as a result of colonization/modernization. A good example of this is a Nigerian scholar O. Oyěwùmi's study of precolonial Yoruba culture and language (Oyěwùmi 1997). The sexist power of Russian would be more blurred and less dimorphic than English, while even a more stunning discrepancy would emerge in case of gender-neutral Turkic (Braun 1999) or some of the Caucasus languages (mainly Georgian; Kikvidze 2001). The principles of gender identification in different languages vary and need to be contextually investigated in their own terms and not in terms of the universalized Western linguistic sexism.

The same discussion refers to the necessity of deconstruction of the internalized Western feminist idea of the visual (masculine) nature of any culture, which in fact is most typical of the Western European "gaze," but not of many other cultures with a different or mixed predominant communication channels: sound, tactile, and so on. Thus, a combination of intonation and phonetic features of the Turkic or Caucasus languages with the specific influence of Muslim culture considerably shifts the role of the visual. The prescribed gender roles that radical feminists so much want to get rid of turn out to be different in non-Western locales (while gender roles themselves are far from being the central division in many societies) and need to be understood before being dismantled.

Most feminist interpretations of gender problematic in Central Asia and the Caucasus remain blind to the imperial/colonial difference and unanimously assume that a progressivist liberal model of gender relations remains normative for everyone. In the logic of imperial difference and its secondary colonial difference, gender discourses in Russia or the Caucasus and Central Asia, with few exceptions, become watered down copies of the Western originals, infected with someone else's zero point epistemology and enunciation, appropriated as their own, thus creating a comical impression of intellectual mimicry. The subjectivity of researchers themselves is carefully hidden in these works, while the reality they analyze, and a part of which they often are, has little to do with the standard revelations of Western feminism. The majority of studies flourishing in and about Eurasian borderlands in the last decade and written by a number of Western scholars, their Russian bleak copies and the works of the colonial gendered subjects who mostly received a Western-style education for lack of anything else (Kamp 2006, Vigmann 2005, Tyomkina 2005, Harris 2000, Solovyeva 2006, Abasov 2005, Zubkovskaya 2007), are based on a simple binary opposition of presumably archaic gender discourses (here conceptualized as Muslim ones) and modernized Western models of women's liberation from the universal patriarchal system. What often remains unaddressed is the complex juxtaposition of several layers and forms of modernization in these locales, which often lead to conflicting subjectivities and negotiating gender forms. The Russian imperial model acts parallel to Muslim countries modernizing influences. The Soviet radical modernity strangles all alternatives, allowing for only a trickster type of passive or cunning resistance and today is itself replaced by the predominant internal colonialist yet also global version, which is projected directly without the Russian/Soviet mediation anymore, together with a possibility of Muslim patterns and role models. In all cases, the epistemic premises largely remain the same—it is the Western categories, value systems, and paradigms, while the cosmology, ethics, and epistemology of the inhabitants of Caucasus and Central Asia are neglected and dismissed as superstition or always negatively coded as traditionalism, while the new old local elites rewrite the Caucasus and Central Asian cosmologies in such a way as to create a convenient national myth—a new master narrative shaping the loyal subjects of the post-neocolonial regimes, including the gender sphere. Therefore, anything traditional is automatically associated with these official national narratives and immediately rejected, while the only option remaining for thinking subjects in the Caucasus or Central Asia is once again, progressivism, modernization, Westernization, leading to another deadend, for no place is reserved for them in this narrative.

It is important to emphasize here that my intention is not to go back to some initial primordialist pure sources when criticizing the negative interpretation of tradition by Western-style disciplines. The indigenous gendered tradition is a living, changing variable within itself and not fixed or given once and for all, not something that one has to go back to. This cosmology slips out of the Western logic of either/or, assuaging what the Western culture would interpret as contradictions in the all-penetrating act of balancing the change and the continuity. So, what is needed is not to go back to tradition but rather to stop gripping it in the vice of Western disciplinary divisions, concepts, assumptions, categories of thought and action. What is needed is to stop denying contemptuously its ways of expression and resistance that would not necessarily be academically sanctioned by the West.

Such categories and compartments of analysis are products of Western feminism that distort gender relations and discourses in other locales. Thus, women's activism in the Soviet colonial period is still measured by their participation in demonstrations and protests or their enrollment and involvement in the Soviet education and ideology, as if they cannot be regarded as full subjects before they started to use the accepted Western form of political and civil activity. This approach is perfectly expressed in a 2006 book by American historian Marianne Kamp, *The New Woman in Uzbekistan* (2006), which incorporates many interesting facts[62] but in the end provides a biased picture, as often happens when a foreign scholar studies the impenetrable other, relying too much and uncritically on his or her disciplinary approaches, political and moral ideals, liberal feminism, and naively believing that surrounding oneself with archival documents can facilitate the difficult task of pluritopic hermeneutics.[63] Of course, I do not mean to blame Kamp, as I think her approach is unconscious and inadvertently linked to the coloniality of knowledge at large. However, applying readymade methodologies or disciplines created in the West in the analysis of the non-Western subject always carries a danger of objectification, an unconscious drive to regard the world and the studied other from some kind of disinterested imagined objective position—the previously discussed epistemology of the zero point.

In the case of Soviet modernity the situation is further complicated by the fact that Western and Western-oriented scholars are still divided between two extremes—the passing extreme of demonization of everything Soviet and the younger generation of scholars who were shaped after the collapse of the Soviet Union and whose problem is often that they trust the Soviet propaganda too much and do not see the gap between propaganda and reality, remaining also blind to the psychological and existential realm. Many leftist Western intellectuals have stepped into this trap before. The younger generation of scholars of Central Asia and the Caucasus in the West often repeats this mistake, sentimentalizing gender slogans of the Soviet empire. A large number of local women intellectuals of all ages also tend to interpret the Russian/Soviet modernization positively, by contrasting the Soviet modernizing projects in the colonies, including the gender ones, and those of the Muslim developing and Third World countries. The favorite argument here is the following: If it were not for Russia, Uzbekistan would be like Afghanistan now or worse. In other words, the symbolic rising to the status of the Second World (instead of the Third) together with the Soviet Union is still regarded by a considerable number of local intellectuals as an unquestionably positive step. While any possible intersections with any women of color or Third World gender discourses are automatically erased as threatening, irrelevant, or humiliating. There is no understanding or meaningful dialogue yet between Third World and women of color feminists and ex-socialist gender studies and discourses, including the colonial ones. In this context, Kalpana Sahni's work mentioned previously is much more rewarding, as it is written from the border and marked by the colonial wound that is lacking in Western works and carefully hidden and suppressed in post-Socialist/post-colonial ones.

On the other hand, it is symptomatic that a large number of post-Soviet feminists tend to deny completely the previous Soviet forms of state-supported gender discourses in their Amazon forms of physical equity (the notorious Soviet women crane operators and asphalt layers were, after all, the modern versions of women warriors) or in their gender forms of inefficient and double-standard quotas, and they promote Western feminist models as an absolute novelty without seeing the common sources of Western and Soviet gender discourses and ignoring and erasing the existing divergent history and genealogy of Soviet gender discourses and practices in both the colonial and imperial forms. As the women question was regarded as solved and forgotten if not forbidden already in the early Soviet history and feminism since then was regarded as a harmful bourgeois influence, gender studies in their critical form indeed emerged in post-Soviet societies only after the collapse of the USSR and the flooding of different Western NGOs, often forcefully indoctrinating women activists with some ideal prescribed set of feminist goals and aims that had little to do with their own history and present situation. It was particularly painful in the case of the non-European ex-colonies, where the newly emerged gender studies remained blind to the geo- and body politics of gendered and racialized knowledge of the colonial others and insisted on the idea of discrimination of women as a result of some abstract male dictate, in this case also intensified by the demonized and in most cases totally invented idea of the Muslim gender system. Thus, one more time in these new works, created in and about Central Asia and the Caucasus, gender as a myth, a contextually determined construct, turned into some absolute universal given.

V.

Gender discourses in post-independence Central Asia and partly in the Caucasus also have been marked by the oversimplified dichotomy of tradition vs. modernization and built on the mechanical application of Western feminism to local material as a direct result of the main feminist indoctrination vector. The majority of the collections of essays, field studies, and oral histories published in the post-independence Caucasus and Central Asia retain a developmentalist approach. This refers to a 2005 Tadzjik collection with a telling name, *Gender: Traditions and Modernity* (Kasymova 2005a), as well as partly to an earlier 1995 Uzbek collection of fascinating oral histories, *Destinies and Time* (Tokhtakhodzhayeva,. Abdurazzakova, and Kadyrova 1995). In the Introduction, the editors mix the unreflected-on Soviet and Western modernization ideologies, marked by stagism and universalist notions of the patriarchal nature of any traditionalist society as the main impediment for women as such. The legitimacy of Western/Soviet modernization for any woman is never questioned in the book (except in the oral histories themselves), as it drags a number of values and features, which were naturalized in the collective unconscious and are associated with modernity/modernization, such as an access to secular Russian (and colonizing) education, to decision making, career, social security—exclusively in the variants prescribed by the Soviet and Western modernity. Zombification by the rhetoric of modernity and its knowledge matrix is obvious in the texts, written by the scholars of gender in Central Asia and the Caucasus. They still cling to the tripartite model of the traditional woman/Soviet half-emancipated one/fully emancipated Westernized woman. Western-style emancipation is often regarded in a mythologized way when, for example, local anthropologists and sociologists seriously consider changes in body care to presumably more Western ones as a manifestation of unproblematic emancipation. It has long become commonplace for feminists that gluing artificial nails or being scared to death of gaining half a pound and losing one's similarity to a Barbie doll are not signs of real emancipation. Yet no one seems to ask this question: Isn't the so-called traditional woman who calmly understands that each of her life stages is associated with a particular body, a certain appearance, who flexibly changes her social identities in different contexts and pays more attention to parameters other than primitive erotic appeal in the way she looks or behaves, isn't she fundamentally much more free than the presumably "emancipated" one?[64] Instead of praising the Central Asian or Caucasus women for finally learning to understand their physical bodies as social entities (thus, erasing the difference between sex and gender altogether), it is important to remember that, in many precolonial societies, in Oyěwûmi's words, the (sexed and/or gendered) body was not the basis of social roles, inclusion or exclusion, it was not a foundation of social thought or identity (Oyěwûmi 1997: x–xi), and it does not have to be today.

However, it would be unfair to fail to mention that a number of Central Asian and Caucasus gender scholars have started to develop an in-between model presented as an alternative for Eurasian borderlands women (Kasymova 2005a). This alternative is still conceptualized mostly in terms of the Western model of turning geography into chronology (Mignolo 2009a), the predominance of time over place, pushing of traditionalism outside the world history and, consequently, the interpretation of border as a deficiency, as a state of being stuck in time, which requires synthesizing or negation in one or the other direction. Understanding of the border not only in temporal sense (between tradition and modernity) but also in spatial-cultural one is not typical of Western thinking. It is necessary to go away from this simple scheme, imposed onto the world by Western social sciences and humanities, and rehabilitate space as a concrete locale, and corporality as a concrete body. The first steps in this direction are already being taken. In August 2006, a summer school on postcolonialism and the prospects of gender studies in Central Asia took place at Lake Issyk-Kul. One of the painful issues discussed was the continuing necessity for the Central Asian scholars to correspond to Western gender theories and assumptions with their hidden Orientalist stereotypes, thus re-Orientalizing ourselves in peculiar ways by, on the one hand, playing the role of the eternal other (a native informant or a native instrument of feminist imperialism; Shu-mei Shih et al. 2005: 145), or studying our own ex-colonial space using the Western area studies or feminist tools.[65] Identity then is being re-essentialized again and again. Central Asian gender activist, ex-director of the gender center in Almaty (Kazakhstan) and a supervisor of the Central Asian Gender Net, Svetlana Shakirova shrewdly pointed out: "The proliferation of such themes as the kidnapping of brides in Kyrgizia, the sexual women traffic in Central Asia, the self-immolation of women in Uzbekistan, the arranged by parents marriages in Tadzhikistan and prostitution in Kazakhstan—what is this all if not following the Orientalist clichés?" (Shakirova 2006).

However, Svetlana's position is dubious and self-negating at times, marked with typically colonial double discourses (one for the ex-metropolis and a different one for Central Asian community) and silences, symptomatic on the whole of gender studies in the region. Shakirova is perfectly aware of the problems and limitations of non-Western feminism connected with self-indoctrination and neo-Orientalist tendencies. Yet, she is clearly a product of mainly Western and Russian feminist sources and traditions. On top of that, Svetlana is well institutionalized within the state, the NGO system, and most important, the academic feminist community, which has managed to rebuild in the post-Soviet space a neoimperial/colonial hierarchy. That is why she is very cautious and evasive when discussing issues that may endanger her place within this hierarchical feminist community. This is obvious in her recent discussion of my book *Decolonial Gender Epistemologies* (Tlostanova 2009) with one of the leading Russian anthropologists of Central Asia, Sergey Abashin, published in a Ukrainian journal, *Gender Studies* (2009). Svetlana's discourse betrays her essentially trickster position on the difficult verge where subjectification finally results in a new subjectivity: She obviously does not agree with the Russian scholar in many points but tends to accentuate similarities instead of bluntly pointing to his blindness or a conscious reluctance to notice various internal issues of the Central Asian problematic closely linked to Russian/Soviet modernity/coloniality. Yet, Svetlana manages to indirectly raise certain painful topics and at least point to her own difference with Sergei Abashin and also the post-Soviet gender scholars, without losing her assigned space in the hierarchy of area studies on Central Asia and post-Soviet gender studies traditionally presided by Russian, Ukrainian, and Belarusian scholars (i.e., those with (pseudo) (secondary) European claims). I am far from trying to discredit Svetlana's position. Yet, I think that institutionalization on any level can effectively disempower contesting discourses and their activists by imposing an invisible set of rules that they are not allowed to transcend. It is clear that we need other forms and ways of coalition and dialogues that would not be co-opted and minced by the dominant structures.

Another interesting and symptomatic example is the works of a diasporic Kalmyk anthropologist and scholar of gender Elza Bair Guchinova, living in Moscow and working in a top academic institute of anthropology and ethnology. She represents a position that is closest to the post-Soviet kind of decolonial and women-of-color feminism. Being well read in these discourses and aware of the postcolonial dimension, having the variegated experience of studying and working abroad, and a decidedly transcultural stance, Elza remains a Kalmyk for whom the experience of her people's forced deportation in 1943–56, including its effect on gender roles and relations, is not a detached subject for research but a lived history of her ancestors, compatriots, and relatives. A specific version of the Soviet/colonial wound allows Guchinova to better sense and understand the gendered version of the historical trauma of dislocation, the effect of Eurocentrism on the idea of the beautiful and appropriate in mixed cultural contexts, the survival strategies of multiply disenfranchised others, and so forth. Elza's position is a border one, as she combines a critical cosmopolitanism with a truly participatory anthropology (Guchinova 2003, 2005).

Gender studies of the Russian/Soviet non-European ex-colonies seldom venture into the spheres of epistemology and theorizing, leaving this privilege to Western feminism and thus agreeing with their own dependency. In this respect they repeat the path already taken and largely rejected by Third World and women-of-color feminists. Disavowing the Eurocentric universal theory often leads to stagnation and fear of any meta-theory as such, hence the proliferation of mini discourses and going into specific and often narrow problems of race, sexuality, class, nation; grounding oneself exclusively in the empirical research of a concrete group of others. Paradoxically, Third World feminism helped reproduce what it was fighting against. Such a position was critically analyzed by Chinese feminists, who managed to overcome the fascination with Western modernity and claim that there is no need to repeat the Western way, that they already went a long way along their own road (Li Xiaojiang 1993: 104). The same impulse is to be found in the radical works of Egyptian gender activist and writer Nawal el Saadawi. She draws attention to the new multicultural forms of gendered Orientalizing and the imperial/colonial asymmetry when she criticizes the organizers of a rigidly structured feminist conference, who "did not understand at all why the Third World women were uncomfortable . . . at their powerlessness to contribute in any meaningful way . . . the well meaning U.S. organizers and panel conveners had and probably still have no idea how maternalistic and condescending they sounded . . . when they read papers or talked at the participants, telling them how to behave . . ." (el Saadawi 1997: 148). Instead of a dialogue, here, we encounter an asymmetrical colonial communication. "The oppressor here blames protest and dissent on the character defects and the hang-ups and the shortcomings of the colonized" (el Saadawi 1997: 149). For el Saadawi, the roots of this approach are clearly colonial and masculine, but the Western feminists willingly reproduce them. Gender discourses generated in the Caucasus and Central Asia unfortunately did not reach this conclusion as yet on any massive scale, silently agreeing to erase the path they have already gone and start again from scratch, mimicking someone else's foreign model, which does not fit yet is considered normative.

The continuing dependency of local gender discourses on the West is not surprising if we take into account that the majority of these works are supported by Western grants and NGOs. What is at work here is what African feminist Obioma Nnaemeka called "the politics of poverty" and "the politics of the belly" (Shu-mei Shih et al. 2005: 159), which makes the work for NGOs the only safe harbor and often the only material means of existence for many local women. We cannot blame them for their position. It only proves again the vitality of the naturalized, universalist Western notions and scholarly categories, models and paradigms, and forms of thinking and subjectivity. This is not just a post-Soviet problem. Oyěwùmi points out similar tendencies in her African colleagues (Oyěwùmi 1997: xv) as well as a Chinese feminist Y. Wu (Wu 2005: 41) and S. Marcos, who claims that she refused the role of the Western feminism mirror (Shu-mei Shih et al. 2005: 145). This role is associated with a number of advantages, not entirely material but also symbolic—the exoticized non-Western women are accepted only if they translate word for word the ideas of Western feminism. Then, they are immediately given a chance to travel around the world, speak at international congresses, and act as legitimate representatives of their cultures and women's movements in academic and political spheres. This problem is in fact a problem of ethical choice, which is harder for non-Western feminists than for Western ones because of the persistent epistemic and economic asymmetry. The expert community not only defines the dominant scholarly discourses but also controls the accessibility and centrality of particular positions and points of view in the academic world, so that the "sanctioned ignorance" about the non-Western paradigms is promoted in the global intellectual community. The works that go beyond the generally accepted mainstream gender notions would be never translated, published, or promoted, remaining known only to selected enthusiasts.

VI.

However, a growing body of works on gender demonstrates a different approach today, unlearning Western feminist ways and notions in a complex border position of gender tricksterism. Representatives of border in-between gender positions and decolonial feminism shape the new transmodern gender discourses, rethinking both Western feminism and traditional (for lack of a better term) cultures. They are based on the principle of dialogic knowledges and constant traveling between the West and the non-West, opening points of confluence between Western philosophy (usually of a contesting kind) and cosmologies, subjectivities and social justice systems of indigenous people. Such is Oyěwùmi's attempt to question the very category of woman as a Western construct imposed on Yoruba culture that previously lacked the category of gender (Oyěwùmi 1997). Instead of biological gender divisions, the society is based on clan and professional principles and a much more flexible seniority principle. In Central Asia and the Caucasus, the woman in indigenous society was also far from being constantly and always discriminated against. Her roles changed dynamically through life, from a relative condition without rights typical for the young wife, to the respected mother of the family with grown-up children and grandchildren who took an active part in the decision making. Adyghean cosmology retains traces of gender parity, women's active participation in politics, their well-defined property rights, the specific gendered division of labor, which was never based on coding one (female) labor as less prestigious than the other (male), even the predominance of female over male in certain spheres, as a result of a longer sustaining of feminocratic systems. Many local histories manifested such traditions of gender egalitarianism and lack of fixed gender divisions. Traces of these alternative relations and models are to be found in the Amerindian and African cultures but were erased from the collective memory of the Caucasus or Central Asian people and hard to restore. In contrast with Mesoamerican cosmology, which always remained a living tradition, in the Caucasus and Central Asia, there were more layers and radical forms of colonization, interacting with each other, each of which added a new wall between the string of indigenous cosmology and the people, preventing from a link with their history and epistemology.

In the Caucasus mythology, the oldest layers tend to be feminocratic, and the later social structure of the northern Caucasus Nart epic still clearly carries traces of gender egalitarianism. In the Caucasus, women remained for a long time outside the patriarchal law, while in the social life of Adyghean community the guiding principle of fluidity and flexible contextuality of gender roles was linked with seniority: the older wise women were no less but often more respected than men and connected with a number of sacred acts and rituals that only they could perform (healing, the control of rain and thunder, rituals at the building of a new house, the initiation rituals, etc.). In the oral poetry and songs of the Adyghe people, created when they fought for their independence from Russia, we find "texts" made by women themselves and from their perspective. These "texts" did not describe them from outside but concentrated on women's feelings and emotions, on their willingness to be active and to make decisions in all spheres of life, including the erotic one. These poems and songs, as was the case with Mesoamerican culture, were later predictably erased or edited by the indigenous tradition itself, which was becoming more and more patriarchal, and by the no-less-patriarchal interpretations by Western and Russian ethnographers and anthropologists, who condescendingly misinterpreted the majority of symbols, images, metaphors, connected with the women's world and their perception of this world (Tekuyeva 2006b).

On a larger scale, everything threatening the colonizers was simply taken out of these texts, from heroic and liberating identities to strong women warriors. This is true about the aforementioned genre of the heroic epic *dastan*. In many *dastans*, the central part belonged to the woman warriors, the Amazons of Central Asia. The subversive tradition survived in other oral forms as well. An example is Khanifa Kazi series of epic poems from the northern Caucasus. Khanifa had a real historical prototype and combined the woman-warrior faculties with healing ones. Her story was closely connected with the Caucasus war—an outstanding situation of colonization of the whole people in which a woman was allowed to cross the usual gender boundaries. As M. Tekuyeva points out, for Khanifa, there was a priority of patriotic motifs over the personal feelings. She served as a role model of selfless devotion to the idea of liberation and a stimulus for the continuation of struggle (2006a: 142).

The idea that the dichotomous structure of gender roles is largely a Western phenomenon naturalized due to modernity worldwide is proven by the practices of marginal Muslim cultures, such as in the Caucasus and Central Asia. In Chapter 3, I mentioned the tradition of the *bacha* cult, which could take male and female forms with a distinct transsexual element. A milder example, which does not cross the boundaries of sexuality, comes from a medieval Muslim culture with its nuanced gender system. Along with the *Sharia* ideal woman and its opposite (a whore), it has a powerful image of a beautiful and sly coquette—the treacherous *Afet* (translated literally as "disaster"). This "beautiful dame" of Eastern poetry, in N. Mekhti's words (2005: 137), takes an in-between position. It is a good example of non-Western cultures' sensitivity and intuition in grasping intermediary transcultural, transvalue, and transgender models, hard to reconcile with Western binary thinking, vacillating between the extremes of the Madonna and the whore or in, this case, the veil and the mini skirt.

In the case of Mexican Zapatistas women, the central goal is decolonization from the Eurocentered racist epistemologies in their creole rendering. In case of Caucasus and Central Asian women, there is a more complex task, as the modernizing/colonizing agents here were multiple and varied, and negotiating women's identities between and beyond neoliberalism, Islam, and their ethnic/national cultures becomes a truly challenging task. What is meant here is not a simple, straightforward negation of one tradition for the sake of the other. A dynamic interpenetration and mutually directed transculturation is at work.

VII.

A lack of understanding between Western feminism and non-Western gender discourses is obvious in the ongoing discussion on the meaning of veiling, which remains unresolvable unless we attempt to unlearn certain Western assumptions on Muslim women and their agency. Wearing a hijab does not always carry the fixed religious meaning of controlling the aggressive manifestations of male sexuality; it can also be a symbol of resistance to colonization and Western cultural influence or carry an openly feminist and anticapitalist meaning (Shaikh 2003). In Central Asia and parts of the Caucasus, the function of hijab is close to the Turkish model, as described by N. Göle (1996). She claims that the very emergence of the civil society in Turkey was linked directly with the beginning of understanding women as humans and citizens and their specific socialization, together with Turkish modernization. The women of Kemalist Turkey were real symbols of the civilizing/ modernizing project (1996: 131). Something similar—although with a Communist ideology at its core and the outward atheism on top of the colonial difference—we find, in southern and eastern provinces of the Soviet Union during the infamous campaigns for the liberation of the women of the East and the mountain women. Later these Soviet republics shaped their own model of the secular educated and socially active working mother.

Soviet modernity, in contrast with the Western one as described by Oyěwûmi in the Yoruba case (Oyěwûmi 1997: 122), was very active in involving the local women in the new life style. But, the Soviet emancipation of racialized gendered others was still based on double standards and attempted to keep the colonized women in a downtrodden state, at the same time making them believe they are liberated. The Bolsheviks' interest in the "Oriental" women was not confined to redeeming them through conversion to the Communist faith. It was necessary to make women enter the public sphere in the capacity of new working hands and reformed voices in the mass construction of the ideal society by the ideally docile workers with maximally erased gender differences. The easiest way of making the change palpable was through appearance and clothes, hence the early Bolshevik campaigns in the non-European parts of the Soviet Union, such as "a coat for a mountain woman" in the Northern Caucasus in the 1920s, which consisted in the supply of European style overcoats to the local women to make them come to the elections, or an anti-paranjee campaign in Central Asia, which was part of the larger "hujum" movement. In both cases, the impetus behind them was similar to Soviet anthropology and biomedicine, based on interfering in the woman's most intimate world, which was in itself a manifestation of imperial violence in the control of sexuality and subjectivity.

When Caucasus and Central Asian women revert to hijab today, they "go back" to what is interpreted in the collective unconsciousness as the "traditional" (though it is not always so) in the form of the protest against modernization in its Soviet, national, or global variant. In Turkey, Central Asia, or the Caucasus, this consciously chosen hijab identity is often appropriated by young and middle-aged urban, educated, professional, and socially mobile women, who are attempting to legitimize the social, political, and cultural changes and the shaping of alternative normative values. The difference with the Turkish model is that the previous national secular modernity in Turkey is opposed to a more religious and presumably independent and authentic version of national identity today, while in the Caucasus and Central Asia, the conflict is between the mothers who were brought up on the ideals of Soviet modernity and daughters who prefer to forget about this secular modernity in its (post-)Soviet or neoliberal forms, turning to a highly constructed notion of the modern Muslim identity instead, yet allowing for the technological sides of Western culture. Besides, in Turkey, the process of radical Islamist revival and the emergence of the new Muslim identity took several decades (from the 1950s on), accelerating toward the end of the twentieth century. The Soviet ex-colonies became independent almost overnight and not of their own will, finding themselves in need of an immediate and often unconscious choice of the new woman identity. In the Caucasus and Central Asia, with their peculiar forms of cultural and ethnic Islam, the local gendered identity could be manifested in the phenomenon of the "virtual hijab," to quote Nijazi Mekhti (2005), which was a compensatory technique of Muslim culture during the Soviet years.

Islam was and still is not a singularly misogynist or women-liberating tradition, the same way as the local pre-Islamic traditions incorporated various contradictory elements. Often, it was the patriarchal society and clergy that distorted Islam (similarly to Christianity) to make it more misogynist than it was. The imposition of Islam was sometimes used by the local men to enforce patriarchy. They artificially muted the genderly egalitarian parts of Muslim culture and reinforced or invented the discriminating ones. In the Arabic countries, there is already a whole tradition of Muslim women theologists, who regard it as their goal to prove that Muslim texts were distorted by male interpreters and are in need of reinterpretation by women (Ali 2003). In the Caucasus and Central Asia, this impulse has not yet been expressed in the academic form, though there is a continuing tradition of Sufi orders linked in a complex way with a well-developed system of pre-Islamic saints who were often women, the institute of modern women healers and otins questioning and destabilizing the Muslim male master narrative from their marginal positions (see Chapter 3). By contrast, the male forms of new Islamism in the northern Caucasus turn women into dispensable lives, as in case of the so-called black widows. This attitude toward women is not an ancient tradition but a rather new one, linked with modernity/coloniality.

VIII.

In the process of unlearning the Western feminist notions and assumptions, a crucial part today is played by women's voices themselves, their oral histories, with rich subtexts and eloquent voids and silences often unnoticed by the interviewers zombified by Western scientific and scholarly principles. Particularly interesting are those oral histories that belong to women born or raised before or outside the Soviet indoctrination. Such is the interview with Muborakhanum Gaffarova (born in 1905) (Tokhtakhodzhayeva et al. 1995: 38–45), a refugee to Sindzyan (which later became a part of China), who came back to Uzbekistan only in the early 1960s. Gaffarova is free from the Soviet ideology and ethnic/nationalist intolerance, generated by reaction to the forced modernization/colonization. She offers an alternative and pluritopic way of reconciling modernization with local ethnic, cultural, epistemic, and religious models, such as Jadidism.

She is clearly a border dweller, open and tolerant to otherness to a much larger degree than any other informants. From the oral history of this elderly woman emerges a different image of the Central Asian Muslim culture, than the one created by Western feminists and endorsed by their local pupils. She does not specifically discuss gender, but her oral history indirectly points to such features of the presumably backward and more traditionalist Sindzyan Uzbek diaspora as an obvious respect for women and children, a lack of gender inequality in the questions of education and career, and even a certain parity between men and women to a larger degree than in Soviet Uzbekistan, where colonial subjects were persuaded that they were free and happy. She stresses that, in the history of Central Asia as well as other colonized spaces, the ugly excesses of patriarchal discourses and practices were not initially inherent in the local or Muslim culture, rather being an indirect result of colonization. Gaffarova seems to be the only informant sensitive to this imperial/colonial side of the problem, while people shaped in and by the Soviet system, even if critical, think entirely within the developmentalist progressivist paradigm, demonizing any traditional culture, and particularly Islam, and remaining unaware of any alternative models. Only Gaffarova openly speaks of the reasons for the degeneration of her people, regarding colonization by Russia as a direct source of the slave psychology of the Central Asians (Tokhtakhodzhayeva et al. 1995: 45), which she was so shocked with after her return from China. As an outsider, she clearly sees the typical colonizing tactics of zombification and is able to detect the darker side of the modern colonial gender system, which is not accessible to other informants—both the colonized and the colonizers.

The women representatives of the colonizing culture, by contrast, remain insensitive to the ethical ambiguity and manipulative nature of their own positions. A. Memmi formulated an opposition of a colonialist and a passive colonizer (1991: 52). The majority of Central Asian or Caucasus Russians are precisely such reluctant colonizers, who are often offended that the aboriginals are not able to appreciate their noble civilizing efforts (Tokhtakhodzhayeva et al. 1995: 107). Their minds unconsciously carry racist and discriminatory ideologies. The colonizers of both genders share a number of typical features, such as the condescending attitude to local languages and the interpretation of Russification as a civilizing norm, as well as the well-known idea of the *conservation* of traditional culture as opposed to *teaching* the locals the new and progressive European/Russian ways (Tokhtakhodzhayeva et al. 1995: 107). For Central Asian and Caucasus Russians alike, it is habitual to compare their ancestors who ended up in the Russian colonies with the North American pioneers and adventurers of the West, a comparison that helps them elevate their own status (and the status of their empire by association) and erase the stigma of colonization and imperialism. There are also important clashes between the Russian and the colonial women in these locales that have not been yet commented on, such as the social status and the economic and sexual differences and asymmetries marked by racism.[66]

IX.

The Soviet empire was Eurocentric and patriarchal in spite of its external rhetoric. But, this does not mean that the women themselves were simply passive victims. The women definitely created ways out of the imposed binarism as well as conscious ways of flexibly (re)constructing their subjectivities within different social discourses. These models offer mediation, an ironic tricksterlike vacillation and play on stereotyping and discrimination, as a way of coping. Such positioning steps beyond the persistent double standard maintained by the coloniality of gender. The modern/colonial gender system has always sustained one ideal for the Western (or Russian in case of Soviet modernity) gendered subject and the opposite ideal for the colonial and ex-colonial spaces, whose women need to be redeemed by means of various discourses and tactics—from Christianity to a civilizing mission, from Socialism to overall consumerism today. A specific variant of the second-class colonial modernity was and is on sale in the Third World/global South, in Socialist colonies and in ex–Second World today. This colonial modernity is a cheap throwback to the culture of modernity zombifying (ex-)colonial people and incarcerating them into a triumphant vector pointed toward emancipation in accordance with stagist heresy. An alarming recent tendency is that more and more locales (including the ex–Second World and its colonial difference) are branded as unreformable and imprisoned within an essentialist (neo-)Orientalist paradigm.

The women marked with difference in cultural, ethnic, religious, sexual, linguistic, and other senses or taking a bordering position between the cultures of several colonies or a colony and a metropolis form a rather large group, particularly inconvenient for anthropology and gender sociology, as it does not fit the readymade categories and conventional schemes. In the context of complicating the simple tripartite scheme of traditional-Soviet-Westernized women, one of the most interesting and understudied phenomena is the Soviet colonial gender trickristerism, whereby the Soviet and the colonial merge and balance on the verge of resistance and re-existence, acting around the power structures to successfully avoid their policing censorship.

The emergence of a well-defined generation of colonial gendered intellectuals in Central Asia and the Caucasus coincides with the massive political decolonization in the world and should be regarded within this crucial context as one of its elements. By the late 1950s, there was already a discursive space of those Soviet colonial women who refused to slide either to the paranjee or to the parachutist with the Young Communist League badge on her chest. How did they negotiate their identity between these binaries and eventually beyond them? They lost the freedom of thinking in their native language. Their link with the local culture, value system, and knowledge was seriously damaged, but it does not necessarily mean that the culture itself was lost, that it was replaced completely with a different and artificial system. The necessity of corresponding to Soviet values was often negotiated in unexpected forms. This became obvious in career trajectories, fashion, hobbies, intersexual relations, and leisure activities. If, in Northrop's book, we find mostly the photographs of the entirely veiled enigmatic Tashkent women, even as late as the 1940s (2004: 319, 322, 236) and Marianne Kamp presents us mostly the official encyclopedia photographs of the New Uzbek women who made their careers through Soviet modernity propaganda, my own mini-field study of the photographs and testimonies of several Uzbek families from Tashkent of the same period shows something more complex. Far from being a massive phenomenon, this particular gendered trickster subjectivity is still symptomatic as it promises the possibility of re-existence around, beyond, and at the crossing of several models—from soviet Orientalism and multiculturalism, to Muslim culture, from ethno-cultural patterns of Uzbek people to Western modernity and today's internal neocolonialism.

There is a flexible change of identities, a play on them, which Soviet educated gendered colonials used with various goals—from mimicry to strategic positioning at the border, giving a double vision and a multidimensional understanding and perception of oneself in the world, a possibility of remaining within the rigid Soviet multiculturalism yet practicing a difference in forms that would be impervious to imperial censorship (Tlostanova 2010a).

It is a much more complex picture than the women wrapped in paranjee from Northrop's book or party activists and Turkmen women crane operators of Soviet multiculturalism, where colonial gendered individuals had to act as symbols of themselves, liberated Oriental women, but always remember not to become better than the Russian originals. Such a colonial gender tricksterism has survived until today both in the ex-metropolis and in the ex-colonies. What is crucial here, according to Lugones, is the multiplicity in the fracture of the locus of the colonial difference that incorporates the enactment of the coloniality of gender and resistance from a subaltern sense of self, of the social, of the self in relation, of the cosmos, all grounded in a peopled memory. For Lugones, as for a decolonial intellectual, it is particularly important to always feel this tense multiplicity and movement, "people moving: the tension between the dehumanization and paralysis of the coloniality of being, and the creative activity of be-ing" (2008).

The locus of imperial difference and a secondary colonial difference marked by the Socialist modernity generates still another response. The well-known feminist slogan "the personal is the political" is not attractive to the women of the (post-)Socialist countries, because the whole social field in these places, including the private and everyday spheres, was so politicized that a natural reaction was precisely an apolitical or a depoliticized stance. In the USSR and China to different extents, an opposite tendency is natural as a reaction against the system, which in many cases is realized in the outward manifestations of conventional femininity, a phenomenon that not many Western feminists have even been able to grasp. Chinese gender theorist Li Xiaojiang elaborates on the discourses of femininity in modern China, which are interesting to compare with the post-Soviet ones. It seems that the resexualizing of woman's body in China after the 1980s is a more distinct and expressive reaction against the Socialist excesses than in the ex-Soviet Union, where there was never such a powerful and successfully implemented discourse of women's desexualizing in all realms (Li Xiaojiang 1993: 104).

X.

The gender sphere, along with the arts and nonrational knowledges, seems to be one of the few remaining areas of colonial subjectivity in the Caucasus and Central Asia, where the revival of indigenous and transmodern models and the building of other trajectories for the future is still possible. Such a revival is necessarily linked with bringing forward the erased histories of resistance and re-existence of the colonized peoples and efforts to establish their dialogue with indigenous movements around the world. The acquaintance of Central Asian and Caucasus gender activists with voices of decolonial feminists is crucial, as it offers them an alternative instead of the prescribed correspondence to only Western standards, an alternative that does not have to be reproduced word for word but awakens the gene of freedom and decoloniality—of being, of gender, of knowledge, of sensing, and so forth. In this respect, one of the most promising areas of the post-Soviet decolonizing is the intersection of gender and the arts. Central Asian and Caucasus women artists, writers, film, and theater directors, little by little, create a decolonial discursive space and agency. As Kazakh artist Saule Suleimenova (2010) pointed out recently,

> [A] true artist is always in a quest for the new formula of the beautiful and is always free and ready to create something that would liberate others as well, while beauty equals freedom, joy and life, but also simplicity and the glowing of truth as it is, and therefore it cannot be a quotation or a mimicking, and is devoid of the annoying factors of cultural discrepancies. It must be your own and not a second hand colonial use of someone else's freedom, or joy. I am trying to reconnect and reconcile the traditional Kazakh culture and the aesthetics of revolt, the modernist artistic devices, the pathos of eternity, and the poetics of everyday. (Suleimenova 2010)

For the development of understanding and cooperation on a global level and coalitions at the points of difference with other racialized, colonized, and gendered subjects, Caucasus and Central Asian women need first of all to decolonize their own thinking. Second, they need a kind of feminism that would not be a clone of the Western (or Russian) one and that would not be a repetition of the Soviet state gender discourses either. It would have to be an independent and critical feminism based on a careful differentiating and empathic grasping of particular values and sensibilities born in historical and cultural contexts of the Caucasus and Central Asia, including the indigenous epistemology. In the case of the Caucasus and Central Asia, there is a danger that having gotten rid of the hijab as a result of Soviet gender politics, the women of these locales can find themselves today in the clasp of a much more hierarchical regime—not of veiling but of silencing and leveling of their opinions and selves—promoted by Western epistemology and Western (and mimicking Russian) feminism as its integral part.

What is important in Maria Lugones's formulation of coloniality of gender and what can and should be taken into account by the emerging decolonial feminism in Central Asia and the Caucasus is oppositional fragmented and coalitional gendered subjectivity and activism projected into the future. The coloniality of gender generates a counteraction, a virus of resistance from the crack and in terms of the colonial difference. Lugones stresses that "from the fractured locus the movement succeeds in retaining creatively ways of thinking, of behaving, of relating . . . Subject, relations, ground, possibilities are continually transformed incarnating a weave from the fractured locus that constitutes a creative peopled re-creation" (2008). Conducting a dialogue under the preservation of difference and multiplicity is a difficult task—money and power remain in the hands of the feminist mainstream, and if they get into the hands of freely thinking and acting gender activists, unfortunately, this can cause a change even in their nature, making their dialogues false and their institutions suffocating (Shu-mei Shih et al. 2005: 150). Echoing the opinions of many gender theorists from D. Haraway to B. Preciado and S. Marcos, Lugones points out that "the emphasis should be on maintaining multiplicity at the point of reduction, not in maintaining a hybridity (as a product, which masks the colonial difference) but in the tense workings of more than one logic, not to be synthesized but transcended . . . The responses from the fragmented loci can be creatively in coalition. This decolonial coalitional resistance generates oppositional consciousness of a social erotics that take on the differences that make be-ing creative, that permits enactments that are thoroughly defiant of the logic of dichotomies" (2008).

Even if it is hardly possible to avoid the dependence on Western grants and NGOs, we can still keep and cultivate a certain degree of freedom and self-reflection, a conscious delinking from the dominant ego politics of knowledge and an attempt to build a geo- and body politics of the gendered border thinking, which can help elaborate an other dynamic of action, a specific transcultural language that would be linked with more symmetrical and dialogic relations between Western and non-Western cosmologies and epistemologies. It does not mean that we need to reject the Western influence altogether or take the position of aggressive and rigid nativism or nationalism. But, having shaped the multiple paradigm of critical other thinking, which can hope to see and adequately reflect the diversity and contradictoriness of various experiences of multifarious global world, we thus exercise our right to keep our dignity and not to plead to be accepted by the West/global North (or Russia).

PART III

CHAPTER 5

Who Speaks for the "Human" in Human Rights?

Dispensable and Bare Lives

I. The Issues: Experience and Philosophical Categories

Chapter 4 raised the issues of gender in non-European ex-colonies. When the gender issues are debated by mainstream feminists in Europe or the U.S., it is de facto assumed that race is not constitutive of gender. However, outside Europe and the U.S., racism and gender are mutually constitutive. When it comes to Human Rights, the same principle applies. Thus, while debates on the issue focus generally on "rights," this chapter shifts the accent toward the "human." Early claims, by non-European nations, to have their own regional declaration next to the Universal Declaration of Human Rights of 1948, reframed in the context of the geopolitics of knowledge, (knowing, and being, i.e., in terms of global racial hierarchies) showed indirectly that the question of "rights" applied to both human beings and regions (e.g., the Third World) (Rana, 2007; Barreto 2009, 2012). This chapter follows up on the intersection of gender and race and focuses on the idea of "human" in Human Rights and the idea of humanity as well as the Humanities in higher education. In the next chapter, we examine the complicity of the concepts of humanity and citizenship in the Western imaginary. In the interregnum, the concept of "rights" emerged at two complementary levels: first in international law, in the Atlantic in the sixteenth century; and second, in the sphere of the legal status of individual citizens (above all, the French Declaration of the Rights of Man and of Citizen). We now concentrate on the question of Human/Humanity in relation to categories such as citizenship, rights, and knowledge.

I.1.

The idea of Human Rights combines an ontological assumption (being human) and a legal question (rights). It would appear that the almost seven billion human beings on the planet are endowed with the "rights," since the declaration says that rights are universal. In this chapter, we concentrate on the "human" aspect of the equation and will question the assumption of the universality of human rights. Three major events of Western modernity prompted the universal declaration of human rights: the genocides in Germany (Nazism) and in Russia (Communism) and the atomic bomb in Hiroshima (the inauguration of the U.S. imperial era).

"Human Rights"—as they were conceived in the Universal Declaration of 1948—presupposes not that "rights" are universal but that "human" is a universal category accepted by all and that, as such, the concept of "human" does justice to everyone. The wrong assumption is that what is enunciated as "Universal" also corresponds to the universality of the enunciation. We have been arguing that a universal enunciation is a mirage; enunciation can emerge only from a local genealogy of thoughts and needs. The only occasion in which the universality of the enunciated coincides with the Universality of the enunciation is through the world of God. It is only in God that the enunciated and the enunciation can be one and the same. When that pretense is assumed by human beings, we have good reason to suspect that it is an excuse and a justification of imperial and totalitarian designs.

The concept of "human" that is used in general conversations, by the media, at universities, and in seminars and conferences is a concept that leaves outside of "humanity" a quite large portion of the global population. That men (and women) are all born equal,,is a statement that, since eighteenth century Europe, we can find in the Bill of Rights and the European and American constitutions. The statement has been made under the presupposition that everybody basically educated, no matter where (in China, in the Middle East, in any region of Africa, Central Asia, and South America, in Russia, etc.), will agree with such a statement. And, indeed, it makes a lot of sense and it can be taken as, if not universal, a global truth. The problem is right there, in the equality status at birth. And, the problem is that if men (and women) are born equal, they do not remain equal the rest of their lives.

The statement I have never seen written as such but implied in countless places is the following: "Men and women are all born equal but they do not remain equal the rest of their lives" should also be globally, if not universally, accepted. It certainly would be endorsed by the majority of the population of the planet, knowing by experience that such a statement is true. Indeed, this should be a basic principle of global governance if democracy/socialism is taken seriously, for there cannot be true democracy or socialism without the decolonization of both concepts. Decolonization of democracy and socialism would be to overcome both of them in building decolonial transdemocratic and transsocialist societies. For all human beings born equal, losing their equality is a humiliating experience. In the modern/colonial world, the humiliating experience has been infringed by coloniality: the colonial wound is both racial and patriarchal.

This time, instead of making Central Asia and the Caucasus the center from which our reflections emerge, our point of reference is the millenarian civilizations of the Americas at the moment they were interfered with and described and controlled by the Spaniards. And we keep Islam (e.g., the Moors) in consideration, since it also has been a point of differential reference for the European humanist to create the notion of Man and Humanity. Man and Human are European differential concepts on which the racial matrix was construed. We do not trace here the history of losing equality since the origin of the world (created by God or emerging from the Big Bang) but examine how, when, why, and which population of the planet was classified and ranked as Human. And above all, *who did it* and who has the legitimacy to classify and speak for all human beings. The classification and ranking was not a "representation" of an already existing world already classified and ranked. Someone invented and enacted the classification. Who did it and how was it legitimized? We also argue that the concept of Man and Human went hand in hand with the emergence of the concept of Rights. In other words, the idea of Human and the idea of Rights both separately and in conjunction have been invented by humanists of the European Renaissance, responding, on the one hand, to the internal history of Western Christianity in what would become Europe in their long-lasting conflicts with Islam and, on the other hand, to an external history of Christianity, indeed a beginning of a historical process with no precedent: the emergence of the New World and new people that forced Renaissance humanists to review their epistemic premises and forced Indigenous intellectuals in Anahuac and Tawantinsuyu, as well as leaders and thinkers of enslaved Africans in the New World to make sense of a history of which they were the real origin: cut off from African histories, enslaved Africans had to start anew in the New World. This is the initial moment in which massive number of people began to loose their equality, their humanness, and their rights.

It shall be repeated, until it is naturalized, that concepts such as Man and Humanity were inventions of European humanists of the fifteenth and sixteenth centuries, an invention that served them well for several purposes. Man and Human are not categories of thought ontologically embedded in entities that have been conceptualized as Man and Human. Both concepts are relational, and the relations in question are based on racial hierarchies. And we know that racial hierarchies are not embedded in people or regions but are an invention of imperial knowledge. Consequently, the universality of both concepts is a pretense and a mirage of the locus of enunciation that asserts the universality of its enunciation; it is an imperial invention that hides its foundation in a relational ontology (racism) and claims that is founded in an essential ontology (humanitas). Because the enunciation was not taken into account, scholars, activists, and politicians have written hundreds of pages about the quarrel of the universal and the particular in the enunciated. A mute point indeed when we shift the geography of reasoning and decolonize Western epistemology. Although the planet was populated by living organisms standing in two extremities, using their hands freely, their brain to communicate and organize in communities and build sophisticated civilizations, all over the planet, there was nothing "essentially human" in the sense that Renaissance philosophers, following on Greek legacies, selected a portion of that population and labeled them "animal rationals," that is, "human." The inhabitants of Anáhuac and Tawantinsuyu did not know that they were being observed and ranked in a classificatory order of which they were not aware and not invited to discuss.

First, then, European humanists introduced the concept of Man to detach themselves (humanists) from the control of the Church and the principles of divine law. For the Church, being Christian counted more than belonging to the class of Man. Humanists began to twist that belief toward a secular idea of humanity. Second, by inventing the idea of Man, the humanists distinguished themselves from coexisting communities they perceived as a threat, challenge, or enemies: Saracens or Easterners and pagans or rustic religions served to establish the difference with Man. These two terms are already revealing: He, the humanist (because it was always a He), who placed himself in relation to the Saracens or Easterner placed himself as Westerner. Westerner then defined the locus of enunciation (not as geohistorically and geopolitically located but as the enunciation of the universal). Easterners became instead the enunciated, to whom the enunciation was denied. Westerners were able to secure the control knowledge and legitimize their universal authority to name without being named in return. He (the humanist) who defined the pagans assumed that his own religion (Christianity, in this case) was the point of reference and the most sophisticated religion in relation to more rustic religions, the pagans. He (the humanist) who named and described the heathen anchored his locus of enunciation in Christianity and Judaism, since "heathen" was used to refer and describe all those who were neither Christian nor Jews. Here, we enter the terrain in which learning to unlearn in order to relearn is of the essence.

We have no doubt that the ones who were labeled as such by Christians and humanists of the Renaissance did not see themselves as pagans, heathens, and Saracens. They were classified, certainly, but being classified by others does not mean that one is what the classifier wants that person to be. First of all, the Arab-speaking population in the East of Jerusalem and in the South of the Mediterranean, on the one hand, and the Latin- and vernacular-speaking population in the West of Jerusalem and North of the Mediterranean did not share the same history, memories, subjectivities, experiences. What we have here, in Western classification, is just half of the story—the regional and provincial history told by Western Christians and Renaissance humanists. However, the Latin and Western vernacular categories have been naturalized in a one-to-one correspondence with the designated entity. I (Walter) am writing this paragraph inhabiting the Latin and Western vernacular cosmology (which is not Madina's dwelling), not in its smooth and uninterrupted history form Athens and Rome, but in its discontinuity: the discontinuity of Western classical tradition disrupted by the emergence of the New World in the consciousness of Western Europeans. Christians repeated with the population of the New World what they had been practicing with their undesirable neighbors and faraway coexisting populations (the Far East, where Marco Polo went): They named as Indians all the inhabitants of the New World and Black people in Africa and enslaved Africans in the New World.

Being and feeling oneself Western Christian meant also having "dominium" over the enunciation (and thus having the right to classify) and assuming that whatever was named and conceived according to Greco-Latin principles and categories of knowledge corresponded to how the world really was. Here, we encounter the regional enunciation that not only pretends to have captured the Universal but indeed invented it. For, the Universal did not preoccupy most of the civilization of the planet before the expansion of Western theology and secular epistemology. The problem is that the force of this belief is with us today, thus, another instance in which learning to unlearn is of the essence. In sixteenth century historiographical treatises, it is often stated that history is made of word and things, an assumption that was analyzed by Michel Foucault. Humanists felt authorized to speak for Man and the Human. The warranty of such belief was religious and epistemological—religious, because it was stated in biblical narratives (which was the dictation of God), and epistemological, because Saint Thomas Aquinas (1224–1275), who brought together Greek philosophy and biblical narratives, framed religious belief in logico-philosophical arguments. Needless to say, while Western Christians in the fifteenth and the sixteenth centuries were demonizing differences that allowed them to create their own identity as Western Christians, Muslims from Africa to Central Asia were living their lives and doing their deeds in the same way as communities and societies in China and India.

It was not quite the same, however, for the communities and societies of Anahuac and Tawantinsuyu. Since the first half of the sixteenth century, they could no longer continue living their lives as they were before that time. Kingdoms of Africa that were broken by the kidnapping and enslavement of their young population and Black communities in America had to rebuild, overcoming the differences of their original Kingdom. It was force and violence on the part of Western Christians and merchants (Portugal, Spain, Holland, France, England), but it was mainly the growing power of their own locus of enunciation that allowed themselves to assume that there was just one God and that they were His representatives on earth. At the top of the human species (humanitas) were Western Christians and placed below the rest: Saracens, Heathens, Pagans, Indians, and Blacks. The assumption here is the belief in the absolute possession and control of knowledge and the denial of it to all the people classified outside and below.

Thus, when the idea and the category of Man came into the picture, it came with a privilege: the privilege of being under the framework already created by Western Christians. If being Christian was, for Christians themselves, the ultimate point of reference of civility and the correct life, then being Man was the ultimate point of reference of beauty, morality, and knowledge for the humanists. Man and Humanities updated the Roman idea of *humanitas* and the sphere of learning. *Humanitas* and *Civitas* (close to the modern idea of citizens) presupposed an educated person. During the European Renaissance, Man was conceived at the intersection of his body and his mind, his body proportion and his intellect. Leonardo da Vinci's *Vitruvian Man* translated into visual language what humanists were portraying in words (Leonardo da Vinci 2009) Man and *humanitas* became the frame of reference allowing the enunciator inscribed in Greco-Latin genealogy of thought to decide who belonged (not just to Christianity) but to Humanity.

During the European Renaissance He who spoke for the Human was the humanist.

II. He Who Spoke for the Human Spoke Also for Rights

In the European Renaissance, the question of "rights" was indistinguishable from he question of "law": divine and natural law. *Jus gentium* served well both to talk about the "rights of the nation" and "international law." However, the question of "rights" became one of the key concepts of international law in the construction of the modern/colonial world and the formation of the colonial matrix of power. The works of Castilian Dominican Francisco de Vitoria (in the mid-sixteenth century) and Dutch jurist Hugo Grotious, are truly founders of a new type of discourse that German political and legal philosopher Carl Schmitt described as *Jus Publicum Europaeum* ([1952] 2003).

The distinction between divine and natural law came from the Roman Empire and the influential works of Cicero. The question of "rights" is properly a question of the modern/colonial world and not of ancient Rome and, even less, ancient Greece. The question of "rights" was inaugurated by and of the historical foundation of modern colonialism—the initial moment of imperial/colonial expansion of the Western world and the "spread" of the ideal of being Christian, the ideal Man and, by the eighteenth century, the ideas of citizen and democracy. From the sixteenth century to the Universal Declaration of Human Rights, He who speaks for the Human is an actor embodying the Western ideal of being Christian, being Man, and being Human. In other words, the "human" in Human Rights is a racial (that is, hierarchical in relation to the standard model of Man and Humanity) invention of Western imperial knowledge rather than the name of an existing entity to which everyone has access, too. Being an invention of Western knowledge means that the idea of Man and Human is controlled by certain categories of thoughts entrenched in particular, regional history and experience—for a Jamaican woman like Sylvia Wynter, the idea and ideal of what does it mean to be Human certainly differs from the same question asked and responded to by Francesco Petrarch, for example.[67]

It is precisely in this regard that "Human" is a Western differential (e.g., vis-à-vis lesser humans) and fictional (e.g., not based on a preexisting essence of humanity) concept based on Greek and Latin categories and translated into modern European vernacular languages (Italian, Spanish, Portuguese, German, French, and English) controls (e.g., owns) the concept of Human. It is not a concept based on Aymara or Mandarin categories of thought and even less based on the "essence" of living organism standing on two legs. If you want to dispute it from the genealogy of thought of Arabic, Urdu, Russian, Aymara, Bambara, or any other language and experience embedded in non-Western history or indirectly related to Western categories of thought (and "indirection" here refers to imperial expansion and colonization), you would have two options: to bend and accept what is Human according to Western knowledge (grounded in Greek and Latin, i.e., not in Greek and Arabic); or you could prefer to delink, to engage in epistemic disobedience, denouncing the provincialism of the universal and engage in a collective, differential, planetary assumption that being Human is not being Vitruvian, Christian, or Kantian but being able first to dispute the imperial definition of humanity and second to engage in building communities and societies in which Human is not defined, rhetorically affirming that we are all equal, but Human is what comes out of building societies on principles that prevent classification and ranking to justify domination and exploitation among people who are supposed to be equal by birth. If you decide for this second option, do not attempt to provide a new truth, a new definition of what it means to be Human that corrects the mistakes of previous definitions of the "human." Since there is no such entity, the second option would be decolonial, that is, it moves away (delinks) from the imperial consequences of a standard model for the human, humanity, and the related ideal of civilization. If you choose this option, it does not mean that you accept that you are not human and you are also a barbarian. On the contrary, placing yourself in the space that imperial discourse gave to lesser humans, uncivilized and barbarians, you would argue for radical interventions from the perspective of those who have been made barbarians, abnormal and uncivilized. That is, you argue for justice and equality from the perspective and interests of those who lost their equality and have been subjected to injustices.

"Rights," then, emerged in the process of building what today is conceived as the modern/colonial world; that is, "rights" is a concept responding to imperial necessity. I sketch three moments of the trajectory of "rights" and conclude by showing that "human rights" today continues to be an imperial, tool at the same time that it became a site to fight for injustices qualified as "violations of human rights." In other words, while we should praise the appropriation of the declaration of human rights by actors and institutions who engaged in dangerous enterprise in the defense of human rights, we do not lose sight of their use to advance imperial agendas. "Humanitarian interventions," which entered the vocabulary of international relations in the past decades, brings back to the present the generally forgotten history of human and rights (Hinkelammert 2004).

II.1

In the first stage, the question of "rights" was treated as belonging to people or nations (e.g., communities of birth, *nation*). Theological and legal theorists at the University of Salamanca, in the sixteenth century, began to address such questions, prompted by the "apparition" (pretty much like the apparition of Virgin Mary) on the intellectual horizon of Western Christians, of people who were not accounted for in biblical narratives. Led by Dominican Francisco de Vitoria, one of the main issues was to solve the problem of *jus gentium,* rights of people or of nations. The question of "natural, divine law and human law" were not new issues; both had a tradition in Christian theology and were laid out by Saint Thomas Aquinas. What is crucial here is not so much the "novelty" within the same classical European tradition (that is, the newness within a unilinear and universal idea of history) but the *discontinuity*—the moment in which the Western genealogy of thoughts that men of the European Renaissance were attempting to build on the legacies of Greece and Rome, was *dislocated* by the emergence of people totally outside Greek-Roman (and Hebrew Jerusalem) legacies. Vitoria had to deal then with the authority of the Pope and the authority of the monarch. He questioned the authority of the Pope, who arrogated himself the power to appropriate and to "give" half of the New World to the Spaniards and half to the Portuguese and the emperor. A second issue Vitoria had to deal with was the relation between "belief" and "right to property." He argued that unbelief does not cancel natural law, and since ownership and dominion are based on natural law, the right to property is not invalidated by unbelief. Indians are not believers, but because of natural law, they have, like the Spaniards, property rights. Vitoria's openness and fairness missed a crucial point: He did not stop to ponder whether Indians care about rights and whether Indians' relationship to land was a relation of property, like the Spaniards, and not something else. In other words, as a good humanist and theologian, Vitoria spoke for Humanity and told half of the story without realizing it, assuming, indeed, that he (and his colleagues) was dealing with the world as is and not as it was for him or them.

The logic of Vitoria's argument was flawless. The premises are suspect. Why would Vitoria assume that Aztecs and Incas (whom he referred to as "Indians") and other communities in the New World would have the same "avarice" toward property as Spanish Christians? Why he did not stop to think for a minute that life and economy, among the inhabitants of the New World, was organized on different principles? He did not. And, therefore, the next step was to justify the rights of the Spaniards to dispose "Indians" (not

Aztecs or Incas) of the "property" that Indians did not have because they did not conceive their relation to land as "property." Remember, "Indians" have property rights, and the question was how to find a way to legitimize Spaniards' appropriation of Indian properties having acknowledged that Indians had property rights. There were two positions among Spanish men of letters about the "nature" (humanity) of the Indians. For the most conservative, Indians were irrational, dirty, immature, barbarians and so forth. For more progressive men of letters, like Dominicans Bartolomé de Las Casas and Francisco de Vitoria himself, Spaniards and "Indians" (and not for them Nahuatls-, Aymara-, Quechua-, Tojolabal-, speaking people) were rational in their own way. Both Spaniards and Indians were bound by a system of natural law; therefore, both Spaniards and Indians were subjected to *jus gentium* (natural law of the people or nations). However, there was something "lacking" among the Indians that placed them in an inferior echelon vis-à-vis Spaniards.

As far as he was Spaniard and not Aymara or Tojolabal, Vitoria managed to articulate the *legal colonial difference,* based on his control of knowledge (e.g., his assumptions on the principle of argumentations as well as the belief that whatever questions were relevant for the Spaniards were also relevant for Indians because his questions were universal).

Siba N'Zatioula Grovogui explored some issues concerning the historical foundation of international law. His summary runs parallel to the analysis of the historical foundation of the colonial matrix of power, for international law is the instrument to ensure the control of authority in international relations.

> I seek to demonstrate that the dependence of international politics on the European dominated political economy and its legal apparatus resulted in two of the most significant paradoxes of decolonization: The first is that only the rights sanctioned by the former colonialists were accorded to the colonized, regardless of the needs and demands of the latter ... The second paradox is that the rules and procedures of decolonization were determined and controlled by the former colonial power to effect specific outcomes. This is a paradox because *the rights to self-determination* is generally understood to mean *the absolute political authority to create rights and obligations for oneself* ... The rules and processes of decolonization not only denied African communities the right to the protection of the law, *they failed to recognize African's need for such protection.* (1995: 96)

There is a straight line, to which we return in the next two sections, in the history interrelating the concept of people, men, citizens, human, and rights, from the *colonial revolution* of the sixteenth century to the *decolonial revolutions* of the second half of the twentieth century (starting with India in 1947). Although Grovogui starts his argument with Hugo Grotius (which is a common beginning for scholars of international law in the English- and French-speaking worlds), it is obvious for most scholars in the Spanish and Portuguese worlds[68] that his two paradoxes are nothing else than two cases of the constitutive and complementary character of modernity/coloniality. What appears as paradox is, and has been, the node, the technological key of the simultaneity, always simultaneity, between the rhetoric of modernity announcing salvation, happiness, progress, development, and the like, and the necessary logic of coloniality, appropriation of natural resources, exploitation of labor, legal control of undesirables, military enforcements of the law to ensure "salvation" through the imposition the interests and worldview inherent to capitalist economy.

II.2

The second moment has been self-fashioned and enacted between the Glorious Revolution in England (and the Bill of Rights), at the end of the seventeenth century, and American (Virginia Declaration of Rights, 1776; the English Bill of Rights, 1689), and the French Revolutions (The Rights of Man and of Citizen, 1789), at the end of the eighteenth century. The main difference between the centuries in which the Bill of Rights and The Rights of Man and of Citizens came to the foreground and the century of Vitoria (in Spain) and Grotius (in Holland), for whom *jus gentium* was integral to the historical foundation of international law, was that the pronunciation that the Bill of Rights and The Rights of Man and of Citizen were no longer intervening in an international arena but, instead, limited to national issues. It was indeed the period in which nation-states were being forged and the advent of the bourgeois ethno-class being legitimized. "Rights" were linked to the construction of nation-states and the coming into being and stabilization of an ethno-class commonly known as the European bourgeoisie. Being Human meant to be rational, and rationality was limited to what philosophers and political theorists of the Enlightenment said it was.

By the end of the seventeenth century, being Human became identified more with being secular bourgeois than with being Christian. That was the Man of the "Right of Man." However, being Christian did not vanish; it remained in the background. Exteriority was no longer a problem. The battle had been already won and the energy was concentrated on an idea of Humanity that was recast as The Rights of Man and of Citizen after the French Revolution. "Nations," in the emerging nation-states displaced the idea of "nation" (*gentium*) in Vitoria and Grotius. A new figure of exteriority was necessary when the concept of "citizen" was introduced: The "foreigner" enriched the list of "exterior Human," that is, of "defective Humans" next to pagan, Saracens, Blacks, Indians, women, and those with nonnormative sexual preferences. The Enlightenment idea and ideal of Man and Humanity was adopted and adapted in the colonies. The so-called American Revolution was in the hands of White men of British descent. They did not have yet the problem of the "foreigner" as in Europe, but the Founding Fathers had the problem of Indian and Black populations, which of course Europe did not have. In other words, Man and Human in the U.S. were defined at the crossroad of British and European philosophy and in contradistinction with Indians and Blacks surrounding the Founding Fathers.

In South America (Spanish and Portuguese colonies and ex-colonies), the situation was similar to that of the U.S. but with significant differences. The similarity was that independence was in the hands of White men of European descent (Spain and Portugal). Leaders of independence movements and nation-state builders of continental South America and the Ibero-Caribbean, too, conceived Man and Humanity in the European tradition and in contradistinction with Indians (mainly continental Spanish America) and Blacks (mainly Brazil and the Caribbean). However, in the dominant discourse of northern European ranking of Man and Human, Spain and Portugal, and their nationals, were already considered second-class Europeans. Immanuel Kant and George W. F. Hegel canonized this view. In short, by the eighteenth century, who spoke for the Human were secular philosophers and political theorists in the heart of Europe (France, Germany, and England). That vision was adopted by creoles of European descent in the U.S., South America, and the Caribbean. And, that vision became constitutive also of the model of Man and Humanity when England and France began their expansion to Asia and Africa. "The civilizing mission" was nothing else but (a) imposing a model of Man and Humanity and (b) assuming (after Kant's and Hegel's canonization) that not only were non-Christian religions inferior but people of color who spoke languages not derived from Greek and Latin were less Human. The Roman legacy of *humanitas* and *civitas* were rehearsed when European men and citizens appointed themselves to carry civilization to the *anthropos* of the planet.[69]

II.3

This view did not go away with the Universal Declaration of Human Rights in 1948. All the talks, problems, and dramas of immigration in the European Union and the U.S. cannot be properly understood, and obviously addressed, without asking who speaks for the Human in the modern/colonial world and cast immigrants in different scales of the subhuman. Old racial categories are being recast when it is no longer the colonist who encounters the anthropos, but the anthropos that is knocking at the door of the colonist in his imperial home.

"Human" in the Universal Declaration was redefined according to a changing world order and the change of hands in imperial leadership, from England to the U.S. Subsuming the nation-state stage of the Bills of Rights and the Rights of Man and Citizen, the Universal Declaration returns to the arena of interstate relations and international law set up by Vitoria and Grotius. In fact, for Grotius, distinct from Vitoria, the problem of international law was twofold: On the one hand, international law meant inter-Europe and Dutch colonies in the East. He was living and writing in the middle of the Thirty Years Religious War. And, at the same time, he was sitting, literally, on Holland's imperial reach in its short-lasting but quite influential imperial moment. Grotius and Descartes, indeed, were in Amsterdam when Holland was gaining its imperial momentum. Grotious' *Mare Liberum* could have been named "universal declaration of rights to the sea in international law." Vitoria did not label the issue he was discussing "universal declaration of rights and international law," but that is what he was doing: defining and profiling the Human by tracing the colonial difference, epistemic and ontological.

After the interregnum of nation-state building in Europe and nation-state imperial expansion (mainly England and France), the Declaration was forged with three horizons in mind, under the leadership of the U.S.: (a) the rebuilding of Europe after the Holocaust and World War II; (b) the "Communist menace," which were added to the old list of pagans, Saracens, Indians, Blacks, and now Communists; and (c) the uprising in the Third World, of which the independence of India was already a strong sign of alert. The bombing of Hiroshima was seldom mentioned next to the Holocaust and Stalin's crimes against humanity, because the bombing was the event that brought "peace" and the end of World War II. The Ougtherson Commiesion Study estimated that 45,000 people out of a population of 255,000 were killed the first day; 19,000 died from radiation poisoning during the next fourth months. It is estimated that several hundred survivors will die of cancer and leukemia in the years to come. As for the Third World, the U.S. politics of foreign relations strongly supported self-determination of colonial locales. The motifs were not so much the right to self-determination but, rather, the U.S. global designs. Very much like the "independence" of South Americans from Spain and Portugal— to build a nation-state that under the fiction of sovereignty depended on France for knowledge, culture, and politics and on England for the economy—decolonized countries in Asia and Africa sooner or later moved under the arm of Uncle Sam.

The idea of "human" in the Universal Declaration was taken for granted: It had been already profiled in the Renaissance and rehearsed in the Enlightenment. What else could be said about what being "human" means? However, a geopolitical remapping took place, with the same hidden assumptions under which Renaissance humanists were operating. Parallel to the Universal Declaration, a reclassification of the planet was taking place: First, Second, and Third Worlds. By the 1970s, Indigenous people from all the Americas, New Zealand, and Australia made themselves heard: Where is our face, they asked, in this world order? A new category was invented to "please them": the Fourth World. Do you think indigenous people of the planet were happy to be a fourth-class global citizen? And, who is talking and celebrating, today, global citizenship? Frequent travelers, has been one answer.

"First World" looked like an objective category, the naming of an existing entity. What was hidden (as stated in the Introduction, Section II) was that the classification was made from the perspective of the First and not from the Second, Third, or Fourth World. The First World controlled the enunciation and therefore knowledge. It was and continues to be both the enunciator and a member of the classified world. Five hundred years separated political scientists and economists after World War II from Renaissance humanists. The logic, however, was exactly the same. Only the content changed. No more pagans, heathens, or Saracens, but Communists, underdeveloped, and—still!—Indians.

The First World was, and continues to be, the place where humanity par excellence dwells. That is why immigration is so disturbing. The rest was inhabited by different kinds of *anthropos*. Liberalism and Christianity set the ideological stage against Communism. Humanity par excellence was surrounded by the dangerous Second World, Communism, in the Soviet Union, in its colonies at the border of Europe (the Caucasus, Belarus, and Ukraine), in Central Europe and the Balkans. And, then, there was the Third World, further away from the model of humanity par excellence. But, since the Declaration of Human Rights was universal, the entire population of the planet has the rights to have rights. This was the First World's gift to the Second and

Third Worlds. But, it was a gift similar to stating that all men and women are born equal. People of the Second and Third Worlds were told that they have the right to have rights. However, they were also told that they were in the Second and Third World, that the latter were underdeveloped and the former were under a totalitarian regime—and that it was mainly in the land of the *anthropos* where it was expected human rights were to be violated. In the First World, there was a struggle among countries that would soon be part of the First World, countries that divided among themselves the entire African continent. Violation of human rights was not a question for Africans; after all, they clearly where not considered to be part of Humanity. It was in the Holocaust that, as Aimé Césaire remarked in 1955, the White man applied against White people the techniques of extermination that Europe learned and practiced through its colonial experience against people of color (that is, not quite human). Thus, at this moment and in this occasion, the question of Humanity was strictly entrenched in the decision to formulate the Universal Declaration of Human Rights. Previous genocides in the name of Christianization and the Civilizing Mission did not move the White Man to think about Universal Declaration of Human Rights.

In other words, the international order was mapped no longer in terms of *jus gentium* and international law but of *human rights*. Until 1989, one of the main functions of Human Rights was to watch closely their violations in Communist countries and countries of the Third World not aligned with the U.S. Human Rights. Violators are to be found, in general, in the non-European world (Second or Third World). That is, they are at the fringe of Humanity and violate the rights of people who are considered human for a while to chastise the non-European violator (generally State officers). However, human rights violators in the Third World (like corporations) are not considered to be violators of human rights but agents of progress and development. At that moment, the victims who protest against the exploitation of labor and contamination of nature are considered "rebels," that is, less than human, and they lose their rights to the corporations.

The violators or perpetrators of human rights were denounced, accused, and if possible penalized. The saviors, in the First World, defended the cause of democracy. It was mainly with Guantánamo and Abu-Grahib that the First World was caught as violator and perpetrator and no longer as—just—a savior. The difference with the Second and Third World was that the violation did not take place in the First World but in Third World territory. Humanity was not, it is not, a transcendental and neutral essence that anyone can appropriate and describe: Humanity has been created on philosophical and anthropological categories of Western thought and based on epistemic and ontological colonial differences. If someone else wants to use Human rights, that person has to specify what kind of Human he or she is. For example, "Indigenous rights" are predicated on the assumption of the difference: "Universal (or White Euro-American) Rights." However, by the sheer fact of naming a set of rights–say, "Indigenous rights"—it becomes clear that it cannot be universal rights and that what passes as universal is indeed "Euro-American White rights." That is, there are two "species" of the Human, by convention, which is spoken by everybody who wants to speak and locate her- or himself in a specific community of rights. *La Via Campesina* put on the table a ground-breaking concept of "right": Food and water are basic Human Rights. The new Constitution of Bolivia and Ecuador made similar claims—a conquest of Indigenous nations for whom water, nature, and food were never commodities but an integral part of living and being alive.[70] In that statement, the entire commercialization of food and water, the economic corporations—Western and transnationals—are called into question as basic violators of Human Rights that Human Rights organizations are not paying attention to: Human Rights has been restricted to politics and law not to the corporations that play the capitalist game of competition and economic gains. In a nutshell, since capitalist economy is based on private property and justified by expansion, growth, and development, anything that gets on the way (like the self-determination of farmers and peasants of the world), shall be eliminated. Thus, corporations incur in double violation of Human Rights: the commodification of life by converting food into a commodity (erasing the fact that food is a Human Right) and eliminating the agencies that act on the conviction and the principles that food and water are Human Rights.

When the Cold War ended, the defense of human rights took a new impulse and it was associated with the second wave of development, which soon turned out to be a project (development) that to be advanced must violate human rights. The first wave took place between 1950 and 1970, and the labels were "development and modernization of underdeveloped countries." The International Monetary Fund and World Bank were the two main institutions in charge of advancing the project. After the fall of the Soviet Union, development came back under the label of "globalization and market democracy."

Human Rights have been recast after the fall of the Soviet Union with one of its consequences: the Washington Consensus and the neoliberal doctrine. This scenario, that dominated the 1990s, was extended to deal with the consequences of 9/11's aftermath. The question of Islam and Human Rights then became central. Basically, the Washington Consensus—a doctrine of about ten points advanced by John Williamson in 1989 (Washington Consensus 2003)—was the second wave of "development and modernization" launched in the 1950s and ending around 1970. In the interregnum, Western rhetoric turned to "modernity" and "globalization," and in the 1990s, modernity and globalization were subsumed under the Washington Consensus. What does all of this have to do with Human and Rights? A lot, indeed.

It has been documented by many that the Washington Consensus and the neoliberal doctrine were a road to global disasters. One well-informed analysis is the classic book by Joseph Stiglitz, *Globalization and Its Discontent* (2002). Parallel to the implementation of the Washington Consensus, a significant expansion of Non-Governmental Organizations took place. Although civil society organizations to help the needy can be dated back to the mid-nineteenth century, it was officially established as a Non-Governmental Organization in 1945 within the charter of United Nations. As far as the growing influence of neoliberal doctrine increased, since Ronald Reagan and Margaret Thatcher, so increased its devastating consequences. NGOs proliferated. The Washington Consensus operated, at the economic level, in the same frame of mind that missionaries operated at the religious level in the sixteenth century. Conquering the soul of the Indians by conversion is equivalent to conquering the soul and labor of underdeveloped countries and people. The differences are also important: Conversion did not imply exploitation. Exploitation, in the sixteenth and seventeenth centuries, was the job of merchants, plantation owners, *encomenderos*, and gold and silver mine owners. However, at that time, they were not attempting to impose their economic behavior but just taking advantage and accumulating wealth.

Thus, parallel to the increase of poverty and widening of the line separating the haves from the have-nots, violations of human rights proliferated under damaging conditions. Whether leaders of the Washington Consensus and NGO officers see the connection or not, the fact remains that NGOs have been working to take care of damages inflicted by neoliberalism and the Washington Consensus. Both the Washington Consensus and NGOs are Western creations under the global mask of the United Nations. The proliferation of nationally based NGOs still depends on the master plan. In the same vein, the Washington Consensus managed to find and found their branches in the underdeveloped world (i.e., Menem in Argentina, Gonzalo Sánchez de Lozada in Bolivia). Consequently, both the Washington Consensus and NGOs were based in the ex–First World and their action directed mainly toward the ex–Second, Third, and Fourth Worlds. Or, if you wish, they were both institutions in the *humanitas* geared toward developing and taking care of the *anthropos*. The consequences of the logic of coloniality (disastrous consequences of the Washington Consensus doctrine) were sold and disguised by updating the rhetoric of modernity (development, market, and democracy). The injuries were inflicted by the logic of coloniality to advance what the rhetoric of modernity promised; someone has to take care of the damage. And, the NGOs were there to help the *anthropos*.

The situation reached a point in which the closed circuit of the rhetoric of modernity, the apparent collateral damages that indeed are the actual consequences of the logic of coloniality, prompted the emergence of a global political society taking destiny in their own hands. In other words, while NGOs operate in the sphere of civil society, repairing the damages of neoliberal capitalism, the political society came into being with a different horizon in mind: decoloniality. While NGOs work to help the *anthropos*, the political society is the *anthropos* in arms and thoughts. This very chapter is located in the sphere of the *anthropos* and of the political society. The concepts of Human, of Rights, of First and Third World, of developed and underdeveloped countries are called into question. Indeed, what are being called into question are not exactly these categories but the epistemic locus of enunciation that created them as if they were universal and good for all. What is being called into question is the saying behind the said. That is, it is a call and a process toward decolonization of knowledge and being, knowledge and being entrapped by the imperial and modern idea of Man, Human, and Humanities. If, then, the Humanities (a field of knowledge since the Renaissance) is in part responsible for the creation and maintenance of the concept of Human, the first step is to engage in decolonial Humanities. Or if you wish, decolonizing the Humanities is tantamount to engaging in practicing decolonial humanities (Transcultural Humanities 2006).

III. Decolonial Humanities and the Question of Rights

Contrary to the global order during the European Renaissance and Enlightenment, the relative success of Western empires to manage discontent today rests in the mainstream media that transforms other ways of thinking into pieces of information. The political society is marching next—and sometimes in confrontation—to the civil society and NGOs. Muslim and Aymara intellectuals are jumping on the debate about human, humanity, and rights. And scholars in the humanities and Chinese history are putting in conversation Confucianism and Human Rights. Afro-Caribbean philosophers are taking front stage. Global projects like *La via campesina* are following

Monsanto's step closer and proposing alternatives for the enhancement and preservation of life rather than initiatives for growth and accumulation and the fertilization of death.

What this means is that Human and Rights are no longer trusted to Western initiatives and its rhetoric of salvation. Decolonizing human rights means to take them out of imperial hands and institutions and place them in a global community of interests, not just the interest of the leading developed countries. Human and Rights have been placed in a different universe of discourse, that of the political society and decolonization. And, what all of this amounts to, with pros and cons that should be analyzed in each case, is that everyone is ready to speak for the Human and for Rights. The premise is to *change the terms and not just the content of the conversation.* To provide a "new" (and satisfy modernity's desire newness) will be more akin to the task of NGOs than to decolonial projects. When, for example, Jamaican intellectual and activist Sylvia Wynter outlined the horizon "after man, toward the human," statement in which the story I told previously is implied, we are already in a change of terrain in our conversation about "what does it mean to be Human" (Wynter's question). Once we asked this question, the one about the rights will follow: What kind of social, legal, and economic organization is required to secure the "rights" of human beings? Who in that society are the violators? Is it possible to think of social organizations in which "human rights" is not necessary because there is no violator? What, if not a society organized on domination and exploitation to produce more and to succeed, can be the "perpetrator" of rights violations and creator of a concept of Human that legitimizes him or her as "savior" when indeed it is a "perpetrator"?

The idea of human, humanity, and rights became a contested arena. The "victims" are not always waiting for the "savior," and the "savior" willingly may or not may work to the benefit of the "perpetrator." Taking their destinies in their own hands, political society's diversity of projects involve actors whose experiences and subjectivities do not match the expectations of NGOs or peripheral European economic investments. Some actors place themselves in the wide array of imperial interests, now widespread.

On another level, that of the nation-states (instead of the sphere of the civil and political society), current conflicts between the U.S. and the European Union, on the one hand, and Russia, China, Iran, India, and Brazil, on the other, are conflicts between two types of nation-states: Western nation-states embedded in imperial history congruent with capitalist economy and nation-states encountering capitalism. A polycentric capitalist world is emerging. The principles of a capitalist economy are the same, but national histories, sensibilities, desires, tensions, and anger with Western imperial arrogance makes the same economic logic be put at the services of particular interests, national or regional. Responses are not always manifested in diplomatic wars among country leaders visiting each other and in many summits among the G7 or G8 or at the United Nations Security Council. Violence, as Frantz Fanon convincingly argued, is a necessary response to violence. The question of human rights emerges here as a place in which the so-called democratic and industrialized states use the rhetoric of human rights violations to confront their economic rivals. Western expansion and capitalist economy is a terrain of "capitalist contention" today. In that contention, a polycentric capitalist world order goes hand in hand with a polycentric discourse on Human and Rights in non-Western histories and sensibilities that cut across Western history of the idea of Human and Rights from the European Renaissance to World War II. The distinction made previously between civil society and NGOs, on the one hand, and political society, on the other hand, is also valid for the following analysis. China has not only built a powerful economy; it is building a powerful discourse unveiling the double standards of Western discourse on human rights.

The political society has been and continues to be formed by dissenters and activists whose goal is not to remedy the damages of the capitalist economy in order to make its functioning smoother but to delink from that system of belief and work toward a society built not on principles of accumulation and the belief that the more produced, the better it is for "the people." There already is enough evidence sustaining and justifying the directions (decolonial, I would say) of the political society.

Let us make clear that the political society cannot be subsumed under decolonial processes. Many sectors and projects advanced in the political society have visions and horizons that are not decolonial: theology of liberation, Marxism, or progressive liberalism. Having said that, it is imperative to remember that the decolonial option (or decolonial options, if you prefer the plural) is *not* the new and only game in town. It is called "option" precisely because it is an option among others. The purpose of decolonial thinking is not to debunk concurrent projects but to capture more converts and become the one and only. Pluriversality, and not universality, is the horizon of decolonial thinking. Under decolonial processes projects are under way, are emerging and proliferating all over the world and delinking from the major spheres of dissension in the West (liberation theology, progressive and critical liberalism, Marxism; white feminism, and white queer activists). Decolonial projects and the political society join forces when the horizon and the vision are guided by the struggle for liberation from Western control of the economy (control of labor and natural resources), authority, knowledge, subjectivity, gender, and sexuality.

Decolonial humanities (or the decolonial option within the humanities) is coming into sight as a consequence and out of the demands of the decolonial political society).[71] Decolonial Humanities assumes, in the first place, that the humanities has been and continues to be a fundamental dimension of Western scholarship. Second, it is assumed that the Humanities (as a set of disciplinary formations) are bound to the Renaissance concept of Human and the Enlightenment concept of Reason. In Western genealogy of thought, the Humanities have a double face: On the one hand, under the name of Humanities, art, literature, philosophy, and to certain degree the social sciences flourished in the West and enchanted the non-Western world. On the other hand, the Humanities were the epistemic site in which it was possible, for social actors, to speak for the human. The humanities naturalized, in the modern/colonial world, the distinction has been brilliantly summarized and argued by Japanese scholar Nishitani Osami (2006), the long-lasting distinction, since the sixteenth century, between *humanitas* and *anthropos*.

Osami's argument can be recast (I hope without causing violence to it) in the language and the purposes of decolonial humanities. The decolonial humanities project is not to take on a new definition of the Human, a definition that *includes* (inclusion is off decolonial discourse) everybody and presents decolonial thinking as *the* point of arrival. Decolonial thinking, in this sense, is naturally non-Hegelian. What the decolonial option proposes, and Osami's article clearly illustrates, is that (a) the concepts of Man, Human, and Humanity are inventions of Western scholarship since the Renaissance; (b) these concepts have links to the concept of Rights, which is also a European Renaissance invention in its colonial expansion (e.g., its darker side); (c) in a world order of polycentric capitalist economies, the concepts of Man, Human, and Humanity became also a polycentric dispute at the level of states (Jordan, Iran, France) and international institutions that followed up after Mohammad Khatami, former president of Iran, who launched the project *Dialogue among Civilizations* to counter Samuel Huntington's *Clash of Civilizations* (Afrasiabi 2006). UNESCO, in 2005, formed a truly international committee, the Alliance of Civilizations (Alliance of Civilizations 2009), whose main charge has been to work toward peace. UNESCO's project is not the only one. Prince Hassan of Jordan has been leading a similar project under the name of *Dialogue of Civilizations,* which follows after Khatami's pronunciation. In the Middle East, Prince Hassan is concerned mainly with dialogue between Muslims, Jews, and Christians All these projects are, I repeat, unfolding at the level of states and institutions of international scope (Dialogue with the Islamic World 2009).

Decolonial projects are closer to grassroots movements than to state and institutions in which, directly or indirectly, the question of Human, Humanity, and Rights is being redressed—which of course does not mean that collaboration between decolonial and state institutional are not possible. It means only that these two kinds of projects operate at different levels: one at the level of state-related institutions and the civil society; the other in the sphere of the political society, where new institutions shall be created.

In decolonial thinking, peace, a peaceful world, a peaceful society require two main conditions:

a. To delink from capitalist economy, organized societies, nationally and internationally.
b. To accept, even if for the ruling minority it will be a hard act to follow, that indeed the vast majority of marginalized human beings are human as well as the privileged economic and political elites, nationally and internationally.

If these two conditions are fulfilled, no one in particular will speak for the Human because the Human will just be taken for granted. And, in such societies, there would be no need for Rights, because there will be no perpetrators violating Human Rights and Life Rights, where the victim is directly the planet and indirectly a limited species of the living that has been cast as Humanity. The ideas of man and humanity, as articulated in Western discourse since the sixteenth century, from Francisco de Vitoria to John Locke to the Universal Declaration of Human Rights, went hand in hand with Francis Bacon's conceptualization of Nature as something that has to be controlled and dominated by Man.

In sum, decolonial thinking is not arrogating on itself the legitimacy of talking for the Human, as the last word, but proposing that there is no need for some specific one to talk about the Human, because Human is what we are talking about. However, what lingers upon us are five hundred years of epistemic and ontological racism constructed by imperial discourses and engrained in the last five hundred years of planetary history (not global, because global reproduces the unidimensional view of history).

CHAPTER 6

Thinking Decolonially

Citizenship, Knowledge, and the Limits of Humanity

I.

In Chapter 3, it was noted that nation building in Central Asia and the Caucasus posses a particular problem of citizenship:

> The inhabitants of Central Asia or the Caucasus, who are so much hated by xenophobic Russians and constitute a larger part of the labor migration today, go mainly to Russia and not to the West (which is possible only for the chosen few) looking for jobs and better life, because in the modern global configuration of power, entering the world economic system as labor force is still impossible. These people can get to Europe or the U.S. through human trafficking or as organ donors, because only for these kinds of activities have the borders become more permeable today if one is an ex-Soviet colonial other. (Chapter 3, section V)

To further explore the relevance of the trickster, it would be useful to revisit the concept of citizenship in a decolonial frame and in Western political culture. In this chapter, we expand on several issues touched upon in the previous one.

When the idea of "citizenship" came into view—and was linked to the materialization and formation of the nation-state in secular northern

Europe—it enforced the formation of communities of birth instead of communities of faith. But, at that time, the imperial and colonial differences were already in place, and both were recast in the new face of Western empires. The figure of the "citizen" presupposed an idea of the "human" that had already been formed during the Renaissance and was one of the constitutive elements of the colonial matrix of power. Henceforth, there was a close link between the concept of Man (standing for human being) and the idea of Humanities as the major branch of higher learning in both European universities and their branches in the colonies (the universities of Mexico and Peru were founded in the 1550s, Harvard in 1636).[72] If Man stood for human being (at the expense of women, non-Christians, people of color, and homosexuals), the Humanities as high branch of learning was modeled on the concept and assumptions of the *humanity* that, in turn, was modeled on the example of *man*. Our goal in this chapter, therefore, is to explore the hidden connections between the imaginary of citizenship, the coloniality of being, and the coloniality of knowledge. Control of knowledge (the coloniality of knowledge) was absolutely necessary to build an imaginary where citizens were defined and noncitizens were cast as the difference (coloniality of being). We describe the veiled connections as the logic of coloniality, and the surface that covers it, we describe as the rhetoric of modernity. The rhetoric of modernity is that of salvation, whereas the logic of coloniality is the logic of imperial oppression. The unfinished project of modernity carries over its shoulders the unfinished project of coloniality. We conclude by suggesting the need to decolonize "knowledge" and "being," advocating that the (decolonial) "humanities" has a fundamental role to play in this process. Truly, "global citizenship" implies overcoming the imperial and colonial differences that have mapped and continue to map global racism and global patriarchy. Changing the law and public policies is not of much help in this process. What is needed is that those who change the law and public policy change themselves.

The problem is how such changes may take place if we would like to avoid the missionary zeal for conversion; the liberal and neoliberal belief in the triumphal march of Western civilization and market democracy; and the moral imperatives and forced behavior imposed by socialism. As we do not believe in a new abstract universal that will be good for the entire world, the question is how people can change their belief that the world today is like it is said to be and that only through the "honest" projects of Christians, liberals, and Marxists/Socialists could it be better for all, and citizenship will be a blessing for all.

The changes we are thinking about are radical transformations in the naturalized assumptions of the world order. The naturalized assumptions in question are imperial/colonial (not universal), and they have shaped the world in which we live over the past five hundred years, when Christianity and capitalism came together and created the conditions for the self-fashioned narrative of "modernity." Hence, the transformations we are thinking about require an epistemic decolonial shift. Not a "new," a "post," or a "neo," which are all changes within the same modern colonial epistemology, but a "decolonial" (and not either a "deconstruction"), which means a delinking from the rules of the game (said many times) (e.g., the decolonization of the mind, in Ngugi Wa Th'iongo's vocabulary) in which deconstruction itself and all the "posts-" for sure are caught. Delinking does not mean being "outside" of either modernity or the Christian, liberal, capitalist, and Marxist hegemony but to disengage from the naturalized assumptions that make of these four macro-narratives "une pensée unique," to use Ignacio Ramonet's expression.[73] The decolonial shift begins by unveiling the imperial presuppositions that maintain a universal idea of humanity and human being that serves as a model and point of arrival and by constantly underscoring the fact that oppressed and racialized subjects do not care and are not fighting for "human rights" (based on an imperial idea of humanity) but to regain the "human dignity" (based on a decolonial idea of humanity) that has and continues to be taken away from them by the imperial rhetoric of modernity (e.g., White, Eurocentered, heterosexual, and Christian/secular). The conditions for citizenship are still tied down to a racialized hierarchy of human beings that depends on universal categories of thought created and enacted from the identitarian perspectives of European Christianity and by White men In the Afro-Caribbean intellectual tradition, the very concepts of the human and humanity are constantly under fire.[74] Would indeed a Black person agree with the idea that what "we" all have in common is our "humanity" and that we are "all equal" in being "different"? I would suspect for one would suspect that the formula would rather be of the type advanced by the Zapatistas: "[B]ecause we are all equal we have the right to be different."[75] The universal idea of humanity is not the same from the perspective of Black history, Indian memories, or the memories of the population of Central Asia.

The humanities, as a branch of knowledge in the history of the university since the European Renaissance have always been complicitous with imperial/colonial designs celebrating a universal idea of the human model (see Chapter 7). The moment has arrived to engage (and to further the process of learning to unlearn in order to relearn) the humanities in decolonial projects in their ethical, political, and epistemic dimensions. To recast the re-inscription of human dignity as a decolonial project in the hands of the *damnés* rather than given to them through managerial designs of NGOs and Human Rights Watch, which seldom if ever are led by actors whose human dignity is at stake. Decolonial projects imply downsizing human rights to its real dimension: an ethical imperative internal to imperial abuses but not really a project that empowers racialized subjects and helps them to regain the human dignity that racism and imperial projects (from the right, the left, and the center) took away from them.

II. The Myth of Global Citizenship

Those of you who have the tendency to trace History to its initial moment and the origin of Humans on earth would find that people have always moved across lands and seas and across continents. However, people moving around the globe before the sixteenth century did not have a "global view" of the globe as we have today, thanks to the world map drawn by Gerardus Mercator and Abraham Ortelius.[76] Furthermore, there are no traces in the long and hazy past of wandering human beings (and wandering living organisms) in which they had to show passports at the frontiers or that there were clear, delineated frontiers. Frontiers that demand passports do not have the same long history of getting lost in the hazy times of the human species. Citizens, foreigners, and passports are part of a short history of the same package that constructed an imperial idea of the "human" and traced the frontiers with "the less humans" and the "nonhumans." The paradigm of the "human" defined by Christian men of letters during the Renaissance became the paradigm of the "citizen" defined by secular philosophers during the European Enlightenment. "Citizens" is the frame that allowed for the definition of the "foreigner," which was the translation, in secular terms, of Christianity's "Pagans" and "Gentiles." Members of the community of faith did not need passports or the administrative identity that was required of citizens (name, birthday, town of residence, and—as technology and urbanization developed—street name and number, driver's license, and telephone number).

If one is stubborn and persists in finding antecedents of citizens as social entities or citizen as a concept, and in that task the origin of humanity proves to be a difficult point of reference, one could take a shortcut back to Roman history and the idea of *civitas* and most likely develop from there an argument showing how the idea of the city and its dwellers, the citizens, evolved.

And, most likely, a large percentage of historians looking at the history of humanity from that "universal" point of origin would jump from Roman *civitas* and the birth of citizenship to the post–French Revolution and find that the citizens are fully grown up and ready to go. The Kantian cosmopolitan citizen was ready to march all over the world—starting from France, England, and Germany (Kant's paradigmatic example of *civitas*, reason, and sensibility) and move at his will (because the idea of the citizen was modeled first at the image of Man), through the globe.[77]

But, let us try another route, neither that of the hazy past of humanity nor that of the partial and provincial Roman origins. Miguel León-Portilla, a well-known scholar of Anahuac (Eurocentered scholarship refers to pre-Columbian Mexico instead of Anahuac) and the transformations of Aztec civilization during the Spanish colonial period, explored the meaning of the word "*Toltecáyotl*" and defined it as the consciousness of a cultural heritage.[78] He pointed out that, in ancient Náhuatl (the equivalent of ancient Greece), the word "*tlapializtli*" means "the action of preserving something" (León-Portilla 2003: 17). It is not something in general that is being preserved but "what belongs to us" (León-Portilla 2003: 17). "*Tlapializtli*" is connected in Nahuatl vocabulary with "*yuhcatiliztli*," which, according to León-Portilla, literally means "the action that drives us to live in a given way" (2003: 18). This is, understandably, the basic knowledge human beings have for building communities. Hegel then Heidegger, for instance, used the term "dwelling" to name a similar kind of experience. We can say now that "dwelling" means a certain way of living in the experience of European history, whereas "*yuhcatiliztli*" means a certain way of living in the experience of the communities of Anahuac.[79] More recently, Afro-Caribbean intellectuals have brought to light the sense of dwelling for African communities that descend from the experience of the massive slave trade by imperial Europe during the sixteenth and seventeenth centuries. An equivalent to Hegel's and Heidegger's dwelling is, at the same time, just the opposite in the hierarchy of the human in the modern colonial world. Thus, what is universal is the human drive to build communities grounded on memories and experiences that constitute the house, the dwelling place of different people and not the way that that experience was defined on the bases of European imperial histories and memories (by which I mean, since the Renaissance, because before then the very idea of "European history" is problematic).

Back to León-Portilla. A third concept is *toltecáyotl* or *toltequidad* (equivalent to *anglicidad* or *hispanidad*; i.e., the word that names the identity of a given community, that defines a sense of belonging and a logic of exclusion). Now, *toltécatl* has been derived from the word "Tollan," a word describing the place where the Toltecas (a community from whence the Aztecs emerged) lived; "*tollan*," in Nahuatl, could be translated as "city" in the Latin tradition. Thus, "*toltécatl*" came to refer to a certain type of dwellers in Tollan that, in translation again, would be the people of wisdom, artists, and intellectuals in modern terminology—briefly, the elite of Tollan. Consequently, "*toltécayotl*" was the expression describing a certain style of life of all those who lived in a Tollan, i.e., in a city. León-Portilla makes the educated guess that "*toltecáyotl*" describes a certain set of habits that, in the West, were described as civilization. Now, if "Tollan" is equivalent to city and "*toltecáyotl*" to civilization, then all the inhabitants of a Tollan who follow the rules of *toltecáyotl* are citizens (from *civitas*, in the West, from which "citizens" and "civilization" were derived). But alas, for Christians, Tollan was a place inhabited by barbarians and pagans; and when the very idea of citizen emerged in the West (in the eighteenth century), the memories of Tollan had already been significantly (if not totally) erased from Mexican indigenous memory. And, of course, there was no particular interest, on the part of Western scholars, to investigate a history that could jeopardize their own roles and disciplinary ground. It is not by chance that a Mexican scholar, León-Portilla, revamped a history buried under the noise of five centuries of imperial/colonial "histories": that is, not a history of Europe grounded in Greece, but histories Europeans wrote about a past that did not belong to them; a past to which they did not belong; a past that did not belong to the knowledge, memories, and being of the historian telling the story.

The logical conclusion is that looking for the ontology of Western and post-Enlightenment concept of the citizen will not do. It would be more advantageous to look for the conditions that, today, make the idea of global citizenship a myth and an illusion, an illusion of the modern or postmodern idea of globalization that even a Marxist like Masao Miyoshi described with certain enthusiasm in the early 1990s as a borderless world. Global citizenship for almost seven billion people, after five hundred years of modern/colonial world order, may be a little to much for a world controlled by perhaps 20 percent of the global population. The need to learn to unlearn becomes crucial in bringing the myth of global citizenship to common sense and learning to relearn a necessary decolonial vision of global futures.

To start with, today, global citizens have to cross colonial and imperial differences; and those two frontiers, apparently invisible and most of the time unconscious, are very much ingrained (like a blue chip) in the brain of gatekeepers in the frontiers of southern and eastern Europe, in the consulate and embassies of western European countries and the U.S. around the world, and in the U.S. South, as well as in the so-called civil society. If you have a Brazilian passport in Japan and you are not an employee of the Brazilian Embassy in that country or a CEO of a Brazilian branch of transnational corporations, your citizenship status is far from flexible. It would be closer to Black citizenship in the South of the U.S. before the Civil Rights movement. All is relative, as the dictum goes, and global citizenship applies to only a very small percentage of the world population, those belonging to the political and economic elite and those of us working and consuming for the ruling elite. The rest, the civil and political society in France and Germany as in Bolivia or Tanzania, Russia, or Uzbekistan, are subjected to the rules of the imperial and colonial differences.

Before describing the noninstitutional frontiers created by the imperial and colonial differences, let us make a disclaimer. We are not assuming that global citizenship shall be defined by the desire of the entire population of the world to be citizens of the European Union or the U.S. And it is not the case that the western European U.S. institutions are knocking the doors of 180+ countries to move over there. Beyond that double directionality, global migrations (to which the very idea of global and flexible citizenship is wedded) are going on everywhere. One could argue that not all migrations in the world move to Western Europe and the U.S. from the rest of the world. There are also migrations between the rest of the world. That is right. But there is no massive migration from Western Europe and the U.S. to the rest of the world and, above all, only in the U.S. and Western Europe that the issue of global citizenship was created as an issue. However, whatever particular case you look at, you see that the rules of the colonial and imperial differences are at work. What is important for our argument is the directionality of migrations for which the very idea of citizenship is today at stake. It is obvious that there are more Nigerians, Bolivians, Indians, Ukrainians, or Caribbeans who want to migrate to Europe or the U.S. than people in the U.S. desiring to migrate to any of those places. We do not know of any stories of Anglo-Americans dying in the Arizona desert when marching to cross the Mexican border.[80]

Similar examples could be found outside the U.S. and Europe. For example, more Bolivians are crossing borders and migrating to Argentina and Chile than Chileans are immigrating in mass to Bolivia. Argentineans and Chileans who move to Bolivia are not people but capital. And, as we know, global capital is much more flexible than global citizenship. The directionality is parallel to the U.S. and Latin America or Europe and North Africa: People move from the south to the north and capital moves from the north to the south. In the case of Chile and Argentina, the geographical parameters do not apply, because capital moves to the north and people to the south—the racialization of the Bolivian population and colonial difference are equally at work. It is estimated that, in Iraq, more than four thousand Americans and more than one hundred thousand Iraqis died in an invasion that was justified for the good of Humanity.[81]

Well, you may say, that is natural: People move to find better living conditions and, right now, better living conditions are in the U.S. and Argentina and not in Nigeria or Bolivia. And better living conditions in this polycentric and capitalist world we are living in mean more money. And, you can argue that democratic states go to war to eliminate the Evil from the surface of the earth. Fair enough. However, better living conditions are also a myth and an illusion for immigrants from a lesser country in the global distribution of wealth that largely would have difficulties enjoying the privileges of the nationals of the better country. We would ask, then, what are the relationships among capitalism (in its current, global form), citizenship, and racism? Why does capital move freely while people do not? We say people and not citizen because not every person is a citizen—and that space (the space between the person and the citizen) is divided by racism, on which the colonial and imperial differences have been built in the social and political imaginary of the modern colonial world. You are not stopped at the gates (of frontiers or embassies) because you are poor but because of your religion, your language, your nationality, your skin, whatever is taken as indicator of the colonial and imperial differences. Being poor and white is not the same as being poor and of color. In a country like Bolivia, the connection between race and poverty is more evident than in the U.S. where, today, poverty is reaching a vast sector of the White population. Racism is the condition under which the agents of the state and of capital decide who shall be poor, because in the capitalistic economic system, poverty cannot be avoided: It is ingrained in the very structure of the system.

III. Racism, the Colonial Matrix of Power, and Colonial/Imperial Differences

We return to colonial and imperial differences, two complementary concepts introduced in Chapters 3 and 4. Before the citizen emerged in the imaginary of the modern/colonial world, there were the heathens, the pagans, the gentiles, and the barbarians. Who defined them, and how were these social roles described? Where was the standard, the model on which these categories were defined? To put forward the question in the way we did already presupposes accepting Christian theology as the epistemic standard to classify the world. If we look at the world from the conceptual eyes of Islamic theology or Arabic philosophy or from Aymara pacha-sophy (as an Aymara equivalent to Greek philosophy has been described),[82] we reach at least two different conclusions.

The categories of pagans, gentiles, heathens, and barbarians are not found in Islamic, Arabic, or Aymara thought. We are not saying that there were no categories by which the intellectual elites and officers of the "states" and the population, in any of these language communities and religions, made a distinction between "insiders" and "outsiders." The question is whether they made it with the virulence we find in many theologians of the Spanish Inquisition as well as progressive intellectuals of the time such as Bartolomé—de Las Casas so fearful of the enemies of Christianity—and with the virulence that was reproduced through the history of the modern colonial world, going through France, England, Germany, and the U.S. A commonly held belief cutting across the most extremely conservative and the most extremely progressive theologians was that heathen, barbarians, pagan, gentiles, and so on all had some kind of deal with the devil (sound familiar?). After the Enlightenment and secularization, the role of the devil receded and lack of civilization took its place.

When theology was displaced by secular philosophy and the monarchic states in complicity with the church were replaced by the secular nation-state, the logic of exclusions that Christians applied to Jews, Moors, Indians, and Blacks was rearticulated. How? Sixteenth-century reclassification of languages and religions in the planet operated mainly in three frontiers. One, the most immediate, was the frontier between the religions of the books that were reestablished when Moors and Jews were expelled from the Iberian Peninsula. The second, in chronological order, was the new question of the limits of humanity. To what extent could the Indians be considered human beings? The question was not asked about African slaves, implying that there was no question that they were not quite human. Secularization, in the eighteenth century, replaced the "friends of the devil" with the "foreigners." Foreigners were not necessarily enemies of the nation. They were just not born (i.e., they were not nationals) in a given language, territory, culture, and blood. The foreigners were not citizens, because they were not under the administration of the secular state, that is, a state no longer controlled by the church and the monarch, but by a state that protected the people against the monarch and the church—a state of the people, for the people, by the people. It was then that the "citizen" was born, ambiguously cast in between the state and the nation in such a way that all modern states were assumed to be mononationals. By this, I mean that those who were not born in a language, a blood, a culture were not considered members of the state—an administrative unit without blood, language, or memory but, instead, with a flag, a national anthem, and an army.

Immanuel Kant is a good case study for our argument. In the historical context of Europe at the end of the eighteenth century, when imperial powers were changing hands from the Christian and Catholic south to the secular and Protestant north, Kant was at the crossroads of several debates and new developments. One of them was to rethink universal history with a cosmopolitan intent. Why rethink?—because universal history, which was the property of Christian theologians, needed now to be rethought in secular terms and in relation to the state.

As any frequent reader of Kant will remember, when thinking about the ideal society and the ideal history, he replaced God with nature. Theologians used to talk—like charlatans on television and best-selling authors claiming that they know how to save the believers—of God's will. They knew what God planned, what God wants for you, and what God knows is good for you. Thus, God was and still is a floating signifier you can appropriate and fill to your taste in private life or in the public sphere. The same thing happened with Kant and nature. Kant knew what nature's designs were for a peaceful society and cosmopolitan peace. Kant's political thought maintains a pyramidal order of society, from the top down, following the Western tradition in political theory. He places, then, between nature's design and the human nation-states, the civil constitution. The civil constitution plays the role of the master, because all human beings need a master, whereas no human being could be master of other human beings (Locke had already developed the same idea). The civil constitution as the supreme document of state management is the document through which citizens are managed. A sort of law-politics, to play with words. law-politics, parallel to bio-politics, manages the "right" and the "legality" of the citizens; not their bodies, but their mind. From the recasting of the idea of civility and citizen, civilization also became the global secular design that took the place of Christianization. Thus, Kant's cosmopolitan order and the universal history he needed to rewrite was the necessary knowledge to back up the state as well as state imperial designs in "propagating" the ideals of civilization all over the globe.

Willingly or not, Kant wrote about anthropology and aesthetics in a way that revealed the underpinning of his abstract universals in philosophy and political theory. Let me quote a couple of examples then elaborate on them. The first comes from anthropology, from a pragmatic point of view:

> The Spaniard who evolved from the mixture of European blood with Ara-

bian (Moorish) blood, displays in his public and private behavior a certain solemnity; and even the peasant expresses a consciousness of his own dignity toward his master, to whom he is lawfully obedient.

The Spaniard's bad side is that he does learn from foreigners [who are the foreigners from whom Spaniard have to learn? Are German learning from foreigners]; that he does not travel in order to get acquainted with other nations; that is he is centuries behind in the sciences. He resists any reform; he is proud of not having to work; he is of a romantic quality of spirit, as the bullfight shows. (Kant [1798] 1996: 231)

Remember that Kant is here describing national characters. And this is what he had to say about the Germans: "The Germans are renowned for their good character; they have the reputation of honesty and domesticity; both are qualities which are not suited to splendor." However, not all is lost in that domesticity, for "Of all civilized people," Kant continues, "the German subjects himself most easily and permanently to the government under which he lives" ([1798] 1996: 233). And here is an interesting complement to the previous characterization:

If he arrives in foreign lands as a colonist, he will soon form with his compatriots a sort of social club which, as a result of unity of language and, partially, of religion makes him part of a little clan, which under the higher authority of the government distinguishes itself in a peaceful and moral way through industry, cleanliness, and thrift from the settlements of other nationalities (1[1798] 996: 233).

So much for Kant's cosmopolitanism—apparently derived from how Germans feel at home and bond among themselves in foreign land when they go as colonists. Kant's national characters, as he himself explains, are based on blood although he will slide color in without justification. First, let us take a look at how Kant connects blood with nature. When Kant gets out of Europe, he encounters the Russian, the Polish, and the European Turks. Let's listen to what he has to say (stand with me for a little bit longer and you will see how global citizenship and the humanities walk parallel to each other and meet in the same corner) about Russian, Polish and Turks: "Since Russia has not yet developed definite characteristics from its natural potential; since Poland has no longer any characteristics; and since the nationals of European Turkey never have had a character, nor will ever attain what is necessary for a definite national character, the description of the nations' characters may properly be passed over here" ([1798] 1996: 235).

In section four of *Observations on the Beautiful and the Sublime*, Kant takes on the Arabs, Chinese, Indians, Africans, and American Indians. But, I do not go into details here. What I am interested in underlining is that, once you get out of Europe, you get into the downhill road of the human scale. What is interesting, however, is that Kant is describing national characters as innate, as natural characters who, so to speak, lie in the composition of the person's blood. And he further adds that, "since we are not talking about the artificially acquired (or affected) characteristics of nations, we must be very cautious in sketching them" ([1798] 1996: 235).

Now, it so happened that nature provides the global designs for the state and the Constitution and the innate national character of the human race. Therefore, because nature provides "natural" designs, it would be very difficult to contest Kant as interpreter of nature's will. What we have here is a sort of secular fundamentalism that brings together the figure of the citizens of both law and blood. For that reason, the nation-state cannot be but a monoracial state and the citizen a composite of an administrative and racially constituted entity.

We have chosen Kant as an example for two reasons. One is that Kant offers the chronological link between sixteenth-century Spanish theologians and their first classification of the world population in racial terms and the twentieth-century updating and transformation of his national characters at a global scale. There is not much difference between what Las Casas thought of the Moors and what Kant thinks of the Arabs. For, beyond the particular descriptions of national characters worldwide, Kant has a scheme in mind that I described elsewhere as the Kantian ethno-racial tetragon. In a nutshell, for Kant, yellow people were in Asia, black in Africa, red in America (he was thinking of the Indians and not of the population of European descent in America), and white in Europe. The ethno-racial scheme, during the Nixon administration, presupposed the Kantian tetragon. It added Hispanics to form what David Hollinger named the "ethno-racial pentagon" (Hollinger 1995). Behind this scheme, we can also recognize—second reason—Kant's transformation of the colonial and imperial differences as racial configurations put in place by Christian theologians and secular philosophers from the sixteenth to the eighteenth centuries. Thus, truly global citizenship presupposes overcoming the colonial and imperial differences, which means that Chicanos/as in the U.S., Aymaras in Bolivia and around the world, and Russians in Europe have the epistemic power to intervene and question the naturalization of an order based on global racism.

Colonial and imperial differences are ingrained in dominant imperial descriptions and justifications of their control over the population in the colonies as well as in imperial superiority over other empires or imperial histories (e.g., Christian and capitalist empires confronted with the non-Christian and noncapitalist empires, such as the Ottoman Sultanate and the Russian and Soviet Empires). For the colonial difference, Indians and Africans offered Spanish theologians the opportunity to remap the configuration of the chain of human being; and Blacks ended up at the lower level of the scale. That is to say, if Indians were suspicious of not fulfilling the requirements established for *humanitas;* Blacks were out of the question simply because they were not considered human. That is the only way to understand why they became a commodity in the global market, and they were the first dramatic example of how the dispensability of human life in the formation of capitalism goes hand in hand with the emergence of the Atlantic commercial circuits. For the same theologians who were disputing the humanity of the Indians and assuming the lack of humanity of the African slaves, Jews, Moors, Ottomans, and Russians were not at the same level. They were not disputed because of their humanity but because of their lack of Latin and Latin alphabetic writing (Las Casas named it "the lack of literal locution"; [1552] 1967: 637) and in their wrong religion. Or, in the case of Christian Orthodox in Russia, they were seen as deviating from true Christianity. Asia was less relevant for Christian theologians.

The Ottoman Sultanate was the closest case in the sixteenth century in relation to which the emerging Christian empires (the Holy Roman Empire of the German Nations and the Castilian Empire) could measure a period of differences. China was a second case in point. The first Jesuits arrived in Japan and China in 1582. But, certainly, Asia was relevant to Kant, because the Dutch and the British, from the second half of the seventeenth century on, have made their entry into the Asian continent. And, at this point, the colonial difference articulated in the Americas (Indians and Blacks) began to be restructured and reinterpreted. France, during the first half of the nineteenth century, made its way to North Africa when the clout of the Islamic Caliphate and Ottoman Sultanate was vanishing. Thus, the colonial difference was rearticulated here, too. And, when that happened, when Asia and North Africa (and the Middle East, since the beginning of the twentieth century) were brought into the sphere of colonial and imperial differences, Orientalism was born. Kant's characterization of the Arabs, the Chinese, and the Indians were part of the transformation of the colonial difference from the foundation of Occidentalism (the Spanish *Indias Occidentales*), to the French and British construction of Orientalism.

Why are we telling you this story? To argue that global citizenship is being vetoed by the colonial and imperial differences and not by gatekeepers working for the U.S. and European embassies or patrolling the borders. Central Asia and the Caucasus are not alien to this nation-building and citizenship (and the emergence of tricksters), all this is articulated through imperial difference and the second-class status of the Russian Empire, the Soviet Union, and their colonies. What we are saying is that these dividing lines (the imperial and colonial difference, based on the racial classification of people on the planet) are still alive and well and preventing the concretization of global citizenship. In other words, global citizenship is part of the rhetoric of modernity (salvation, development, progress, well-being for all, and democracy), whereas the imperial and colonial differences are the invisible divides that maintain the logic of coloniality (oppression, domination, exploitation, and marginalization). Gatekeepers are the tools of a historically formed belief that has been naturalized and transmitted from generation to generation of schools, colleges, universities, state institutions, tourism agencies, and the like. For this reason, you cannot change subjectivities and the principle of knowledge by means of public policies that maintain the existing subjectivities and principle of knowledge. Reforms are better than nothing, but the result is making more palatable the chronicle of an announced dead. It may improve but not change the situation. If changes cannot come from new laws and public policies, they should come from changes in people's minds, in their understanding of the historical roots that have formed their sensibilities and beliefs. And, to that end, the decoloniality of being and knowledge is of the essence.

It is our contention that global citizenship today is being challenged by the underground history of racism that impinges on the subjectivity of the population of white countries as well as policy makers and their preferential attitude toward who gets in and who does not. It is true that the needs of the market produce the effect that technologically trained people from the Third World or non-Western imperial countries are less dark to the eyes of employers and passport control. The control over the global circulation of people, particularly from the European Union and the U.S. administration (although the example of the "terrorist's menace" is spreading to other countries) is enacted not only in the borders but also in the countries of origin. Consulates and embassies act like frontiers over there, as the first scanner. The racial structure with which the imperial and colonial differences have been historically founded (i.e., the foundation of the colonial matrix of power) is the major impediment today to thinking seriously of global citizenship. Once again, decoloniality of being means to regain the dignity that *humanitas* took away from other humans casted as *anthropos*. Citizenship can be global only once the colonial and imperial differences are erased and with it the superiority of humanitas over the anthropos. To achieve this goal it is necessary to delink from the imperial hegemony of the *humanitas* and, therefore, from the hegemony of modern/colonial racial classifications. But, to reach this point, we need the decolonial epistemic shift—not a "new turn" (linguistic, pragmatic, or what have you) within the epistemic perspective that does not admit other epistemic perspective; not a new post (modern or colonial) that recasts the old within a new vocabulary, but a decolonial delinking from the hegemony of Western thought from the Renaissance and the Enlightenment to the postmodern and the postcolonial.

IV. The Role of the Humanities and the Decolonial Option

How can we bring the Humanities into the previous historical scheme and toward encountering the decolonial option? Well, let us go back to Kant, this time to his *The Contest of the Faculty* ([1798] 1955). Three aspects are relevant to my argument. The first is that *The Contest* introduced an internal shift in the history of modern Europe since the Renaissance, replacing theology with secular philosophy. He assigned to theology a very important role, next to medicine and law. The three primary disciplines had the responsibilities of ensuring the well-being of society: theology to take care of the soul, medicine of the body, and law of the society. The second aspect is the role Kant gave to philosophy: On the one hand, philosophy was itself one among many secondary disciplines; on the other hand, he assigned to philosophy the role of policing the practice of the three primary disciplines (very similar to the role Jacques Derrida gave to grammatology). And the third aspect introduced in *The Contest* is the reorganization of knowledge. In this regard, philosophy fulfilled the function that theology had in the Renaissance university (Kant [1798] 1955). Kant is with good reason one of the masterminds of what has been called the Kantian-Humboldtian University (Readings 1996), a new university and a new curricular organization at the service of the state and no longer at the service of the monarch or the church.

Basically, the Kantian-Humboldtian University, which is contextualized in the next chapter, was a university in which the crucial role the humanities played in the Renaissance became secular but equally important. It was a mutation from theological to secular humanities. In both cases, the university was no longer a European business but an imperial/colonial one as well: The imperial expansion since the Renaissance and the formation of colonies had in higher education a major way to control knowledge and subjectivity. The humanities and science (Copernicus, Galileo, etc.) shared the same house of knowledge in the sixteenth and the seventeenth centuries and were cast under a curriculum composed by the *trivium* and the *cuadrivium*. After the Enlightenment, in the reorganization of the curriculum—which had in Kant's work an exemplar articulation—science and the humanities began to take separate routes. At the end of the nineteenth century, Wilhelm Dilthey distinguished between ideographic and nomotetic sciences, between understanding and explanation, between the natural and the human sciences (*les sciences humaines,* in French vocabulary) or the sciences of the spirit, as Dilthey would have it (1991). After World War II, three important changes were introduced in the tradition of the Kantian-Humboldtian University. First, the social sciences gained ground in complicity with the transformation of capitalism. Corporations began to intervene in the transformation of the university, particularly in the last twenty years, in various forms known to us. Second, the division between the social sciences and the humanities (which in Europe were lumped together as human sciences) gained ground, and the three hard social sciences (political science, sociology, and economics) came to dominate the scene. The humanities receded to a secondary role: Philosophy, no longer the queen of the human sciences, is now an exotic practice among the humanities that is struggling for survival in Europe (western and eastern) and has been reduced to analytic philosophy and logic in the U.S. The same could be said about literature, art history, and the like. And third, and this is the direction in which I move and conclude, an epistemic decolonial shift emerged simultaneously with the social movements of political decolonization during the Cold War. These periodizations in the history of the European university always had consequences in the colonies or ex-colonies (Mignolo 2002b).

However, Kant has also the merit of articulating the concept of critique that in Karl Marx and Sigmund Freud (both European Jews) took a decisive turn: The underlying logic of capital and the underlying logic of consciousness became the target of critical examination. Some thing has changed between Kant, on the one hand, and Marx and Freud, on the other. In 1937, Max Horkheimer (also a German Jew) articulated that change in terms of traditional and critical theory (1937). By "traditional," he did not mean to value one type of theory over the other but, rather, to distinguish between two types of theorizing. One type of theorizing, what he called "traditional theory," occurs when theory is constructed on facticity, i.e., on assumptions that the world is as it looks to us, and theories are necessary to organize and explain what is disorganized and not understood. Natural and social sciences, particularly of the positivist kind, operate at this level. The second type of theorizing, which he called "critical," examined the underlying logic and the social consequences of social phenomena and scientific knowledge. Basically, Horkheimer followed the path opened by Marx and Freud in unveiling the darker side of nineteenth-century modernity, the exploitative nature of capitalism, and its consequences in the (de)formation of subjectivity. Marx, Freud, and Horkheimer followed, in Europe, a critical path in the humanities that had started in the colonies three centuries before them.

Neither of them, in fact, has much to say about coloniality, a concept that was not available or even thinkable, although decolonial thinking and doing (as well as thinking by doing) was already in place in European colonies in the Americas. And, the reason was that European thinkers were aware of colonialism but not of coloniality or the fact that the responses to coloniality were not limited to the European critique of colonialism. This is yet another instance showing the need for learning to unlearn. Marx saw colonialism as a derivative phenomenon. Freud was quite unaware of it, and after an initial enthusiasm about the global role of psychoanalysis in India, as has been shown by Ashis Nandi in *Savage Freud and Other Essays on Possible and Retrievable Selves* (1995), Freud's critical diagnosis remained operative in the domain of European subjectivities. In the 1950s and 1960s, Frantz Fanon showed the limits of psychoanalysis for subjectivities formed in the African diaspora since the sixteenth century and the massive slave trade as well as for North African Arabs and Berbers. What has been forgotten from the eighteenth century on was the critique of colonialism by Bartolomé de Las Casas and the decolonial shift taken by indigenous intellectuals like Waman Puma de Ayala in the Viceroyalty of Peru imposed over the Inca's Tawantinsuyu (e.g., their social and historical organization conceived as the land of the four corners). Decolonial thinking in South, Central America, and the Caribbean as well as among Latino(a)s in the U.S., builds on what was silenced, partly because not understood and partly because to recognize it would have been dangerous not only for imperial forces but also for critics like Las Casas himself, who would have had to recognize that his critique of colonialism, as important as it was, was equally limited to his dissenting and critical Christian and European perspective. Waman Puma was dwelling in a different memory, in a different language, in a different epistemology, and, when confronting the imperial control by Spanish men of letters and missionaries, he naturally took the decolonial shift: He delinked from the supremacy of theological categories of thought and included them within indigenous (Quechua and Aymara) categories of thoughts. Border thinking was the consequence of Guaman Poma's doing—his historical narrative and his political proposal to reorganize the Tawantinsuyu and not, of course, the

Viceroyalty of Peru, which was the colonizing job of the Spanish monarchy to which precisely Guaman Poma was decolonially responding.

The emergence of imperial internal critique (Las Casas, Kant, Marx, Freud, and Horkheimer) silenced the emergence and continuation, since the sixteenth century, of the decolonial option, as the critique of modernity from the perspective of coloniality, of which Waman Puma, in the Viceroyalty of Peru under Spanish rules, is one of the foundational examples. Mahatma Gandhi is a second case in British India, under British imperial rule. And, after World War II, the genealogy expanded through the works of Amilcar Cabral (in the Portuguese colonies), Aimé Césaire and Frantz Fanon (in the French Caribbean), Fausto Reynaga (in Bolivia), and Gloria Anzaldúa (in the U.S.). Our own argument is inscribed and follows this later genealogy. We are now in the middle of a decolonial epistemic shift; and it is from this shift that the role of the humanities could be not only imagined but also reoriented. How shall we understand the decolonial epistemic option? The next question we ask is this: What are the relationships between the decolonial epistemic shift, the humanities, and global citizenship?

The decolonial epistemic option is both geopolitical and body political; that is, it respond to the needs and perspectives of people and regions who do not see that plans and designs made for them by developed countries and corresponding institutions (IMF, World Bank, Monsanto, etc.) as really "convenient" for their regions and the people who live in the region. The decolonial epistemic option is becoming also, for similar reasons, an option for immigrants to developed countries who organized themselves to work to participate (instead of assimilate or accommodate) in the democratization of knowledge, of economy of political life. In other words, the decolonial is an option for all those human beings who want to participate and share rather than be managed and integrated to master plans that are not theirs or to be expelled and marginalized.

The geopolitics of knowing brings to the foreground the relationship between geohistorical locations and epistemology. It came to the foreground during the Cold War and its point of origination was the Third World, not Europe. Argentinean philosopher Enrique Dussel in 1977 launched his philosophy of liberation by asking for the relationship between geopolitics and philosophy and established a correspondence between economic and epistemic dependency in the history of the modern colonial world. In the mid-1990s, Franco Cassano, Italian philosopher from Bary (south of Italy), raised the question of the relationship between the sea and epistemology. And during the same years, Portuguese sociologist Bonaventura de Sousa Santos advanced the idea of an "epistemology of the South," which became integrated into the philosophical platform of the World Social Forum, initiated in Porto Alegre, Brazil. The three of them raised their voices to claim that there is no knowledge detached from experience. But, more important, that "experience" cannot be reduced to the universality of Human Experience, which was claimed by Kant: "Experiences" have been marked and continue to be marked by the imperial/colonial modern world order. Whether you have been born and raised in London or Beijing, and whether you have been put in those places or move around the world, you cannot escape from "experiencing" the world order you received when you were born and educated—the experience and memories in question are part of the modern colonial world, structured by the colonial and imperial differences. You can try to narcotize imperial and colonial differences if you are trying to assimilate to a dominant culture or to emulate ideas that emerged from bodies embodied in local histories (like Germany or France) and languages that are not the histories and languages in which—unfortunately—your skin and brain were formed. Or you can accept—with pride—what you are, to embody the place you occupy in the colonial matrix of power (metaphorically similar indeed to the places that people occupy in the film *The Matrix*)

Learning to unlearn becomes then of the essence, since what you have learned was already established by theological and egological (e.g., secular nation-state education) rules of the game. The geopolitical and body-political shifts are decolonial in the sense that they delink (i.e., it is no longer an internal critique, like those of Marx, Freud, or Horkheimer) from the hegemonic history of Western civilization and the corresponding categories of thoughts founded in Greek and Latin and expanded in the six modern European imperial languages (Italian, Spanish, Portuguese, French, German, and English).

The geopolitical shift emerged in the Third World (during the Cold War) and in the south of Europe (the post-USSR Europe that lost the train of the Enlightenment). The body-political epistemic shift surfaced instead in the U.S., during the Cold War but, above all, after and as a consequence of the Civil Rights movement. The question prompted by the Civil Rights movement was not the relationship between geopolitics and epistemology but, rather, that between identity and epistemology. New spheres of knowledge came into being (women's studies, gender and sexuality studies, gay and lesbian studies, Afro-American studies, ethnic studies, Latino/Latinas studies, etc.). What do all of them have in common? First, all of them incorporate the knower into the known, the personal and collective memory of communities configured around race, gender, and sexuality. Second, they all introduced into the social sphere of knowledge the perspective from the *damnés*, those disposed by colonial racism and patriarchy. And, third, they introduced a new justification of knowledge: knowledge not at the service of the church, the monarch, or the state, but knowledge for liberation, that is, for subjective and epistemic decolonization.

Now, we invite you to think about this double shift in relation to the story we told before on the making of the colonial matrix of power and the colonization of knowledge and being. You would be able to make the connection, on the one hand, between the stumbling block for global citizenship and the structure of knowledge, and on the other, between the coloniality of knowledge and being (which prevents global citizenship) and the critical role the humanities can play to demolish the stumbling block built on the colonial and imperial differences. The ultimate question, then, would be to determine the role of the humanities in dismantling global racism that prevents the full achievement of global citizenship. However, the task is not possible without changing the current common sense, in which happiness is related to accumulation; well-being is predicated on increasing production; and competition and meritocracy are the final destinations of human beings for their full satisfaction. All these goals predicated in the rhetoric of modernity imply running over, exploiting, and killing others; that is, they imply the logic of coloniality without which the ideals of modernity could not be carried out.

The map we draw of the internal critique and decolonial option suggests that there are two different tasks, although complementary, for the humanities. The internal critique (i.e., a critique that maintains the theo- and egopolitics of knowledge) is very prominent in the U.S. and Europe. In the first case, foundations supporting the humanities (Ford, Mellon, Rockefeller, McArthur, etc.) allow for a fundamental critique of the increasing dominance of corporate values within the university. The internal critique is also very prominent, within and outside of the university, in the works of the Euro-American left (followers of Marx, Freud, and the initial years of the Frankfurt school). The decolonial shift brings another critical dimension of the humanities, this time the geo- and body politics of knowledge (the epistemology of the South and of the color of reason) as epistemic and political projects from historical agents, experiences, and memories that were disqualified epistemic subjects. If global citizenship requires the dismantling of global racism, it is from the decolonial shift (from the geo- and body politics of knowledge) that such a task will have its leadership. Last but not least, the decolonial option is at odds with the liberal dictum that we should emphasize what we have in common rather than the differences, for the "commonality" is predicated on an idea of the human whose paradigmatic example is a White European heterosexual man.

I heard a dictum (I do not have a scholarly reference, just oral saying, undocumented but no less relevant) attributed to Spanish writer Fernando Savater that goes like this: "We are all equal in that we are different." Whether Savater said it or not, the formula is very common: It presupposes and defends the commonality of human beings—which means that Human Beings are what hegemonic knowledge allows you to say what they are. The Zapatistas prefer—instead—the following version: "Because we are all equal, we have the right to the difference." My argument and the task I see for the decolonial humanities goes with the Zapatistas's dictum. This is one of the fundamental tasks for the decolonial humanities in the twenty-first century: to acknowledge that global citizenship is a myth while global racism is not overcome and to work toward the decolonization of imperial knowledge that engendered the coloniality of being.

CHAPTER 7

Globalization and the Geopolitics of Knowledge

The Role of the Humanities in the Corporate University

IN CHAPTERS 3 TO 6, we explored different aspects of the modern/colonial world order, focusing on the coloniality of knowledge and being and, simultaneously, the attempts and decolonial possibilities in which the formation of global political societies and scholarship are engaged. Ethnic (Chapter 3) and gender decolonial formations (Chapter 4) in Central Asia and the Caucasus were followed by a decolonial readings of the complicities in Western imperial imaginary of the concepts of Human(ity) and citizenship. In this closing chapter, we make a case for education, particularly higher education, to engage the Humanities as a branch of learning from the perspective of decoloniality.[83] We further claim that the Humanities shall not be conceived as a branch of knowledge next to Natural and Social Sciences and the professional schools (engineering, law, medicine, business administration) but as the overarching ethical horizon of research and learning. Nevertheless, thus conceived, the Humanities can offer and follow different trajectories. One of them would be the Humanities in line with and dependent on market ideologies of progress, development, capitalist accumulation, and the like. The other, would be more in tune with theology of liberation and liberal ideals of a democratic and just society ,without calling into question the basic principles of capitalist economy. And, the third trajectory would be the one we are arguing here: learning to unlearn the previous two hegemonic options and engage in decolonial Humanities. To argue this point, we review the history of the University in the Western world and take Amawtay Wasi [House of Learning] in Ecuador as a model of learning to unlearn in order to relearn, that is, to engage in decolonial education.

To start with, two kinds of histories of the university as an institution may help us understand the dilemmas now confronting universities all over the world. The Plan Bologna in Europe and the meeting in Davos on the future of the University (Mignolo 2009b) are turning learning into a tool for efficiency and economic development, giving to "learning to manage" the central role in the corporate university. The task of learning to unlearn becomes urgent as far as management and efficiency are the terms of the rhetoric of modernity and progress that conceals the logic of coloniality and domination. For whom are management and efficiency beneficial? In the recent past, the world witnessed or is witnessing two failures of management and efficiency: the invasion of Iraq and the collapse of Wall Street. That route of knowing, the belief under which knowledge is created and argument built, is no longer tenable. To imagine nonmanagerial futures based on the principle of "living well" rather than in efficiency and belief (or make belief) that good management and efficiency bring happiness to all is an ideal that benefits the elite, who put forward the idea and can maintain it through various means (institutions, money, media). We need then to recap the history of higher learning in Western civilization. Since the history of the university has been linked to colonial expansion, since the sixteenth century, and therefore the imperial, learning to unlearn is a decolonial endeavor in two senses: It is necessary to decolonize imperial education and it is of the essence to work toward decolonial education.

Since the European Renaissance and European colonial expansion in the sixteenth century—that is, the foundational moment of the modern/colonial world—the accumulation of money has gone hand in hand with the accumulation of meaning and of knowledge. Today "historical/structural dependency" still structures the world, both economically and epistemically. How did that happen? How was it possible that a local conception of knowledge, grounded on Greek and Roman experiences and categories of thought, become hegemonic through various stages of five centuries of imperial expansion? In what follows, we sketch how that happened, and in the end, we advance some ideas of how to delink from that imperial legacy and engage in epistemic disobedience. Before engaging in this task, we need to identify the logic and the consequences of imperial thinking.

Western categories of thoughts (let us remember, grounded in Greek and Latin and translated into the six modern European imperial languages: Italian, Spanish, Portuguese, French, German, and English) put any other category in a double bind: they are either "incorporated" (and their singularity erased) into Western categories (e.g., transforming Hinduism and Buddhism into " religions") or dismissed and rejected (all economies based on capitalist principles and knowledges that cannot be assimilated to Western normativization of life and subjectivities, from governments to "popular" knowledge, e.g., Vandana Shiva's report on traditional knowledge of the forest or the administration of water in conditions of water scarcity).

The logic of Western imperial epistemology consists in a meta-discourse that validates itself by disqualifying the difference. That is, it consists of making and remaking the epistemic colonial difference: Barbarian, primitives, Orientals, Indians, Blacks, and so on, are qualified as people "outside" or "behind" who need to be brought in and to the modern present. Modernity then is not a historical epoch but an imperial category of self-validation and disqualification of the epistemic difference. Take philosophy of science, for example. Once these categories of knowledge have been institutionalized in Western scholarship and translated into common sense (or in Western appropriation of Greek and Roman legacies), they become totalitarian, preventing any other kind of knowledge to be recognized at the same level as philosophy and science. Similarly with political theory (democracy) or political economy (capitalism), after the financial crisis of 2008–2009, the main issue in the media and high learning institution was how to save capitalism, not to propose an-other economy (based on reciprocity instead of gain and accumulation that promotes destruction and killing in all forms, from war to food crisis). Learning to unlearn means to delink from the illusion that knowledge in all spheres of life is bound to one set of categories that are both universal and Western.

To start shifting the geopolitics of knowledge, delinking and engage in epistemic disobedience, it is necessary to excavate the foundation of Western categories and principles about the knowledge itself and the values attached to a certain kind of knowledge used to devalue epistemic differences, that is, building and maintaining the epistemic colonial difference that reverts to and complements imperial epistemic differences: Mandarin, Russian and Arabic, to name a few languages spoken by billions of people are not languages epistemically sustainable in the epistemic world order. Knowing how and critical thinking can be found in any community of living organisms that can use their hands to do while thinking and thinking while doing. Knowing how is a matter of surviving and living in community. But with knowing how comes knowing, *that*, which is the first level of theoretical knowing. If you know how to make shoes, it is not the same as birds knowing how to make a nest. Making shoes implies already a level of doing that goes beyond living on the basis of what nature gave you, feathers, fur, or renewable leaves. Knowing *what* projects theoretical knowing that into a level of complexity in which other doings and thinking enter into consideration: Knowing what is the theoretical level that operates in the domain of options. One, perhaps, could say that the Greek breakthrough was to move from knowing that to knowing what and the achievement of Western civilization was to capitalize on it: Theology, philosophy, and sciences are three disciplinary formations responding to the same basic principles on which knowing what has been built. Exploring and unveiling such principles became an urgent task for decolonial humanities in confrontation with the corporate values of management and efficiency. Therefore, decolonial humanities means epistemic disobedience (since critiquing the foundation of Western knowledge accepting Western epistemic rules of the game does not go very far—it remains within an obedient kind of criticism) and delinking. It means learning to unlearn (delinking, epistemic disobedience) in order to relearn (inventing and working out decolonial categories of thought that allow building noncapitalist and nonimperial values and subjectivities.

We say the "humanities," and not just "the humanists" (as a species distinct from natural scientists and scholars in professional schools) for the reasons stated previously regarding the role of the Humanities and decolonial Humanities. Since all knowledge and understanding is *human understanding* (from genomics to dance, from electrical engineering to literature, from mathematical models in economy to political economy), every scholar, academic, and scientist has a responsibility toward the humanities; in other words, he or she has *critical, ethical,* and *political* responsibilities in the *production, dissemination, transformation,* and *enactment* of knowledge. The Humanities can and must do something else in relation to what they have been doing in the past. If the Humanities, since the Renaissance, has contributed enormously to the expansion of the realm of interactions and imaginations of human beings, it was oblivious to what laid out beyond the realm of a regional concept of the Human that was projected as universal. Unfortunately, the achievements in the Humanities were the brighter side that hid from view the Humanity that was being negated. Therefore, the task of decolonial Humanities is to redress the lost balance for which imperial Humanities was responsible. In other words, the Humanities have to be recognized in their contribution to the very idea of Modernity as well as for the creation of its negated side: the idea of the Unhuman.

As we said, the accumulation of money, in the constitution of Europe, the West, or Western civilization, went hand in hand with the accumulation of meaning. The role of imperial Humanities was crucial in this regard. Think about "museums of natural history," for example. They are a clear example of the accumulation of meaning and knowledge; and the "histories" of museums of natural history parallel those of capitalism and European expansion all over the globe. Let this serve as a paradigmatic example in the sketching of two kinds of histories, the proper knowledge of which is beyond my reach at this point. As I said earlier, I am not interested in history per se, or in covering all the important details that would satisfy the empiricist scholar, but in underlining two historical trajectories: first, the linear history of the Western university, and second, the fractured histories of universities in colonial, Third World, and "emerging countries."

Redressing the balance in decolonial education, we have the case of Amawtay Wasi, showing all of us a way out of these two histories, those of the Western universities and of the West's colonial surrogates. In describing colonial universities as "colonial surrogates," I do not ignore the fact that universities embedded in colonial histories are centers where critical scholars and intellectuals have emerged and continue to emerge.[84] What we say is that critical scholars, scientists, and intellectuals trained in the universities of colonial, Third World, or emerging countries do not fail to recognize their position vis-à-vis Western universities. In fact, the concept of "colonial surrogates" emerged from my encounters and conversations with critical scholars, scientists, and intellectuals working in Bolivia, Ecuador, Argentina, Venezuela, South Africa, North Africa, and South Asia.

In other words: universities, in the Americas since the sixteenth and the seventeenth centuries, were created and run by Spanish and British immigrants and their creole (Anglo and Spanish) descendants. In Russia, the Soviet Union, and the Russian Federation, higher education and universities were Western models that displaced, as in other parts of the world, original schooling, nurturing as if Western universities offered the latest and most "advanced" model, good for all over the world. Thus, in the history of this place (America), a group of transplanted Europeans ignored and marginalized indigenous knowledge from Patagonia to Labrador and destroyed the African memories that the slaves brought with them. They started a type of institution (the university) and a kind of education that was rooted in European history since the Middle Ages. The colonial universities both were and were not European universities; they aspired to be but were not quite. The colonial difference implied in this relationship explains the long, historical inferiority complex, in both Anglo-and South America, with respect to Europe. The theory embedded in the creation of the Universidad Intercultural led me to review the history of the university in the Western world and its links to colonialism—or, better yet, to coloniality. It is argued today that "colonialism" is no longer a valid description of our "postmodern" era. I argue, however, that although "colonialism" as a system of historical and geographical structures of power may have ended, "coloniality" is alive and well.[85] "Global coloniality" is an appropriate description, in my view, of the current restructuring of the colonial patterns (e.g., coloniality) that shaped the modern/colonial world, from the sixteenth to the twenty-first century. "Global coloniality" does not imply a global university but, rather, the reproduction of coloniality at a global scale under neoliberal values and principles of education.

An important chapter in the history of the university in the modern/colonial world (through the different phases of colonial and imperial European and U.S. expansion) was written in the nineteenth century, during the transition from the Renaissance to the Kantian-Humboldtian era, when secular philosophy and science triumphed over Christian theology and rhetoric. The nation-state became the prevailing form of government, displacing despotic political regimes (which reappeared in the twentieth century as different forms of totalitarianism and dictatorship) and the foundation of the modern nation-states in Europe and in modern/colonial states elsewhere. The first wave of "postcolonial" states emerged in the Americas. The colonial Renaissance university, organized around the trivium and the quadrivium in the service of the church and the Crown, gave way to the colonial Kantian-Humboldtian university, organized around philosophy and sciences in the service of the emerging nation-states. However, in the seventeenth century several temporalities coexisted that were not alien to the planetary transformations of the Renaissance university. While, in the Americas, the university was part of the process of decolonization and the construction of colonial nation-states, in South Asia and (North and sub-Saharan) Africa, which were falling under the colonial control of Great Britain, France, Germany, and Italy, the Renaissance university did not have the same strong institutional stature.

The university was and still is part of this set of changing processes, which maintains the logic of coloniality through "nation building." Nation-states are not the end of coloniality; they are simply its restructuring. British education in India in the nineteenth century (Viswanathan 1989), for example, followed a logic similar—although with different content—to the one that organized the study of Latin and rhetoric in Mexico in the sixteenth century: In both cases, the university was crucial to the introduction, and eventual displacement, of existing forms of knowledge that were labeled "traditional" and measured against the "modernity" of secular philosophy in European science. The practice of science in nineteenth-century India[86] and the creation of state universities in Latin America (Argentina, Chile, Uruguay,

Brazil) were processes complementary to both nation building and the different temporalities in the restructuring of coloniality of power and knowledge.[87] The difference was that, in Latin America, the new universities, built according to the Kantian-Humboldtian model, coexisted with universities from the colonial/Renaissance period, which entered into a process of radical transformation. In nineteenth-century Latin America, the state universities were linked to the process of nation building, although this occurred in "dependent" countries—or, if you prefer, under conditions of "internal colonialism." Decolonization meant, in the nineteenth and twentieth centuries, that an elite of "creoles" or "natives" took power and reproduced the patterns implanted by colonial rulers. In this sense, nation-building was a form of colonialism, of internal colonialism. That is, it was a pattern of coloniality in the hands of creoles of Spanish descent or *mestizos* of Spanish and Indian mixture. The university of the nineteenth century, in British India as well as in Spanish America, followed the Kantian-Humboldtian model of the European university.[88]

The "corporate" university is the type of university that, in industrialized countries, has been displacing the Kantian-Humboldtian tradition since the 1970s. Its exemplar model is the U.S. university (see Wallerstein 1997). In ex–Third World countries, the "model" began to be imposed in the late 1980s but more clearly after the collapse of the Soviet Union. The initial manifestations of the newly imposed "quality control" of the faculty as well as of departments and special programs, in Argentina or in Mexico, were the demands that professors publish in refereed journals, account for their research and publications periodically, and so on. Another manifestation has been the progressive deterioration of major state universities and the parallel and complementary divergence between accumulation of money and accumulation of meaning, characteristic of capitalism and Western universities. In Latin America, state universities had been the home of the humanities or the human sciences of critical thinking (sociohistorical, ethical, and political) and, of course, major centers of political upheaval against the various versions of dictatorship. The deterioration of state universities has been mirrored by the proliferation of private "universities," the majority of which are centers for professional and technical training only. Philosophy and other humanistic disciplines either have a low profile or are not part of the curriculum in the private "universities" emerging in Latin America. They are, so to speak, the latest manifestation of "modernization," in which local elites see the university as both a business like any other and a sign of "modern" status. A new facet of coloniality manifests itself in the turn that higher education is taking in both developed and emerging countries. Historically, Italy and the

Iberian Peninsula provided the model of the Renaissance university, while Germany and France provided the model of the Enlightenment university, in the tradition of Immanuel Kant and Alexander von Humboldt. Today, the U.S. that is mainly leading the way in the transformation of the latter model into that of the corporate university, a phenomenon that should be seen in the context of other neoliberal developments in Latin America, such as the Free Trade Area of the Americas (FTAA) and Plan Colombia.[89]

Let us consider the three moments in the histories of the university and the *temporal* epistemic fractures in its European version then look at the *spatial* epistemic fractures emanating from its colonial version. We also examine spatial epistemic fractures in the emergence of the Universidad Intercultural, which has been led by indigenous intellectuals with the collaboration, of course, of mestizos and Whites. It may be objected that we are trying to cover too much ground in too few pages. Not really, since our goal is not to describe in detail the full history of the European and colonial universities but to highlight three epistemic fractures of the institution. The temporal one fits Michel Foucault's conceptualization of "epistemic breaks" in the history of Western thought. The other two largely escaped Foucault's model, at the same time, as they allow for a critique showing the regional limits of his "epistemic breaks."

One of the spatial fractures, in the Americas, is the history of the colonial university in the hands of Hispano-, Luso-, and Anglophone creoles as well as *mestizos*, particularly in South America, where the first four major modern/colonial universities were created. By "spatial fractures," we mean that the colonial university (in its Renaissance, Kantian-Humboldtian, and corporate versions) was always coeval with and dependent on the metropolitan university, while at the same time disrupting the memories of the colonies. It was not the same thing to read Aristotle in Salamanca or Paris as in Mexico City/Tenochtitlan or Cuzco. Similarly, it was a different experience to read Rousseau in Paris than to read him in Nigeria or Bolivia in the middle of the nineteenth century. In contrast to the Renaissance and (Kantian-Humboldtian) Enlightenment universities, which generated two colonial fractures (one when the university was at the service of the monarchy and church and the other when it served the metropolitan or colonial state), and to the corporate university, which expanded and introduced a new set of values over the state university (both in the metropolis and in the ex-colonies or independent states), Amawtay Wasi, the Universidad Intercultural de las Nacionalidades y los Pueblos Indígenas, introduced a fracture of a different kind. For the first time in the history of the modern/colonial world, a university was created whose epistemic foundation (e.g., the principles and the type of knowledge) was no longer that of the European Renaissance university and its medieval and classical (Greek) foundations. The foundation of the Universidad Intercultural is not Greece but the Tawantinsuyu. "What is that?" you may ask. If you indeed asked yourself this question, that is the point I am trying to make, since you would not have asked it if I referred to Ancient Greek society and cosmology or to the Greek polis, doxa, and episteme ("Tawantinsuyu" is the Quichua word for "the Four Territories," a map of the world for the Inca Empire; Barja 2001). Of course, Western knowledge and civilization is part of the curriculum of the Universidad Intercultural. It will be duly "included" and processed. The radical difference here is that we are talking about the "inclusion" of Western civilization within a curriculum grounded in indigenous philosophy and not about the "inclusion" of indigenous knowledge within the state (and corporate) university, whose foundations remain in the Renaissance and the Enlightenment types of universities.

The history of the European university since the Renaissance has been framed as part of the larger macro-narrative of Western civilization. In this narrative, history originated in Greece, spread through the northwest of the Mediterranean, then crossed the Atlantic to culminate in the U.S. Samuel Huntington's "clash of civilizations" is as good an example as any other in rehearsing such macro-narratives, although he mainly covers the twentieth century. In this framework, the university is an invention of the Middle Ages, of the High and Late Middle Ages around the twelfth century, to be more precise. The creation of the university as an institution was the culmination of a process of scholastic learning. There were continuities, writes Marcia Colish (1997), linking the revival of speculation in the eleventh century with the interests and methods of masters and cathedral schools and universities in the twelfth century and after. One of the major links was the belief and the confidence that reason could shed light on any subject and that the increasing use of logic and semantics would take medieval philosophy well beyond its classical roots (Colish 1997: 266). Since the university, today, is rooted in a tradition of learning originating *from* monastic and cathedral schools, the university is complicit with both philosophical universalism and Christianity. The mottoes of many universities, inscribed on their official seals in Latin, with that language's corresponding legacy in the conceptualization of knowledge, is an obvious reminder. Latin was not only the language of learning; it was also the language of power. Previously, Arabic and Hebrew had been pushed out of the temples of learning in favor of Greek, which supported a Greco-Latin tradition in learning parallel to the Judeo-Christian tradition in religion. These centuries-old epistemic power struggles have clear ramifications in the history of Israel, and the Israeli-Palestinian conflict, as well as, of course, for the most recent history of colonialism, from the British Empire to U.S. imperialism. The medieval university, in other words, laid the foundation for the geopolitics of knowledge under whose hegemony much of the world still lives.

In the university of the European Renaissance scholastic learning was displaced by humanistic learning. Accordingly, the role and profile of the humanist replaced that of the *scriptor* and *notarius* as well as new roles that had emerged in the twelfth century, the *magister* and the *grammaticus* (Gil Fernández 1981: 231–428). At the top of the pyramid were theologians and the "masters" of the law. The names they received at the time were *literaratus* and *jurisperitus*. The appearance of these social actors in the Middle Ages is linked to "the emergence of written culture" (Stock 1983: 30–88). In the late Renaissance, the towering symbolic image of the humanist, the Renaissance man, cut across the redistribution of knowledge in jurisprudence, political philosophy, history, grammar, rhetoric, poetics (or literature, as we say since the Enlightenment), mathematics, music, and dialectics. Latin was still the master language, and the *trivium* and the *quadrivium* remained as a general frame for the organization of knowledge.

But an *extraordinary* series of events intervened in the history of the Renaissance. And here is where the second kind of history begins. The out-of-the-ordinary event I refer to is the colonization of the New World and the creation of New World universities. The colonial university, in the Americas, had a function different from that of the European Renaissance university. It had a mission that was clearly "out of place"; that is, the university in the New World did not have the medieval university's *burden of the past* (hence, the temporal epistemic fracture). It had the *burden of the present*, since it was implanting itself over the institutions devoted to education in the Aztec and Inca "empires," as well as over the remains of Mayan knowledge in astronomy and mathematics (hence, the spatial epistemic fracture). The colonial university was a university without history, so to speak, a university out of place, since it did not include the educational tradition of the Aztecs but did include that of the Greeks and Romans. Nahuatl, in other words, was not considered as valuable as Greek and Latin. Indigenous knowledges and epistemologies neither corresponded to the history of the West nor were recognized by the missionaries and men of letters who founded the Universidad de México and the Universidad de San Marcos in Lima, Peru. The model of the Renaissance university, on the contrary, contributed to the eradication of the Aztecs' and Incas' educational institutions and the displacement and subalternization of their ways of knowing. Inca and Aztec knowledges, in the minds of missionaries and men of letters, were dictates of the devil and consequently should be eradicated. What the Spaniards called the "extirpation of idolatry" was in fact an epistemic lobotomy. The mission of the Universidad Intercultural is precisely to ground itself in the knowledge tradition that was marginalized and disrupted by the installation of the colonial/Renaissance university in the New World. But, of course, the mission of the Universidad Intercultural is not a *recuperation* of ancient knowledge but its *reactivation* in the process of appropriating Western technical contributions, although not Western values of education, which are increasingly complicit with capitalism.

The second spatial epistemic fracture is harder to understand. To some, it may sound "New Age" or "new Rousseauian." Those who think thus may be limited by the very frontiers of "modernity" that allowed for the successful invention of "traditions" to bolster the epistemic position of "modernity." Other skeptics may not know that the Universidad Intercultural is a political project—as were the Renaissance and Kantian-Humboldtian universities—grounded in many years of indigenous social movements and emerging from the 1987 reform of the Ecuadorian constitution. Still other doubters will remain unconvinced because they cannot accept that indigenous people and people of African descent can meet their own needs instead of waiting for the Whites and *mestizos* in power to generously offer what they—as inferior people—need. In other words, one of the difficulties in truly understanding the radical nature of the project, of the Universidad Intercultural, is coming to terms with the fact that there are other forms of knowledge (beyond the Western tradition) that are equally valid. One of the impediments to overcoming the blindness of the ideology of modernity and modernization is understanding that the great intellectual and scientific achievements of the West are indeed great achievements, but that, at the same time, *there is no reason why the rest of the world has to bend to them*. Linked to the need to uncouple the recognition of achievements from imperial motivations is the fact that the complicity between the accumulation of money and the accumulation of meaning (knowledge) are two sides of the same coin. "Knowledge," in the prevailing view, is still conceived of as, above all, a kind of materiality and geopolitics available to everyone, regardless of sex and sexuality, color, belief, or the part of the world where one was born, grew up, and went to school and the university.

The "conquest" of America meant the demolition of indigenous educational and economic systems. Universities in the New World were located in the land of people whose languages and histories bore no relationship to either Greek and Latin or Arabic and Hebrew. In sixteenth-century Mexico, a very interesting and intense effort was made to teach Latin to the Nahuatl-speaking Indians. The Crown soon came to believe that this was a risky proposition (since indigenous people might use what they learned against the Spanish institution for their own liberation), and by the seventeenth century, teaching Latin to the Indians was a forgotten episode of the early stage of colonization. Frederick Douglass told a similar story, later on, in the context of African slaves' relationships with their masters in the U.S. There is here a "discontinuity of the classical tradition" (Mignolo 1992), a discontinuity that can be attributed to colonialism (Mignolo 1995, 2000), which I identified as one of the two spatial epistemic fractures. The second, and radically different, fracture is the Universidad Intercultural.

Before going into more detail about the Universidad Intercultural, let us look at the internal colonial transformation of the colonial Renaissance university into the colonial Enlightenment one, that is, at the first temporal epistemic fracture in the history of the university within Western civilization. Toward the end of the eighteenth century, secularization and the French Revolution, together with a redistribution and reconceptualization of knowledge, led to the emergence of what is known in the history of learning as the Kantian-Humboldtian university, that is, the university at the service of the emerging nation-states. The nineteenth century witnessed the birth of the social sciences—required by the need to organize government and civil society—and also the consolidation of political economy. Wilhelm Dilthey, at the end of the nineteenth century, conceptualized the distinction between the natural and the human sciences, between the nomothetic and the ideographic forms of knowledge, between explanation and understanding. Knowledge of nature became detached from knowledge of society and of human beings. Such a conception of knowledge is alien to the indigenous histories in the Americas, as well as to concepts of knowledge and understanding beyond European modernity. The transition, across the Americas, from the colonial to the national period implied the transformation of both the colonial Renaissance university into the colonial Kantian-Humboldtian university and the colonial provinces into nation-states. The colonial elites that controlled the economy, the church, and the government were not bourgeois elites, as in Europe. There were significant differences between the Anglo- and Spanish-American revolutionary elites; in both cases, however, coloniality was a physically invisible but always present force among the creoles in both Anglo-and Spanish America.

While this transformation was under way in the Americas, the British in India were beginning their version of a process that the Spanish and Portuguese had started in the "New World" almost three centuries earlier and the Anglo-Americans a century after that with the foundation of Harvard and other early universities in what would become the U.S. (see Viswanathan 1989, Prakash 2000, Gortari 1979, and Jardine 1999). A similar process would unfold in the nineteenth century in other places in Asia, Africa, and the Caribbean, where the British and French Empires extended their colonial administration. These processes were part of the second modernity, the Enlightenment. In the ex-colonies, the story evolved somewhat differently depending on whether the metropole was Spain, Portugal, France, or England. Between 1776 and 1831, approximately, these colonies became independent from their former masters and began the process of building themselves into nations. The colonial Renaissance university founded in the sixteenth and the seventeenth centuries had to transform itself under new social demands and a New World order. New universities were created. The University of North Carolina, the first state university in the U.S., was chartered in 1789 and opened its doors in 1795. The point here is that, while the model of the Kantian-Humboldtian university was that of higher education under new forms of colonialism, in the emerging nation-states of the Americas, the same type of university began to replace the model established during the Renaissance. But, of course, the process in the Americas, particularly in South or Latin America, was not the same as the process in Europe. Europe and the Americas were separated by the colonial difference ("the colonial difference" meaning not only that people in the colonies are "different" but that they are "inferior" and need to be "civilized," "modernized," or "developed"), a difference that is in place today, although their histories have followed divergent paths. The university, in other words, played a fundamental role in nation building. However, while for England and France, and of course for Germany, nation-building was part of Western expansion and the civilizing mission in the Americas, it was linked to nation building and the articulation of a new form of colonialism, "internal colonialism." In India, as well as other places in Asia and Africa, the university was instead part of the colonial regime. This was also the period in which philology, in the European universities, contributed to the creation of the idea and the images of the "Orient," as well as the idea of the "South" of Europe (e.g., see Dainotto 2000). The Kantian-Humboldtian university was, in other words, the university in what Hegel labeled as "the heart of Europe" (Germany, England, and France), while the Renaissance university was, mainly, the university in what became the "South" (Italy, Spain, Portugal).

And now, at the intersection of the two histories (the colonial and the modern), we come to the period after World War II. The U.S. started to assume the role played until then by England, France, and Germany. This was the era of the Cold War and the Cold War university (Wallerstein 1997), the era in which the social sciences, in the U.S., gained preeminence over the humanities. It was also the era of decolonization in Asia and in Africa, and the era of the Cuban revolution and dictatorship in various Latin American countries. The social sciences in the U.S. were associated with the materialization of "area studies." Even if there were conflicts between those who defended the purity and rigor of the disciplines and those who became experts in the "content" of certain areas, the fact remains that "area studies" was an affair of the social sciences as much as "Orientalism" was an affair of the humanities. It was also the heyday of the social sciences in the sense that they were part of the project of the "development and modernization" of the Third World. In Latin America, the social sciences are a recent addition. Although there were *cátedras* of sociology before 1950, the social sciences as a branch of knowledge were introduced in or after the late 1950s. Interestingly enough, the report of the Gulbenkian Foundation, *Open the Social Sciences* (Wallerstein et al. 1996), emphasized the crisis of these disciplines not only in the "central countries," where they were born and prospered, but also in the Third World. The "Gulbenkian report" was followed by thirteen small volumes in which the future of the social sciences in various regions of the former Third World was discussed.

But, this was also the period when the corporate university began to displace the Kantian-Humboldtian model. The more technologically oriented social sciences (economics, political science, and sociology) remained the exemplars of rigorous and useful knowledge, while the humanities and the interpretive social sciences (history, cultural anthropology, and interpretive sociology) lost their previous standing in the hierarchy of efficient knowledge required by corporate values associated with knowledge. The consequences of the corporate university's emergence became apparent after the end of the Cold War. In the former Third World, including Latin America, the principles of "excellence" and "efficiency" became guiding tenets of knowledge production. Parallel to these processes, the large state universities in various Latin American countries started a process of disintegration (see Chomsky et al. 1997 and North American Congress on Latin America 2000). The *fuga de cerebros*, or "brain drain," accelerated in various countries, as well-regarded intellectuals, scholars, and scientists migrated to Europe and the U.S. Scientists in former Third-World nations also voiced their discomfort with the deprived and meager conditions under which they had to do their jobs. The "network society" (i.e., the world society connected through the internet more than by means of transportation), as Catalan sociologist Manuel Castells calls it, does not have the same intensity in the South as in the North. Until 1996 or so, Africa and Latin America were not yet on the map of this society. "Excellence" and "efficiency" turned against the scientific and scholarly production of the Third World. And, once again, the possibilities for technological expansion have been restricted by the demands and expectations of economic designs.

The preceding story is a blueprint of two kinds of histories of the university. However, we are often reminded of the canonical names in the history of Western thought (Diderot, Smith, Marx, Freud) but not of those whose intellectual production was part of the canon not of "modernity" but of "coloniality." A few examples of the latter are Guamán Poma in Peru (in the late sixteenth and early seventeenth centuries), Mohandas Gandhi in India, Aimé Césaire and Frantz Fanon in the Caribbean, Nelson Mandela in South Africa, and Subcomandante Marcos and the Zapatistas in Mexico. In all these cases, the production and transformation of knowledge and understanding was not restricted to the university.

Here are the issues from the previous narrative that I consider relevant to our discussion:

1. Our main thesis is that the history of capitalism runs parallel to the history of knowledge. Also, an implicit distribution of values and labor places knowledge in relation to nature. Asia, Africa, and Latin America became the providers of "natural" resources to be processed in the countries in which the Industrial Revolution took place and prospered. These three continents were also placed in the role of providing information and culture but not knowledge. Or, the knowledge produced in the regions that were either colonized or remained outside the scope of colonial expansion was considered relevant only in and for those regions. The situation today is not radically different from the one that began to unfold five hundred years ago, when the Renaissance university was transplanted to the New World. Of course, since then, numerous "nation-states" have been considered "developing countries." Universities are institutions that depend, today more than ever, on the economy. Thus, in "developing countries" one can surmise that we also have "developing universities." There is not yet a transnational institution for higher education with the function that the World Bank and the International Monetary Fund perform in relation to the state in developing countries. The United Nations Educational, Scientific, and Cultural Organization (UNESCO) may be the closest we can get to a transnational institution related to research and education.

2. The histories, as I have told them, imply a relation of "dependency" that is not just economic but also epistemic (that is, cultural, intellectual, scientific in a larger sense of the word, and technological, as well

as related to the natural and social sciences) and manifests itself at the level of the disciplines. This was one of the concerns of the Gulbenkian report. Dipesh Chakrabarty, a South Asian historian now teaching at the University of Chicago, noted the particular kind of epistemic dependency in the domain of history as a discipline. Chakrabarty remarks that the "history" of the Third World cannot be written on "its own," since history (as a discipline) is a European invention. Consequently, the history of the world "depends" on European history. In this regard, Chakrabarty (2000) underscores that, while European historians do not need to quote, mention, or take into account the history of India when they write the history of Europe, Indian historians cannot write their own history without taking into account European history. My own understanding of "epistemic dependency" runs parallel to economic dependency and touches all areas of knowledge, as I suggested earlier in describing colonialism as disruption of the epistemic and economic organization in the Andes and Mesoamerica. You may be thinking that I ignore the fact that "dependency theory" has been harshly criticized. But, I am aware of that. However, just because "dependency theory" has been criticized and because "dependency" does not "depend"—so to speak—on the evil designs of foreign capitals (only), it does not follow, necessarily, that we should *not* think in terms of "dependency." How else can one describe the situation of Argentina today? As I finished an earlier version of this essay, Eduardo Duhalde was the president and the Argentine crisis seemed to be hitting bottom. It would be difficult to ignore that, while the "financial dependency" of Argentina on the IMF and the government of the U.S. is not the only explanation for the crisis, "structural interstate dependency" is a foundational factor of capitalism at the international level. Capitalism functions not only by exploiting the labor of individual workers but by taking advantage of interstate export and import, natural resources in "Third World" countries (oil, for example), and financial flows of capital and interest.

3. If the map I just traced has a grain of truth, what then are the needs and possibilities for interuniversity cooperation, given the framework of the corporate university and the need to think in terms of international and interdisciplinary relations and cooperation? To address these questions, we need to remember that, while the Kantian-Humboldtian university was linked to nation building, the corporate university appeared at a time when certain nation-states are being rendered less and less relevant. That is, the corporate university is linked to a

global and, in a certain sense, postnational era. How are the conditions of knowledge production changing today in terms of the invention of new tools (e.g., the internet and other technologies that are opening up new avenues for the production and distribution of knowledge traditionally supported by the book)? How are these changes challenging and perhaps making obsolete the conceptualization of knowledge we inherited from the Kantian-Humboldtian university (natural sciences, social sciences, and the humanities)? And, what would be the humanities' role in the response of the corporate university to the needs of globalization?

The story is not over yet, however: a crucial chapter—the second spatial epistemic fracture (that is, a fracture from the European legacy as well as from the creole/*mestizo* colonial version of that legacy)—began to unfold with the creation in Ecuador of Amawtay Wasi. This university, conceived from the perspective of indigenous knowledge but not for indigenous people only, constitutes a reversal, but not an opposition, of and to the history of the university in the Western world and its colonies that I outlined previously. From the perspective of the European university, whether in its Renaissance or Enlightenment model, whether in Europe or in the colonies, indigenous knowledge was, at best, an interesting object of study, but never part of what was considered true, sustainable, or generative knowledge. The project of Amawtay Wasi radically reverses these relations. However, while, in the European model of the university in Europe and the colonies, indigenous knowledge was an object of study, from the perspective of Amawtay Wasi, modern (Western) knowledge is incorporated as sustainable and generative knowledge. This is a paradigmatic example, in my view, of the epistemic potential of border thinking. From the perspective of subaltern knowledges, all knowledge and understanding is potentially sustainable and generative, while from the perspective of Western hegemonic knowledge, the only generative and sustainable knowledge is founded on the canon of Western thought and scholarship.

Let me address first, then, the notion of "interculturalidad" as the indigenous intellectuals leading the project and the implementation of the Universidad Intercultural are using the term. "Interculturalidad" refers not to the universality of certain phenomena but, rather, to the singularity of the perspective from which intercultural (epistemic, political, ethical) relations are being conceived. We should dispel from the outset the suspicion that "interculturalidad" is just another name for what in the U.S. is called "multiculturalidad" (in Spanish) or "multiculturalism" (in English). To avoid misunderstanding and false alarms, it should be said first that the meanings of "interculturalidad" and "multiculturalism" are similar when used in the discourse of the state. The differences are historical. That is, they lie in how multiculturalism and *interculturalidad*, as seen from the perspective of the state, have been formed.

Multiculturalism is, in the U.S., an updated version of the "melting pot." Both terms have been prompted by massive immigration transforming the U.S. society. However, the "melting pot" refers to a society transformed by European immigration at the end of the nineteenth and beginning of the twentieth centuries, while "multiculturalism" refers to a society transformed by massive migration from the Third World and by the internal transformation prompted by the Civil Rights movement at the end of the 1960s. The differences between "multiculturalism" in the U.S. and "interculturalidad" used from the perspective of the state in Ecuador or Bolivia are based on the configuration of the ethnoracial maps in those countries.

In the U.S., the first three sides of the ethnoracial pentagon were formed by the colonial history of Native Americans, African slaves, and European Protestant Whites. To this basis was added the largely Catholic and Jewish European immigration of the end of the nineteenth and the beginning of the twentieth centuries. The fifth side of the pentagon has been added since 1970, with the extensive immigration from the Third World. This is the point at which the "melting pot" has transformed into "multiculturalism." Furthermore, with the sudden "visibility" of Muslim Americans since 9/11, it has become clear that the pentagon is being transformed by public immigration-control policy into an ethnoracial hexagon.

In Ecuador, and more generally in the Andean region of Latin America, the ethnoracial foundation was laid out by the Indians, that is, the population under the administration of the Inca Empire, and by the Spaniards. Creoles/*mestizos*, that is, people of Spanish (or European) descent (mixed with "Indian blood"), became the third component of the ethnoracial configuration. Later on, with the end of slavery, the Afro population that was concentrated mainly in the Caribbean began to migrate to other areas of Latin America, chiefly to the west of modern Colombia and Ecuador. The European immigration of the late nineteenth and early twentieth centuries did not greatly affect the ethnoracial composition of Ecuador. The bottom line is, then, that Indians (about thirty-five distinct groups) form 40 percent of the country's population, estimated at around twelve million. Mestizos constitute another 40 percent. People of Spanish descent, that is nonmestizos, are calculated to be 15 percent, and people of African descent make up the remaining 5 percent. The meaning of interculturalidad should be understood in this context. Moreover, it should be remembered that the Indian population has a strong organization, the Confederación Nacional de Indígenas del Ecuador (CONAIE) and that its representatives have occupied and continue to occupy important positions in the government. There are thirty-three cities, at this writing, governed by indigenous leaders, and many indigenous people have been members of the Congress; an indigenous woman, Nina Pacari, was vice president of the Congress until recently (Consejo Nacional de Cultura del Ecuador 2000). Luis Alberto Macas, a lawyer by training, was very influential in the foundation of the CONAIE and is currently director of the Instituto Científico de Culturas Indígenas, or ICCI-Rimmai. He is also the leading figure in the instrumentation of the Universidad Intercultural.[90]

The government conceives of interculturalidad as a generous move toward the inclusion, in education as well as in other spheres of life, of the population that has not been included during the long years of nation building and creole/*mestizo* concentration of power. The university in Ecuador, state or private, complemented the construction of the nation-state, which, in Ecuador as in any other country in Latin America, North America, or Europe, is a uninational state. However, from the indigenous perspective, the Universidad Intercultural should lead toward a plurinational state. The aims and goals of the Universidad Intercultural, from the perspective of the indigenous people, are not the same as the goals and principles of the creoles/ *mestizos* who created the nineteenth-century university in Ecuador on the European Kantian-Humboldtian model.

The Universidad Intercultural is not framed on a "campus" but disseminated throughout the country, among the communities, like a net. The nodes of the net are mainly in areas with high concentrations of indigenous population. However, the university is for everybody and not for indigenous people only.

All the degrees that the university offers are named in Quichua. The official language of all universities in Spanish America is (still) Spanish, although the colonial languages of the second modernity (English, French, and German) are, in relation to Spanish, what Spanish is to Aymara. That is, "valuable" knowledge nowadays is produced in English, French, or German, not Spanish. There are significant grammatical (not to mention historical) differences among these languages, but it is still "easier" to translate between Spanish and German than between Quichua and Spanish or German. By the same token, translation between Quichua and Aymara or Nahuatl is easier than translation between any of these languages and German or Spanish, and so on. As one example of the difficulty, for a speaker of modern European languages, the future is "in front" of the speaker, thus the possibility and the importance of the idea of "progress." For Quichua or Aymara speakers, the future is "behind," because it cannot be seen. The past can be remembered and therefore "seen"; it is thus "in front" of you, hence the difficulty among Quichua or Aymara speakers of naturally inventing an idea like "progress."

Let's give an example from the organization of graduate studies. The name of the program is "Amautai," *amauta* meaning a person of wisdom in ancient Quichua and Aymara. The program is composed of cycles: "Amautai Kallari" (general wisdom, first cycle) and "Sumak Amautai" (particularized wisdom, second cycle, equivalent to the PhD). The first focuses on specific knowledges, either practical or reflexive. The second is devoted to the process of researching and writing the doctoral dissertation. The two cycles are linked through the axis of "communitarian practice" in the sense that, while preparing the doctoral dissertation, the candidate has to do work in the community. The other two cycles are "Runa Yachaikuna" (cycle of indigenous sciences) and "Shuktak Yachaikuna" (cycle of universal sciences). The second is seen as "complementary" to the indigenous sciences that are the main component of the curriculum. The first cycle, "Runa Yachaikuna," has as its main objective "to socialize indigenous knowledge to allow the students to consolidate their identity and to strengthen their self-valorization. That is, *the goal is to allow student learning to be*" (Boletín ICCI-RIMAI 2000: 53).[91]

Tinku is an Aymara-Quichua word meaning a conflict of power, contrary as well as contradictory, a dialogue of feelings as well as a conceptual struggle, a dialogue of experiences and conceptions of life. *Tinku* alludes to physical as well as conceptual encounters that are embedded in the history of colonialism and, certainly, in the installation and survival of the Renaissance and Kantian-Humboldtian universities in the history of (Latin) America. The very conceptualization of the Universidad Intercultural is redirecting the future, and changing the path of history. It is a *tinku*, but now one performed by indigenous agents instead of one performed on them, as was the case with the Renaissance and Kantian-Humboldtian universities. The Universidad Intercultural opens up a wide range of opportunities but, above all, it makes possible an education from the perspective of those knowledges that have been subordinated and displaced in the history of the Western and colonial universities, from the Renaissance university to the corporate one. At this juncture I see two types of university for the future, and a wide range of possibility in between. I say "two types" and not "two universities." Each type may have a variety of manifestations, but there is a "difference" between the two types that cannot be transcended without serious negotiation. That difference is "the colonial difference," which has been historically articulated in a wide array of configurations, through the diversity of colonial experiences. The two "types" of possibilities I see are the following. At one extreme is the potential of improving the university within the neoliberal ideals of civilization and democracy. That is, a society in which democracy is managed from above, by "skillful and efficient managers," and in which 30 percent of the population enjoys prosperity and the remaining 70 percent is left out of the social order. At the other extreme is the promise offered by the Universidad Intercultural as a model reproducible around the world. This type of university is guided by the ideal of a "critical cosmopolitanism," that is, an education whose final goal is to generate, simultaneously with positive knowledge (medicine, law, economy, technology), a critical understanding that balances "efficiency" and "justice," "development" and "democracy," "freedom," and "violence to defend freedom," and so on.

The role of the humanities in the corporate university is larger than the role it may play within one history, that of the modern (European) university. The critical role of the humanities should be involved with the critical legacies within the colonial university and the radical transformation being enacted by projects like the Universidad Intercultural. At this point, the humanities cease to be the "humanities" of the European tradition and its colonial legacies. They become something else, a space of "border thinking" and political transformation in which the Western contribution to universal knowledge is only one, as important as any other, but regional, not itself universal. And in the same way that the Western and modern epistemology and its institution, the university, built itself by absorbing and integrating other legacies (e.g., Arabic epistemology, so crucial to European modernity), the myriad subaltern knowledges around the world are a living example that Western legacies survive by dying in the womb of those knowledges that modernity itself had to subdue in order to survive as modernity. The next step in the transformation toward a better world, where knowledge no longer is controlled by corporations and imperial states and the *uni*-versity becomes a *pluri*-versity, can no longer emanate from Western modernity. The incomplete project of modernity can no longer be completed by and from the ideals under which European modernity was built. Modernity belongs to the planet, and it is up to the rest of the planet to complete the project that European modernity can no longer finish. The total collapse of morality and expertise that we have been witnessing with Enron, WorldCom, the Catholic Church, the IMF in Russia, Turkey, and Argentina, and the silent secrecy of the Pentagon and the CIA vis-à-vis 9/11 are all signs of the limits of Euro-American modernity. More than the accumulation of knowledge and an information superhighway, what is valid are new principles of understanding. In that regard, Western humanities can join forces with the reactivated subaltern knowledges in the modern/colonial world, as the example of Amawtay Wasi illustrates.

AFTERWORD

IT IS TIME to return to our main line of argument: learning to unlearn in order to relearn, the decoloniality of knowledge and of being, and the decolonial option. How are these three concepts related and how do we relate to them?

First of all, the principle of learning to unlearn in order to relearn is, as explained in the Introduction, the starting point of Amawtay Wasi. Therefore, it is a proposition of Indigenous philosophical and decolonial thinking. As neither of us is an Indian in blood or in the way of life, philosophy, or education, what would the consequences be of taking this principle as the first step? We are not trying to appropriate and expropriate the proposition of learning to unlearn and by so doing contribute to reactionary forces that would be happier if such an institution (Amawtay Wasi) did not exist and the traditional imperial/colonial universities (e.g., state universities) or private and corporate ones were the only options. On the contrary, rather than appropriating the breakthrough, advanced by Amawtay Wasi, we submit to it, in the same way as other intellectuals prefer to submit to the Hegelian or Marxist options instead of submitting to Indian epistemology and wisdom. By so doing, we shift our own epistemic geography and contribute to shifting the geography of reasoning and the geopolitics of knowledge. As stated previously, by geopolitics of knowledge, we are spatializing epistemology and delinking from the idea that there is only one house of knowledge, that being the one built on two classical and six modern Western European imperial languages.

Second, in which way does the argument advanced in this book contribute to learning to unlearn and to the decoloniality of knowledge and being? The first chapter introduced border thinking and border epistemology ingrained and embodied in colonial and imperial differences. It then framed the entire argument that was developed in two types of local histories responding to imperial local histories and Western locally based global designs. Central Asia and the Caucasus, on the one hand, and South America and the Caribbean, on the other, are not objects we studied, "applying" border epistemology, but are precisely the local histories from where border epistemologies emerge, very much like the local histories of Western Christendom transmuted into secular European philosophy and science. The difference is that border epistemologies around the world advance decolonizing projects while Western Christian and secular epistemologies advance national European formations and their imperial expansion. The concept of "humanity" was crucial in that endeavor, since it was a key concept to classify and rank the world according to races, gender, and sexuality. Chapters 3 and 4 describe, through the imperial and colonial differences, what needs to be unlearned and what the horizons are for relearning and, therefore, for decolonial education and agency. Chapters 5 to 7 focus on the concept of humanity within Western imperial histories and its complicity with the idea and practice of citizenship. Thus, our argument closes with a history of the Western modern and colonial university, on the one hand, and the breakthrough, the discontinuity introduced by Amawtay Wasi.

Border epistemologies, very much like Western hegemonic and territorial ones, emerge from political, epistemic, and ethical needs. Territorial epistemology directly and indirectly contributed to found and consolidate the modern/imperial world order, the diversity of local histories that had to deal with the encroachment of Western political, economic, epistemic, and subject (trans)formation, where the need to emancipate, liberate, and decolonize becomes a question of fighting for human dignity that Western imperial ambitions needed to negate to advance the project of one world united by one global design. Border epistemology should be distinguished from anti-Western and anticapitalist doing and thinking. Anti-Western options are forms of resistance, while border epistemologies, in and from different local histories confronting imperial Western designs, not only oppose but mainly think forward, imagining and building a pluriversal and nonimperial world order(s). Thus, learning to unlearn becomes the starting point of border epistemologies and border epistemologies are the origination for delinking from what hegemonic education tells us (all of us) to learn and for what, instead of claiming for recognition and inclusion.

We have been working on the final version of this book during the financial and economic crisis that shook the world. We are not economists. But the crisis is not just an economic and financial problem to be solved by economists, bankers, and presidents of the G8 or the G20, or the G8 and the "emerging countries." It is a civilizational crisis that affects all levels of life, and crisis is also a good time for initiating the rethinking and delinking from the neoliberal model that has demonstrated its complete failure. As the economy has become increasingly the guiding horizon of Western civilization, subjectivities were formed and transformed according to economic and financial values based on the belief that development (that is, increasing production) is the road to freedom because it offers more options to people, but these options are of the same kind and in the same sphere of belief and values: Happiness has been tied to consumption and accumulation. Development is supposed to put more money in the pockets of people, from the multimillion-dollar salary of the CEO to the working class and the middle class—the entire spectrum of society dancing in the happiness of an infinite growth.

Instead we have been arguing for decolonial options. While development argues for increasing economic options, decoloniality argues that development is the latest rhetoric of modernity and the new modulation of coloniality. The question then is not how to make development work for all, to defend globalization or save capitalism. The argument of the book focuses on particular cases in which the civilization model has been analyzed from the margin of developed countries before the crisis, to be sure but in retrospect, in instances that were already signs of a nonsustainable world order structured, over the past five hundred years, on the making and remaking of imperial and colonial differences. If the management and control of economy within the colonial matrix of power established hierarchies on the bases of material wealth manifested in buildings, banks, corporations, institutions, monuments, museums, universities, and above all, national reserves, the discourses naturalizing such a world order and forming subjectivities permeated all other spheres of the colonial matrix: management and control of knowledge, subjectivities (citizens and consumers), and gender/sexuality. The financial crisis that started in 2008, and in 2011 affected the core of the system (The European Union and the U.S.), is another indication that the West (meaning the core of the EU and the U.S.) can no longer control the colonial matrix of power. The international dispute of our time is, indeed, for liberation, be it at the level of the States (cf. the BRIC countries) who are disputing who controls the matrix; or be it at the level of the political society (e.g., decolonial social movements and projects, like The Zapatistas and La Vía Campesina), which is aiming to delink from the colonial matrix of power.

What options are available to imagining a world beyond the colonial matrix of power? The world is linked today by a common conception of what the economy is and should be, let us call it "capitalism." The struggle takes place at the interstate level and centers on the control of authority. Iran and Venezuela base their strength on oil and dispute the control of authority in the name of Islam and Socialism of the twenty-first century, respectively. Bolivia joins forces but with a different claim: indigenous concepts of life, and therefore of politics and economy to move toward nonindividualistic, non-self-serving model, not governed by success through competition and killing, which is ingrained in Western conceptions under the name of democracy. China and India, two countries that account for half the population of the world, have been moving toward political disobedience in relation to Washington, the European Union in the Doha Round, and joining other emerging countries (Brazil, Australia, Mexico, South Africa) in rejection of the G8 plan for emission control. However, beyond the interstate system and the transstate network of the corporations, the novelty in the past thirty or so years is the growing forces of the global political society (i.e., the social movements). While the civil society has remained dependent and obedient to the dictates of the states, the corporations, and the supporting international institutions (UN, IMF, World Bank), the political society began to delink, to disobey the uniform conception of life based on individual success, accumulation, gains, growth of the GNP (Gross National Product), securing consumers to buy commodities with the single function to increase gains for the makers of these commodities, who, to do so, need to exploit labor, destroy the natural balance of Pachamama/Gaia as a living organism, and invent, in a very creative manner, the financial structures based on subprime mortgages that generated the most dramatic expanded moment for the majority of about 30 percent of the global population who "benefit" from a philosophical conception of life based on overproduction and overconsumption. For the rest of the world population, about 70 percent, the changes are not significant: They have been living under the level of poverty, increasingly, since 1820, the symbolic date of the Industrial Revolution and the splendid takeoff of Western civilization and industrial production.

All of this is what needs to be unlearned in order to relearn and to imagine a world not driven by the survival of the fittest in a society created by a handful of people, who constructed a world for the fittest and defined fitness according to their own will to power. The fact is that the majority of the population, who are not interested in the will to power, suffered the consequences of a world in which the will to power was naturalized. The time has come to build a world according to the needs and visions of those who are not driven by the will to power and the survival of the fittest.

The decolonial option proposes and promotes social organizations globally interconnected but not globally dominant or hegemonic, based on cooperation rather than competition, and on a horizon in which institutions are at the service of life rather than life at the service of institutions. Today, for example, the restructuring of the state and "saving" the capitalist economy are the two main concerns, at the expense of life in general, not only of human beings but of life of which human beings share in minimal proportion because life is much and very much larger than just human life.

It has been reported that, in industrialized countries, the crisis motivated people to go to church and find comfort in religion. Religious movements have been also instrumental in supporting people in stressful situations. However, religious options created by the need of the people do not necessarily match and correspond to the religious options promoted by the theologians (the Pope or theologians of liberation) in their will to help. If the papacy shares some features with liberal and democratic government and institutions concerned with "the end of poverty," theologians of liberation share some features with NGOs: NGOs present themselves as saviors, but the vision of NGOs seldom coincides with the vision of the people and communities they want to help. NGOs are embedded in the rhetoric of modernity, while the communities they are helping are victims of the logic of coloniality.

Another option is Marxism. As we stated previously, in Russian and Soviet ex-colonies, Marxism has become a difficult and complex option—contrary to the West, where it still has some purchase. Because of lack of information and the continuing zombification by the rhetoric of modernity and its binary division into right and left, these people have not yet perceived the decolonial option as a viable alternative, as it is, for example, for the countries of South America, where colonial Marxism (i.e., Marxism transplanted into the history of countries in which Amerindians and peasants live at the margins of industrialization and the formation of an industrial working class) has been in crisis for at least three decades.

Learning to unlearn, delinking from the naturalized conception of life that has been increasingly dominant in the past five hundred years, is the starting point of decolonial agency and thinking. The decolonial option emerges from that horizon. But, contrary to existing options based on universal assumptions and the drive to collect adepts as members of the institution (Christianity in its various forms, liberalism in its many variants, Marxism in all its modulations, Islamism in its different manifestations), the decolonial option does not offer a readymade horizon, like the options just mentioned: The decolonial option starts from delinking, learning to unlearn that the objectivity and truth without parentheses in which universal options are grounded, have been exhausted. The decolonial option is not a new universal, a convenient project for the future but, on the contrary, a starting point where the future has to be made in the process of learning to unlearn. This is precisely what the Zapatistas meant in their dictum: a world in which many worlds will coexist.

We are not offering a blueprint of how to learn to unlearn, because learning to unlearn is the constant process of delinking rather than a revolutionary act. The modern concept of revolution is being displaced by the transmodern and decolonial process of delinking and rebuilding (to relearn). We are ourselves in the process of unlearning, conceptualizing new categories of analysis that would not be infected by the rhetoric of modernity, but it is a difficult task and an open field that we invite everyone to join. Our book was one of the first attempts at learning to unlearn.

Since our anchor has been Amawtay Wasi, we do not imply that learning to unlearn is a process limited to the academy and higher education. To start with, Amawtay Wasi, as we explained, is a different type of academy, an other university, which is not competing on the same level as the modern and corporate universities are competing with each other (to get more grants, to have more students, national and international, to promote development, etc). Rather *it is moving in a different direction,* shifting the history of the university toward the needs of people who do not partake of the idea that rewards and recognition should be based on money and political position. If the bourgeoisie was the ethno-class that emancipated itself from the monarchs (European monarchs) and the Christian European church, we are living at the time in which the global political society is no longer contained in one ethno-class governed predominantly by males, but in a world in which the human dignity of the *damné* is at stake. The main social actors in the present and pointed toward the future are the many decolonial projects designed and enacted by the global political society, whose members share more than gender or ethnicity—the commonality of the colonial wound that makes them/us less human or less able to take their/our destiny in their/our own hands.

Learning to unlearn is an activity and thinking processes taking place not merely in the sphere of higher learning but in all spheres of life. The Zapatistas have a lot to offer, in a different domain of the social, the same way as Amawtay Wasi has in the sphere of higher education (Universidad de la Tierra). We made several passing references to the Zapatistas throughout the book. We would like to close by invoking the four domains in which the Zapatistas initiated, in their own movement, the process of learning to unlearn in order to relearn.

The first one, in random order, was initiated by the "urban intellectuals," such as Rafael Guillen, a group of Mexican activists who went to the Lacandon Jungle in the mid-1980s. In that process, Rafael Guillen became subcomandante Marcos and understood (learning to unlearn) that the Marxist ideals of the urban intellectuals were of little significance to communities who have been in the struggle for five hundred years, much before, and in a different context from, the Industrial Revolution in Europe and the emergence of the ethno-class of proletarians. Learning to unlearn was followed by a long and creative process—for and by the urban intellectuals—of learning to relearn. The teachers or better yet the people of wisdom were Indians from the south of Mexico, of the Maya region and Mayan languages. In other words, the people who have been classified from the initial days of the conquest as humanly deficient and in need of "learning" what Christians had to teach them, became the teachers. 'Governing by obeying at the same time" is simply a political treatise that is being unfolded in the very deeds of the Zapatistas.

From this political treatise, "Juntas de Buen Gobierno" or "Los Caracoles" emerged (González Casanova 2006). The name of this decolonial organization invokes the initial step taken by Guaman Poma de Ayala, in the Viceroyalty of Peru/Tawantinsuyu in his by now well-known historiographical and political treatise, *Nueva Coronica y Buen Gobierno*. "Los Caracoles" is just the enactment of the radical and decolonial political treatise in one sentence. Indians/Mexicans now have the option of managing their own life and destiny rather than casting votes for Mexican presidents who will ignore them and prevent them from taking their life into their own hands. That is they are learning to unlearn, delinking, in order to relearn, re-exist.

Correlative and complementary to the political principle and its enactment, is another well-known and powerful Zapatistas's statement: "Because we are all equal, we have the right to be different." The dictum shifts the naturalized Western modern (Christian and secular) hegemonic idea that, since we are all equal and humans, we should forget the differences. Such principles go badly with the very practice of Christian and liberal deeds, where differences are always repressed, suppressed, disavowed in their support for a homogeneous world that guards the interest of the global bourgeois ethno-class.

Last but not least (and introduced in "La segunda campaña") is the Zapatistas' reversal of any missionary will of conversion into existing ideologies (Christianity, liberalism, Marxism, Islamism) and their emphasis on the open orientations of decolonial options. This principle was expressed as "Andar preguntando" rather than "andar predicando" ("walking while asking rather than walking and conversing"). It should be understood as bi- or pluridirectionally. In other words, it is not a privilege of the Zapatistas to ask questions while walking, focusing on what the Zapatistas are interested in and preventing other "walkers" (i.e., the actors of converging but different decolonial projects) to do the same. If the process of asking while walking was unidirectional, it would not be a contribution to learning to unlearn but, rather, an enactment of missionary principles, only giving a false impression of contesting them. Learning to unlearn in order to relearn is a difficult process due to the fact that Western modernity is inscribed in all of us (Westerners or non-Westerners). But it is already an ongoing process enacted by many of us, because while recognizing that modernity is in all of us, we also recognize that coloniality is constitutive of modernity. Western contributions to world history must be celebrated, but the self-appointed role of modern actors and institutions to demand that the rest of the world follow their example has been and will always be totally illegitimate. The emerging global political society is responding to this false demand in a variegated process of delinking, learning to unlearn, and engaging in relearning.

APPENDIX

Amawtay Wasi, Universidad Intercultural de los Pueblos y Naciones Indigenas del Ecuador[1]

The Political Trajectory

The political process that eventually created UIAW (Universidad Intercultural Amawtay Wasi) goes back to the 70s when "los pueblos originarios" in the Américas, and in the world, began a new stage in their long-lasting struggles (500 years in the Américas, 300 years in New Zealand, Australia, Africa, and Asia) to survive under the increasing pressure of Western imperial Powers (Spain, Portugal, the Netherlands, France, England, the U.S.). Amawtay Wasi emerged from specific local histories of the Andean regions that were conquered first by the Spaniards and that lately are engaged in political, military, and economic entanglement with the U.S. Above all, it depended on the Euro-centered categories of knowledge, institutions of learning, and social actors that, in Ecuador, provide the local continuity of global designs under the rhetoric of modernity, progress, and development.

    1. The diagrams are here reproduced in black and white. In the original version, the colors are very important. Red invokes planet earth, orange—culture and society; yellow suggests energy and strength and sustains the moral principles of Andean runa (human being in the West); white points toward time becoming, the permanent transformation of the world (physical constitution) and society (politics, ethics, economy). Green appeals to the economy and the nurturing of life, the territory that includes the soil, the sky, and the air. The color blue calls for the cosmic space, and violet evokes the political and ideological spheres. Interested readers should consult the Amawtay Wasi web page.

In this most recent cycle of struggles, land claims acquired priorities in the 70s, followed by claims of linguistic and cultural rights. However, toward the end of the 70s, Indigenous intellectuals and political leaders understood that without claiming epistemic rights, the previous claims were subject to arguments based on epistemic principles of Western epistemologies. They understood that it was not possible to go very far thinking with the tools of the master, so to speak.

Thus Amawatay Wasi was born not from the idea that Indigenous people also shall have a university following the model of European institutions adopted and adapted by the Creole elite in Ecuador. On the contrary, it was born from the idea that they needed to have their own educational institutions, just as their ancestors had. For why would Indigenous societies have an education based on the education of the ancestors of Creole and Mestizos of European Origin? Only a Western prejudice that Greek and Roman ancestors are the universal model could deny the Indigenous the right to organize education responding to their needs and not to the needs of Creole and Mestizos, as it is the case today in the Andes, in all South America, in New Zealand and Australia, and in the U.S. and Canada. However, the creation of educational institutions was disrupted by the direct invasion of Spanish conquerors and, during the republic period, by French, German, British, and U.S. ideas mediated by the Creole elite that created the republic, the nation-state, and the university, emulating the Renaissance and the Kantian-Humboldtian model.

Amawtay Wasi emerged at the confluence and entanglement of political and cosmological ways of thinking and doing, of being in the world in the Andes and in Europe. Politically, the Andes (and the ancient Tawantinsuyu, which is somewhat analogous to ancient Greece), have been constantly disrupted in its social and economic organization by the social and economic organization of the Spaniards directly, and indirectly, with the emerging imperial states since the eighteenth century. All of them replaced Incas by incorporating Spanish institutions, concepts, and socio-economic organizations. However, what was replaced was indeed displaced, and it never died: it is alive and well in the Andes. Amawtay Wasi is a consequence of that long-lasting survival of the displaced, and that means that Amawtay Wasi is not a return to the past. Such return is impossible, and Indigenous peoples know that better than non-Indigenous peoples accusing the Indians of wanting to live in the past. That is not the point for most of Indigenous visions of the future, a future of which they will take control rather than waiting for a future made for them by new colonial programs (like development). In such case, Indigenous cosmologies must be articulated with Western cosmologies (the mixture of ideas coming from Greece and Rome, through the Renaissance and the Enlightenment), and Western cosmologies had to be subsumed within Indigenous ones. And that is precisely what Amawtay Wasi intends to do: to appropriate and subsume whatever can be appropriated and subsumed into their needs, vision, philosophy, and way of life, from the Western archive and contribution to human civilization. Subsuming does not mean replacing, and therefore inverting, what the Spaniards directly did and then what the French, British, and U.S. indirectly did. It means that the present articulation of Indigenous cosmologies in the future will coexist with the Euro–U.S. cosmology in their diversity. It means that now there are two types of options, whereas for 500 years only one was presented as diverse—the diversity of sameness. The mirage of diversity in the struggles remains the same: the struggles of secular against sacred forces, and the struggles between the left and the right within secular political parties. But all such belief was within Western cosmology adopted and adapted by Creoles and Mestizo elites.

Epistemically and philosophically, the process was similar and parallel to political processes. Amawtay Wasi is neither an adaptation of Western university structure nor a return to the education of the Incanate. It simply requires common sense to understand that for better or worse we are living in a world built and dominated by Western institutions, actors, and categories of thought. However, domination (and even hegemony) is not equivalent to the totalization of the totality. That is, domination and hegemony give only the impression that there is no way out. Amawtay Wasi is showing us that there are ways out by delinking from the entanglement and building an-other option. By building an-other option, we learn that the dominant or hegemonic is only an option that convinced us that it was not an option but the one and only truth. The academic structure of Amawtay Wasi was modeled on the idea of "centers or nodes of knowledge/wisdom" that comes from the ancestry of Andean civilizations: the center or node of political knowledge/wisdom, Atiy.

In the presentation of Amawtay Wasi, in the publication Boletin ICCI-Rimai (Publicacion del Instituto Cientifico de Culturas Indigenas), it is specified that:

> The university was established to be a space of both reflection and action, and grew out of a project of the nationalities and peoples of Ecuador and of all Abya Yala (the Americas). Our university works towards the decolonization of knowledge and is committed to reconstructing the concept and meaning of intercultural knowledge. The UIAW is an intercultural project

whose purpose is to serve as a foundation stone in construction of a plurinational state and an intercultural society. (http://www.amawtaywasi.edu.ec/web/index.php?option=com_content&view=article&id=23&Itemid=34&lang=en).

What was and is the Americas in the frame of Western knowledge was and is Abya Yala in the frame of Indigenous knowledge. They coexist. The need to decolonize knowledge, mentioned above, and the need to create intercultural knowledge, arise from the awareness that the mirage of epistemic universality since the European Renaissance was indeed imperial knowledge, a type of knowledge and subjectivity (way of being) that is becoming unsustainable by the minute as we have been witnessing in the years 2007–2011.

Amawtay Wasi was born in the frame of the history of Indigenous struggles for liberation since the sixteenth century. Currently, Amawtay Wasi is anchored in and supported by (jointly and separately) the Confederation of Indigenous Nationalities of Ecuador (CONAIE), the Scientific Institute of Indigenous Cultures (ICCI), and Amawta Runakunapak Yachay (ARY). The decision to create a House of Wisdom, higher education based on Indigenous cosmology instead of Western cosmology, emerged from the awareness that unless they controlled their own knowledge, Indigenous peoples would fail in claiming Indigenous rights. It became clear that the axis upon which Indigenous peoples work to liberate themselves from the chain of the Creole and Mestizo State is their own education, not a claim that they have the right to be educated by the State that oppresses them. The recovery of land and territories, the reconstitution of Indigenous nationalities and memories, are unthinkable without a structure of knowledge based on Indigenous epistemology that supports the advocacy to obtain Western knowledge. Anchored in the colonial State and University, Western knowledge prevents Indigenous peoples from reconstituting a fractured civilization, but the knowledge at the service of imperial/colonial expansion is reproduced through internal colonialism. Amawtay Wasi is showing us that it is necessary and possible to delink, epistemically, politically, and subjectively. And it is showing us how this can be done, not as a universal model, but as one of the roads to pluriversal futures.

The antecedents in the struggle to consolidate autonomous structure of education can be traced back to the 30s and 40s in Ecuador and Bolivia, but, more specifically, 12 November 1996 remains a key moment. That very day, the first meeting toward the organization of Amawtay Wasi took place at the office of Dr. Luis Macas, at that point holding the office of National Deputy of the Government of Ecuador. The process began. Committees were formed, and a working project was structured during the subsequent months. Three workshops were held with the participation of Indigenous organizations, Indigenous and non-Indigenous ONGs, intellectuals, professionals, and officers of the State. By 1998, the first projects of Amawtay Wasi were laid out in six volumes, and it was agreed that the managers of such projects will be the CONAIE and the ICCI. The project was then presented to the National Parliament that very year. And the official process began.

Ethics of Education, Epistemic Structure, and Political Orientation

We will make several disclaimers before entering the epistemic foundation and the system of ideas that animates and structures Amawtay Wasi.

It is called "University." As such, it is connected to the tradition of European universities at the same time delinking from them. Its foundation is neither Christianity (medieval and renaissance university), nor the Kantian-Humboldtian university inaugurated during the Enlightenment; even less the corporate university that, in the West, subsumes the Christian and the Kantian-Humboldtian legacies, a story we summarized in Chapter 7. Amawtay Wasi is a case of border thinking par excellence: revamping Indigenous cosmologies and ways of life by subsuming European contributions into their own models. Border thinking means that precisely—that the restitution of disavowed and broken knowledge had to be articulated in the idiom of the invaders (Spanish, French, Portuguese, English, Italian, German, as the case may be in the past 500 years), but no longer in their language, their epistemology, and their institution, even if the name is appropriated. Decoloniality needs border thinking. Both are necessary conditions for delinking from the mirage of imperial thinking and being. Amawatay Wasi is indeed a radical delinking from the history of the Renaissance/Kantian-Humboldtian/Corporate University of the Western world. That delinking is expressed in one of the processes through which students had to go: learning to unlearn in order to relearn.

What is the genealogy of Amawtay Wasi, if it is not Greco-Roman or coming from the Renaissance and the Enlightenment? This genealogy stems from the Southern Cross. As we explained in the introduction and chapter 7, there is a correlation between the Southern Cross, Tawantinsuyu, and the conceptual structure of Amawtay Wasi. Like Tawantinsuyu, Amawtay Wasi added a center to the four parts composing the structure. In Tawantinsuyu it was Cuzco, the belly of the world. For Amawtay Wasi it is Kawsay (wisdom, life, plenitude, estar siendo). The very foundation of the Amawtay Wasi conceptual structure is a combination of the Chacana and the four elements of life: water, fire, air, land. At the center is life. But life is not an entity: it comes out of the relations between the four elements which, in their turn, find their distinctiveness not by their essence but by their mutual interrelations. For this reason, Indigenous ontology is relational, but it radically differs from the Western claim for relational ontology. Relational ontology is a Western response to Western essential ontology, the ontology of Being (Heidegger) that encountered its critique in Levinas (the ontology of relations, the face to face, the dialogue). Indigenous relational ontology comes from their own ancestral epistemology parallel but unrelated until the arrival of Spanish missionaries, who brought with them the ancestral Greek epistemology based on the essence of objects, ideas, and denotation; not of relation but of denotation.

The Amawtay Wasi conceptual structure consists in layers of the same basic structure shown in figure 1. What changes in each case are the four components and the characteristics that the center acquires in relation to those specific components. Thus one can imagine that "on top" of the "four elements of life" the basic categorial structure of Amatay Wasi consists in the four nodes of learning.

The overall structure thus consists in these four nodes of institutes (see figure 2):

Yachay: wisdom, knowledge, epistemic training
Munay: love, passion, intuition
Ruray: doing, experiencing, and building
Ushuay: potency, energy, power

The four nodes organize ancestral knowledge of Indian, not Western, cosmology. Greeks and Romans have nothing to add here, or, in any case, not as a model or influence but as inconvenience: Amawtay Wasi has no choice but to define itself, and redefine indigenous ancestral knowledge, in relation to the Western ancestral knowledge. The reverse is not true: Europe does not have to respond to Indigenous knowledge to re-invent itself. Or, if it does, it is to dismiss any epistemology that is alien to Western epistemology. Thus, modeled on the Southern Cross, we have the node of political knowledge, or Ushay; the node of spiritual knowledge, or Munay; the node of practical knowledge, or Ruray; and the node of technical/technological knowledge, or Yachay. At the center of the four nodes, or the Center of the centers, is Kawsay—wisdom, life, humanity, and culture.

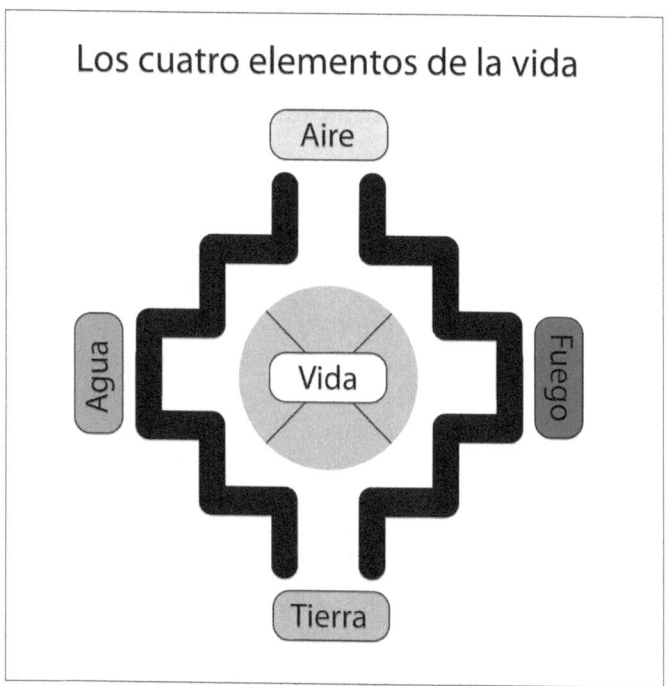

FIGURE 1

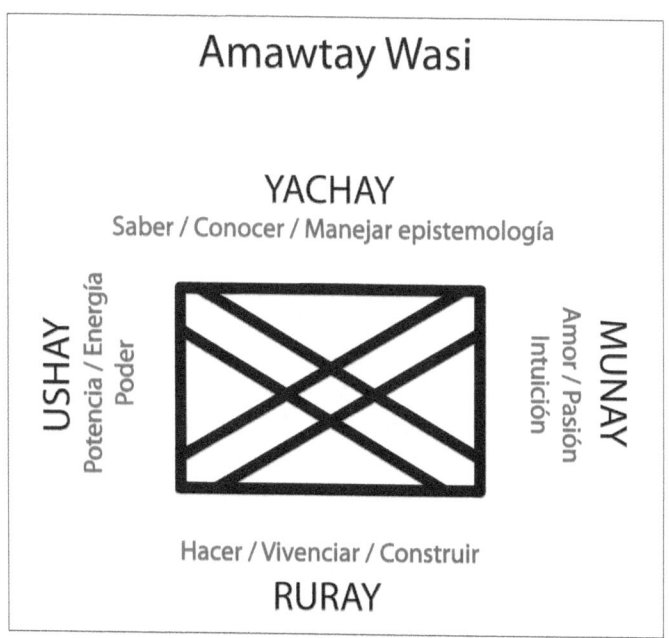

FIGURE 2

Now, crucial to academic and scholarly organization is the principle of *vincularidad*. This principle is vital for understanding the Indigenous relational epistemology. How to translate this term? Sometimes it appears as "relational," but that translation is confusing, for "relational ontology" is already a concept that moves away from both ontology and dialogism and focuses on relational ontology as the foundation of complex structures. But that definition is still within Western debates. "Vincularidad" shall then be translated as co-relationality—connections between the four nodes and, above all, connections with the center upon which each and all of the nodes depend. The expression "vincularidad como ser," which appears in figure 3, is indeed a difficult expression to translate. It means that being is constituted by and in vincularidad. The concept of "being" is maintained and is at the same time radically transformed when transplanted from Western to Indigenous ways of thinking and of "being." Thus, as the figure makes clear, "vincularidad como ser" (at the center) emerges from the correlations between "complementarity," "reciprocity," "correspondence," and "proportionality." A phenomenology of Being, as found in Continental philosophy, is unthinkable in any Indigenous languages and structures of thought. Seen in this light, the diagram is still abstract. But when we project "vincularidad" on the four nodes and the respective center, it acquires all its epistemic potential. Thus each node is interrelated with the agro-ecological, and vitally and organizationally with the four elements of Pachamama—air, fire, land, and water—and, furthermore, with the four basic symbolic colors of Tawantinsuyu—red, yellow, green, and blue. The four basic colors correspond to the four "suyus" of Tawantinsuyu. Qollasusyu, on the West and the Pacific, is blue (water); Antisuyu, in the Northeast, the jungle, is green; Chinchaysuyo, in the North, the desert region with strong sunlight, is yellow; and Collasuyu, in the Southeast, the region of argillaceous earth or land, is red.

When it comes to the four nodes of knowledge, the interconnections create pairing on each side of the nodes. And so we have in the node of Yachay/Widsom/Knowledge the challenge of Interculturality that interconnects Yachay with Ushay. On the other hand, we have the challenge of the Cosmovision that interrelates Yachay with Munnay. At its turn, Munay interrelated with Ruray take us to the ecological challenge: to make the habitat livable. In correspondence, Ruray and Ushay present the challenge of technoscience. Now, Ushay (and any of the four nodes) is interrelated with the nodes next to it; for example, Ushay interrelated with Yushay presents the challenge of interculturality, whereas when interrelated with Ruray, it takes us to the challenge of technoscience. Thus we enter a house of knowledge where neither the sense of being in one single domain nor the sense of Western holism

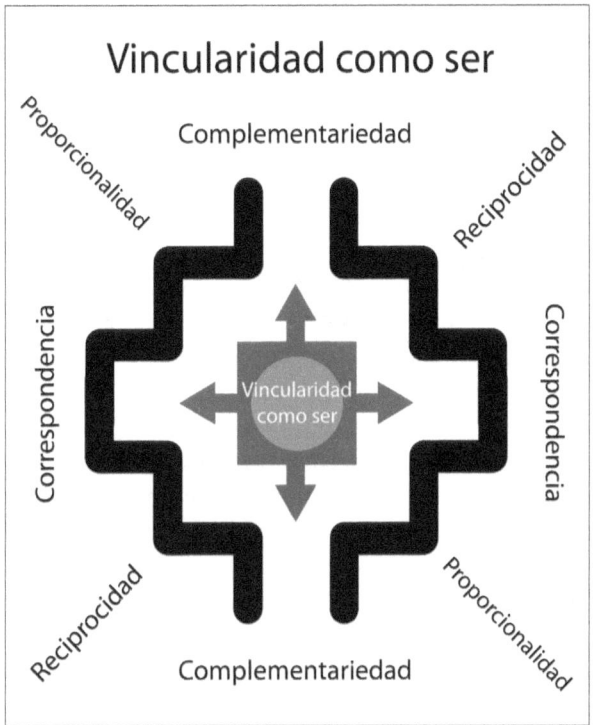

FIGURE 3

obtains. In this house, the wholes and the parts belong to one specific epistemology. We enter a house of wisdom whose components come from a non-Western cosmovision, knowledge, wisdom, and way of life, but always in forced relation with it (which is another dimension of Indigenous relational epistemology that was not in place or needed before the Spanish invasion and, in other part of the world, before the French, British or U.S. invasion and intervention. That both systems have been entangled for 500 years, and that one dominates over the other, does not mean that Indigenous cosmologies should continue to surrender to something that is not their own. Why would Indigenous or any other non-Western peoples have to live as others want them to live? To understand the ethical dimension of this observation, it is suffice to remember many situations in which a Western person would say "I do not want to live as the communists want me to live!" Well, the reverse is also true. There is no reason to pretend that it is the true and the preferable. Furthermore, the curricular structures and the five-year program make sure that students also understand the relations between Ruray and Yashay (complementarity between knowing and doing), Ushay and Munay (correspondence between power and love), Proportionality between Interculturality, and Reciprocity between Cosmovision and Technology.

Let us come back to Amawtay Wasi. Each node in itself has its own goal, beyond the interrelation that each node has with the other nodes (e.g., Yushay–Ushay and Yushay–Munay). Thus the main goal of Yushay–Munay (Wisdom, Knowledge, Cosmovision), in complementarity, is to strengthen the identity (linguistic, cultural, spiritual, memory) of Nacionalidades y Pueblos Indigenas. Training is offered in Cultural Knowledge, History, Psycho-pedagogy, Health, and Intercultural Medicine. The training personnel of this center is composed of Uwishining, Yachaks, Shamans, Midwives, and Cultural Trainers.

Ruray–Munay (to do, to experience, and to build) is the economic node. The goal of this node is the organization of the economic structure of indigenous communities and the formation of micro-organizations run by the families and the communities. Students are trained in agro-ecology, sustainable tourism, economic principles, and economic administration. This node is governed by a Council of Amawtas and formed by personnel from the communities in charge of the administration and organization of communal economy.

Ushay–Yushay (Energy, Potency, Power, Interculturality) is in charge of education dedicated to the political strengthening of Nacionalidad y Pueblos Indígenas in their respective and relevant organizations. The goals are the advancement of plurinational societies; the conformation of cultural autonomies; the consolidation of territorialities; counseling to local governments; and the conceptualization and unfolding of Indigenous Law and Indigenous Legal Administration.

Ruray–Ushay (experiencing, doing, potency, energy) is oriented toward the expansion of technological learning in the communities. It is related to the organization of the territories and the construction and building of infrastructures, with training in architecture and engineering. It is governed by a Council of Amawtas formed by Indigenous builders, textile makers, goldsmiths, and communication–technology experts.

IN SUMMARY, Amawtay Wasi focuses on the following basic needs for decolonization of knowledge and generation of decolonial knowledge. The center of the entire project is life and "learning to be," a term that refers to the long experience in which Indigenous peoples have been treated as inferior and of inferior knowledge. Amawtay Wasi has begun a long process to redress what was unjustly disregarded and how the people were mistreated. Thus decolonization of knowledge and of being goes through wisdom/knowledge (science); knowing to do (technology); knowing to be/ser (individual and the community); knowing to be/estar (service, society, community); and harmony and balance (with nature) to live in plenitude (buen vivir). All four trajectories centered on Kawsay (plenitude, life, wisdom). Decolonization of knowledge and of being, to which Amawtay Wasi is contributing, consists in delinking from Western epistemology (essential ontology and relational ontology) and rebuilding an Indigenous, relational ontology that puts life above institutions and above the myth that development and growth lead to freedom and happiness.

Figure 4 summarizes the Strategies and the four formative levels. The Strategies consist of Challenges (Desafios), Competences (Capacidades), and Approaches (Enfoques). The three of them constitute the General Proposal of Amawtay Wasi. The four formative levels are:

- Learning to think by communal doing
- Learning to learn
- Learning to unlearn in order to relearn
- Learning to undertake

Amaway Wasi is today (January of 2012) well and running. It has become an important point of reference contributing to numerous new beginnings: higher education is in the hands of the people who have had until now to submit to the higher education managed by actors and institutions that denied them the right to think on their own. Memories are local and cannot be controlled by global designs. When global designs attempt to control memories that are not the memories of the actors and institutions upon which global designs are imagined and enacted, they become imperial modes of domination; designs to induce or force people to live according to the desires and designs based on the memories that are not theirs. Learning to unlearn in order to relearn is precisely this kind of project: the project of the people who become epistemically and politically disobedient, who realize that knowledge cannot be framed and packaged in the bags of Greece, Rome, France, Germany, England, and the U.S. This is of course a very important genealogy of thought and memories for Euro-American citizens. But not for 80% of the world now close to 7 billion people. Learning to unlearn is of the essence to build democratic, non-imperial, non-violent, non-legally delinquent futures. Amawtay Wasi is a small star in the universe of new beginnings.

La estrategia

Desafíos:
- Lograr Sabiduría
- Construir Cosmovisión
- Construir un Mundo vivo
- Tecnociencias para la vida
- Lograr Interculturalidad

Capacidades:
- Centro Yachay Munay
- Centro Munay Ruray
- Centro Ruray Ushay
- Centro Ushay Yachay
- Centro Kausay

Enfoques:
- Relacionalidad
- Construir Cosmovisión
- Antropo -eco-socio-cultural
- Multicultural
- Transdisciplinario
- Pedagogía del aprendizaje

Propuesta A.W.

El camino complejo esta estructurada en base al desarrollo y adquisición de competencias de aprendizaje:

Niveles de formación

Nivel 1
Aprender a pensar haciendo comunitariamente

Nivel 4
Aprender a emprender

Nivel 5
Aprender a Ser

Nivel 2
Aprender a aprender

Nivel 3
Aprender a desaprender y reaprender

FIGURE 4

NOTES

Introduction

1. We mean here the parallel march of the—better known in the West—colonization of South America and the first Russian colonies in Volga region and Western Siberia. Moscow was declared the Third Rome in the early sixteenth century, inheriting from the Byzantine empire a specific providential theocratic imperial consciousness, with the state viewed as a metaphysical principle of sacred cosmology. The sixteenth century also brought the ascension of Ivan IV (Ivan the Terrible) as Tsar of all Russia in 1547 and the succeeding colonization of territories that almost equaled Europe in their size. Hernan Cortés managed to control the Aztec Tlatoanate in 1520, and Francisco Pizarro did the same in the Andes, taking over and dismantling the Incanate. When Philip II replaced his father, Charles I, as King of Castile, he initiated a well-thought-out managerial project to organize the Spanish possessions in Indias Occidentales. In the meantime, Portugal was following suit in managing its Brazilian possessions.

2. For the colonization of time and the invention of the Middle Ages, see Dagenais and Greer (2000). For the transformation of barbarians in space into primitives in time, see Walter D. Mignolo, "Coloniality at Large: Time and the Colonial Difference" In *Time in the Making and Possible Futures*. (Rio de Janeiro, Unesco—ISSC—Educam, 2000), 237–73.

3. For the complete cycle of learning and a summary of the political process that led to the foundation of Amawtay Wasi and its overall philosophy, see the appendix in this volume. Information on Amawtay Wasi can be found in the Internet. There is a publication by UNESCO, in Quichua, Spanish, and English, (Amawtay Wasi. Sumak Yachaypi, Alli Kawsaypipash Yachakuna: Aprender En La Sabiduria Y El Buen Vivir = Learning Wisdom and the Good Way to Live. UNESCO, Universidad Intercultural Amawtay Wasi, 2004; Catherine Walsh, 2005).

4. The reader not familiar with Amawtay Wasi can find a more detailed description in the appendix of this volume.

5. For the relevance of the concept, in Ecuador and Bolivia, related to the state and the rewriting of the constitution, see Catherine Walsh (2008).

6. Along with the general meaning of shifting the geography of reason from its established European place to other locales, what is important in Lewis Gordon's idea is the

constructive criticism of the disciplinary decadence with the claims of the disciplines at their closed, absolute, and deontological nature, as well as the teleological suspension of the disciplines as the ends in themselves (Gordon 2006: 183). As a result, the thinker who attempts to shift the geography of reason takes a position objectively close to the philosophy of education and knowledge practiced in Amawtay Wasi, which we share. It is to see the issues, the crucial problems to pursue, whose solving is more important than the loyalty to one's discipline, method, school, or a system of knowledge. Instead of studying an object from the position and with the help of the instruments of different disciplines, we attempt to build a dialogue between different knowledges on what is knowledge as such. Hence, the object in the understanding of Western philosophy disappears, giving place to problems discussed from various positions and the question of what kind of knowledge we need to make the world a more fair and just place for us all.

7. There is one institute of nanotechnology in Monterrey, Mexico, and another one in Brazil, but they are ancillary of similar institutes in the U.S.

8. Chicana intellectual and activist Gloria Anzaldúa described the borders between Mexico and the U.S., as "una herida abierta." We see in this metaphor, an expression of the global "colonial wound" inflicted by georacial classification of regions and people through five hundred years of Western theological and egological politics of knowledge: Racism is a politics of humiliation, of wounding people by making them feel inferior, both as human beings (ontological colonial difference) and as rational beings (epistemic colonial difference). Geo- and body politics of knowledge emerge from the colonial wound and not from Aristotle, Saint Thomas Aquinas, and Descartes. See Anzaldúa 1987.

9. See, for example, decolonial arguments in business schools and in the area of management in South America by Eduardo Ibarra Colado (2007), in Australia by Subhabrata Bobby Banerjee (2008); in the area of health, between Morocco and southern Spain by Isabel Jiménez-Lucena (2008).

10. There is an obvious line connecting Paulo Freyre's *Pedagogy of the Oppressed* (1970) and Chela Sandoval's *Methodology of the Oppressed* (2000).

Chapter 1

11. The bibliography on the concept of coloniality is extensive by now, including: a summary in Anibal Quijano (2000); on coloniality of knowledge, Edgardo Lander (2000); on coloniality of being, Enrique Dussel (1977); and on being and geopolitics of knowledge, Nelson Maldonado-Torres (2008). "Coloniality" contributed to the move from Eurocentered works on the sociology of knowledge toward the geopolitics of knowledge as decolonization . On this, see Walter Mignolo at www.incommunicado.info/node/view/18.

12. As far as we (Madina and Walter) carried within us the memories of being born and raised in Moscow (with ties with Uzbekistan and Caucasus) and Argentina (with ties with Northern Italy), respectively, the postcolonial academic talk in the United States remained somewhat—and for different reasons—outside the realms of our imperial/colonial experiences and our sociohistorical formation of subjectivity. Interestingly enough, we found in Gloria Anzaldúa (1987) and Frantz Fanon (1952) (who are neither Eruasian nor of European descent) a guide for our thoughts and reflection of our subjectivities.

13. The idea that "globalization," as understood today, is a process that starts with the "discovery" of America is shared by European political theorists such as Carl Schmitt

who, in Schmitt 2003 [1952] makes a clear distinction between the "preglobal" and the "global" age. "Globalization" in this view is not a human phenomenon from time immemorial but a historical qualitative turn in appropriation of land, massive exploitation of labor, and international law that is concentrated both in the hands of European and capitalist imperial countries.

14. The concept of body politics of knowledge is radically different from Michel Foucault's biopolitics. While, in Foucault, biopolitics is conceived in terms of management of power (and is still anchored in the modern—and imperial—conception of knowledge), the body politics of knowledge displaces epistemology from its Eurocentric location to the places (geopolitics) and racialized bodies of the colonies (men and women of color, gays and lesbians of color, indigenous people and Muslims, Arabic and Aymara languages instead of Greek and Latin, etc.). "Body politics of knowledges" refers to epistemic and philosophical creativities in places, bodies, languages, and memories that have been disqualified as thinkers and philosophers, and in this regard, shall not be confused with the imperial body politics of knowledge that—in seventeenth-century political theory in England—conceived the social structure as an analogy of the human body. "Border thinking" refers precisely to the articulation of the displaced appropriating the global expansion of Western categories of thinking and principles of knowledge. Decolonial thinking emerges from all of this, which does not mean that all Blacks and Indians, Muslims and Aymaras, women and men of color endorse it. Assimilation is the alternative to decolonial thinking and decolonial option. See the next chapter "Theorizing from the Borders," for a more detailed elaboration of this concept.

15. There is already a significant bibliography addressing such issues. For example, *"Double Critique: Knowledges and Scholars at Risk in Post-Soviet Societies,"* edited by Walter Mignolo and Madina Tlostanova, *South Atlantic Quarterly,* 105/3, 2006; *Globalization and the Decolonial Option,* special issue of *Cultural Studies* (21/2–3, 2007). A recent volume edited by Mabel Moraña, Enrique Dussel, and Carlos A. Jáuregui, *Coloniality at Large: Latin America and the Postcolonial Debates,* which clearly shows that epistemic universality is no longer viable in a decolonial world. In contrast, Madina Tlostanova has shown the differences between South America on the one hand and Central Asia and the Caucasus on the other ("Imperial Discourse and Post-Utopian Peripheries: Suspended Indigenous Epistemologies in the Soviet Non-European Ex-Colonies" 2006).

16. For more details about these basic and important distinctions, see the special issue of *Cultural Studies, Globalization and the Decolonial Option,* edited by Walter Mignolo in collaboration with Aruro Escobar, 21/2/3, March 2007.

17. Intellectuals such as Malek Bennabi (Algeria) and Abdelkhebir Khatibi (Morocco) devoted their works to the problems of decolonization in the sphere of knowledge and being (Bennabi 2003a, 2003b and Khatibi 1983). Even if French poststructuralist thinkers developed some of their ideas in France as a consequence of the war in Algeria, their problems were not the same as those of Bennabi or Khatibi, but rather problems emerging from the regional history of Western thought. When Robert Young suggests in *White Mythologies* (1990) the links between French poststructuralism and decolonizing processes in Algeria and Tunisia, he does so with still another (third) set of problems at hand: the problems set by postcolonial agendas approximately since the mid 1980s. Thus, the geopolitics of knowledge allows us to see three regional projects, each characterized by a set of specific issues and questions. From a decolonial perspective (which is the fourth project in this scenario, emerging from historical process in South America and the Caribbean), none of them can be reduced to another.

18. We write "capital/modernity" instead of "capitalism" because the latter is a term of Marxist discourse while the former belongs to decolonial discourse. We make a distinction between capitalism and the colonial matrix of power. In this particular case, "capital/modernity" links the sphere of control of an economy with the sphere of knowledge and subjectivity. A distinctive feature of capital/modernity is the dispensability of human lives disguised under the discourses of progress, development, and modernization. Capitalism, instead, focuses on the economic aspects and leaves aside the "cultural" dimension that we translate into the control of knowledge and subjectivity in the colonial matrix of power.

19. David Chioni Moore suggested that we locate the post-Soviet world within the postcolonial realm (Moore 2001). He is quite right to point out that postcolonial scholars usually do not include the ex-Socialist block into the sphere of their interests and there are no postcolonial studies in ex-Soviet Union or former Socialist countries. But Moore lumps together eastern and southeastern European countries and the USSR, which have had distinctly different histories and imperial and colonial discourses. It might have been a good idea to explore the hidden reasons of why postcolonial discourses do not exist in the ex–Second World. To do that, it might have been important to get better acquainted with the actual contemporary situation in this quite diverse area. Probably, then, he would not put together, in a purely rhetorical way, Algeria and Ukraine or Hungary and Philippines, which have very different colonial histories. What is lacking in this article, written from the distinctly outsider's perspective, not at all familiar with internal cultural, linguistic, religious differences, and nuances of this locale, as well as contemporary artistic/cultural/linguistic expressions of postcolonial, postimperial, transcultural sensibilities, is a strong universalizing bent in trying to use the umbrella term "postcolonial," regardless of possible differences (Moore 2001).

20. What we mean by "second-class" empire can be seen today in the cases of Georgia and Ukraine. President Mikhail Saakashvili denounces Russia's imperial ambitions, but he himself has no quarrel with joining the Western imperial designs, even if in the capacity of a groveler. A similar case is Ukraine. In the South American and Caribbean countries, the situation is radically different, because from their independence in the nineteenth century, they all wanted to join France and England, and now the United States, which form the history of Christian and liberal capitalist empires of the West.

21. Until the beginning of the nineteenth century, "Latin America" did not exist and there was no such a thing as "Latin American" countries. We refer here mainly to the Spanish (and indirectly to the Portuguese) colonies in the New World. The Spanish colonies extended to today's California and Colorado, including Texas, New Mexico, and to a certain point, Louisiana and Florida. It is common, however, to repeat the mistake of labeling the period between 1500 and 1800 "colonial Latin America." What we have are "Spanish colonies in the Indias Occidentales," sometimes also called New World and America.

22. Within the socialist modernity was an internal and external civilizing and modernizing rhetoric as well. The first was intended for the Soviet non-European colonies and was expressed in the reinvention of the old Lenin myth that had typically Eurocentric origins of the heroic civilizing efforts of the great Russian people in backward Central Asia. In the 1960–1980s, it was used to divert attention from the deteriorating living standards by looking for an imagined enemy—the Muslim colonies that the poor Russians presumably had to feed. In the external rendering, the same mythology referred to the Third World countries who were the objects of the continuous Western and Soviet rivalry.

23. For more details available in English, see an interesting though ambivalent discussion on racial politics in the USSR in *Slavic Review,* vol. 61, no 1, spring 2002, and Kalpana Sahni's book on Russian Orientalism (Sahni 1997).

24. We could think here also of transnational corporations in a transnational unified economy (capital/modernity) in which contending states are moving toward a polycentric capital/modernity (or capitalism in Marxist terminology). Therefore, transnational corporations are not undermining the state but forcing its transformation. The European Union is a case in point; the emerging UNASUR (the projected union of Latin American countries to defend their interests in front of U.S. and the European Union) is another. Therefore, the argument that opposes transnational corporations to national states should be revised in the light of the international and competitive relations between the states (G8, G5). This scenario may not be clear enough if we think in terms of "capitalism," but it becomes clear if we think in terms of "capital/modernity"—the emerging states are no longer willing to follow the dictates of U.S. or the European Union to modernize but, rather, follow the dictates of their own experiences and needs. It is in this new scenario that a global political society is emerging, calling for decolonial thinking and decolonial political and epistemic options.

25. Brazil most likely will take the leadership in the constitution of UNASUR (Unión Suramericana), which would only resemble the European Union, with its dominating "heart of Europe" (in Hegel's metaphor), "integrating" the periphery. UNASUR would be like a Central or Eastern European Union in confrontation with England, France, and Germany, as UNASUR is being created basically to avoid the U.S. (as well as other intrusions) into the region.

26. Capital (from the Online Etymology Dictionary) c.1225, from L. capitalis "of the head," from caput (gen. capitis) "head" (see head). A capital crime (1526) is one that affects the life, or the "head." The noun for "chief town" is first recorded 1667 (the O.E. word was heafodstol). The financial sense (1630) is from L.L. capitale "stock, property," neut. of capitalis. Of ships, "first-rate, of the line," attested from 1652. Capital letters (c.1391) are at the "head" of a sentence or word. Capitalism first recorded 1854; originally "the condition of having capital;" as a political/economic system, 1877. Capitalist is 1791, from Fr. capitaliste, a coinage of the Revolution and a term of reproach.

27. The arguments asserting and enacting "de-Westernization" are already well advanced in East and Southeast Asia. See Kishore Mahbubani. *The New Asian Hemisphere: The Irresistible Shift of Global Power to the East,* 2008.

28. This story told by Nebrija himself in the prologue to his grammar of Castilian languages (printed in 1492) is well known. In connection with this argument, it is analyzed in Walter D. Mignolo, 1995, *The Darker Side of the Renaissance: Literacy, Territoriality and Colonization,* Chapter 1.

29. A useful counterpart for the Atlantic empires is Anthony Pagden's *Lord of All the World: Ideologies of Empires in Spain, Britain and France c. 1500–c. 1800,* 1995.

30. A system of charges in the Spanish colonies, by means of which a group of individuals owed retributions to other groups (the colonizer) in terms of labor or other means.

31. It is perhaps worthwhile to state that we limit the meaning of "imperial differences" to the formation of the modern/colonial world sustained and structured by the colonial matrix of power. In this regard, "imperial differences" do not apply, for example, to the relations between the Ottoman and the Mughal Sultanates, in the same way that "colonial difference" does not apply to their internal organization. By "imperial" and

"colonial difference," we mean a racial (ontological and epistemic) difference that began to be construed by Christian theology in the sixteenth century, then extended itself, and transformed into secular philosophy. "Imperial difference" implies, for instance, to describe the relations between Western imperial formations and the Ottoman Sultanate (or today between the West and China, on the one hand, and Russia, on the other), but not the other way round.

Chapter 2

32. Any dictionary would have something like this as a definition of epistemology: a branch of philosophy that investigates the origin, nature, methods, and limits of human knowledge. But, who were the philosophers who contributed to that definition; what were the sociohistorical conditions in which their thought unfolded; and what were the needs to which their thought responded? Border thinking and epistemology emerges from bodies and subjects that "human knowledge" cast as to be not human enough to have knowledge. Border thinking is always thinking in conflictive dialogue with imperial epistemology, "the dominant branch of human knowledge." Border thinking emerges from bodies dwelling in the border between an epistemology that was not theirs, which they cannot avoid, and an epistemology that was theirs, which was disqualified. Border thinking thinks from the awareness of disqualification.

33. For example, John Milbank's (1993) theological critique of the social sciences reverts the order of the secular and the sacred in epistemology, but the geohistorical location of his thought as well as the unspoken male, white, and Christian identity of his discourse are grounded in Greek and Latin categories of thought and articulated in the English language. On the other hand, when W. E. B. Du Bois asked "how can one be American and Black at the same time?" he established the foundation of a "double consciousness" as an epistemic foundation grounded on the racial colonial difference ([1904] 1995).

34. "Third World nationalism" (e.g., India or Algeria) reproduced in the ex-colonies the model of "Imperial nationalism" (e.g., England or France), and all ended up in the impasse we all know about. "Internal colonialism" was the result, since the first-colonial nation-states, in the modern/colonial world, which emerged in the Americas at the end of the eighteenth and first decades of the nineteenth centuries. Bolivia now is going through an interesting process of border thinking and constitutional decolonization. And, we may see a similar experience in Iraq. "Third World nationalism" furthermore remained within the monotopic and exclusionary imperial logic, just in the hands of the "locals or natives." Frantz Fanon, instead, opened up the possibility and the need of a double consciousness and border thinking of and from the experience of the *damnés de la terre*. His thoughts were far removed from national fundamentalisms.

35. For example, Deng Zhenglai (http://cuscps.sfsu.edu/Events/deng_zhenglai.htm) also claims, in *Development of Chinese Social Sciences in the Era of Globalization*, that Chinese social sciences should keep the open-minded or global orientation as its strategy of development and enhance the dialogue with the West. But at the same time, social scientists should also recognize that China is now a country of global significance and no longer a country secluded from the dominant/Western discourse. Therefore, globalization is a chance for China and Chinese academe to challenge the overtowering Western discourse and promote the Chinese interpretation of Chinese history and experience

and envision Chinese ideals and world ideals. Problematization and exploration of new methods and theory in Chinese social sciences should stem from Chinese history, Chinese modernity, and Chinese transformation. We owe this information to Chunjie Zhang (Duke University). See also the robust arguments advanced by Kishore Mahbubani, 2009.

36. In his ironic travelog, *Five Rivers of Life,* contemporary Russian postmodernist writer Victor Yerofeyev points out: "A Russian in Europe is like a cockroach. He is running, moving his whiskers, nervously smelling. He is scandalous for Europe's clean surface. Europe can contemplate with interest the exotic insects, it would like some kind of poisonous tarantula or a caterpillar, ladybirds are a touching site for it, but there are no good cockroaches" (Yerofeyev 2000).

37. A Turkish ironist Orhan Pamuk, in *The Black Book,* says: "The customer,—one of the shop-keepers said,—does not want to put on an overcoat that he sees every day in the street on the shoulders of mustached, bow-legged and emaciated compatriots. He wants to put on a jacket that arrived from a distant unknown country, and that is worn by new and beautiful people. He wants to believe that once he puts on this jacket he will transform himself, he will become a different person . . . It is for this reason that they invented revolution in dress, shaved off the beards and even changed the alphabet . . . The customers in fact are buying not clothes, but dreams. They wish to buy a dream to be the same as those who wear the European dress" (Pamuk 2000).

38. The Ottoman Sultanate and Russia had a lot in common. The Ottoman territorial expansion was stopped early in history because, to unite with their ethnic and cultural "relatives" in Central Asia, the Turks already in the sixteenth century had to (and could not) bypass Shiite Persia, which later on resulted in the clash of Russian and Ottoman interests in the Balkans. The multiethnic, multiconfessional, and multilinguistic Russian Empire, with its extensive principle of conquering the space, started to lose its position in the eighteenth and nineteenth centuries in the presence of capitalist Western empires of modernity and had to satisfy its expansionistic appetites mainly in the East and South (i.e., in the locales that were drastically different in an ethnic-religious sense from the metropolis). Each of these empires was born in the outskirts of its religious-cultural oecumena, but with the passing of time, each proclaimed as its imperial mission to take the central place: In Russia, it was the famous Moscow as the Third Rome doctrine, according to which the ex outskirt of Byzantine empire, which became Christian relatively late, claimed the role of Orthodox Christian center, and in Turkey, it was the Central Asian, and hence relatively remote from Muslim centers and shrines, origin of Turks, who became Muslim only in the tenth century and began to inhabit Anatolia even later but soon turned into the most powerful Muslim empire—even if for a relatively short period of time. The Ottoman Sultanate had to correspond to this new role, turning from the eclectic, in the cultural and religious sense, marginal state into the center of Islamic civilization. Embracing Islam, the Turks became the heirs of the ancient high Islamic culture and here, as well as in Russia, a complex religious configuration of juxtaposing itself to both Islam and Christianity was obviously at work. If, in the Russian Empire, it was a juxtaposition with Islam (an other religion) and a contrast between Orthodox and Western Christianity (i.e., an internal Christian difference), then in the Ottoman Sultanate, the juxtaposition was done not only along the obvious division into Christians and Muslims but also within Islam, which was reflected in the rather negative attitude of the Sunnite Ottoman Sultanate to Shiites. Religious identification of both Russians and Turks at that time was relatively perfunctory, syncretic, and border but was presented certainly as the

only true religion on the basis of which the Ottoman and the Moscow imperial myths were slightly later created. For more details, see Goodwin (1998), Lieven (2000).

39. At the time of writing the first version of this chapter, the FAO Summit on the food global crisis just ended. During the summit, it was reported that *Monsanto, DuPont,* and *Syngenta,* the largest companies controlling transgenic seeds and fertilizers, declared huge profits. The UN, IMF, and WB concurred that the crisis was human-made and could be fixed. It is not a paradox: It is ingrained in the rhetoric of modernity, based on progress and salvation of all kinds, while increasing capital accumulation and, in this case, "using" people risking starvation as "bodies to feed," to increase food production, and hence the profits of the corresponding corporations. Look around and you will see the same seeming "paradox": a rhetoric that maintains the faith in progress and development as salvation, while increasing the mechanisms of economic and political control, by maintaining a structure of knowledge that justifies development as the only way to freedom and happiness. Any alternative *to* such structure of knowledge is condemned as antidemocratic. *La Via Campesina* and *Food Sovereignty,* the two global organizations in the sphere of political society working toward the decolonizing knowledge that controls and manipulates the global food crisis, were not invited to this summit. It was limited to transnational corporations and international organizations (UN, IMF, World Bank).

Chapter 3

40. The name "Eurasian studies" itself sounds highly ambiguous. In the Russian mind, it immediately evokes Eurasianism as a philosophic-cultural movement of the early twentieth century, going through periodic revivals at the times of nationalist and imperial booms, like today. This is not what is meant by the name "Eurasian studies" in the West. It rather designates just a presumably objective geographic phenomenon—Eurasia. However, geography here hides a geopolitical myth. Eurasia in geography means the whole continent, which comprises Europe *and* Asia. Geography does not recognize Berlin walls and divisions between Protestantism and Orthodox Christianity or Latin- and Cyrillic-based languages. Therefore the term "Eurasian studies" is meaningless in a geographic sense, because it would mean to study France along with Turkmenia and Spain along with China. What is meant by "Eurasian" here is rather a geopolitical and civilizational myth of not Europe and not Asia, which Russia stands for. Thus, although Russia itself stopped being interesting for Western area studies, its specter is still present in the very name of "Eurasian studies." However, this euphemism seeks to erase Russia and replace its name (and former power) with a "new" geopolitics of knowledge.

41. Several attempts have been made by Russian scholars working within the Frankfurt school tradition in the last decade to apply postcolonial theory to post-Socialist discourse by turning it upside down and assigning the role of the subaltern to the ex-Russian colonizer in the newly independent states. However, the old geopolitical models are still obvious in these constructs, as they look mainly at those colonies that have always claimed their closeness to Europe (the western Ukraine, the Baltic countries) in contrast with Russia coded as an Asiatic empire. This is a cunning rhetoric, as it attempts to transfer the Russian imperial guilt and responsibility to the ex-colonial others (Penzin 2011).

42. Even the best of the Western experts on Central Asia suffer this Orientalist bent, which is clearly seen in the titles of their articles, in the visual representations of the

people adorning the covers of their books, which stress the sensational and the exotic and abuse the modernity vs. tradition and civilization vs. barbarity dichotomy. See, for example, Sahadeo and Zanca 2007.

43. The *mardikors* were and are today, in post-Soviet Central Asia, the day laborers with no permanent jobs. After the 1916 Turkistan massive revolts against the Czarist Empire, connected among other things with the Russian attempt to force the local population to public front-line work, a whole subculture of mardikor insurgent songs and poems emerged, many of which remain only in oral form and only recently were collected and presented in the Uzbek Memorial of the victims of repression. The usual tactic was to collect the oral histories, as if for the future publication, then hide them in inaccessible archives and get rid of their reciters (the ozans or shamans), attempting to buy them into Socialism by asking them to write odes to the tractor and kolkhoz, or later, to publish the *dastans* in distorted forms, where the liberatory heroic impulse was amputated (Paksoy 1995a, Tekuyeva 2006a).

44. This is a question that recently caused a heated discussion among the Western ex-Sovietologists, who started to question the formula of divide and rule and attempted to prove the presumable good intentions of the Soviets in drawing the Turkistan borders by stating that the Bolsheviks were thinking not only about defending the intactness of their new empire but also about activating their nation-building and, later, gradual nation-dissolving theories and creating a new brand of colonialism. This is the opinion of Francine Hirsch (2000) among others. To anyone who has experienced the Soviet power from within, this rationale sounds not only simplistic and easily bought into the Soviet ideological clanking but also highly cynical, as it presupposes that one can somewhat excuse the USSR if one proves that it was building a new and better brand of colonialism! In all such reasoning invariably alienated from history and from the indigenous subjectivity, there is a crucial element missing—that of race.

45. The yard of my Moscow apartment complex, as well as the majority of other Moscow yards, has been cleaned over the last five years by a family of Uzbeks from Namangan. Both the husband and wife have university degrees. He is an engineer and she is a doctor. They brought three children, out of five, to clean Moscow streets as well. The children are segregated at a Moscow school. The family resides in a construction trailer that, as they explained to me, is much better than before, when they stayed in a basement infected by rats. The municipal authorities employ them half legally, with a $100 monthly salary, and no Moscow "registration," which makes them vulnerable to any policeman in the street. Today, when the economic crisis hit Moscow violently, the Uzbek families are risking quick deportation and subsequent starvation at home.

46. The resistance tactics of the Central Asian peoples were and are similar to those of the Caribbean intellectuals, who also resorted to fiction instead of forbidden historiography or philosophy, to tell the truth and preserve the link with the past, with the ancestral beliefs, with their freedom-fighting legacies. It is resistance in the disguise of fiction that we find, for example, in the works of Alisher Ibadinov and other Central Asian writers of the Soviet time, most of whom perished in Stalin's purges. Unfortunately, today, after the Central Asian states became independent and it is seemingly the indigenous people who are in power there, the same logic of repression persists. A telling case is the fate of Mamadali Mahmudov, a writer who, having suffered in Soviet times, received a prize for his resistant literary works after the gaining of independence, but then in the 1999 was imprisoned again, this time, apparently by the new government, which promotes its freedom-loving and democratic image (Paksoy 2002).

47. Kalpana Sahni correctly points out a process of gradual popularization of racism and Eurocentrism in the Soviet period, linked with the erasing of the difference between the elite and popular culture. If, in Czarist Russia, Eurocentrism arguably was restricted by the aristocracy and middle class strata, in the Soviet Union, it became a commonplace discourse among the Soviet people (Sahni 1997: 162). Today, we can trace the remnants of the Brezhnev era myth interiorized by Russians and used as a justification for the colonization excesses and neocolonialism. It is a myth first formulated in Lenin's time and depicting the sacrifices of the "great Russian people" for the development of the backward nations. Soviet economists and ideologists of the 1970s revamped this myth by adding pseudo-scientific grounds to it. In the last decades of the Soviet rule, it was necessary to take attention away from the deteriorating living standards of the soon to collapse empire. The economic stagnation was then presented to the Russian majority as entirely a fault of Central Asia, which presumably the heroic Russian people constantly dragged to their own higher status, risking their own well being and prosperity. This myth continues to live today in both Russia and Central Asia and the Caucasus zombified by the Soviet propaganda and still generates colonial complexes.

48. The situation started to visibly change when I was working on the second revision of this chapter—the indigenous social movements in practically all former and present colonies of Russia/Soviet Union have begun to raise their voices due to various internal and external factors.

49. See a thorough and unbiased report of the event by Shirin Akiner (2005).

50. In the last several years, an armed resistance has been emerging in the territory of historic Circassia. Analysts both in Russia and abroad viewed the Nalchik bloody uprising of October 2005 as Circassia's entry into a war of liberation. The recent decision making Sochi the place of the 2014 Winter Olympics and the large scale preparations for this event have stirred up the Circassian resentment globally. Circassian organizations point out that, by an irony of history, the 2014 Olympic Games will mark the 150th anniversary of the Circassians' defeat by Russia in 1864 (Tlisova 2007). One of the possible scenarios is that the Olympics, if they ever happen in Sochi, might be the match that would light a major uprising in the Caucasus, this time centered on the Cherkess people.

51. In Andijan, it was particularly graphic, as the incident started with the insurgents breaking into a local prison and forcibly freeing the prisoners (killing and wounding those who refused to obey) then marching them down the main road toward the National Security Service, where they were made to stand as a human shield as the insurgents fired on the building behind them. The bodies of those killed earlier in prison were thrown in front of the railings. See Akiner (2005) for more details.

52. However, there were links between religion and social movements in Latin America in the past, for instance, in the Peruvian anticolonial movement of *Aky Onkoy.*

53. This sentiment is expressed in the attempts to apply the postcolonial discourse to an analysis of the Russian situation of the "new subalterns" in the ex-colonies. See, for example, Alexei Penzin's works on this problem (2011).

54. Thus, in 1851 American popular writer, globetrotter, and publisher Maturin Murray Ballow (Lieutenant Maturin Murray) wrote a sensational exoticist tale *The Circassian Slave, or the Sultan's Favorite. A Tale of Constantinople and the Caucasus* (Murray Ballou 2006), in which he presented Circassia as a prototypal South of Europe populated by noble savages: "Circassia, the land of beauty and oppression, whose noble valleys produce such miracles of female loveliness, and whose level plains are the vivid scenes of such terrible struggles; where a brave, unconquerable peasantry have, for a very long period,

defied the combined powers of the whole of Russia, and whose daughters, though the children of such brave sires, are yet taught and reared from childhood to look forward to a life of slavery in a Turkish harem as the height of their ambition—Circassia, the land of bravery, beauty and romance, is one of the least known, but most interesting spots in all Europe" (Murray Ballou 2006: Chapter 4).

55. Nakshbandi was born near Bukhara, where now stands his shrine and mausoleum to which thousands of people have been paying homage for six centuries. Nakshbandi Sufism was one of the main versions of Islam in this locale for a long time, predictably banned in Soviet years. This order was different from other Sufi orders, as it did not stress the ascetic life and turning from the real world to the transcendent one but rather spoke for the equality of both worlds, the real and the mystical, their existence in each other and through each other. This philosophy is marked with a special tolerance and rejection of orthodoxy: It regards women as equal to men and allows them into the main parts of the mosques along with men.

56. There are many parallels between the non-European borderlands of Eurasia and other locales marked with transcultural impulses. One of them is the idea of a hybrid, impure ethnicity, mixed blood. It was the Russian imperial scholars that built the convenient—pure in blood—classification of people living in Central Asia. In reality, they never existed. And, even the imperial ideologues themselves realized that. The first Turkistan general-governor, von Kaufman, lamented that the local population is mixed and often impossible to define in ethnographic terms (Abashin 2004: 49). Moreover, there was a specific variant of Central Asian Creoles—the "Sarts"—half Uzbek and half Tadzhic, in an ethnic sense and in some elements of the way of life resembling the Tadzhic but speaking a Turkic language (new Uzbek) and not Farsi. And, again, as in the Caribbean or in Latin America, a supraidentity made these internal names unimportant for the people themselves, because they knew that a certain pan-Turkic identity is working for the unity of all Central Asian tribes. The latter was dangerous for the Russians, and Russia fought this threat in many ways, from the forceful change of linguistic hierarchy to a population census based on binary principles.

57. *Ilkhom* comes from an Arabic word meaning "inspiration which God sends to the creators." In 1976, a half-underground club of young artists, musicians, and poets called *Ilkhom* founded a theater studio—the first independent theater in the whole Soviet Union—which was to become the center of Tashkent's alternative aesthetics. Its first performance was at attempt at a transcultural link, as it combined the traditions of the Uzbek street theater Maskharaboz with the latest theatrical experimentation, which gradually resulted in the creation of specific *Ilkhom* theatrical principles and school of acting based on constant improvisation.

58. When I was writing the second version of this chapter, *Ilkhom* brought to Moscow theater festival *The Golden Mask*, the two last Weil shows—the most ambitious and provocative of his projects. I was lucky to attend one of them, *Ecstasy with the Pomegranate*, a sensuous parable of yet another trickster, a Russian by origin, modernist painter Alexander Nikolayev, fascinated with the Orient. He came to Uzbekistan, later became a Sufi and turned into Usto Mumin, always driven by an angst and attracted by a transsexual *Bacha* [boy] dancer. This performance is a virtuoso transcultural, transmedia, and global phenomenon, not only in its presentation but also in its creation. The androgynous *batcha* dances were directed by a famous American dancer, writer, director, and founder of the modern interracial and intercultural dance group *Reality*, David Roussève. A talented young Uzbek artist, Babur Ismailov, did a fascinating work of adapting Nikolayev's paint-

ings for video and animation presentation during the show. An interesting Korean by origin composer, Artyem Kim, created a delicate, sensuous, and suggestive soundtrack of the *Ecstasy*, based on rhythmical leitmotifs repeated in various media—from traditional musical instruments to voice and even pebbles in a big metal pot. As a result, a border performance emerged, always balancing on the edge of various art forms, languages (Weil uses Anzaldúa's type of bilingual repetition with variation when a phrase is first said in Uzbek then repeated in Russian but with a deviation), rhythms (traditional Uzbek mixing with Caribbean), symbols (e.g., queer semiotics interchanges with Sufi).

59. The abundance of English-speaking universities in Central Asia is particularly symptomatic in relation to the Amawtay Wasi phenomenon, as it demonstrates how easily indigenous cosmology, knowledge, and thinking can be appropriated, neutered, and used as a new multicultural edition of mind colonization. A perfect example of such initiative from above (as opposed to Amawtay Wasi, as the indigenous people project from below) is the regional internationally charted University of Central Asia, cofounded in 2000 by the heads of Kazakhstan, Kyrgyzia, and Tajikistan under the supervision of and with the money from "his highness" the Aga Khan, the Imam [spiritual leader] of the Shia Imami Ismaili Muslims since 1957 and a representative of a small expatriate Muslim top elite in the West (UCA 2011). The university is positioned as promoting the Central Asian Mountain Societies and their cultural and economic heritage in the new world order. Yet, the curricula and specializations, the tuition in English, and other telling details demonstrate that the university is going to make Western style experts and new local elites according to the new old formula: ethnic-national-regional in its form, neoliberal-capitalist in its essence.

Chapter 4

60. In 2002, the *Slavic Review* organized a discussion on the meaning of race in the USSR, where opinions differed from Eriz Weitz's (2002) parallel between Nazi and Soviet racial politics, even if there was no clearly defined idea of race in the Soviet Union, in his view, and Francine Hirsch's (2002) opposite idea of the clear Soviet definition of race accompanied by an incoherent and often inconsistent racial politics. In good faith, the American scholars tried to analyze Soviet modernity without paying much attention to its darker colonial side or listening to the colonized/racialized/gendered voices. In reality, the Soviet racial othering is not unique for any modernity/coloniality, as it is based on the familiar operation of divesting the (unreformable) enemy of its human nature to justify its annihilation. On top of that, there was always a gap between the official racial ideological discourses and rhetoric in the USSR and the real practices of the Janus-faced empire.

61. The exception in this case was the Orientalistic interpretation of the homosexual problematic, particularly, homosexuality between grown men and young boys, especially in the form of the "bacha cult," which was ostracized by the Russian empire and later banned by the Soviet authorities and presented as an inherent part of Central Asian law. It was not directly linked to Islam though. Lesbianism figured in these accusations much less frequently, although it also was regarded as a direct and unhealthy result of female seclusion and a harmful medieval or bourgeois survival.

62. For instance, she makes a viable comparison of the Uzbekistan national gender project and those of Turkey, but she fails to mention that both cases represent the realm of

subaltern empires and their colonies and the specific identity generated catching up with modernity.

63. The majority of Kamp's elaborations can be found in earlier books and articles by Uzbek gender activist M. Tokhtakhodzhayeva, published in Uzbek and in Russian (Tokhtakhodzhayeva 1996, 1999, 2001), with only a brief reference in Kamp's book. This testifies to the asymmetry of knowledge production and distribution—as anything that Kamp would write will be by definition more reliable in the academic world than Tokhtakhodjayeva's or Shakirova's works, as they are assigned the role of native informants and diligent pupils of Western feminists and gender theorists. Therefore, their knowledge is appropriated by the West and reproduced under a sanctified Western name, or sometimes a name that is non-Western but still sanctified by Western education or tenure at a Western university. Chandra Mohanty and Jacqui Alexander address this issue in their seminal *Feminist Genealogies, Colonial Legacies, Democratic Futures*: "Token inclusion of our texts without reconceptualizing the whole white, middle-class, gendered knowledge base effectively absorbs and silences us. This says, in effect, that our theories are plausible and carry explanatory weight only in relation to our *specific* experiences, but that they have no use value in relation to the rest of the world" (Alexander and Mohanty 1997: xvii).

64. See an interesting article on body and gender by a Tadzhik scholar Gulnora Beknazarova, who nevertheless clings to the outdated pattern of the traditional vs. emancipated women (Beknazarova).

65. Area studies and Western-style ethnography lie in the basis of an interesting book written by the northern Caucasus scholar Madina Tekuyeva, *Man and Woman in Adygean Culture: Tradition and Modernity* (2006a), where one has to read in between the lines to fight the methodological constructions that do not fit the described material.

66. For example, in the Russian and early Soviet Empires, the colonizers demonstratively ignored possible sexual partners from the colonized women as being below their status, while the colonial men who chose the Russian/Soviet modernity also preferred to marry Russian women, thus elevating their own status by acquiring a more desirable (Whiter) partner. Later, the situation reversed, in the sense that the local elites and the middle class started to regard the Russian women as sexually accessible and socially emancipated but definitely preferred to marry local women from good families who were educated and enlightened enough yet continued to act as the bearers of the sanctified local tradition.

Chapter 5

67. On Sylvia Wynter's ideas on the subject and bibliography, see *After Man, Towards the Human: Critical Essays on Sylvia Wynter*, ed. Anthony Bogues, Kingston and Miami: Ian Randle Publisher, 2006.

68. There are some exceptions, like German Catholic Carl Schmitt, for whom Catholic Spanish intellectual tradition takes precedence over Protestantism, which was crucial for his co-national Max Weber who argued for the connection between capitalism and Protestant ethics.

69. On the distinction *humanitas/anthropos*, see Nishitani Osamu, "Anthropos and Humanitas: Two Western Concepts of 'Human Beings,'" in *Translation, Biopolitics, Co-*

lonial Difference, ed. Naoki Sakai and Jon Solomon. Hong Kong: Hong Kong University Press, 2006, pp. 259-74.

70. See Constitution of Ecuador, Titulo II, Derechos; Capitulo 2, Derechos del Buen Vivir (http://pdba.georgetown.edu/Constitutions/Ecuador/ecuador08.html); Constitucon de Bolivia, capitulo cuarto, Derecho de las naciones y pueblos indigenas originario campesino, http://pdba.georgetown.edu/Constitutions/Bolivia/bolivia09.html. See also Annette Aurélie Desmarais, *La Vía Campesina: Globalization and the Power of Peasants.* London and Ann Arbor: Pluto Press, 2007.

71. An example of how decolonial humanities are being thought out in Russia, see http://www.jhfc.duke.edu/globalstudies/currentpartnerships.html; http://www.jhfc.duke.edu/globalstudies/Tlostanova_how%20can%20the%20decolonial%20project.pdf,

Chapter 6

72. See Walter D. Mignolo, "Globalization and the Geopolitics of Knowledge: The Role of the Humanities in the Corporate University," *Nepantla: Views from South* 4.1 (2003): 97-119. (Chapter 7 is a modified version of this article.)

73. See Ngugi Wa Th'iongo, *Decolonizing the Mind: The Politics of Language in African Literature* (1986) and Ignacio Ramonet, "La Pensé Unique," *Le Monde Diplomatique* (1992): 1.

74. To make a long story short, I refer only to Lewis Gordon's *Fanon and the Crisis of European Man: An Essay on Philosophy and the Human Sciences* (1995).

75. About the Zapatistas' theoretical revolution, see Walter D. Mignolo, "The Zapatistas' Theoretical Revolution: Its Historical, Ethical and Political Consequences," *Review. Fernand Braudel Center* 25.3 (2002a): 245-75.

76. A copy of Abraham Ortelius's map can be found at <http:// image.sl.nsw.gov.au/cgi-bin/ebindshow.pl?doc=crux/a127;seq=11>; this map was published for the first time in his atlas titled *Theatrum Orbis Terrarum* (1570).

77. For a useful, Eurocentered narrative of citizens and foreigners, see Julia Kristeva, *Strangers to Ourselves,* trans. Leon S. Roudiez (1991).

78. I am following here a less-known narrative of another conceptualization connecting people to "cities": see León-Portilla, 2003, 15-35.

79. I explored this issue in Andean history (and in Aymara's categories of thought) in "Decires fuera de lugar: sujetos dicentes, roles sociales y formas de inscripción," *Revista de Crítica Literaria Latinoamericana* 21.41 (1995): 9-32. A decolonizing foundation of philosophy leading to the epistemic and hermeneutical shift delinking Greco-Latin categories of thought reinscribed in the imperial languages of modernity could be found in the pioneering work of Rodolfo Kusch, an Argentinian philosopher of German descent. See his *La negación en el pensamiento popular* (1975) and *El pensamiento indígena y popular en América* (1971) in *Obras Completas,* Vol. II (2000), 255-546.

80. Stories are being told of Chinese people going to the West then returning to China, being welcomed, and initiating companies, small and large, which in part explains the Chinese economic boom in the past twenty years. That is not the case for those from countries like Bolivia, Tanzania, or Tunisia. The various types of frontiers and citizen mobility are strictly related to colonial and imperial differences and to the economic world structures that the colonial and imperial differences contributed to creating and maintaining.

81. Arguments are often advanced that sound like a reaction to the situation in the U.S. rather than an analysis of racism in the modern colonial world. Poverty, in the sense that the term has in the modern colonial and capitalist world and racism are two sides of the same coin: The Industrial Revolution would not have been possible without the Colonial Revolution in the sixteenth century.

82. As with any key category of thought, the decolonial shift needs to be articulated within the conceptual package of Western epistemology (i.e., Greek and Latin translated into modern imperial languages—Italian, Spanish, Portuguese, French, German, and English) and to work out the displacement, the fracture, the colonial or imperial differences rearticulated from the perspective of coloniality. As Ali Shariati would say, why shall we study the *Q'uran* with the instrument and principles of the social sciences and the humanities and not reflect on the social sciences and the humanities from the instruments and epistemic principles we find in the Q'uran? (See Alí Shariati, *On the Sociology of Islam* [1979], 44–45.) Something similar happens with *pacha-sophy*, looking at the Greek philosophical legacy from the categories we find in the Aymara language.

Chapter 7

83. On October 20, 2010, a meeting was held in Canada to consider the possibility of a common higher-education framework, similar to the European Plan Bologna (http://chronicle.com/article/A-Common-Higher-Education/125062/). In February 2011, the government of the U.S. appointed a National Commission on the Humanities, http://www.dukenews.duke.edu/2011/02/rhbhumanities.html.

84. See Natalia Vinelli's interview with Felipe Quispe (2002). Quispe, also known as El Mallku, is a Bolivian indigenous activist and leader. Now in his fifties, he is finishing a PhD in history at the Universidad Mayor de San Andrés.

85. To make a long story short, each time that I write "coloniality," just think about the other side, the darker and obscure side of "modernity." And remember that there is not and cannot be modernity without coloniality. The reason why "coloniality" sounds odd and remains invisible is that the histories of modernity have been told from the perspective of modernity itself! As is often said, it is difficult to understand and feel poverty while standing in the marina in Marseilles, looking at the sun set in the Mediterranean. Of course, you can "conceive" of colonialism and "know" that there are poor people around. But, that is a different story.

86. As far as the history of science is concerned, Mexico provides a good example to be contrasted with that of India; see Prakash 2000; see also Gortari 1979. As for the "original" scientific revolution, that is, the metropolitan one that gets exported to and imported into the colonies, see Jardine 1999.

87. See Tünnermann Bernheim 2001. On "coloniality of knowledge," see Lander 2000.

88. For a critical and historical overview of the modern (that is, postindependence) university in Chile, see Thayer 1996. For a historical and critical historical overview, see the classic Readings 1996. Both books generated interesting debates. The one on Thayer's book was published in *Nepantla* 1 (Quijano 2000): 229–82. The debate on Readings's book was published in Smith 1996. See also Sousa Santos [1987] 1998, on "the idea of the university," and Hinkelammert 2002. For an analysis of the United States and Japan, see Miyoshi 2000.

89. For the peculiarities of the U.S. university during the Cold War, see Chomsky et al. 1997. For the crisis of the university in Latin America during the post–Cold War years, see North American Congress on Latin America 2000.

90. For more information about the structure and goals of the Universidad Intercultural, see Macas 2000, Macas and Lozano 2000, and "Universidad Intercultural" 2002.

91. See also Multinational Monitor 2002. The special issue of the *Boletín ICCI-RIMAI* from which the quotation is drawn is devoted entirely to the Universidad Intercultural and provides ample information related to the issues I bring up here.

BIBLIOGRAPHY

Abashin, Sergei. 2004. "Naseleniye Ferganskoy Dolini" [The population of Ferghana Valley]. In *Ferganskaja Dolina. Etnichnost. Ethnicheskie Protsessy. Etnicheskie Konflikty* [Ferghana Valley. Ethnicity. Ethnic Processes. Ethnic Conflicts]. Moscow: Nauka, pp. 38–101.

———. 2007. *Natsionalizmi v Srednei Azii: v Poiskakh identichnost*i [Nationalisms in Central Asia: In quest of identity]. Saint Petersburg: Aleteya.

———. 2009. :Mustakillik i Pamyat ob Imperskom Proshlom: Prokhodya po zalam tashkentskogo muzeya pamyati zhertv repressii: [Mustakillik and the memory of the imperial past: Passing through the halls of Tashkent Memorial to the victims of repression]. *Neprikosnovenny Zapas. Debaty o Politike i Kulture* [Reserved funds: Debating politics and culture] no. 66, pp. 37–54.

Abasov, Ali. 2005. Genderny Analiz Sotsialno-poiliticheskoi Zhizni Azerbaidzjana [Gender analysis of the social-political life of Azebajdzhan]. Gender Studies. Central Asian Network. http://www.genderstudies.info/magazin/magazin_02_01.php, 08.25.06.

Abergel, E. A. 2005. "Technological Sovereignty and Food Security: The Global Politics of Agricultural Biotechnology." Paper presented at the annual meeting of the International Studies Association, Honolulu, Hawaii, 5 March 2005, http://www.allacademic.com/meta/p_mla_apa_research_citation/0/6/9/6/6/p69668_index.html.

Ab Imperio. Studies of New Imperial History and Nationalism in the Post-Soviet Space, 2000–2009.

Adams, Laura L. 2005. "Modernity, Postcolonialism and Theatrical Form in Uzbekistan." *Slavic Review* 64.2: 333–54.

Afrasiabi, Kaveh. 2006. "Conversation with Mohammad Khatami on the Dialogue among Civilizations." *UN Chronicle* online edition: http://www.un.org/Pubs/chronicle/2006/webArticles/102006_Khatami.htm.

Akiner, Shirin. 2005. "Violence in Andijan 13 May, 2005: An Independent Assessment." Central Asia-Caucasus Institute. Silk Road Studies Program. John Hopkins University, Uppsala University.

Aksartova, Sada. 2005. "Civil Society from Abroad: U.S. Donors in the Former Soviet Union." PhD Dissertation, Princeton University.

Alban Achinte, Adolfo. 2006. *Texiendo Textos y Saberes. Cinco Hijos para Pensar los Estudios Culturales, la Colonialidad y la Interculturalidad.* Popayán: Editorial Universidad del Cauca, Colección Estiodios (Inter)culturales.

Alexander, Jacqui M. 2005. *Pedagogies of Crossing*. Durham, NC, and London: Duke University Press.

Alexander, Jacqui M., and Chandra Mohanty, eds. 1997. *Feminist Genealogies, Colonial Legacies, Democratic Futures*. New York: Routledge.

Ali, Kecia. 2003. "Progressive Muslims and Islamic Jurisprudence." In *Progressive Muslims on Justice, Gender, and Pluralism*, ed. Omid Safi. Oxford, UK: Oneworld, 2004, pp. 163–89.

Al Jabri, Mohammed Abed. 1999. *Arab-Islamic Philosophy: A Contemporary Critique*. Austin, TX: Center for Middle Eastern Studies.

Alliance of Civilizations. 2009. http://www.unaoc.org/.

Allione, Constanzo. 1997. *Habiba: A Sufi Saint from Uzbekistan*. Documentary. New York: Mystic Fire Video.

Allworth, Edward. 1998. "History and Group Identity in Central Asia." In *Nation-Building in the Post-Soviet Borderlands. The Poltics of National Identities*, ed. G. Smith, V. Law, A. Wilson, A. Bohr, E. Allworth. Cambridge: Cambridge University Press.

Ampiah, Kweku. 2007. *The Political and Moral Imperatives of the Bandung Conference of 1955: The Reactions of the US, UK and Japan*. Folkestone, UK: Global Oriental.

Andijan Massacre Linked to Local Power Struggle. 2005. Source: 09/29/05. Eurasianet.org, http://www.eurasianet.org/departments/insight/articles/eav092905.shtml.

Antelava, Natalia. 2008. "Crossing Continents: Uzbekistan." BBC News. BBC Radio 4's *Crossing Continents* broadcast on Thursday, 3 April 2008 at 1102 BST; repeated on Monday, 7 April 2008 at 2030 BST. http://news.bbc.co.uk/2/hi/programmes/crossing_continents/7325384.stm.

Anzaldúa, Gloria. 1999. *Borderlands/La Frontera. The New Mestiza*. San Francisco: Aunt Lute Books.

Aranaga, Carlos. 2009. "University Studies Introduce Central Asia to Americans. Indiana University among U.S. Leaders in Central Asia Studies." America.gov. 12 February 2009.

Arrighi, Giovanni. 1995. *The Long Twentieth Century*. London: Verso.

Ashwin, Sarah. 2000. *Gender, State, and Society in Soviet and Post-Soviet Russia*. London and New York: Routledge.

Ballinger, Franchot. 1991–92. "Ambigere: The Euro-American Picaro and the Native American Trickster." *Melus* 17.1 (Spring).

Banerjee, S. B. 2008. "Live and Let Die: Colonial Sovereignties and the Death World of Necrocapitalism." Reartikulacija. Arsticstic-Political-Theoretical-Discoursive Platform. No. 3, March. http://www.reartikulacija.org/dekolonizacija/dekolonizacija3_1_ENG.html.

Barja, G. 2001. "Tawantinsuyu." Accessed online at members.tripod.com/˜Gialma/Tawa.html, 28 October 2002.

Barreto, José Manuel. "Human Rights and the Crisis of Modernity." *Critical Legal Thinking*. October 19, 2009. http://www.criticallegalthinking.com/?p=70

———. 2012. "Conquest, Independence and Decolonisation." In J M. Barreto, *Human Rights from a Third-World Perspective: Critique, History and International Law*. Newcastle: Cambridge Scholars Publishing, forthcoming 2012.

Bataillon M. [1950]. 1967. *Erasmos en España*. México City: Fondo de Cultura Económica.

Baudrillard, Jean. 1979. *De la Seduction*. Paris: Les Éditions Galilée.

Beissinger, Mark R. 2008. "The Persistence of Empire in Eurasia." *Newsnet: News of the American Association for the Advancement of Slavic Studies* 48.1: 1–8.

Beknazarova, Gulnora. "Transformatsija normi—osobennosti perekhodnogo perioda" [The transformation of the norm—features of transition period]. *Gender Studies. Central Asia Network*, http://www.genderstudies.info/telo/telo_sexs16.php.

Bennabi, Malik. 2003a. *The Question of Culture*, trans. Abdul Wahid Lu'lu 'a, revised, annotated, and with a foreword by Mohamed El-Tahir El Mesawi. Kuala Lumpur: The International Institute of Islamic Thought.

———. [1390 Ramadan AH; 1970 A.D.] 2003b. *The Question of Ideas in the Muslim World*, translated and with a foreword by Mohamed El Tabir El Mesawi. Kuala Lumpur: Islamic Book Trust.
Bertran, Frederic. 2003. "Nauka bez obyekta? Sovetskaya Etnografiya 1920-1930 godov" [A science with no object? Soviet ethnography of the 1920-1930s]. *Jurnal Sotsiologii i sotsialnoi antropologii* [Journal of Sociology and Social Anthropology] 6.3: 90-104.
Blumenbach, Johann Friedrich. [1795]. 1865. *The Anthropological Treatises of Johann Friedrich Blumenbach: De Generis Humani Varietate Nativa*, ed. and trans. Thomas Bendyshe. New York: Bergman Publishers.
Bobrovnikov, Vladimir. 2000. "Abreki i gosudarstvo" [Abregs and the state]. *Vestnik Evrazii* [Acta Eurasica]. Nezavisimy Nauchny Zhurnal. Institut Vostokovedeniya RAN, 1.8: 19-46.
Bogues, Anthony. 2003. "C. L. R. James and W. E. B. Du Bois: Heresy, Double Consciousness and Revisionist Histories." In *Black Heretics, Black Prophets: Radical Political Intellectuals*. London: Blackwell, 69-94.
Boletín ICCI-RIMAI. 2000. Publicación mensual del Instituto Científico de Culturas Indígenas. October.
Botiakov, Yuri M. 2004. *Abreki na Kavkaze. Sociokul'turnyj aspekt javlenija*. St. Petersburg: Peterburgskoe Vostokovedenie.
Braun, Friederike. 1999. "Gender in a Genderless Language. The Case of Turkish." In *Language and Society in the Middle East and North Africa*, ed. Yasir Suleiman. London: Routledge, 190-203.
Candau V., ed. 2009. Educacao Intercultural hoje en América Latina: conceptoes, tensoes e propostas. Florianápolis: Universidad Federal Santa Catarina, 12-44.
Caroe, Olaf. 1967. *Soviet Empire. The Turks of Central Asia and Stalinism*. New York: Macmillan.
Castro-Gómez, Santiago. 2000. "Traditional and Critical Theories of Culture." *Nepantla* 1.3: 503-18.
———. 2007. "The Missing Chapter of Empire: Postmodern Reorganization of Coloniality and Post-Fordist Capitalism." *Cultural Studies* 21.2-3 (March/May): 428-48.
Catherine, David. 2007. *Nature, Theophany and the Rehabilitation of Consciousness*. Ufudu Medicinal Arts. http://www.workingwithoneness.org/PDF/Nature_Theophany.pdf. 12.10.11.
———. 2004. *The Green Fingerprint*. Ufudu Medicinal Arts. http://khidr.org/Green_Fingerprint.pdf. 12.10.11.
Césaire, Aimé. [1955]. 2000. *Discours sur le colonialism*. English translation, *Discourse on Colonialism*, trans. Joan Pinkham. New introduction by Robin D. G. Kelley. New York: Monthly Review Press.
Chakrabarty, Dipesh. 2000. *Provincializing Europe: Postcolonial Thought and Historical Difference*. Princeton, NJ: Princeton University Press.
Chatterjee, Partha. 2004. *The Politics of the Governed: Considerations on Political Society in Most of the World*. New York: Columbia University Press.
Chomsky, Noam, et al. 1997. *The Cold War and the University: Toward an Intellectual History of the Postwar Years*. New York: New Press.
The Circassians. 2008. Special Issue. Research and Analytical Supplement. Issue No. 43 (May), ed. Stephen D. Shenfield. http://www.circassianworld.com/RAS_Circassians.html.
Circassian Genocide. 2008. http://circassiangenocide.org/.
Colish, Marcia L. 1997. *Medieval Foundations of the Western Intellectual Tradition, 400-1400*. New Haven, CT: Yale University Press.
CONAIE. 1997. *Proyecto Político*. Quito, Ecuador: CONAIE.
Consejo Nacional de Cultura del Ecuador (CNCE). 2000. "Nina Pacari y los pueblos indios." Accessed online at http://www.cultura.com.ec/HTM/ NPACARI-PINDIOS.HTM, 09/2702.
Constitución de Bolivia, http://pdba.georgetown.edu/Constitutions/Bolivia/bolivia09.html.

Constitución de Ecuador, http://pdba.georgetown.edu/Constitutions/Ecuador/ecuador08.html.
Crenshaw, Kimberle. 1991. "Mapping the Margins: Intersectionality, Identity Politics, and Violence against Women of Color." *Stanford Law Review* 43.6 (July): 1241–99.
Cusicanqui, Sylvia Riviera. 1990. El potencial epistemológico y teórico de la historia oral: de la lógica instrumental a la descolonizacion de la historia. *Temas Sociales* 11: 49–75.
Dagenais, John, and Greer, Meg. 2000. *Decolonizing the Middle Ages.* Special issue of *Journal of Medieval and Early Modern Studies* 30.3.
Dainotto, Roberto M. 2000. "A South with a View: Europe and Its Other." *Nepantla: Views from South* 1: 375–90.
Dawisha, K., and B. Parrot. 1994. *Russia and the New States of Eurasia: The Politics of Upheaval.* Cambridge: Cambridge University Press.
———. 1996. *The End of Empire? The Transformation of the USSR in Comparative Perspective.* International Politics of Eurasia, Vol. 9. New York: M. E. Sharpe.
"De-Colonizing the Digital/Digital De-Colonization." 2009. Convened by Dalida María Benfield, WKO, spring, http://www.jhfc.duke.edu/wko/forthcoming.php.
Deng, Zhenglai. 2009. *Development of Chinese Social Sciences in the Era of Globalization,* http://cuscps.sfsu.edu/Events/deng_zhenglai.htm.
Desmarais, Annette Aurélie. 2007. *La Vía Campesina. Globalization and the Power of Peasants.* London and Ann Arbor, MI: Pluto Press.
Dialogue with the Islamic World. Qantara.de. 2009. http://www.qantara.de/webcom/show_article.php/_c-476/_nr-983/webcom/show_article.php/_c-478/_nr-742/i.html?PHPSESSID=ad16a32480e888ca549942f86da5191e.
Dilthey, Wilhelm. 1991. *Selected Works.* Volume I. *Introduction to the Human Sciences.* Princeton, NJ: Princeton University Press.
Dostoyevsky, Fyodor. 1977 [1881]. "Geok-Tepe. Chto takoye Azia dlya nas?" *Dnevnik Pisatelja,* Sobranije Sochineniy, tom 27 ["Geok-Tepe. What is Asia for us?" *Writer's Diary,* Complete Works, Volume 27].
"Double Critique: Knowledges and Scholars at Risk in Post-Soviet Societies." 2006. Ed. Walter Mignolo and Madina Tlostanova. *South Atlantic Quarterly* 105.3.
Driscoll, Mark. 2010. "Looting the Theory Commons: Hardt and Negri's Commonwealth." *Postmodern Culture* 21. September 1. http://muse.jhu.edu/journals/postmodern_culture/toc/pmc.21.1.html
Du Bois, W. E. B. [1904]. 1995. *The Souls of Black Folks.* New York: Penguin Group.
Dussel, Enrique. 1977. *Philosophy of Liberation.* Maryknoll, NY: Orbis Books.
El Saadawi, Nawal. 1997. *The Nawal el Saadawi Reader.* London and New York: Zed Books.
Escobar, Arturo. 2007. "Worlds and Knowledges Otherwise." The Latin American Modernity/Coloniality Research Program. *Cutural Studies* 21.2–3: 179–210.
Espiritu, Yen Le. 1997. "Race, Class, and Gender in Asian America." In *Making More Waves,* ed. Elaine H. Kim, Lilia V. Villanueva, and Asian Women United of California. Boston: Beacon Press.
Eurasian Space in the Eyes of the Young, or, a New Generation About . . . . 2004. An Almanac of the School of the Young Author, Nos. 1–2, Natalis.
Eze, Emmanuel Chukwudi. 1997. "The Color of Reason: The Idea of 'Race.'" In *Postcolonial African Philosophy: A Critical Reader.* London: Blackwell, 103–40.
Fanon, Franz.1952. *Peau noire, mask blanches.* Paris: Maspero.
———. 1967. [1961]. *The Wretched of the Earth.* London: Penguin.
Ferguson, Neil. 2004a. *Empire: The Rise and Demise of the British World Order and the Lessons for Global Power.* New York: Basic Books.
———. 2004b. *Colossus: The Price of America's Empire.* New York and London: Penguin Press.
Foucault, Michel. 1968. *Les mots et les choses.* Paris: Gallimard.
Franke, Patrick. 2000. *Begegnung mit Khidr.* Beirut and Stuttgart, Germany: Ergon.

Freyre, Paulo. 1970. *Pedagogy of the Oppressed*, trans. Myra Bergman Ramos. New York: Continuum.
Friedman-Rudovsky, Jean. 2011. "Bolivia's Long March Against Evo Morales: An Indigenous Protest." *Time World*. October 17. http://www.time.com/time/world/article/0,8599,2097142,00.html
Fukuyama, Francis. 1992. *The End of History and the Last Man*. New York: Avon Books.
Garcia, Jorge. 2004. Sumak Yachaypi, Alli Kawsaypipash Yachakuna: Aprender En La Sabiduria Y El Buen Vivir = Learning Wisdom and the Good Way to Live. UNESCO, Universidad Intercultural Amawtay Wasi.
Gender Studies. Journal of the Kharkiv Center for Gender Studies. No. 19, 2009. http://www.gender.univer.kharkov.ua/gurnal/19/.
Giddens, Anthony. 1992. *The Consequences of Modernity*. Stanford, CA: Stanford University Press.
Gil Fernández, Luis. 1981. *Panorama social del humanismo español, 1500–1800*. Madrid: Alhambra.
Glissant, Eduard. [1990] 1997. *Poetics of Relation*, trans. B. Wing. Ann Arbor: The University of Michigan Press.
Göle, Nulifer. 1996. *The Forbidden Modern: Civilization and Veiling*. Ann Arbor: The University of Michigan Press.
González Casanova, Pablo. 2006. "Las razones del Zapatismo y la Otra Campaña." www.bibliotecavirtual.clacso.org.ar/ar/libros/osal/osa119/38Casano.pdf/.
Goodwin, Jason. 1998. *Lords of the Horizons. A History of the Ottoman Empire*. New York: Henry Holt and Company.
Gordon, Lewis R. 1995. *Fanon and the Crisis of European Man: An Essay on Philosophy and the Human Sciences*. London, UK: Routledge.
———. 2006. *Disciplinary Decadence: Living Thought in Trying Times*. Boulder, CO, and London: Paradigm Publishers.
Gortari, Eli de. 1979. *La ciencia en la historia de México*. Mexico City: Grijalbo.
Globalization and the Decolonial Option. 2007. Special issue of *Cultural Studies*, ed. Walter Mignolo in collaboration with Aruro Escobar, 21/2/3, March.
Greer, Meg, Walter Mignolo, and Maureen Quilligan. *Rereading the Black Legend. The Discourse of Religious and Racial Differences in the Renaissance Empires*. Chicago: The University of Chicago Press, 2008.
Griffiths, Richard T., and Durmus Özdemir. 2004. *Turkey and the EU Enlargement: Processes of Incorporation*. Istanbul: Bilgi University Press.
Grovogui, S. N'Zatioula. 1995. *Sovereigns, Quasi Sovereigns, and Africans*. Minneapolis: University of Minnesota Press.
Guchinova, Elza Bair. 2003. *Postsovetskaya Elista: Vlast, Biznes i Krasota* [Post-Soviet Elista: Power, business and beauty]. Saint Petersburg: Aleteya.
———. 2005. *Pomnit, Nelzya Zabyt: Antropologia Deportatsionnoy Travmy Kalmykov* [Remember, not possible to forget: Anthropology of Kalmyk deportation trauma]. Stuttgart, Germany: Ibidem.
Habermas, Jürgen. 1998. *The Inclusion of the Other. Studies in Political Theory*, ed. C. Cronin and Pablo De Greiff. Boston: MIT Press.
Haraway, Dona. 1991. "A Cyborg Manifesto: Science, Technology, and Socialist-Feminism in the Late Twentieth Century." In *Simians, Cyborgs and Women: The Reinvention of Nature*. New York: Routledge, 149–81.
Hardt, Michael, and Antonio Negri. 2000. *Empire*. Cambridge, MA: Harvard University Press.
Harris, Colette. 2000. *Control and Subversion. Gender and Socialism in Tajikistan*. Manchester, UK: Pluto Press.
Harris, Wilson. 1981. "History, Fable and Myth in the Caribbean and the Guianas." *Explora-

tions: A Selection of Talks and Articles 1966–81, ed. H. Maes-Jelinek. Mundelstrup: Dangaroo.

Hegel, Georg W. F. [1822] 1991. *The Philosophy of History*, trans. J. Sibree. Buffalo and New York: Prometheus Books.

Hinkelammert, Franz. J. 2002. "La universidad frente a la globalización." In *El retorno del sujeto reprimido.* Bogotá, Columbia: Universidad Nacional.

———. 2004. "The Hidden Logic of Modernity. Locke and the Inversion of Human Rights." WKO, http://www.jhfc.duke.edu/wko/dossiers/1.1/HinkelammertF.pdf.

Hirsch, Francine. 2000. "Towards an Empire of Nations: Border Making and the Formation of Soviet National Identities." *Russian Review* 59 (April): 201–226.

———. 2002. "Race without the Practice of Racial Politics." *Slavic Review*, Vol. 61, No 1: 30–43.

Hobson, John A. [1902]. 1965. *Imperialism.* Ann Arbor: The University of Michigan Press.

Hollinger, David. 1995. Post-Ethnic America: Beyond Multiculturalism. New York: Basic Books.

Horkheimer, Max. [1937]. 1999. "Traditional and Critical Theory." In *Critical Theory: Selected Essays.* New York: Continuum Publishing, 253–72.

Hynes, William J., and William G. Doty. 1993. *Mythical Trickster Figures.* Tuscaloosa: The University of Alabama Press.

Ibarra Colado, Eduardo. 2007. "Organization Studies and Epistemic Coloniality in Latin America: Thinking Otherness from the Margins." *World and Knowledges Otherwise, A Web Dossier.* Fall 2007. http://www.jhfc.duke.edu/wko/dossiers/1.3/documents/ibarra-coladofin.pdf.

Ilkhamov, Alisher. 2005. "Arkheologiya Uzbekskoy Identichnosti" [Archeology of Uzbek identity]. Etnograficheskoye Obozreniye [Ethnographic survey] No. 1.

Ilkhom. 2009. http://www.ilkhom.com/english.

Jaimoukha, Amjad. 2010. "The Nart Tales of the Circassians." International Centre for Circassian Studies (ICCS), http://iccs.synthasite.com/nart-epos.php, 10/11/10.

Jardine, Lisa. 1999. *Ingenious Pursuits: Building the Scientific Revolution.* New York: Nan A. Talese Doubleday.

Jersild, Austin. 2002. *Orientalism and Empire.* Montreal and Kingston, ON: McGill-Queen's University Press.

Jiménez-Lucena, Isabel. 2008. "Gender and Coloniality: The 'Moroccan Woman' and the 'Spanish Woman' in Spain's Sanitary Policies in Morocco." *Worlds and Knowledges Otherwise, a Web Dossier* (Spring). http://www.jhfc.duke.edu/wko/dossiers/1.3/documents/JimenezWK02.2_002.pdf.

Kamp, Marianne. 2006. *The New Woman in Uzbekistan. Islam, Modernity and Unveiling under Communism.* Seattle and London: University of Washington Press.

Kandiyoti, Deniz. 2002. "Post-Colonialism Compared: Potentials and Limitations in the Middle East and Central Asia." *International Journal of Middle Eastern Studies*, 34.2: 279–97.

Kant, Immanuel. [1798] 1955. *Le conflit des facultés en trois sections*, trans. into French with an introduction and notes by J. Gibelin. Paris: J. Vrin.

———. [1798]. 1996. *Anthropology from a Pragmatic Point of View*, trans. Victor Lyle Dowedel. Carbondale: Southern Illinois University Press, Book II, Section II.

Karimov, Islam. 1993. *Uzbekistan na Poroge Buduschego* [Uzbekistan at the threshold of the future]. Tashkent, Uzbekistan: Government Printing House.

Kasymova, Sofia, ed. 2005a.*Gender: Traditsii i Sovremennost.* [Gender: Traditions and modernity]. Dushanbe, Tadzhik: Shkola Gendernogo Obrazovanija.

Kasymova, Sofia. 2005b. "Genderny Poryadok v Postsovetskom Tadzhikistane" [Gender order in post-Soviet Tadzhikistan]. In *Gender: Traditsii i Sovremennost* [Gender: Traditions and modernity], ed. S. Kasymova. Dushanbe, Tadzhikistan: Shkola Gendernogo Obrazovanija, pp. 177–97.

Katz, Katarina. 2001. *Gender, Work and Wages in the Soviet Union: A Legacy of Discrimination*. London: Palgrave Macmillan.
Khalid, Adeeb. 1999. *The Politics of Muslim Cultural Reform: Jadidism in Central Asia*. Comparative Studies on Muslim Societies. Berkeley: University of California Press.
———. 2007. *Islam after Communism: Religion and Politics in Central Asia*. Berkeley: University of California Press.
Kharitonov M. S. 1986. *Dvadtsat Chetyre Nasreddina* [Twenty-four Nasreddins]. Moscow: Nauka.
Khatibi, Abdelkhebir. 1983. *Maghreb Pluriel*. Paris: Denoel.
———. 1990. *Love in Two Languages*, trans. R. Howard. Minneapolis: University of Minnesota Press.
Kikvidze, Zaal. 2001. "On the Sex-Preferential Order of the Components in Some Dvandva Compounds in Georgian." In *Papers of the First International Conference, Gender: language, culture, communication. November 25-26 1999*. Moscow, 209-12.
Kimmage, Daniel. 2005. "Uzbekistan: Bloody Friday." In *The Ferghana Valley*. Radio Free Europe. Radio Liberty. May 14. http://www.rferl.org/content/article/1058869.html.
Klyuchevsky, Vassily. 2009. *Kurs Russkoy Istorii* [A course in Russian history]. Moscow: Alfa-Kniga.
Khun, Thomas. 1962. *The Structure of Scientific Revolutions*. Cambridge, MA: Harvard University Press.
Kosmarskaya, Natalya. 2006. *Deti Imperii v Postsovetskoy Tsentralnoy Azii* [Children of empire in the post-Soviet Central Asia]. Moscow: Natalis.
Kosmarsky, Artyom, ed. 2004. *Yevraziiskoe Prostranstvo Glazami Molodykh, ili Novoye Pokolenie O* [Eurasian Space as seen by the young, or a new generation about]. An Almanac of the school of young authors. Moscow: Natalis.
Kotkin, Stephen M. 1995. *Rediscovering Russia in Asia: Siberia and the Russian Far East*. New York: M. E. Sharpe.
———. 2003. *Armageddon Averted: The Soviet Collapse, 1970-2000*. Oxford: Oxford University Press.
Kristeva, Julia. 1994. *Strangers to Ourselves*. New York: Columbia University Press.
Kudryashov, Andrei. 2007. "Novaya vystavka v Tashkente." http://www.ferghana.ru/article.php?id=4883, 03/02/07.
Kusch, Rodolfo. 1978. *Esbozo de una antropología filosófica americana*. Buenos Aires: Crisálida.
Lafitau, Joseph François. 1724. *Mœurs des sauvages amériquains comparées aux mœurs des premiers temps*. Paris: Chez Saugran L'Aine.
Lander, Edgardo. 2000. *La colonialidad del saber: Eurocentrismo y Ciencias Sociales*, trans. [1985] Aquilina Martinez and Christine Morkovosky. Eugene: OR: Wipf and Stock.
Las Casas, Bartolomé de. [1552] 1967. *Apologética Historia Summaria*, ed. Edmundo O'Gorman. Mexico City: Universidad Autónoma de México, Vol. II, "Epilogue."
La Via Campesina. *International Peasant Movement*. 2008. http://viacampesina.org/main_en/index.php, 06/30/08.
Lenin, Vladimir. [1917] 1963. "Imperialism, the Highest Stage of Capitalism." *Selected Works*. Moscow: Progress Publishers, Vol. 1, 667-766.
Leonardo da Vinci. 2009. http://leonardodavinci.stanford.edu/submissions/clabaugh/welcome.html.
Leon-Portilla, Miguel. 2003. *Totlecáyotl: Aspectos de la Cultura Nahuatl*. México City: Fondo de Cultura Economica.
Lieven, Dominic. 2002. *Empire: The Russian Empire and Its Rivals*. New Haven, CT: Yale University Press.
Li Xiaojiang. 1993. *Zouxiang nuren—Zhongguo (dalu) funu yenjiu jishi* [Heading towards women—A true account of women's studies in Mainland China]. Hong Kong: Qingwen

Shuwu. Quoted in Wu Y., 2005, "Making Sense in Chinese 'Feminism'/Women's Studies." In *Dialogue and Difference: Feminisms Challenge Globalization*. New York: Palgrave, 2005, pp. 29–52.

———. 1999. "With What Discourse Do We Reflect on Chinese Women ? Thoughts on Transnational Feminism in China." In *Spaces of Their Own: Women's Public Sphere in Transnational China*, ed. Mayfair Mei-hiu Yang. Minneapolis: University of Minnesota Press, pp. 261–77.

Lugones, María. 2003. "Playfulness, 'World'-Traveling and Loving Perception." In *Pilgrimages/Peregrinajes. Theorizing Coalition against Multiple Oppression*. Lanham, MD: Rowman and Littlefield, pp. 77–100.

———. 2007. "Heterosexualism and the Colonial/Modern Gender System." *Hypatia* 22.1 (Winter): 186–209.

———. 2008. "The Colonial Difference and the Coloniality of Gender." A talk presented at Drew Transdisciplinary Theological Colloquium VIII, Decolonizing Epistemology: New Knowing in Latina/o Theology, 20–23 November 2008, Madison, NJ. http://depts.drew.edu/tsfac/colloquium/2008/presenters2.html.

Luxembourg, Rosa. [1913] 1951. *The Accumulation of Capital*, ed. W. Stark. London: Routledge.

Macas, Luis. 2000. "Como se forjó la Universidad Intercultural?" *Boletín ICCI (Instituto Científico de Culturas Indígenas) "RIMAY,"* October. Accessed online at icci.nativeweb.org/boletin/19/macas.html, 27 September 2002.

Macas, Ambuludi Luis, and Alfredo Lozano. 2000. "Reflexiones en torno al proceso colonizador y las características de la educación universitaria en el Ecuador." Accessed online at uinpi.nativeweb.org/docs/macas1/macas1.html, 27 September 2002.

Mahbubani, Kishore. 2008. *The New Asian Hemisphere: The Irresistible Shift of Global Power to the East*. New York: Public Affairs.

———. 2009. http://www.mahbubani.net/.

Malashenko, Alexei. 1993. "Islam versus Communism." In *Russia's Muslim Frontiers. New Directions in Cross-Cultural Analysis*, ed. Dale F. Fickelman. Bloomington and Indianapolis: Indiana University Press, 63–78.

Maldonado-Torres, Nelson. 2007. "On the Colonaility of Being." *Cultural Studies* 21.2–3 (March–May): 240–69.

———. 2008. *Against War: Views from the Underside of Modernity*. Durham, NC: Duke University Press.

Mamedov, Afanasy. 2000. *Khazarsky Veter* [Khazar wind]. Moscow: Text.

———. 2010. "U menta byla sobaka" [A cop had a dog]. *Druzhba Narodov* 9 (2010): 7–32.

March, Andrew F. 2002. "The Use and Abuse of History: National Ideology as Transcendental Object in Islam Karimov's Ideology of National Independence." *Central Asian Survey*, No. 21 (4).

Marcos, Sylvia. 2005. "The Borders Within: The Indigenous Women's Movement and Feminism in Mexico." In *Dialogue and Difference: Feminisms Challenge Globalization*. New York: Palgrave, pp. 81–112.

———. 2006. *Taken from the Lips: Gender and Eros in Mesoamerican Religions*. Leiden and Boston: Brill.

Mariátegui, José Carlos. [1928]. 1971. *Seven Interpetative Essays on Peruvian Reality*, trans. Jorge Basadre. Austin: University of Texas Press.

Marozzi, Justin. 2006. *Tamerlane: Sword of Islam, Conqueror of the World*. N.Y., Da Capo Press.

Massel, Gregory. 1974. *The Surrogate Proletariat: Moslem Women and Revolutionary Strategies in Soviet Central Asia, 1919–1929*. Princeton, NJ: Princeton University Press.

McClintock, Anne. 1995. *Imperial Leather: Race, Gender and Sexuality in the Colonial Contest*. New York: Routledge.

McGlinchey, Eric M. 2007. "Divided Faith: Trapped between State and Islam in Uzbekistan." In *Everyday Life in Central Asia. Past and Present*, ed. J. Sahadeo and R. Zanca. Bloomington and Indianapolis: Indiana University Press, 305–18.
Meddeb, Abdelwahab. 2003. *The Malady of Islam*. New York: Basic Books.
Mekhti, Niazi. 2005. "Virtualny Hijab" [Virtual hijab]. In *Gender: Traditsii i Sovremennost* [Gender: Tradition and modernity]. Dushanbe, Tadzhikistan: Shkola Gendernogo Obrazovanija, 136–145.
Memmi, Albert. [1957]. 1991. *The Colonizer and the Colonized*. Boston: Beacon Press.
Meyer, Karl. 2004. *The Dust of Empire. The Race of Supremacy in the Asian Heartlands*. London: Abacus.
Mignolo, Walter D. 1992. "On the Colonization of Amerindian Languages and Memories: Renaissance Theories of Writing and the Discontinuity of the Classical Tradition." *Comparative Studies in Society and History* 34.2: 301–33.
———. 1995. *The Darker Side of the Renaissance. Literacy, Colonization and Territoriality*. Ann Arbor: The University of Michigan Press.
———. 2000. *Local Histories/Global Designs. Coloniality, Subaltern Knowledges and Border Thinking*. Princeton, NJ: Princeton University Press.
———. 2002a. "The Enduring Enchantment: (or the Epistemic Privilege of Modernity and Where to Go from Here)." *South Atlantic Quarterly* 101.4 (Fall): 927–54.
———. 2002b. "Geopolitics of Knowledge and the Colonial Difference." *South Atlantic Quarterly* 101.1: 57–96.
———. 2003. "Globalization and the Geopolitics of Knowledge: The Role of the Humanities in the Corporate University." *Nepantla: Views from South* 4.1: 97–119.
———. 2007. "From Central Asia to the Caucasus and Anatolia: Transcultural Subjectivity and De-Colonial Thinking." *Postcolonial Studies* 10.1: 111–20.
———. 2009a. "Coloniality at Large: Time and the Colonial Difference." In *Enchantments of Modernity. Empire, Nation, Globalization*, ed. Saurabh Dube, Foreword by Veena Das. Critical Asian Studies. London: Routledge, 67–95.
———. 2009b. "The End of the University as We Know It." http://waltermignolo.com/2009/05/07/at-the-end-of-the-university-as-we-know-it-world-epistemic-fora-toward-communal-futures-and-decolonial-horizons-of-life/.
Milbank, John. 1993. *Theology and Social Theory. Beyond Secular Reason*. London: Blackwell.
Miyoshi, Masao. 2000. "The University and the 'Global' Economy: The Cases of the United States and Japan." *South Atlantic Quarterly* 99: 669–97.
Miziano, Victor. 2006. *Art of Central Asia. An Actual Archive*. Exhibition catalogue. Moscow.
Moore, David Chioni. 2001. "Is the Post- in Postcolonial the Post- in Post-Soviet? Toward a Global Postcolonial Critique." *PMLA* 116.1: 111–28.
Moraña, M., Enrique Dussel, and Carlos A. Jáuregui. 2009. *Coloniality at Large: Latin America and the Postcolonial Debates*. Durham, NC: Duke University Press.
Multinational Monitor. 2002. "'Fueling Destruction in the Amazon': Interview between the *Multinational Monitor* and Dr. Luis Macas, president of the Confederation of Indigenous Nationalities of Ecuador (CONAIE)." Accessed online at www.hartford-hwp.com/archives/41/042.html, 27 September 2002. Originally published in *Multinational Monitor*, April 1994.
Murray Ballou, M. 2006. *The Circassian Slave, or, the Sultan's Favorite*. Gloucester, United Kingdom: Dodo Press.
Nandi, Ashis. 1995. *The Savage Freud and Other Essays on Possible and Retrievable Selves*. Princeton: Princeton University Press.
Natho, Kadir. 2009. *Circassian History*. Bloomington, IN: Xlibris Corporation.
Navailh, Françoise. 1996. "The Soviet Model." In *A History of Women in the West. Towards a Cultural Identity in the Twentieth Century*, ed. Françoise Thebaud. Cambridge and London: The Belknap Press of Harvard University Press, 226–54.

Niño Becerra, Santiago. 2009. *El crash del 2010. Toda la verdad sobre la crisis*. Barcelona: Los Libros del Lince.
North American Congress on Latin America (NACLA). 2000. "The Crisis of the Latin American University." Special issue of *NACLA: Report on the Americas* 33.4.
Northrop, Douglas. 2004. *Veiled Empire: Gender and Power in Stalinist Central Asia*. Ithaca, NY, and London: Cornell University Press.
Nortsov, Alexander N. 1904. Materyaly dlya istorii tambovskogo, penzenskogo i saratovskogo dvoryanstva [Materials for the history of Tambov, Penza and Saratov nobility], Vol. 1. Tambov, Russia: Private Printing House, 111–18.
Olcott, Martha Brill. 1993. "Central Asia's Political Crisis." In *Russia's Muslim Frontiers: New Directions in Cross-Cultural Analysis*, ed. Dale F. Fickelman. Bloomington and Indianapolis: Indiana University Press, 49–62.
Osamu, Nishitani. 2006. "Anthropos and Humanitas: Two Western Concepts of 'Human Beings.'" In *Translation, Biopolitics, Colonial Difference*, ed. Naoki Sakai and Jon Solomon. Hong Kong: Hong Kong University Press, 259–74.
Oyěwùmi, Oyèrónke. 1997. *The Invention of Women: Making African Sense of Western Gender Discourses*. Minneapolis and London: University of Minnesota Press.
Özbudun, Ergun, and E. Fuat Keyman. 2002. "Cultural Globalization in Turkey. Actors, Discourses, Strategies." In *Many Globalizations. Cultural Diversity in the Contemporary World*, ed. Peter L. Berger and Samuel P. Huntington. New York: Oxford University Press, 296–320.
Padgen, Anthony. 1995. *Lord of All the World: Ideologies of Empires in Spain, Britain and France c. 1500–c. 1800*. New Haven, CT: Yale University Press.
Paksoy Hasan B. 1995a. "Dastan Genre in Central Asia." *Modern Encyclopedia of Religions in Russia and the Soviet Union*. Academic International Press, Vol. V. http://vlib.iue.it/carrie/texts/carrie_books/paksoy-6/cae05.html, 10/07/06.
———. 1995b. "'Basmachi': Turkistan National Liberation Movement 1916–1930s." *Modern Encyclopedia of Religions in Russia and the Soviet Union*. Academic International Press, Vol. 1, 5–20; http://vlib.iue.it/carrie/texts/carrie_books/paksoy-6/cae12.html. July 6.
———. 1995c. "The Basmachi Movement from Within: An Account of Zeki Velidi Togan" Nationalities Papers, 23.2 (June): 373–99. Reprinted in *Turkistan Newsletter* (ISSN: 1386-6265) 97.1 (November 1997).
———. 2002. "Literature in Central Asia." *Encyclopedia of Modern Asia*, ed. D. Levinson and K. Christensen. New York: Charles Scribners, 478–82.
Pamuk, Orhan. 2000. *Chernaja Kniga* [Black book]. St. Peterburg: Amfora.
Pannikar, Raimundo. 2000. "Religion, Philosophy and Culture." *Polylog*, http://them.polylog.org/1/fpr-en.htm.
Penzin, Alexey. 2011. "Post-Soviet Singularity and Codes of Cultural Translation." The Latvian Center for Contemporary Art. http://old.lcca.lv/e-texts/17/ (last accessed 04/08/11).
Polat, Haci Bayram. 2008. "The Institutional Face of Collaborationism: International Circassian Association." Paper presented 13 April 2008, William Paterson University, New Jersey, USA. Available at: http://www.circassiandiaspora.com/forum/showthread.php?t=35.
Posadskaya, Anastasia. 1994. *Women in Russia. A New Era in Russian Feminism*, trans. Kate Clark. London and New York: Verso.
Prakash, Gyan. 2000. *Another Reason: Science and the Imagination of Modern India*. Princeton, NJ: Princeton University Press.
Quandour, Mukhammad. I. 2006. *"Muridism." A Study of the Caucasian Wars 1819–1859*. New York: Book Surge.
Quijano, Anibal. 1992. "Colonialidad y modernidad-racionalidad." In *Los conquistados. 1492 y la población indígena de las Américas*, ed. Heraclio Bonilla. Quito, Ecuador: Tercer Mundo Editores/FLACSO/Libri Mundi, 437–47.
———. 2000. "Coloniality of Power, Eurocentrism and Latin America." *Nepantla* 1.3: 533–80.

Quijano, Anibal, and Immanuel Wallerstein. 1992. "Americanity as a Concept, or the Americas in the Imaginary of the Modern World-System." *International Journal of Social Science* 134.
Quispe, Felipe. 2002. "Los ayllus versus el capitalismo: Entrevista a Felipe Quispe, El Mallku— 'Los ayllus y el capitalismo son sistemas antagónicos,'" interview by Natalia Vinelli. Centro de Medias Independientes. 20 June 2002. Accessed online at bolivia.indymedia.org/es/2002/06/109.shtml, 27 September 2002.
Ramadan, Tariq. 2003. *Globalisation Muslim Resistances*. Paris, Lyon: Éditions Tawhid.
Ramonet, Ignacio. 1995 "La pensée unique." *Le Monde Diplomatique*. http://www.monde-diplomatique.fr/1995/01/RAMONET/1144 - janvier 1995.
Rana, Rajat. "Symphony of Decolonization: Third World and Human Rights Discourse." *The International Journal of Human Rights*. Vol. 11.4 (2007): 367–79.
Rasanayagam, Johan. 2004. Etnichnost, Gosudarstvennaya Ideologia i Ponyatie 'Obschina' v Uzbekistane" [Ethnicity, state ideology and the concept of community in Uzbekistan]. *Ferganskaja Dolina. Etnichnost. Ethnicheskie Protsessy. Etnicheskie Konflikty*. Moscow: Nauka, 145–63.
Readings, Bill. 1996. *The University in Ruins*. Cambridge, MA: Harvard University Press.
Safaraliev, Oleg. 2006. *Good Bye, Southern City*. Russia, Azerbaijan: Azerbaijanfilm.
Safi, Omid. 2003. "'Introduction: The Times They Are a-Changin"—A Muslim Quest for Justice, Gender Equality and Pluralism." In *Progressive Muslims on Justice, Gender, and Pluralism*, ed. Omid Safi. Oxford, UK: Oneworld, pp. 1–32.
Sahadeo, Jeff. 2007. *Russian Colonial Society in Tashkent: 1865–1923*. Bloomington: Indiana University Press.
Sahadeo, Jeff, and Russel Zanca, eds. 2007. *Everyday Life in Central Asia: Past and Present*. Bloomington and Indianapolis: Indiana University Press.
Sahni, Kalpana. 1997. *Crucifying the Orient*. Bangkok: White Orchid Press.
Said, Edward. 1978. *Orientalism*. New York: Vintage Books.
Sandoval, Chela. 2000. *Methodology of the Oppressed*. Minneapolis and London: University of Minnesota Press.
Schmitt, Carl. [1952]. 2003. *The Nomos of the Earth in the International Law of* Jus Publicum Europeaum, trans.and annotated by G. L. Ulmen. New York: Telos Press.
Schop Soler, Ana Maria. 1971. *La relaciones entre España y Rusia en la época de Carlos Quinto*. Barcelona: Cátedra de Historia General de España.
Shaikh, Sa'diyya. 2003. "Transforming Feminisms: Islam, Women and Gender Justice." *Progressive Muslims: On Justice, Gender, and Pluralism*, ed. Omid Safi. Oxford, UK: Oneworld, 147–62.
Shakirova, Svetlana. 2005. "Zhenschini.SU-Zhenschini.KZ: osobennosti perekhoda" [Women. SU-women.KZ—features of transition]. In *Gender: Traditsii i Sovremennost. Sbornik Statei po Gendernim Issledovaniyam* [Gender; Traditions and Modernity], ed. S. Kasymova. Dushanbe, Tadzhikistan: Shkola Gendernogo Obrazovanija, 92–135.
———. 2006. "Zhenskoye Dvizheniye: ot nuteshitelnogo diagnoza k effektivnym strategiyam." [Women's movement: From the unconsoling diagnosis to the effective strategies]. In *Central-Asian Gender Net*, www.genderstudies.info (11.27.2006).
———. 2007. *Sredny Klass Almaty: uroven zhizni, gendernye razlichiya, identichnost* [Almaty middle class: Standard of life, gender differences, identity]. Almaty: Gender Studies Center.
———. 2008. *Feminism from West to East*. Almaty: Gender Studies Center.
Shenfield, Stephen D. 2008. The Circassians—A Forgotten Genocide? // CircassianWorld.com, http://www.circassianworld.com/A_Forgotten_Genocide.pdf.
Shu-mei Shih. 2005. "Towards an Ethics of Transnational Encounters, or 'When' Does a 'Chinese' Woman Become a 'Feminist'?" In *Dialogue and Difference: Feminisms Challenge Globalization*, ed, Margueritte Waller and Sylvia Marcos. New York: Palgrave Macmillan, 3–28.
Shu-mei Shih, Sylvia Marcos, Obioma Nnaemeka, and Marguerite Waller. 2005. "Conversation

on 'Feminist Imperialism and the Politics of Difference.'" In *Dialogue and Difference. Feminisms Challenge Globalization.* New York: Palgrave, 143–62.
Simanovsky, Nikolay. 1999. "Dnevnik, 2 aprelya—3 oktyabrja 1837 goda. Kavkaz. [Diary 2 April–2 October, Caucasus] I. Grozova" [publication, introduction, commentary]. *Zvezda* 9: 184–216.
Slavic Review 61.1 (Spring 2002).
Slezkine, Yuri. 1994. "The USSR as a Communal Apartment, or How a Socialist State Promoted Ethnic Particularism." *Slavic Review* 53.2 (Summer): 414–52.
———. 2000. "Imperialism as the Highest Stage of Socialism." *The Russian Review* 59.2: 227–34.
Smith, Linda Tuhiwai. 1999. *Decolonizing Methodologies: Research and Indigenous Peoples.* London and New York: Zed Books.
Smith, Neil. 2003. *American Empire. Roosevelt's Geographer and the Prelude to Globalization.* Berkeley and Los Angeles, CA, and London: University of California Press.
Smith, Terry, ed. 1996. *Ideas of the University.* Sydney: Research Institute for the Humanities and Social Sciences, University of Sydney.
Solovey, Tatyana. 1998. *Ot "Burzhuaznoi" Etnologii k "Sovetskoy" Entografii: Istoriya Otechestvennoi Etnologii Pervoi Treti 20 Veka* [From "bourgeois" ethnology to "Soviet" ethnography: The history of Russian ethnology of the first third of the 20th century]. Moscow: Russian Academy of Sciences, Institute of Ethnology and anthropology named after N.N. Miklukho-Maklay.
Solovyeva, Greta. 2006. "Gender i Dekonstruktsija Territorialnoi Politiki" [Gender and deconstruction of territorial politics]. Gender Studies. Central Asian Network. http://www.genderstudies.info/politol/6.php, 08.25.06.
Sousa Santos, Boaventura de. [1987] 1998. *Um discurso sobre as ciências.* Text of the Magisterial Lecture at the Universidad de Coimbra to initiate the scholarly year 1985–86. Porto: Afrontamiento.
———. 2006. "De la idea de la universidad a la universidad de las ideas." In *De la mano de Alicia: Lo social y lo político en la postmodernidad.* Bogotá: Universidad de los Andes.
Spivak, Gayatri Chakravorty. 1999. *A Critique of Postcolonial Reason: Toward a History of the Vanishing Present.* Cambridge, MA: Harvard University Press.
Stiglitz, Joseph E. 2002. *Globalization and its Discontents.* N.Y.: W. W. Norton and Company.
Stock, Brian. 1983. *The Implications of Literacy: Written Language and Models of Interpretation in the Eleventh and Twelfth Centuries.* Princeton, NJ: Princeton University Press.
Suchland, Jennifer. 2011. "Is Postsocialism Transnational?" *Signs. Journal of Women in Culture and Society.* Vol. 36.4 (Summer): 837–62.
Suleimenov, Olzhas. 1975. *Az i Ya. Kniga Blagonamerennogo Chitatelja.* Alma-Ata, Kazakhstan: Zhazushi.
Suleimenova, Saule. 2010. E-mail interview with Madina Tlostanova. 05.11.10.
Suny, Ronald Grigor. 1997. *The Soviet Experiment: Russia, the USSR, and the Successor States.* New York: Oxford University Press.
Tekuyeva, Madina. 2003. "Nazir Katkhanov." *Izvestiya Kabardino-Balkarskogo Nauchnogo Tsentra Rossiiskoy Akademii Nauk* No. 1 (9): 112–13.
———. 2006a. *Muzhchina i Zhenschina v Adygskoi Kulture. Traditsii i Sovremennost* [Man and woman in Adygean culture: Traditions and modernity] Nalchik, Kabardino-Balkaria: El-Fa.
———. 2006b. Praktiki zhenskoy povsednevnosti [Everyday women's practices]. In *Text: Humanities Discourse Yesterday and Today. A Collection of Essays.* Nalchik, Kabardino-Balkaria: Poligrafservis i T, 105–12.
Thayer, Willy. 1996. *La crisis no moderna de la universidad moderna: Epílogo del conflicto de las facultades.* Santiago, Chile: Cuarto Propio.
Th'iongo, Ngugi Wa. 1986. *Decolonizing the Mind: The Politics of Language in African Literature.* Portsmouth, NH: Heinemann.

Tishkov, Valery. 1992. The Crisis in Soviet Ethnography. *Current Anthropology* 33.4 (August–October): 371–94.
———. 2003. *Rekviem po Etnosu* [Requiem for ethnos]. Moscow: Nauka.
Tkhagapsoev, Khazhismel. 2006. "On the Way to Mirage: Russian Metamorphoses of Liberalism and the Problem of Their Interpretation." Double Critique: Knowledges and Scholars at Risk in Post-Soviet Societies. *The South Atlantic Quarterly.* Special issue, ed. Walter Mignolo and Madina Tlostanova, 105.3 (Summer): 501–26.
Tlisova, Fatima. 2007. "The Challenges of the Sochi Olympics and Russia's Circassian Problem." *North Caucasus Weekly* 8.33. http://www.jamestown.org/single/?no_cache=1&tx_ttnews%5Bswords%5D=8fd5893941d69d0be3f378576261ae3e&tx_ttnews%5Bany_of_the_words%5D=Tlisova&tx_ttnews%5Bpointer%5D=1&tx_ttnews%5Btt_news%5D=4382&tx_ttnews%5BbackPid%5D=7&cHash=792ae76c17.
Tlostanova, Madina. 2003. *A Janus-Faced Empire.* Moscow: Blok.
———. 2004a. *Postsovetskaja literatura i estetika transkulturatsii: Zhit nigde, Pisat niotkuda* [Living never, writing from nowhere: Post-Soviet fiction and the trans-cultural aesthetics]. Moscow: Editorial URSS.
———. 2004b. "University in the Time of Globalization." In *Higher Education for the 21st Century,* Conference Proceedings, ed. I. Ilyinsky. Moscow: Moscow Humanities University Press, 285–93.
———. 2005. *The Sublime of Globalization. Sketches on Transcultural Subjectivity and Aesthetics.* Moscow: URSS.
———. 2006. "Imperial Discourse and Post-Utopian Peripheries: Suspended Indigenous Epistemologies in the Soviet Non-European Ex-Colonies." In *Desarollo e Intercultural, Imaginario y Diferencia: La nacion en el Mundo Andino.* XIV Conferencia International, Academia de la Latinidad. Textos de Referencia. UNESCO and Universidad Candido Mendes, Rio de Janeiro, 296–332.
———. 2008. "The Janus-Faced Empire Distorting Orientalist Discourses: Gender, Race, and Religion in the Russian/(post)Soviet Constructions of the Orient." *Worlds and Knowledges Otherwise/A Web Dossier.* On the Decolonial (II)—Gender and Decoloniality. Vol. 2, Dossier 2, (Spring), http://www.jhfc.duke.edu/wko/dossiers/1.3/contents.php.
———. 2009. *Dekolonialnye Gendernye Epistemologii* [Decolonial gender epistemologies]. Moscow: Maska.
———. 2010a. *Gender Epistemologies and Eurasian Borderlands.* New York: Palgrave Macmillan.
———. 2010b. "A Short Genealogy of Russian Islamophobia." In *Thinking through Islamophobia: Global perspectives,* ed. S. Sayyidm and Abdoolkarim Vakil. London: Hurst and Co., 165–84.
Togan, Zeki Velidi. 1967. *Memories: Struggle for National and Cultural Independence of the Turkistan and Other Moslem Eastern Turks.* Comprised in Istanbul, trans. H. B. Paksoy. http://www.spongobongo.com/zy9857.htm.
Tokhtakhodzhayeva, Marfua. 1996. *Docheri Amazonok: Golosa iz Tsentralnoy Azii* [The daughters of Amazons: Voices from Central Asia]. Tashkent, Uzbekistan: Women's Resource Center.
———. 1999. *Mezhdu lozungami kommunizma i zakonami islama* [Between the slogans of Communism and the laws of Islam]. Tashkent, Uzbekistan: Women's Resource Center.
———. 2001. *Utomlennie Proshlym. Reislamizatsija obschestva i polozhenie zhenschin v Uzbekistane* [Tired with the past. Reislamization of society and the condition of women in Uzbekistan]. Tashkent, Uzbekistan: Women's Resource Center.
Tokhtakhodzhayeva M., D. Abdurazzakova, and A. Kadyrova. 1995. *Sudbi i Vremya.* [Destinies and time]. Tashkent, Women's Resource Center.
Traho, Ramazan. 1956.*Circassians.* Munich: Institute for the Study of the USSR.
"Transcultural Humanities—Between Globalization and Postcolonial Re-Readings of History."

2006. First Annual International Workshop in the Duke-Bremen Series. http://www.fb10.uni-bremen.de/inputs/tagungen/bericht2006.htm.
Tünnermann Bernheim, Carlos. 2001. *Universidad y sociedad: Balance histórico y perspectivas desde América Latina*, 2nd ed. Managua, Nicaragua: Hispamer.
Tyomkina, Anna. 2005. "Genderny Poryadok: Postsovetskiye transformatsii (Severny Tadzhikistan)" [Gender order: Post-Soviet transformations (northern Tadzhikistan)]. In *Gender: Trditsii i Sovremennost.* [Gender: traditions and modernity], ed. S. Kasimova. Dushanbe, Tadzhik: Shkola Gendernogo Obrazovanija, pp. 6–91.
Tyomkina, Anna, and Elena Zdravomyslova. 2005. "Gendered Citizenship in Soviet and Post-Soviet Societies." In *Gender and Nation in Contemporary Europe*, ed. Vera Tolz and Stephanie Booth. Manchester: Manchester. University Press, 96–115.
UCA (University of Central Asia). Official Website. http://www.ucentralasia.org/about.asp, 10.04.11.
"La Universidad Intercultural." 2002. Accessed online at uinpi.nativeweb.org/folleto/folleto.html, 09/27/02.
Useinov Vyacheslav. 2009. Art Works, http://www.useinov.sk.uz/index_eng.html.
Van Cot, Donna Lee. 1995. *Indigenous People and Democracy in Latin America.* New York: Palgrave Macmillan.
Vigmann, Gunda. 2005. "Tadzhikskie Zhenschini i Sotsialnie Izmenenija—vzgljad s Zapadnoi Storoni" [Tadzhik women and social change—A view from the West] In *Gender: Trditsii i Sovremennost* [Gender: traditions and modernity], ed. S. Kasimova. Dushanbe, Tadzhikistan: Shkola Gendernogo Obrazovanija, 162–76.
Viswanathan, Gauri. 1989. *Mask of Conquest: Literary Study and British Rule in India.* New York: Columbia University Press.
Wallerstein, Immanuel. 1997. "The Unintended Consequences of Cold War Area Studies." In Chomsky, Noam, et al., *The Cold War and the University: Toward an Intellectual History of the Postwar Years.* New York: New Press.
Wallerstein, Immanuel, et al. 1996. *Open the Social Sciences: Report of the Gulbenkian Commission on the Restructuring of the Social Sciences.* Stanford, CA: Stanford University Press.
Walsh, Catherine. 2004. "Geopolíticas del conocimiento, interculturalidad y descolonización," *Boletín ICCI-ARY Rimay*, 6,60 (March), http://icci.nativeweb.org/boletin/60/walsh.html.
———. 2005. "Interculturalidad, conocimiento y decolonialidad." *Signos y Pensamientos* 46: 40–60.
———. 2008. "Interculturalidad, plurinationalidad y decolonialidad. Las insurgencias política-epistémicas de refundar el estado." *Tabula Rasa.* Bogotá, 9, 131–52.
———. 2009. Interculturalidad, Estado, Sociedad. Luchas (de)coloniales de nuestra época. Quito, Ecuador: Universidad Andina Simón Bolívar.
Washington Consensus. 2003. In *Global Trade Negotiations Home Page.* http://www.cid.harvard.edu/cidtrade/issues/washington.html.
Weber, Max. 2002. *The Protestant Ethics and the Spirit of Capitalism* (1904/1905). New York: Penguin Group.
Weil, Mark. 1996. *The End of an Era. Tashkent.* A documentary by Mark Weil. Stichting Doen, Dagofilm Studio, Ilkhom Studio.
Weitz, Eric. 2002. "Racial Politics without the Concept of Race: Reevaluating Soviet Ethnic and National Purges." *Slavic Review* 61.1: 1–29.
Wood, Elizabeth A. 2000. *The Baba and the Comrade. Gender and Politics in Revolutionary Russia.* Bloomington: Indiana University Press.
Wu, Yenna. 2005. "Making Sense in Chinese 'Feminism'/Women's Studies." In *Dialogue and Difference. Feminisms Challenge Globalization.* New York: Palgrave, 29–52.
Yagan, Murat. 1984. *I Come from behind Kaf Mountain.* N.Y.: Threshold Books.
———. Official Website. http://www.muratyagan.com/english/en1.htm, 10.04.11.

Yehia, Elena. 2006. "Towards Decolonizing Encounters with Social Movements' Decolonizing Knowledges and Practices." Center for Global Justice: Workshop Papers, http://www.globaljusticecenter.org/papers2006/yehiaENG.htm.
Yerofeyev, Victor. 2000. *Pjat Rek Zhizni* [Five rivers of life]. Moscow: Podkova.
Yordan, M., R. Kuzeev, and S. Chervonnaya, eds. 2001. *Islam v Yevrazii* [Islam in Eurasia]. Moscow: Progress-Tradition.
Young, Robert. 1990. *White Mythologies: Writing History and the West*. London and New York: Routledge.
Zea, Leopoldo. 1958. *América en la historia*. México: Universidad Autónoma de México.
Zihia—Circassian Web-Portal. 2009. http://www.zihia.org/list.php?c=hist_en.
Zubkovskaya, Olga. 2007. Postkolonialnaya teorija v analize postsovetskogo feminizma: dilemmy primenenija [Postcolonial theory in the analysis of post-Soviet feminism: dilemmas of application]. *Ab Impero*, No. 1: 395–420.

INDEX

Abashin, Sergey, 136
Abdurazzakova, D., 134–35
Abkhazia, 114
Abreks, 108
Abu-Grahib, 167
academy. *See* disciplines and the academy; universities and the history of knowledge
adab ethics, 117
adaptation without assimilation, 66–67, 70
Adyghe. *See* Circassian (Adyghe; Cherkess) people
Adyghean Princes Union, 94
Afet figure, 141
Africa, 124, 158, 162–63
Africans, enslaved, 5, 124–27, 155
Afro-Caribbean intellectuals, 170, 177, 179
agonistics, 89
Ahmsta Kebzeh, 114
Akiner, Shirin, 108
Aksartova, Sada, 86
Alexander, Jacqui, 249n63
al-Hadir, Saint (the Green Man), 116–17
Al-Jabri, Mohammed, 75
Alliance of Civilizations, 173
Amawta Runakunapak Yachay (ARY), 228
Amawtay Wasi (Universidad Intercultural de los Pueblos y Naciones Indigenas del Ecuador): the colonial university and, 200–201; ethics of education, epistemic structure, and political orientation, 229–34; formative levels, 235; geography of reason and, 237n6; *interculturidad* and, 13–14, 212–14; learning to unlearn and, 217, 222; mission and radical nature of, 206; model of education, 12–17, 214–15; political trajectory, 225–29; Quichua language and, 214–15; spatial epistemic fracture and, 203–4, 212; as *tinku*, 215
America, "discovery of," 9, 44, 238n13
American Revolution, 163, 164
Americas Social Forum, 19
Anahuac (pre-Columbian Mexico) and the Aztecs: knowledges of, 205–6; Man and Humanity and, 155, 156, 158; overruling of systems of, 44–45; property rights and, 161–62; renaming and, 5; *Toltecáyotl* and *toltécatl*, 179–80
Andizhan insurgency (Uzbekistan), 107–8, 246n51
anthropos, 164–67, 170, 173, 188–89
Anzaldúa, Gloria, 192; on border thinking, 72; on colonial wound, 238n8; colonial wound and, 35–36; as guide, 238n12; Suleimenov compared to, 67; transculturation and, 88; Weil and, 248n58
appropriation, 16–17, 72, 217
area studies, 10–11, 83–86, 209, 249n65
Argentina, 181, 211
Aristotle, 64, 75, 76
arts: border thinking in fiction, 75; of the Caucasus and Central Asia, 100, 102–3, 114, 119–20; *dastans* (heroic epics), 95,

140; gender and, 148; resistance in fiction, 119–20, 245n46
As I Ya (Suleimenov), 67–68
assimilation, 66, 70, 239n14
Atabekov, Said, 100
authority, struggle for control of: diversification and, 48–49; economic control and, 24; media and, 22; polycentric capitalism and, 18; racism and, 55; sphere of, 44
Azerbaijan, 87, 92, 97. *See also* the Caucasus
Azeri people, 92
Aztecs. *See* Anahuac (pre-Columbian Mexico) and the Aztecs

bacha cult, 140–41, 247n58, 248n60
Bacon, Francis, 76, 174
Baku, 115, 116
Bandung Conference (1955), 31
Basmachi, 108
Baudrillard, Jean, 119, 120
Beknazarova, Gulnora, 249n64
Bennabi, Malek, 239n17
Bestuzhev-Marlinsky, Alexander, 125
Bhabha, Homi, 35
Bill of Rights, English, 163
biopolitics, 239n14
"Blacks": Caucasus and Central Asian people renamed as, 6, 98; chain of human being and, 187; enslaved Africans renamed as, 5; gender and, 124. *See also* Africans, enslaved
Blumenbach, Johann Friedrich, 50
body politics of knowledge: area studies and, 86; biopolitics vs., 239n14; from borders, 59; Civil Rights movement and, 193–94; colonial wound and, 238n8; decolonial thinking and, 23; displaced inversion and, 66; double consciousness and, 68; gender studies and, 134; local histories and, 11; postcolonial theory and, 34; social entities and the physical body, 135; spatial epistemic break and epistemic shifts, 57–59; theopolitics and egopolitics vs., 24; as U.S. concern, 33; zero-point epistemology and, 71. *See also* racism and racial politics
Bolivia: border thinking in, 242n34; indigenous concepts, 220; mobility and, 181; Morales government, 13, 19, 24, 78
borders: the Caucasus and Central Asia as paradigmatic border spaces, 87–90; creation of divides between people, 58–59. *See also* geopolitics of knowledge
border thinking (border epistemology): Amawtay Wasi and, 14, 229; the Caucasus and Central Asia and, 110; critical, 69, 71; defined, 6–7, 239n14; delinking and, 6; dwelling in the borders, 72–77; as epistemic, 62–72; epistemic potential of, 212; fictional, 75; Gaffarova and, 144; gender studies and, 135; gender tricksterism and, 139–41; genealogy and history, need for, 71–72; geo- and body political potential and, 59; Guaman Poma and, 191–92; Humanities and, 216; human knowledge vs. imperial epistemology and, 242n32; learning to unlearn and, 217–18; local histories, alternative modernities, global designs, and, 77–79; role of, 60; transculturation and, 87–88; zero point, languages, and, 61–62
brain drain (*fuga de cerebros*), 209
Brazil, 193, 241n25
busurman, 5, 98

Cabral, Amilcar, 192
capitalism: as alternative to Socialism, 113; Atlantic exploitation of labor, 52–53; "capital," defined, 241n26; citizenship, racism, and, 182; "discovery" of America and, 44; education and, 199–200, 210; as hegemonic, 48; "Human Rights" and, 168, 171–72; imperial-colonial relations and, 17–18; and imperialism, in colonial matrix of power, 39; mobility of capital, 181–82; modernity and, 8; primitive accumulation and, 41; structural interstate dependency and, 211; transmuted form in Russia, 54. *See also* polycentric capitalism
capital/modernity, 40, 240n18, 241n24
Caracoles, Los, 223
Caribbean: Afro-Caribbean intellectuals, 170, 177, 179; post-independence imperialism, 4–5; resistance in fiction, 245n46

Cassano, Franco, 192–93
Castells, Manuel, 209
Castile, 50
Castro-Gómez, Santiago, 43
the Caucasus: Adyghean Princes Union, 94; Adyghe Diaspora, 101; colonial and imperial differences and, 52; modern colonial discourses and, 5; multiple colonizations of, 92; mythology of, 139–40; Olympics (2014, Sochi), 246n50; racial reclassification in, 5; self-racialization and self-Orientalizing, 55. *See also* gender and coloniality in the Caucasus and Central Asia; nation building and indigenous resistance in the Caucasus and Central Asia
Central Asia: civilizing mission and, 240n22; cultural mixing in, 87; English-speaking universities in, 248n59; migrations to and from, 97; modern colonial discourses and, 5; modernization in, 92–93; Orientalism and, 244n42; racial reclassification in, 5; self-racialization and self-Orientalizing, 55. *See also* gender and coloniality in the Caucasus and Central Asia; nation building and indigenous resistance in the Caucasus and Central Asia
Césaire, Aimé, 71, 192, 210
Chakrabarty, Dipesh, 211
Charles V, Holy Roman Emperor (Charles I of Castile), 42, 50, 51, 237n1
Chatterjee, Partha, 21
Cherkess. *See* Circassian (Adyghe; Cherkess) people
Chile, 181
China: adaptation without assimilation in, 66–67; femininity discourses in, 147; gender equality in, 130; globalization, and academe in, 242n35; imperial difference and, 187; mobility and, 250n80; political disobedience by, 220
Chinese Dynasties, 51
Christianity: capitalism and, 52–53; Communism vs., 166; control of subjectivity and, 45; hubris of the zero point and, 43; humanist concepts of Man and Human and, 156–58; mission of conversion, 46; "rights" and, 163–64; Russia, transmuted form in, 54; Russian claiming of Orthodox Christianity, 40, 51, 243n38; Russian modernity and, 40; Spanish Inquisition, 183; zero-point epistemology and, 64
Cicero, Marcus Tullius, 159
Circassia, in fiction, 246n54
Circassian (Adyghe; Cherkess) people: Adyghean cosmology, 139–40; in diaspora, 101, 114; identity, 101–2; Olympics and, 246n50; racialization and dehumanization of, 50; resistance by, 94
Circassian Slave, or the Sultan's Favorite, The (Murray Ballou), 246n54
citizenship: birth of, 183–84; global, and colonial/imperial differences, 186, 188; global, myth of, 178–82; labor migration and, 100; nation-state formation and, 175–76; women and, 141
civilizing mission, 46, 128, 164
Civil Rights movement, 193–94
civil society, 21, 22, 110
civitas, 158, 164, 178–79
clothing and the hijab, 141–43
Cold War, 34
Cold War university, 208–9
Colish, Marcia, 204
colonial differences. *See* difference, colonial and imperial
colonialism: end of, 201; knowledge and, 42; Marx on, 191; modernity/coloniality vs., 39; rhetoric of modernity and logic of coloniality vs., 9–10
coloniality: colonialism vs., 201; development and, 37–38; as disturbing concept, 39–41; epistemic break and, 58; global, 7–8, 41, 201; hidden by modernity, 8–9; imperial internal critique, 190–92, 194; meaning of, 8; misanthropic skepticism and, 57; modernity and, 37–38, 251n85; revolution of, 39–40; of Russia, 40; splendors and miseries of, 38. *See also* modernity/coloniality
Coloniality at Large (Moraña, Dussel, and Jáuregui), 239n15
coloniality of gender, 122–23. *See also* gender and coloniality in the Caucasus and Central Asia
colonial matrix of power: area comparison and, 2–3; border thinking and, 7; citizenship, humanities, knowledge, and, 194; colonial and imperial differences and, 41–42; decolonial option and, 20;

decolonial thinking and, 17, 18; imagining beyond, 220–21; imperialism and capitalism joined in, 39; knowledge assumptions and, 11; local histories and, 6; modernity and, 37–39; objects vs. problems, emphasis on, 20; political society and, 24; religious vs. economic control, 79; revolution and, 18; spheres of, 44–46; successive, cumulative periods of, 46–49; Western control, loss of, 48–49, 219–20. *See also* logic of coloniality; *specific topics*
colonial university, 200–201, 203, 205–6
colonial wound: Gandhi, Fanon, Anzaldúa, and, 35; geo- and body politics of knowledge and, 238n8; Guchinova on, 137; "Human Rights" and, 155; modern achievements and, 49–50
Colonizer and the Colonized, The (Memmi), 33
color line and epistemic line, 73
Communists, 165
communitarian societies, 130
competition, 25, 66, 70–71
CONAIE (Confederation of Indigenous Nationalities of Ecuador), 105–6, 214, 228–29
constitution, civil, 184–85
conversion, 46, 142, 169, 176
"Cop Had a Dog, A" (Mamedov), 116
corporate university, 202–3, 209–10, 216
corporations, 167, 168, 190, 241n24
Cortés, Hernan, 237n1
cosmopolitan order (Kant), 184–87
critical cosmopolitanism, 216
critical theory, 190–91

damnés, les, 19, 23, 79, 222, 242n34
dastans (heroic epics), 95, 140
decoloniality: decolonial thinking and, 18; epistemic decolonial shift, 177, 189–95; knowledge of colonial subalterns and, 58; political society and, 22; postcoloniality and, 31–32; solidarity and, 12. *See also specific topics*
decolonial option(s): Bandung Conference (1955) and, 31; colonial matrix and, 20; competition vs., 12; decolonial thinking and, 17, 18–20; delinking and, 23; development vs., 219; "Human Rights" and, 173; internal critique and, 192, 194; learning to unlearn and, 221–22; as option, 172; origination of, 33; postcoloniality and, 31
decolonial thinking: actional thinking and, 35; as already critical, 69; in Americas, 191; Bolivia and, 24; civil society and, 22; decolonial option and, 18–20; expertise and, 20, 22; imperial-colonial relations and, 17–18; locations of, 35; political society and, 21–25; postcolonial studies and theory vs., 32–37; on problems vs. objects, 19–20; Soviet Union and, 34; U.S. vs. Soviet Union and, 34
decolonization: appropriation of, 72; border thinking and, 66; demodernization and, 78; empowerment and, 63; of human rights, 171; limits of, 24–25; transdemocratic and transsocialist, 155
decolonization of being, thinking, and knowledge: the academy and, 23, 32–33; Amawtay Wasi and, 15, 235; border thinking and, 7; citizenship, racism, and, 188–89, 194–95; political society and, 22; radical social movements and, 19. *See also* decoloniality
deimperialization, 78
Deleuze, Gilles, 116
delinking: Amawtay Wasi and, 14; border thinking and, 6, 79; decolonial feminism and, 124, 177; decolonial options and, 23, 222; defined, 14; geography of reasoning and, 10; "Human Rights" and, 172; knowledge and, 11–12, 32; political society and, 220. *See also* decoloniality; learning to unlearn
democracy: the Caucasus and Central Asia and, 103; market democracy as period of colonial matrix of power, 46; second wave of development and, 168; transdemocratic societies, 155
demodernization, 78
Deng Zhenglai, 242n35
dependency: the Caucasus and Central Asia and, 103, 105; epistemic, 210–11; gender and, 130; structural, 197, 211
Derrida, Jacques, 34, 189
Descartes, René, 56–57, 71, 75, 165
de Sousa Santos, Bonaventura, 192–93
developmentalism: the Caucasus and Cen-

tral Asia and, 104–5, 110; decolonial option vs., 219; "Human Rights" and, 167; modernity and "underdevelopment," 37–38; as period of colonial matrix of power, 46; Washington Consensus and second wave of development, 168–70
diaspora: Adyghe (Circassian), 101, 114; decolonial thinking from, 114; Sindzyan Usbek, 143–44
difference, colonial and imperial: borders created by, 58–59; border thinking and, 6–7, 62–63, 66–70, 74; the Caucasus and Central Asia and, 52, 86, 104, 106; colonial matrix of power and, 41–42; defined, 241n31; disqualification of epistemic difference, 198; feminist analysis and, 131; gender and, 147; global citizenship and, 180–83; global coloniality and, 7–8; internal and external imperial difference, 2–3; Kant's cosmopolitanism, racism, and, 182–89; legal colonial difference, 162; linear history and, 9–10; logic of coloniality and, 8–9, 38–39; marginal empires and, 3–5; modernity/coloniality and world of imperial differences, 52–55; mutations of, 49–52; racism as device in, 56; racist renaming and reclassification, 5–6; Russian Empire and, 33–34, 53–55; spatial and temporal, 8–9; universities and, 208, 215
Dilthey, Wilhelm, 190, 207
disciplines and the academy: Amawtay Wasi and, 238n6; in China, 242n35; decolonial thinking and, 17, 23; disobedience to, 32; experience vs., 11; native informants and legitimacy, 249n63; transformations in 1970s, 32–33; Western feminism and coloniality of gender, 129–34, 138. *See also* Humanities; universities and the history of knowledge
"divide and rule," 96–101, 119, 245n44
Dostoyevsky, Fyodor, 36
double consciousness, 68–69, 73, 242n33
Douglass, Frederick, 207
Du Bois, W. E. B., 26, 68, 73, 242n33
Duhalde, Eduardo, 211
Dussel, Enrique, 192–93, 239n15
Dust of Empire, The (Meyer), 87
"dwelling," 179

Eastern question, 94
economic and financial crisis, global, 219
economic control, struggle for: the Caucasus and Central Asia and, 103–5; polycentric capitalism and, 24; racism and, 55; sphere of, 44. *See also* capitalism
Ecstasy with the Pomegranate (Weil), 247n58
Ecuador, 13, 213. *See also* Amawtay Wasi
education. *See* Amawtay Wasi; universities and the history of knowledge
efficiency, 197, 209–10
"ego cogito" and "ego conquiro," 57
egology, 56–57
egopolitics of knowledge: border thinking and, 64; displaced inversion of, 66; displacement of, 59; geopolitics and body politics vs., 24; imperial and colonial differences and, 58; suppressed knowledge and, 58; zero-point epistemology and, 64
El Saadawi, Nawal, 137–38
End of an Era, The: Tashkent (film; Weil), 115–16
Enlightenment (Kantian-Humboldtian) university, 189–90, 201–2, 207–8
enunciation and enunciated: area studies and, 10–12; feminism and, 131; First World and, 166; "humanity" and, 156–58; "Human Rights" and, 154, 170; postcolonial theories and, 34; spatial epistemic break and, 57–58; zero-point epistemology and, 43
epistemic dependency, 210–11
epistemic fractures, temporal and spatial, 203–10, 212
epistemic line, 73
epistemologies. *See* knowledges and epistemologies
equality status at birth, 154–55
Erasmus, Desiderio, 75
espiritualismo, 118
ethnicity: ethno-racial tetragon/pentagon, 186, 213; hybrid, 247n56; introduced, in the Caucasus and Central Asia, 97; Islam transformed into, 98. *See also* racism and racial politics
ethnicity-building tactic, 97–99, 105
ethnic-nationalism, 102
Eurasian studies, 84–85, 244n40
Eurocentrism: body politics of knowledge

and, 239n14; decolonization, appropriation of, 72; feminism and, 28, 137; modern-traditional bias and, 129; postcolonial studies and, 35; secondary, 55, 67, 68, 70, 109; Soviet Union and, 92, 103, 111, 145, 246n47
experience, human, 193
expertise, 20, 22, 138
exteriority, 54

Fanon, Frantz, 192; coloniality canon and, 210; colonial wound and, 35–36; "damnés de la terre" ("wretched of the earth"), 19, 33, 66, 242n34; on decolonial political society, 22–23; as guide, 238n12; on psychoanalysis, 191; on violence, 172
feminism: decolonial, 123, 124; independent and critical, 148; Third World and women-of-color feminists, 137; Western feminism and coloniality of gender, 129–34, 138
fiction: border thinking in, 75; resistance in, 119–20, 245n46
financial and economic crisis, global, 219
First, Second, Third, and Fourth worlds, 166–67
Flights of Mashrab (Weil), 120
food and water as human rights, 168
food crisis, global, 244n39
Food Sovereignty, 244n39
"foreigners," 164, 178, 183
Foucault, Michel, 34, 57, 158, 203, 239n14
French Revolution, 163
Freud, Sigmund, 190–91
Freyre, Paulo, 238n10
frontiers, epistemic, 43
fuga de cerebros ("brain drain"), 209
Fukuyama, Francis, 9–10

Gaffarova, Muborakhanum, 143–44
Galilei, Galileo, 76
Gandhi, Mahatma, 35–36, 192, 210
Gasprinsky, Ismail, 67
gatekeepers, 187–88
gender and coloniality in the Caucasus and Central Asia: alternate discourses, 147–49; border position and gender tricksterism, 136, 139–41; colonial gender paradox and racial/gender stereotypes, 124–27; coloniality of gender concept, 122–23; gendered trickster identity, 145–47; the hijab and, 141–43; local gender studies, 134–39; modern-traditional binary and, 129–30, 131–32, 134–35; Soviet modernity and, 127–29, 133; voices and oral histories of colonial and Russian women, 143–45; Western feminism and, 129–34, 138
gender roles: contextuality of, in Adyghean community, 140; non-Western difference in, 131; racism and, 55; as sphere of control, 44–45
geography of reasoning, shifting: Amawtay Wasi and, 237n6; delinking and, 14; indigenous wisdom and, 217; Man and Humanity and, 156; from object/area to subject, 10–11, 19–20
geopolitics of knowledge: from borders, 59; colonial wound and, 238n8; decolonial thinking and, 23; displaced inversion and, 66; double consciousness and, 68; gender studies and, 134; geohistorical locations and, 192–93; learning to unlearn and, 217–18; local histories and, 11; postcolonial theory and, 34; spatial epistemic break and epistemic shifts, 57–59; theopolitics and egopolitics vs., 24; as "Third-World" concern, 32–33; zero-point epistemology and, 71. *See also* decolonization of being, thinking, and knowledge; knowledges and epistemologies; universities and the history of knowledge
Georgia, 240n20
Ghazali, Abu Hamed Mohammad ibn Mohammad al-, 75–76
Giddens, Anthony, 38–39, 78
Glissant, Eduard, 119
global coloniality, 7–8, 41, 201
globalization, 77, 168, 238n13
Göle, Nulifer, 141
Good bye, Southern City (film; Safaraliev), 115
Gordon, Lewis, 10, 35, 237n6
Gozzi, Karlo, 119–20
Gramsci, Antonio, 33
grassroots movements, 174
Greco-Latin categories of thought, 159–60, 204–5, 250n79

Grotius, Hugo, 159, 163, 164, 165
Grovogui, Siba N'Zatioula, 162–63
Guaman Poma de Ayala, Felipe, 191–92, 210, 223
Guantánamo, 167
Guattari, Félix, 116
Guchinova, Elza Bair, 86, 137
Guest Workers Flight, A (Useinov), 100
Guha, Ranahit, 33
Guillen, Rafael (subcomandante Marcos), 210, 223
Gulbenkian report, 209, 211

Habermas, Jürgen, 73
Habiba, 117–18
Haraway, Donna, 89, 149
Harris, Wilson, 117
Harvard, 45
Hassan, Prince of Jordan, 173
healer figures, 117–18, 128
heathens, 157
Hegel, Georg W. F., 4, 9, 50, 51, 63, 69, 74, 164, 179, 208
Heidegger, Martin, 179, 230
hijab wearing, 141–43
Hiroshima bombing, 165–66
Hirsch, Francine, 245n44, 248n60
histories, local. *See* local histories
History as linear process, 9–10
history of knowledge. *See* universities and the history of knowledge
Hobson, John A., 18
Hollinger, David, 186
Holocaust, 165, 167
homo ludens, 89
homosexuality, 248n60
Horkheimer, Max, 60, 72, 190–91
hubris of the zero point, 43, 73
humanists, European, 155–59, 205
humanitas, 158, 164, 169, 173, 187, 188–89
Humanities: border thinking and, 216; decolonial, 173–74, 177–78, 195; delinking and, 32; the Human and the Unhuman in, 199; humanity and, 176; imperial difference and, 52; postcolonial contributions to, 33; reorganization of knowledge and role of, 189–90; trajectories for, 196
humanity, the human, and Human Rights: accepting vs. delinking, 160; Bill of Rights and Rights of Man and of Citizen, 163–64; the Caucasus and Central Asia and, 94; citizenship and, 176, 178, 183; decolonial humanities and, 173–74; divine and natural law and, 159; European humanist creation of "Man" and "Humanity," 155–59; First, Second, Third, and Fourth worlds classification, 166–67; as Greek/Latin-based concept, 159–60; Grovogui on paradoxes from African perspective, 162–63; international law and, 159; political society and, 170–73; Universal Declaration of Human Rights (1948), 154, 165–66; universality and equality presuppositions, 154–55; violations and violators, 167–68; Vitoria and *jus gentium* (rights of people or nations), 159, 161–62; Washington Consensus, neoliberal doctrine, NGOs, and, 168–70
Huntington, Samuel, 173, 204

Ibadinov, Alisher, 245n46
Ibn Rushd, Abu al-Walid Muhammad, 75–76
Ibn Sina, Abu Ali al-Husayn ibn Abd Allah, 75–76
ICCI-Rimmai (Instituto Cientifico de Culturas Indígenas), 214, 228–29
I Come from Behind Kaf Mountain (Yagan), 114
identity politics, 69
Ilkhom theater (Tashkent), 119–20, 247nn57–58
immigration. *See* migrants and migration
imperial differences. *See* difference, colonial and imperial
imperial internal critique, 190–92, 194
imperialism: and capitalism, in colonial matrix of power, 39; modernity and, 8; modernity/coloniality vs., 39; rhetoric of modernity and logic of coloniality vs., 9–10; Russia and Spain as marginal empires, 3–5. *See also specific topics and places*
imperial wound, 36–37
"imperium," 51
Incas. *See* Tawantinsuyu and the Incas
India, 25, 33, 64–65, 163, 165, 192, 201–2, 207–8

"Indias Occidentales," 5, 240n21
indigeneity and modernity, 94
indigenous resistance. *See* nation building and indigenous resistance in the Caucasus and Central Asia
"Indigenous rights," 168
inorodets, 5, 98
Instituto Científico de Culturas Indígenas (ICCI-Rimmai), 214, 228–29
interculturality (*interculturidad*): Amawtay Wasi and, 13–14, 212–14; the Caucasus and Central Asia and, 105–6, 118
interiority, 54
internal colonialism, 202, 208, 242n34
internal others, 50, 69, 71, 86
international law, 159, 162–63, 167
Iran, 220
Iraq, 167, 182, 242n34
Islam: *adab* ethics, 117; the Caucasus and Central Asia and, 97, 98, 106–9; epistemic erasure of Muslim contributions, 75–76; gender and, 143; hijab identity, 141–43; Ottoman Sultanate and, 243n38; resistance from, 102, 106; rhetoric of modernity and, 10; Sufism, 116, 117–18, 143; "Tatars," Muslims as, 5–6; transformed into ethnicity, 98
Islamism, 99, 107, 108
Ismailov, Babur, 247n58
Ivan IV ("the Terrible"), 4, 42, 237n1

Jadids, 97, 128
Jáuregui, Carlos A., 239n15
Jews, 6, 190
Juntas de Buen Gobierno, 223
jus gentium (rights of people or nations), 159, 161–62, 167

Kabardino-Balkaria, 107–8
Kamp, Marianne, 132, 146, 248n62–249n63
Kant, Immanuel: border thinking and, 63, 64; Cartesian subjectivity and, 56; *The Contest of Faculty*, 189–90; cosmopolitanism, 179, 184–87; geo- and body political knowledge and, 71; on human experience, 23, 193; internal others denied by, 69; Newton and, 76; southern Europe and, 164

Kantian-Humboldtian university, 189–90, 201–2, 207–8
Karabakh conflict, 97
Karagulova, Lira, 118
Kasymova, Sofia, 86
Katkhanov, Nazir, 95
Kazi, Khanifa, 95, 140
Khakim, Khashim ibn, 102–3
Khalid, Adeeb, 86
Khatami, Mohammad, 173
Klyuchevsky, Vassily, 4
knowledges and epistemologies: Amawtay Wasi and, 12–16; Bolshevik elimination of indigenous knowledges, 96; Cartesian logic, 56–57; the Caucasus and Central Asia and, 109, 111; citizenship, humanities, and, 194; Civil Rights movement and, 193–94; of colonial subalterns, 58; decolonial epistemic shift, 177, 189–95; definition of epistemology, 242n32; disobeying common assumptions on, 11–12; disqualification of epistemic difference, 198; double bind of non-Western categories of thought, 197–98; epistemic borders and, 61; epistemic frontiers, 43; gender and, 129; human knowledge vs. imperial epistemology, 242n32; knowing how, knowing that, and knowing what, 198–99; language and, 61–62; Muslim contributions, erasure of, 75–76; native informants and legitimacy, 249n63; as plural, 11; racism and, 55, 56; reorganization of, 189–90; Russian epistemology, Eurocentric, 74; shifting ethics and politics of, 57–59; as sphere of control, 45; submitting to indigenous wisdom, 217; zero-point epistemology, 42–43, 61, 64, 65, 66, 71, 78. *See also* body politics of knowledge; border thinking; decolonization of being, thinking, and knowledge; geopolitics of knowledge; universities and the history of knowledge
Koroglu (Turkic Dastan), 95
Kuhn, Thomas, 57
Kusch, Rodolfo, 10, 250n79

labor exploitation: Atlantic, 52–53; conversion and, 169; "human rights" and,

167, 171; logic of coloniality and, 39; struggle for economic control and, 44; women in Turkistan and, 126
Lacan, Jacques, 34, 35
languages: Amawtay and Quichua language, 214–15; in the Caucasus and Central Asia, 119; epistemology as woven into, 61–62; feminist wars against sexism in, 130; Greek and Latin categories, 159–60, 204–5; humanity and, 183; meta-languages, 42–43; Nahuatl, Aymara, and Quechua, 57, 179–80, 205, 214; translation, 214; universities and, 204–5
Las Casas, Bartolomé de, 68, 162, 183, 186, 191
Latin, 204–5, 206–7
"Latin *America*," 240n21. *See also* South America
"law": divine and natural, 159, 161; international, 159, 162–63, 167
learning to unlearn: in all spheres of life, 222–23; Amawtay Wasi principle, 12–17; border thinking and, 7, 218–19; citizenship and, 180; decolonial options and, 219–20; decolonial thinking and, 25, 193; delinking and, 36; disciplinary disobedience and, 32; geopolitics of knowledge and, 217–18; Humanities and, 196; learning to manage vs., 197; as proposition of Indigenous philosophical and decolonial thinking, 217; Zapatistas and, 220–24
Lenin, Vladimir, 18, 107
León-Portilla, Miguel, 179–80
Lermontov, Mikhail, 125
Levinas, Emmanuel, 230
liberalism, 21–22, 166
liberation theologians, 221
liberation vs. freedom, 130
Lieven, Dominic, 51
Li Xiaojiang, 147
local histories: area comparisons and, 2, 11; decolonization and, 7; gender egalitarianism and, 139; global or universal histories vs., 64, 77
Locke, John, 66, 174
logic of coloniality: delinking and, 23; hidden, 8–10, 20, 46; imperial and colonial differences and, 188; imperialism/colonialism vs., 9–10; knowledge and, 176; postcolonial studies and, 37; racism and, 56; Soviet Union and, 47; universities and, 201; visibility of, 38. *See also* colonial matrix of power
Lugones, María, 27, 45, 89–90, 122–23, 147, 148–49
Luxembourg, Rosa, 18

Macas, Luis Alberto, 214, 228
Mahmudov, Mamadali, 245n46
Maldonado-Torres, Nelson, 57, 123
Mamedov, Afanasy, 75, 115, 116
management, learning for, 197
Mandela, Nelson, 210
Marcos, subcomandante (Rafael Guillen), 210, 223
Marcos, Sylvia, 118, 130, 138, 149
mardikor songs, 95, 245n43
Mariátegui, José Carlos, 33
market democracy, 46, 168. *See also* capitalism
market economy, 21, 104–5
Marx, Karl, 41, 68, 69, 190–91
Marxism, 36, 37, 221. *See also* Socialism
McClintock, Anne, 124
Meddeb, Abdelwahab, 109
media, 22
medieval university, 204–5
Mekhti, Niazi, 141, 143
Meldibekov, Yerbossyn, 100–101
"melting pot," 213
Memmi, Albert, 33, 144
Mesoamerican cosmology, 139–40. *See also* Anahuac
mestizos, 213
meta-languages, 42–43
Mexico, pre-*Columbian*. *See* Anahuac
Meyer, Karl, 87
Middle Ages, idea of, 9
migrants and migration: border thinking and, 60; global citizenship and mobility, 181–82, 188, 250n80; labor migration to Russia, 100; multiculturalism and, 213; Tashkent and, 115; transculturation and, 89
Milbank, John, 66, 242n33
misanthropic skepticism, 57, 123
Miyoshi, Masao, 180
modernity: alternative modernities vs. alternatives to modernity, 78; coloniality

silenced under, 8; development and, 37–38; gender in the Caucasus and Central Asia and, 127–32; as imperial category of self-validation and disqualification of epistemic difference, 198; indigeneity and, 94; liberal/capitalist and Socialist/statist, 47; logic of coloniality and, 37–39, 251n85; mission of modernization, 46; postcolonial studies and, 35; Soviet, 40, 47–48, 131, 133, 142; spatial and temporal differences and, 8–9; traditional-modern binary, 129–30, 131–32, 134–35; transmuted forms within imperial difference, 54–55; zero-point epistemology and, 42–43

modernity, rhetoric of: delinking and, 23; global citizenship and, 188; knowledge and, 176; linear history and imperialism/colonialism vs., 9–10; logic of coloniality hidden by, 8–10, 46

modernity/coloniality: border thinking and, 62; defined, 8; dependency relations, types of, 70–71; imperialism/colonialism vs., 39; New World, building of, 39–40; "rights" and, 159, 160; world of imperial differences and, 52–55. *See also specific topics*

modernization: of the Caucasus and Central Asia, 92–93, 96–101, 104, 110–11; gender and, 131, 133; as mission, 46; private universities and, 202; Soviet "divide and rule" tactics, 96–101, 119, 245n44

Mohanty, Chandra, 249n63
Moore, David Chioni, 240n19
Morales, Evo, 13, 19, 24, 78
Moraňa, Mabel, 239n15
Moscow: as Third Rome, 40, 51, 237n1, 243n38; Uzbeks in, 245n45
Mozart, Wolfgang Amadeus, 120
multicultural colonial cities, 115–16
multiculturalism, 47, 66, 212–13
Munay, 230–34
Murray Ballou, Maturin, 246n54
Muslims. *See* Islam

Nahuatl language, 205, 206–7
Nakshbandi, Bahauddin, 117–18, 247n55
Nalchik uprising (2005), 107–8, 246n50
Nandi, Ashis, 191

Nasreddin, Hodja, 89
national characters (Kant), 185–86
nationalist ideologies, 98–99, 102
nation building and indigenous resistance in the Caucasus and Central Asia: absence or invisibility of decoloniality, 105–13; anti-spaces or nonspaces and Russian modernization, 90–93, 116; area studies and, 83–86; border spaces and tricksterism, 87–90; "divide and rule" modernization and ethnicity building, 96–101, 119; economic system and, 103–5; epistemic revolution, possibility of, 113–14; genealogy of resistance movements, 93–96; suspended indigenous activism, 101–3; transculturation and border thinking, 114–21; women's activism, 132

nation-states: citizenship and, 175–76; competitive relations between states, 241n24; Kantian-Humboldtian university and, 201–2, 207–8; monoracial assumption, 183–86; political society and, 21; "rights" and, 163–64, 171–74, 173

nature, God replaced with, 184–85
Nebrija, Elio Antonio de, 50, 241n28
neocolonialism, 34–35, 109
neoliberalism: the Caucasus and Central Asia and, 103, 104–5, 109; the corporate university and, 203; expertise and, 22; as period of colonial matrix of power, 46; Russia and, 36; universities and, 215–16; Washington Consensus, "Human Rights," and, 168–70

network society, 209
Newton, Isaac, 76
New World: colonial universities and, 205–6; "discovery of America," 9, 44, 238n13; "humanity" and, 155; "Latin America" and, 240n21; revolution of coloniality and, 39–40; universities and, 205–6, 208, 210; Vitoria on pope and, 161; Western classical tradition disrupted by, 157

NGOs (nongovernmental organizations), 221; expansion of, 169; gender discourse and, 138; "Human Rights" and, 169–70

Nnaemeka, Obioma, 138
Northrop, Douglas, 146

Observations on the Beautiful and the Sublime (Kant), 186
"Observatory of the Bereaved" (Atabekov), 100
Olympics (2014, Sochi), 246n50
oppositional dependency relation, 70
oral histories, 95, 245n43
Orientalism: birth of, 187; Central Asia and, 244n42; Eurasian studies and, 84–85; external colonial difference and, 6; homosexuality and, 248n60; secondary, 55; self-Orientalizing, 55, 68, 136; sexual stereotypes, 125–27; Tamerlane semiotics and, 92; theater and, 119–20
Osamu, Nishitani, 173
Osh conflict, 97
otins (women clerics and healers), 128
Ottoman Sultanate: assimilation and, 70; the Caucasus and, 52; imperial difference and, 187; Islam and, 243n38; Russia and, 69–70, 243n38; as second-class empire, 42
Oyěwùmí, Oyèrónke, 130, 135, 138, 139, 142

Pacari, Nina, 214
pacha-sophy (Aymara), 183, 251n82
pagans, 157
Pamuk, Orhan, 243n37
pan-Turkic identity, 96, 99, 247n56
patriarchy. *See* gender and coloniality in the Caucasus and Central Asia
peace, conditions for, 174
Peter I (the Great), 4
Petrarch, Francesco, 159
Philip II of Castile, 237n1
Pizarro, Francisco, 237n1
"Playfulness, 'World'-Traveling, and Loving Perception" (Lugones), 89
plurinational state, 113
pluriversality: Amawtay Wasi and, 13–14; border thinking and, 65–66; decolonial thinking and, 172; knowledges as plural, 11; options and, 12; universities and, 216; zero-point epistemology and, 66
Polat, Haci Bayram, 102
political society, 21–25, 79, 110, 170–73, 220, 241n24
polycentric capitalism: authority disputes in, 24; as diversification, 48–49; "Human Rights" and, 171–72; neo-liberalism and, 8; revolution and, 18
postcoloniality, 31
postcolonial studies and theory: the Caucasus and Central Asia and, 85; decolonial thinking vs., 32–37; historicity of, 41; logic of coloniality and, 37; Russia and, 41, 240n19, 244n41
postmodernity, 33
poststructuralism, 33
poverty: colonial matrix of power and, 19; human rights and, 169; politics of, 138; racism and, 182, 251n81; social sciences and, 20
property rights, 161–62
Pushkin, Alexander, 125

quadrivium, 190, 201, 205
Quijano, Anibal, 44, 79, 122–23

racism and racial politics: border thinking and, 63; colonial wound and, 238n8; decolonization of, 194–95; defined, 55–56; ethno-racial tetragon/pentagon, 186, 213; gender and, 124–27; "great Russian people" myth, 246n47; "Human Rights" and, 164; Islam, racialization of, 98; Kant's cosmopolitanism, colonial and imperial differences, and, 182–89; Man and Humanity and, 156; poverty and, 251n81; reclassification, racial, 5–6; Russian imperial expansion and, 4; self-racialization, 55; Soviet, 47, 124–27, 248n60; Turks and Russians as not quite human, 63
Ramadan, Tariq, 109
Ramonet, Ignacio, 177
rape, 126
Rasanayagam, Johan, 97
religion. *See* Christianity; Islam
religious differences, replacement of, 5–6
Renaissance, European: "les anciens et les modernes," 10; humanists, 155–59, 205; Humanities and, 189; "Man," "Humanity," and "Human," concepts of, 155–59, 166, 173; meta-language and macro-narratives, 42–43, 78
Renaissance university, 45, 189, 207

renamings, racial and ethnic, 5–6
resistance movements. *See* nation building and indigenous resistance in the Caucasus and Central Asia
revolution, 18, 39–40, 163–64, 222
Reynaga, Fausto, 192
rights, human. *See* humanity, the human, and Human Rights
Roman concepts, 158, 164, 178–79
Roman Empire, 51
Ruray, 230–34
Russia (post-Soviet): global coloniality and neocolonialism and, 34–35; imperial wound and decolonial thinking in, 36–37; postcolonial studies and, 41, 240n19, 244n41
Russian/Soviet Empire: border thinking and, 65, 74–75; civilizing and modernizing rhetoric in, 240n22; Cold War and, 34; collapse of, 23, 48, 103, 111; decolonial openings repressed by, 34; decolonial thinking and, 34; establishment of colonies and imperial difference, 51–52; imperial and colonial difference and, 33–34, 53–54, 53–55; as marginal or second-class empire, 3–5, 42, 47, 53, 76; Marxism, version of, 36; modernity in, 40, 47–48; Moscow as Third Rome doctrine, 40, 51, 237n1, 243n38; Orthodox Christianity and, 40; Ottoman Sultanate and, 69–70; religious identification, compared to Turkey, 243n38; Roman Empire and, 51

Saakashvili, Mikhail, 240n20
Safi, Omid, 117
Sahadeo, Jeff, 86
Sahni, Kalpana, 133, 246n47
Said, Edward, 33
Saidov, Utkam, 102
salvation rhetoric: border thinking and, 7, 60; coloniality hidden by, 20; Human Rights and, 171; idolatry, extirpation of, 8; languages and, 62; rhetoric of modernity and, 46, 176, 188, 244n39
Samarkand, 119–20
Sandoval, Chela, 89, 90, 238n10
Saracens, 156
Sarts, 247n56
Savater, Fernando, 195

Schmitt, Carl, 32, 159, 238n13, 249n68
scholastic learning, 204–5
Schop Soler, Ana María, 4
second-class empires, 42, 76, 92
Second World, 104, 133, 166–67
secularization, 183–84
self-determination, paradox of, 162–63, 166
Seven Interpretive Essays on Peruvian Reality (Mariátegui), 33
sexuality: *bacha* transsexuality, 140–41, 247n58, 248n60; colonial vs. Russian partners, choice of, 249n66; homosexuality and Orientalism, 248n60; sexual normativity, 44–45, 55; stereotypes in the Caucasus and Central Asia, 125–27. *See also* gender and coloniality in the Caucasus and Central Asia
Shakirova, Svetlana, 86, 129, 136–37, 249n63
Shamil, imam, 106
Shariati, Ali, 251n82
Shih, Shu-mei, 84
Shiva, Vandana, 198
Simanovsky, Nikolay, 125
skepticism, misanthropic, 57, 123
slaves, African, 5, 124–27, 155
Smith, Linda Tuhiwai, 32
Socialism: capitalism as only alternative to, 113; civilizing and modernizing rhetoric in, 240n22; competition with U.S. mission, 46; logic of coloniality and, 47; Stalin's model of, 54; transsocialist societies, 155
social sciences: after World War II, 190; area studies, 10–11, 83–86, 209, 249n65; Chinese, 243n35; coloniality and, 83; delinking and, 32; in Latin America, 209; postcolonial contributions to, 33
solidarity, 12
Sosruko, 89
South America: the Caucasus and Central Asia compared to, 93, 102, 105–6, 111; external colonial difference and, 5; "Indias Occidentales," naming of, 5; nation-state building in, 164; postindependence imperialism, 4–5. *See also* Tawantinsuyu and the Incas
Southern Cross, 15, 229
Soviet Union. *See* Russian/Soviet Empire; Socialism
Spain, 3–5, 53, 75
Spanish Inquisition, 183

spatial difference and modernity, 9
spatial epistemic break/fractures, 57–58, 203–7, 212
states. *See* nation-states
Stiglitz, Joseph, 169
structural dependency, 197, 211
subaltern empires, 27, 53–55, 60, 65, 68–72, 86–87, 249n62
Subaltern Studies, 33
subjectivities: Cartesian, 56–57; critical blindness to otherness, 69; displaced inversion and, 66; double consciousness, 68–69, 73, 242n33; gendered trickster, 146; racism and, 55, 56; self-Orientalizing, 55, 68; as sphere of control, 45
Sufism, 116, 117–18, 143
Suleiman the Magnificent, 42
Suleimenov, Olzhas, 67–68
Suleimenova, Saule, 148
"Sumak Kawsay" (living the fullness of life), 15

Taken from the Lips (Marcos), 118
Taky Onkoy, 246n52
Tamerlane (Timur), 91–92
Tashkent, 115–16, 119–20, 146, 247n57
Tatars, 5–6, 98
Tawantinsuyu and the Incas: Amawtay Wasi curriculum and, 15, 229; as foundation, vs. Greece, 204; Guaman Poma and, 191–92; knowledges of, 205–6; Man and Humanity and, 155, 156, 158; overruling of systems of, 44–45; property rights and, 161–62; renaming and, 5
Tekuyeva, Madina, 86, 140, 249n65
temporal difference and modernity, 8–9
temporal epistemic fractures, 203–10
The Contest of Faculty (Kant), 189–90
theologians of liberation, 221
theopolitics of knowledge: border thinking and, 64; displaced inversion of, 66; displacement of, 59; geopolitics and body politics vs., 24; imperial and colonial differences and, 58; suppressed knowledge and, 58; zero-point epistemology and, 64
Th'iongo, Ngugi Wa, 177
Third World: assumptions about, 3; borders and, 69; decolonial option and, 33; feminism and, 133, 137; geopolitical shift and, 193; geopolitics of knowledge and, 32–33; "Human Rights" and, 166–67; migration from, 213; multiculturalism and, 213; second-class modernity and, 145; self-determination policies and, 166; Socialism and, 112–13; universities and, 209–10
Third World nationalism, 242n34
THOA (Taller Historia Oral Andina), 86
Thomas Aquinas, Saint, 158, 161
Timur (Tamerlane), 91–92
tinku (conflict of power), 215
Tkhagapsoev, Khazhismel, 54, 100
Tlostanova, Madina, 239n15
To Discover a Hero (Saidov), 102
Togan, Zeki Velidi, 95, 107
Tokhtakhodzhayeva, Marfua, 86, 134–35, 249n63
Tollan, 179–80
toltécatl, 179–80
Toltecáyotl, 179–80
"tradition" and the "traditional": hijab and, 142; modern-traditional binary, 129–30, 131–32, 134–35; traditional-Soviet-Westernized schema, 145–46
transculturation: border space and, 87–89; border thinking and, 114–21; hybrid ethnicity and, 247n56
transnational corporations, 241n24
traveling as mode of existence, 90, 123
tricksterism: gender and, 136, 139–41, 145–47; resistance and, 88–90, 115, 116, 247n58
trivium, 190, 201, 205
Turkey, 141–42. *See also* Ottoman Sultanate
Turkistan National Liberation Movement, 95
Turkistan National Unity, 106–7

Ukraine, 240n20
UNASUR (Unión Suramericana), 241n25
UNESCO (United Nations Educational, Scientific, and Cultural Organization), 173, 210
United States: American Revolution, 163, 164; body politics of knowledge, postcolonial studies, and, 33; Civil Rights movement, 193–94; Cold War and, 34, 208–9; the corporate university and, 203; Hiroshima bombing, 165–66; migration and decolonial thinking, 35;

mission of development and modernization, 46; self-determination and, 166
Universal Declaration of Human Rights (1948), 154, 165–66
"universal history," 54–55, 77
universality: border thinking and, 65–66; of "human" and "rights," 154–55, 172; human experience and, 193; "Man" and "Human" and, 157
Universidad Intercultural de los Pueblos y Naciones Indigenas del Ecuador. *See* Amawtay Wasi
universities and the history of knowledge: overview, 196–97; appropriation and, 16–17; capitalism and, 199–200, 210; Christian colleges and control of knowledge, 45; the Cold War university, 208–9; the colonial university, 200–201, 203, 205–6; the corporate university, 202–3, 209–10, 216; English-speaking universities in Central Asia, 248n59; epistemic dependency and, 210–11; future possibilities, 215–16; instruction and nurturing, in liberal model vs. decolonial, 21–22; interuniversity cooperation, 211–12; the Kantian-Humboldtian University, 189–90, 201–2, 207–8; knowing how, knowing that, and knowing what, 198–99; learning to manage vs. learning to unlearn, 197; logic and consequences of imperial thinking and, 197–98; the medieval university and scholastic learning, 204–5; private universities, 202; radical changes in field of education, 35; the Renaissance university, 189, 207; temporal and spatial epistemic fractures, 203–10, 212. *See also* Amawtay Wasi; disciplines and the academy; Humanities
University of Central Asia, 248n59
University of North Carolina, 208
Useinov, Vyacheslav, 100
Ushuay, 230–34
Uzbekistan: Andizhan insurgency, 107–8, 246n51; ethnic solidarity rhetoric, 105; migration from, 100; Timur figure and, 91–92
Uzbeks: in Moscow, 245n45; Sindzyan Usbek diaspora, 143–44

Venezuela, 220
Via Campesina, La, 168, 244n39
vicularidad, 232
violence, culture of: in the Caucasus and Central Asia, 107, 110; Orientalist assumption of, 125–26; violence as response to violence, 172
visual nature of culture, 131
Vitoria, Francisco de, 159, 161–62, 164, 165, 174

Waldseemüller, Martin, 5
Wallerstein, Immanuel, 44
Walsh, Catherine, 106
war against terrorism, 49
Washington Consensus, 168–70
Weber, Max, 18, 249n68
Weil, Mark, 115–16, 119, 120, 247n58
Weitz, Eric, 248n60
Williamson, John, 169
World War II, 165–66
Wretched of the Earth, The (Fanon), 33
Wu, Yenna, 138
Wynter, Syliva, 159, 171

Yachay, 230–34
Yagan, Murat, 114
Yeltsin, Boris, 111
Yerofeyev, Victor, 36, 243n36
Young, Robert, 239n17
yuhcatiliztli, 179

Zan, Saferby, 67
Zapatistas: "andar preguntando" (walking while asking), 224; anthropologists and, 86; "a world in which many worlds will coexist," 79, 222; on equality and difference, 177, 195; Eurasian colonized spaces contrasted with, 102; learning to unlearn and, 222–24; women and decolonization, 141
Zea, Leopoldo, 4
zero-point epistemology, 42–43, 61, 64, 65, 66, 71, 78
Zhakomikhova, Fatima, 118

TRANSOCEANIC STUDIES
Ileana Rodriguez, Series Editor

The Transoceanic Studies series rests on the assumption of a one-world system. This system—simultaneously modern and colonial and now postmodern and postcolonial (global)—profoundly restructured the world, displaced the Mediterranean *mare nostrum* as a center of power and knowledge, and constructed dis-centered, transoceanic, waterways that reached across the world. The vast imaginary undergirding this system was Eurocentric in nature and intent. Europe was viewed as the sole culture-producing center. But Eurocentrism, theorized as the "coloniality of power" and "of knowledge," was contested from its inception, generating a rich, enormous, alternate corpus. In disputing Eurocentrism, books in this series will acknowledge above all the contributions coming from other areas of the world, colonial and postcolonial, without which neither the aspirations to universalism put forth by the Enlightenment nor those of globalization promoted by postmodernism will be fulfilled.

Oriental Shadows: The Presence of the East in Early American Literature
 Jim Egan

www.ingramcontent.com/pod-product-compliance
Lightning Source LLC
Chambersburg PA
CBHW020641230426
43665CB00008B/260